FLORENCE, ROME AND THE ORIGINS OF THE RENAISSANCE

FLORENCE, ROME

AND THE

ORIGINS

OF THE

RENAISSANCE

GEORGE HOLMES

CLARENDON PRESS · OXFORD

Oxford University Press, Walton Street, Oxford OX2 6DP

Oxford New York Toronto
Delhi Bombay Calcutta Madras Karachi
Petaling Jaya Singapore Hong Kong Tokyo
Nairobi Dar es Salaam Cape Town
Melbourne Auckland
and associated companies in
Beirut Berlin Ibadan Nicosia

Oxford is a trade mark of Oxford University Press

Published in the United States
by Oxford University Press, New York

First published 1986
First published as a paperback 1988

British Library Cataloguing in Publication Data
Holmes, George
Florence, Rome and the origins of the
Renaissance.
1. Italy—History—13th century
2. Italy—History—1268–1492
I. Title
945'.04 DG531
ISBN 0–19–822576–8
ISBN 0–19–822153–3 (Pbk)

Library of Congress Cataloging in Publication Data
Holmes, George, 1927–
Florence, Rome, and the origins of the Renaissance.
Includes index.
1. Florence (Italy)—History—To 1421.
2. Italy—Church history—476–1400.
3. Arts, Renaissance—Italy. 4. Renaissance—Italy.
I. Title.
DG737.26.H644 1986 945'.51 86–12698
ISBN 0–19–822576–8
ISBN 0–19–822153–3 (Pbk)

Printed in Great Britain by
Butler & Tanner Ltd,
Frome, Somerset

TO ANNE

PREFACE

THE Italian Renaissance is sometimes thought to begin with the blossoming of classical scholarship under the aegis of Salutati and Chrysoloras in early fifteenth-century Florence. A period, however, which excludes the innovations of Dante, Petrarch and Boccaccio, Giotto and Giovanni Pisano leaves out the origins of the prolonged outpouring of art and thought which the word 'Renaissance' evokes in our minds. The enrichment of artistic and philosophical conceptions which we owe to the Tuscan imagination runs in a line, interrupted but not broken and always standing out from the general development of European civilization, from the late thirteenth to the early sixteenth centuries. I have, therefore, ventured to apply the idea of the Renaissance to the lifetime of Dante, 1265 to 1321, when Tuscan creativity first appeared.

I have aimed in this book to put the major developments of the literary and visual arts in a more general historical setting which includes their political and economic environment. I do not imagine, of course, that they can be explained in this way. The historical explanation of artistic creativity is always imperfect, even when the sources for it are very much better than they are in the thirteenth century. Nevertheless, there are reasons why the enterprise seems to be worth attempting. Tuscany in the age of Dante is the place and time when the arts began to emerge as a separate area of activity independent of ecclesiastical or secular domination. The ultimate result of this movement, which we see in the work of painters and novelists centuries later, is a notable feature of European civilization, arguably as important as science or the nation state. If the beginning is to be seen in perspective it has to be seen in both literature and the visual arts, which develop with a striking simultaneity around 1300. And for the historical imagination, it is tempting to try to see artistic change against the background of the social circumstances in which the artists lived. I have tried, therefore, to write about this episode in the history of painting and poetry as part of the history of Tuscany, adding a rather strong emphasis on the relations between the Tuscans and the papal court, which is essential to the story of the arts.

Apart from the inherent difficulties of writing history of this kind, I am also conscious of the amateurism which is the fate of a writer who attempts to embrace a number of widely different kinds of human activity, each of which has attracted the lifelong specialization of the experts. To attempt, even to a very limited extent, to see significant events of the distant past in a meaningful perspective in which different aspects of society are related, the historian must accept his deplorable ignorance in many of the fields with which he deals and hope that the result of his work will have a certain interest even though it will often seem to the truly knowledgeable to lack precision. There is a pleasure to be gained from the most exact investigation of particular episodes, but if this book has any value it is of a different kind: it is deliberately an attempt at synthesis.

The civilization of Tuscany and the papal court in the period around 1300 has been studied in its different aspects by very varied groups of historians during the last hundred years. The international character of the scholarship in this part of Italian history has been so marked as to make it different from the history of France, Germany, or England. I have learnt a great deal not only from the Italian elucidators of Dante and of Florentine society but also from the French editors of the papal registers and the German art historians. The wealth of international interest in the field means that it is in some ways a particularly rich area of study. My relatively few footnotes give an inadequate impression of the debts I owe to earlier writers, and I could name a number of scholars whose works have been inspiring. Among them is one name that must be singled out for special mention: Robert Davidsohn, whose history of Florence down to the early fourteenth century, published between 1896 and 1927, is still the most elaborate study of a medieval or Renaissance city ever undertaken, and also the fullest account of the international politics of Tuscany during the period it covers. Davidsohn's knowledge of the Tuscan sources remains quite unsurpassed. I occasionally make specific reference to his book, but its scholarship stands unmentioned behind all I have written about political and social history.

It is impossible to aspire to an understanding of the history of this subject without spending time in the churches and art galleries and the extraordinarily rich archives of the Tuscan cities and of Rome. This requires financial support for which I am greatly indebted to the Leverhulme Foundation, the British Academy, the History Faculty of Oxford University, and St Catherine's College. I should like also to express my gratitude for the help given to me by the staffs of the Archivio di Stato and Kunsthistorisches Institut in Florence, the Archivio di Stato, Siena, the Archivio Segreto Vaticano, the Bodleian Library and the libraries of the Ashmolean Museum and the Taylorian Institution. Finally, I should like to thank two colleagues learned in specialized fields who read three of the chapters for me: Joanna Cannon (Chs 6 and 9) and David Robey (Ch. 5). They are not responsible for views that have been retained in spite of their scrutiny.

CONTENTS

LIST OF PLATES

ACKNOWLEDGEMENTS

The author and publishers thank the following for permission to reproduce plates:

Archivi Alinari: nos. 4, 5, 6, 7, 8, 10, 12, 14, 16, 17, 20, 22, 30, 31, 38, 39, 40, 41, 42, 43, 44, 45; Ilario Bessi, from *Giovanni Pisano* by Michael Ayrton and Henry Moore, published by Thames and Hudson, London 1969: 11, 13; Biblioteca Apostolica Vaticana: 2; Conway Library, Courtauld Institute of Art: 9; Foto de Giovanni, Assisi: 32, 33, 34, 35, 36; Foto Grassi, Siena: 21, 25, 27, 28, 29; Istituto Centrale per il Catalogo e la Documentazione, Rome: 3 (neg. 1608); Istituto Centrale per il Restauro, Archivio Fotografico, Rome: 26 (neg. 7558); The Trustees, The National Gallery, London: 18; Scala, Florence: 19, 37; Foto Vasari, Rome: I; The Trustees of the Victoria and Albert Museum: 15; Professor John White: 23, 24.

Enfer ou Ciel, qu'importe?
Au fond de l'Inconnu pour trouver du *nouveau*!

BAUDELAIRE

Il fallait que ces Vertus et ces Vices de Padoue eussent en eux
bien de la réalité puisqu'ils m'apparaissaient comme aussi
vivants que la servante enceinte, et qu'elle-même ne me
semblait pas beaucoup moins allégorique.

PROUST

In Dante dwells the whole spirit of the Renaissance. I love
Dante almost as much as the Bible. He is my spiritual food,
the rest is ballast.

JOYCE

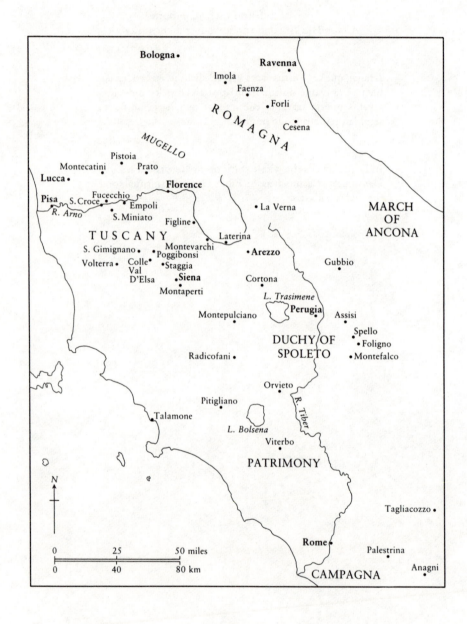

Bologna•

Ravenna•

Imola•

Faenza•

Forli•

Cesena•

R O M A G N A

MUGELLO

Pistoia•

Montecatini•   Prato•

Lucca•

Florence•

Pisa•   S. Croce   Fucecchio•

S. Croce•   •Empoli

R. Arno   S. Miniato•

Figline•

La Verna•

MARCH
OF
ANCONA

Laterina•

T U S C A N Y

Montevarchi•

S. Gimignano•   Poggibonsi•

Volterra•   Colle•   •Staggia

Val

D'Elsa   •Siena

Arezzo•

Gubbio•

Cortona•

Montaperti•

L. Trasimene

Montepulciano•

Perugia•

Assisi•

Spello•

•Foligno

DUCHY OF
SPOLETO

•Montefalco

Radicofani•

Orvieto•

Pitigliano•

R. Tiber

Talamone•

L. Bolsena

Viterbo•

PATRIMONY

N

Tagliacozzo•

Rome•

Palestrina•

0   25   50 miles

0   40   80 km

Anagni•

CAMPAGNA

PART I

Tuscany and the High Medieval Papacy

I

Guelf Ascendancy, 1265–1277

IN 1300, the year of the great indulgence instituted by Pope Boniface VIII, Giovanni Villani, the future chronicler of Florence, went to Rome as a pilgrim and, 'beholding the great and ancient things' at Rome, conceived the idea of imitating the work of the historians of the classical city.

But considering that our city of Florence, the daughter and creature of Rome, was rising, and had great things before her, whilst Rome was declining, it seemed to me fitting to collect in this volume and new chronicle all the deeds and beginnings of the city of Florence, in so far as it has been possible for me to find and gather them together . . . and thus in the year 1300, having returned from Rome, I began to compile this book.[1]

The chronology of Villani's composition of his chronicle presents difficult problems, and modern commentators have doubted whether this romantic recollection of 1300 is true. But the impressions it records are an accurate reflection of how a Florentine would have seen the two cities a few years after 1300, when Rome had been reduced to comparative insignificance by the papal settlement in France. Florence had long been regarded as the 'daughter of Rome', founded by Romans in the first century B.C. and drawing its political virtues from the civilization of the creators of the greatest of empires. The remains of the Colosseum towered over a vast settlement whose ancient grandeur was evident in its ruins, but from which the life had fled. Rome was not a centre of commerce or industry, and after 1304 it was not even the ecclesiastical capital of Europe; it was the home of symbolic vestiges, haunted by the recollection of a greatness far beyond that of any modern city. Florence, on the other hand, was a city with no civilized past but an apparently infinite capacity for expansion fed by its industrial workshops and its mastery of international finance.

In the late thirteenth century the balance had been different. Medieval Rome was the creation of the popes, and its administrative importance resulted from the simultaneous emergence in the thirteenth century of the papal state, which gave the papacy control over substantial parts of Central Italy, and the unified Western church. The papal court drew into Rome vast tributes from all over Europe to fill the exchequers of the pope and the cardinals, and attracted the ambassadors of kings and innumerable postulants

[1] G. Villani, *Cronica*, VIII. xxxvi. (I have used the version printed in *Croniche di Giovanni, Matteo e Filippo Villani*, i, Trieste, 1857.)

for ecclesiastical privileges. The year of the Indulgence of 1300 was the summit of medieval Rome's command of Europe, after an extremely chequered political history. There had been long periods when the popes were driven out of Rome, to Orvieto or Viterbo. But there were also periods, like the pontificates of Nicholas III and Boniface VIII, when they were settled at Rome, and when the revenues of popes and cardinals were channelled into the city and used in part to rebuild its churches and palaces and to embellish them in a manner appropriate to a great capital. Most of that work has vanished in the decay of the Avignon period and the rebuilding of the late Renaissance, but down to 1304 it must have impressed a visitor in the way that the more lasting creations of the Renaissance and baroque papacy do today.

The history of civilization in Florence, whose citizens gave Renaissance conceptions their first and sudden birth soon after 1300, is thus inseparable from the history of Rome, the contrasting and balancing wielder of political and aesthetic authority before 1304. The importance of this symbiosis does not result only from the fact that Florentines could never think of political or ecclesiastical theories without invoking the Rome of the distant past—the home of the republic and the Caesars, and of the expansion of Christianity—but also from Rome's practical importance in the late thirteenth century. At that time Rome had been a centre of artistic patronage at least as important as Florence, a great instigator of original ideas in the new visual arts. It had been the home of the ecclesiastical finance on which many of the richest Florentine merchants depended for much of their wealth. It had been the chief centre of political power in central Italy, and the promoter of the *coup d'état* which led to Dante's exile in 1301. After 1304, power and wealth left Rome for more than half a century. But to understand the dramatic creations of Dante and Giotto one must look at Tuscany during the earlier part of their lives against the background of its relationship with the authorities of the city of Rome.

In the mid-thirteenth century the most prominent inhabitants of the Tuscan towns—Florence, Siena, Lucca, Pistoia, and lesser places—were divided into sharply antagonistic groups of Guelfs and Ghibellines. The origins of these divisions are not to be found in the support for Papacy and Empire which the enthusiasts professed. At Florence the Guelf–Ghibelline conflict was traditionally thought to be derived from a dispute which arose in 1215 when Buondelmonte de' Buondelmonti was murdered by the Amidei after jilting a bride from that family. As a result of this dispute, powerful clans—such as the Buondelmonti and Donati on the Guelf side and the Amidei and Uberti on the Ghibelline—joined together in close friendships and violent feuds. As reported by the chroniclers this episode is no doubt lifted into unjustified prominence from among the many causes which produced friendship and feud within the wealthy groups, but its fame reflects the realities of city life. Living side by side in the narrow streets, forced to marry their not-far-distant neighbours, anxious to maintain their honour, accustomed to fighting, able to draw on support from many members of a *consorteria* (a loosely connected but wide group of families bearing the same name), it is not surprising that the gentry of the towns were both intensely friendly and intensely quarrelsome. Their violent disputes arose out of the permanent circumstances of their ordinary lives and took on only accidentally the colouring of large political issues. Not only the causes but also the extreme results of Guelf–Ghibelline conflict are best explained as manifestations of the society in which they arose. Men were expelled from the city permanently in large numbers—as the Guelfs were from Florence in 1260 and the Ghibellines in 1267—because bloodshed made it impossible to live close to enemies. The properties the exiles left behind were seized or destroyed. Sometimes a community that had caused exceptional resentment by its persistent enmity was wiped out by the razing of all its buildings, as the Florentines destroyed Semifonte in 1202 and Poggibonsi in 1270. The ferocity of city-state society leaves permanent marks of indelible bitterness both within cities and between them.

In recent years historians have emphasized more strongly than before that the medieval Italian cities are not to be equated with the bourgeois cities of Northern Europe. They were not 'boroughs' formed by merchants for the purpose of ensuring commercial freedom and independence, but the homes of landowners whose property was often in the country and whose family customs were indistinguishable from those of the rural aristocracy. Though the cities of thirteenth-century Tuscany derived much of their wealth and political importance from industry and trade, and the commercial supremacy of the Tuscans over the whole of Europe is the feature of their way of life which seems most prominent, this was a recent economic growth grafted onto an ancient system of social customs which retained its dominance over families and their rivalries. The commune, the political system of republican government, was not the original framework of the city but a complex structure imposed upon city life by the citizens in a desperate and often unsuccessful attempt to contain the conflicts arising from the rivalry of families and classes, and to make a tolerably peaceful life possible in spite of the social instincts militating against it. We have also to take account in Italy of the importance of the family clan or *consorteria*, which often acted as a unit in disputes with other *consorterie*. The clan is again a social feature which distinguishes Italian society from the smaller families of both town and country which are characteristic of Northern Europe.[2]

The Guelf–Ghibelline conflict came to dominate the political life of Tuscany in the thirteenth century, partly because of the absence of effective political control in Central Italy; monarchy, as it was known to the subjects of

---

[2] P. Jones, 'Economia e società nell'Italia medievale: il mito della borghesia' in his *Economia e società nell'Italia medievale* (Turin, 1980); J. Heers, *Le Clan familial au moyen âge* (Paris, 1974); J. Larner, *Italy in the Age of Dante and Petrarch 1216–1380* (London, 1980), chs 4–7.

the kings of England or France, did not exist. Central Italy was dominated by independent communes and independent nobles. The southern part of it—a band across Italy mostly to the north of Rome, including Orvieto, Spoleto, Perugia, Fermo, and Ancona—owed an uncertain allegiance to the pope and was organized by him as the provinces of Campagna and Marittima, the Patrimony in Tuscany, the Duchy of Spoleto, and the March of Ancona. It was a weak state in which the pope's rule had constantly to be enforced against rebellious and fighting towns and nobles. But to the north of this, on either side of the Apennines, were the two provinces of Romagna and Tuscany, in which neither pope nor emperor had established any effective control and the absence of central authority was total. Particularly after the death of Emperor Frederick II in 1250, Romagna and Tuscany were for practical purposes without rulers. The multifarious disputes of gentlemen in the cities and nobility in the mountainous countryside were controlled only by the governments of communes, which exercised a limited power over small areas. The result was continual disorder.

The unification of local disputes into the general division between Guelfs and Ghibellines was due originally, however, to the intervention of would-be monarchs, and especially to the ferocious conflict between Frederick II and the popes. The reliance of those who called themselves Ghibellines on the support of Frederick's Hohenstaufen family, with its claim to the kingdom of Naples and to imperial rights in other parts of Italy, including Tuscany, and the reliance of Guelfs on the support of the hostile papacy, defined the external political allegiances of the two parties all over Italy. Though Florence was by this time a city of growing industrial and commercial power in which the government of the *primo popolo* minted the florin, the first gold coin of modern Western Europe, in 1252, its politics were dominated by disputes between ancient city families linked with papal–imperial rivalry. Frederick's illegitimate son Manfred established control over the southern kingdom of Naples and Sicily in 1258. Support for him in Tuscany led to the most dreadful of the conflicts of the two parties on 4 September 1260, when the bloody battle of Montaperti took place about eight kilometres south-east of Siena. Montaperti was fought between, on one side, the exiled Florentine Ghibellines led by Farinata degli Uberti, the Sienese, the troops of Manfred's vicar in Tuscany, and the Ghibellines of Grosseto and Poggibonsi; on the other the Guelf towns of Florence, Lucca, Perugia, and Orvieto. It was a Ghibelline victory. The power of the recollections it left echoes in Dante's *Inferno* half a century later.

After Montaperti, Tuscany was dominated by the Ghibellines for six years until the defeat of Manfred at the battle of Benevento in 1266, which in spite of a minor revival in support of Conradin in 1268, turned out to be the end of effective Ghibellinism in much of Central Italy until the time of Henry VII and Lewis the Bavarian in the fourteenth century. The disputes between the two parties never ceased but the Guelf victory of 1266, leading eventually to half a century of general Guelf hegemony, had a profound significance for the Tuscan cities. It meant that, with the exception of the persistently Ghibelline Pisa and Arezzo, they were controlled by Guelf oligarchies. It involved most of the cities in adherence to a Guelf league which included the pope, France, and the Angevin king of Naples. It facilitated the involvement of Tuscan Guelf merchants in the business of the wealthiest parts of Europe (that is, Northern France and Flanders) and in the lucrative trade with the under-developed kingdom of Naples. It made Tuscan Guelfs the natural bankers of the popes. It encouraged Tuscan interest in the writings and arts of France. The Guelf hegemony is thus an indispensable part of the environment which at the end of the thirteenth century became the world of Dante and Giotto. Its establishment is the first part of that world which we must attempt to describe.

The success of the Guelfs was the result of the efforts of two French popes, Urban IV (1261–4) and Clement IV (1265–8), to overcome the Hohenstau-fen threat to control not only the kingdom of Naples but also Italy to the north as well, and thus to render the papacy impotent in its insecure Central Italian state. Urban IV devised a way of saving the papacy which was eventually successful, though in the years 1268–77 it looked as though it might have the result merely of substituting another ruler equally dangerous in both Naples and Tuscany. The plan was to import as king of Naples a French prince whose expedition to Italy could be paid for with the proceeds of papal taxation of the clergy imposed in the areas in Northern France where it was most lucrative. Thus was set up the essential link of the papacy with a French king of Naples, supported by money advanced by Tuscan Guelf bankers who were to be repaid from taxation in France: the original framework of the Guelf alliance. When Urban IV died in October 1264 this plan was already in existence and accepted by the prince chosen to replace Manfred, Charles Count of Anjou, brother of King Louis IX of France. Charles had already in 1264 become senator of Rome, and a lieutenant sent with a small force to represent him there was holding his own with considerable difficulty. The imposition of the necessary triennial tenth in France to provide funds had been announced. But the position of the papacy was in some ways extremely weak—Rome was surrounded by hostile Ghibelline forces, and the papal court was at Perugia. Charles of Anjou had not himself moved towards Italy.

Clement IV was elected on 5 January 1265. He was Guy le Gros, a Provençal lawyer who had been a councillor of King Louix IX, an appropri-ate man to deal with the Count of Anjou. The political letters which survive from his pontificate were written with a uniformity and idiosyncratic strength of style which suggests they were his own compositions.[3] They give their

---

[3] E. Martène and U. Durand, *Thesaurus Novus Anecdotorum* (Paris, 1717), ii; summarized and dated in *Registres de Clément IV*, ed. E. Jordan (Paris, 1893–1945), Appendix ii.

reader a picture of an intellectual with determined and clear political aims, in keeping with the passionate face on the effigy of his sepulchre in San Francesco, Viterbo. His ally, Count Charles, also has a monument in the Palazzo dei Conservatori on the Roman capitol. It shows a powerful, dominating but rather empty expression, which again seems appropriate to what chroniclers tell us of this immensely ambitious and acquisitive nobleman, successful, and honest but silent and unsmiling.[4] After the death of Urban these two men carried out the destruction of the Hohenstaufen power in Italy.

Charles of Anjou sailed from Marseilles in May 1265 with a force of five hundred knights and a thousand archers. A storm forced him to put in at Portovenere on the headland below La Spezia, and his enterprise might have been nipped in the bud if it had not been for the poor state of relations between Ghibelline Pisa, its enemy Lucca, and the Ghibelline leader in Tuscany, Count Guido Novello, who could not mobilize Pisan help against Charles in time. Eleven days later Charles was at the mouth of the Tiber, having avoided the Ghibellines of Tuscany and the galleys of Manfred. On 28 June he was invested at Rome with the kingdom of Naples by four cardinals, on the condition that he should abandon the senatorship of the city after he had conquered the kingdom. At present Rome was the only territory he governed in Italy, and the future was extremely uncertain. Some places to the north of Rome, particularly Orvieto to which Charles sent help, were friendly to the pope and presented a barrier to Ghibelline Tuscany; but to the south Manfred threatened attack, and he had many friends around Rome itself.

There followed six months in which Charles clamoured for papal help in raising money, and waited for his main army to come down Italy by land. Eventually, in November, the army crossed the Alps, moving through Lombardy with surprising ease to reach Rome the following month. On 6 January 1266 Charles was crowned king of Naples by cardinals with papal authority. A fortnight later he took his French army, together with a body of Tuscan Guelfs led by Count Guido Guerra and Stoldo di Jacopo de' Rossi of Florence, to the south to attack Manfred. On 26 February he destroyed Manfred's army and killed Manfred himself at the Battle of Benevento a few miles inside the kingdom of Naples. The way was open for him to take over the whole kingdom.[5]

Ghibelline power in Tuscany had depended partly on the presence of a body of five hundred German knights under Manfred's vicar, Guido Novello, and one hundred retained by Florence, whose future could not be independent of the fate of the Hohenstaufen. After Manfred's defeat and

---

[4] Villani, VII. i.
[5] E. Jordan, *Les Origines de la domination angevine en Italie* (Paris, 1909), pp. 524–602; Davidsohn, *Storia di Firenze* (Florence, 1956–68, trans. from *Geschichte von Florenz*, Berlin, 1896–1927), II, ii, pp. 777–805; E. G. Léonard, *Les Angevins de Naples* (Paris, 1954), pp. 51–9.

death it became attractive to come to terms with the pope and the new king. Already on 16 March 1266 the Florentine council decided to accept papal directions in order to escape from the pope's interdict.[6] In the curious resulting situation, in which the pope's wishes were partly accepted in a Ghibelline-controlled city, Clement IV was anxious to bring about a pacification and reconciliation of the two sides rather than a Guelf victory. He took upon himself the appointment of the supreme magistrates, and on 12 May 1266 nominated as rectors of Florence two Bolognese, Loderingo degli Andalò and Catalano de' Malavolti, who were prominent members of the pious lay order of *Frati Gaudenti.* This was not a good way of controlling the turbulent city. The pope's demands that Florence should expel the German soldiers and let in the exiles were not carried out. Later in the year Clement tried to improve his control by appointing as *podestà* a Roman baron, Jacopo di Collemezzo, but the Florentines would not have him.[7]

On 11 November 1266 Florence was unexpectedly in upheaval. A popular rising, whose origins are unknown but which was led by the Ghibelline Soldanieri family, procured the expulsion of Guido Novello and his German knights. Guido behaved in a pusillanimous fashion, retreating to Prato and then attempting to return; but eventually he and his knights fled to the countryside between Florence and Prato.[8] Surprised by this upheaval, which does not seem to have been a Guelf movement, the pope sent a new envoy, a priest called Elia Peleti, to represent him beside the *Frati Gaudenti.* The pope appears to have been anxious to prevent further violent popular upheavals, and indeed to restrict popular power in Florence and to promote a genuine pacification of the city with a peaceful re-entry of the exiled Guelfs. Change along these lines seems to have been taking place in the early months of 1267, but even the power the pope had was taken out of his hands and placed in those of King Charles and the Guelfs by the influence of new external events.

The new factor was the threat posed in the autumn of 1266 by the very last legitimate Hohenstaufen, Conradin, nephew of Manfred and a precocious boy of only fourteen living in Germany, who clearly intended to attempt to revive his family's power in Italy. There was now a stronger argument for Charles to secure control of Tuscany quickly in order to prevent Conradin's advance towards the south. At the beginning of April, therefore, Charles came to Tuscany himself with troops imported with papal permission, and with the role of peacemaker, *paciarius,* officially conferred on him by the pope. The forces of the exiled Guelfs, led by Count Guido Guerra, strengthened by a body of hundreds of French knights under King Charles's representative Jourdain de l'Isle, appeared before Florence on Easter Day 17 April 1267;

---

[6] Davidsohn, *Forschungen zur älteren Geschichte von Florenz* (Berlin, 1896–1908, reprint Osnabrück, 1973), iii, p. 19.

[7] Martène and Durand, ii, cols 321, 361–2, 378, 418; Davidsohn, *Storia,* 11. i, pp. 817, 824–5.

[8] Davidsohn, *Storia,* 11. i, pp. 829–33; idem, *Forschungen,* iv, pp. 171–83.

thousands of Ghibellines fled and the Guelfs entered the city, never to leave it again.[9]

'Refloret Tuscia', the pope wrote after Benevento, 'tota demum Italia reviviscit': let Tuscany flower again that all Italy may revive. In the spring of 1266 he expressed the hope that he would be able to return to Rome for the winter.[10] The conflicts of towns and parties in Tuscany remained, however, extremely difficult to wrest into unity on the Guelf side, and Pope Clement died on 29 November 1268 without ever reaching Rome, and without seeing Tuscany all Guelf. Pisa's permanent tendency to confrontation with Lucca and with Florence was an insoluble problem. As long as Florence and Lucca were Guelf, Pisa would make an alliance with any imperialist or Ghibelline intruder. Pisa, however, lay on the borders of Tuscany; more dangerous at this period was Siena, which after Easter 1267 was the chief Ghibelline power. The pope had tried at Siena, as he had tried at Florence, to guide affairs after Benevento by introducing his own representative into the city. In this case it was a French priest, Bernard Languissel, canon of Toulouse, who went to Siena in the summer of 1266. He had little success in his attempts at mediation between Guelfs and Ghibellines because Siena was dominated by a powerful native opponent of the Guelfs, Provenzan Salvani. In May 1267 it looked briefly as though papal persistence in negotiation might win over Siena. The envoys of the city came to an agreement with the pope, now at Viterbo. But it was a bad moment: Conradin had just appeared in Tuscany, and the Ghibelline reaction in Siena in the same month put an end to the hope of peace with the Guelfs before it had been tried.[11]

Charles was in Tuscany for approximately a year, from April 1267 to April 1268. The pope was more frightened of the coming of Conradin than of the dangers of Angevin power, and therefore permitted Charles to use the title of 'imperial vicar', wielder of the imperial authority in Tuscany at a time when there was no emperor, a style which he seems to have adopted at the beginning of May 1267. During that year he acted at times with a cruelty which repelled Italian observers and carried out some destruction, but he did not manage to change the balance of power in Tuscany very substantially. His forces helped to bring about the fall of the Ghibelline fortress at Sant'Ellero in the Arno Valley in June 1267, killing many defenders. He took part in the siege of the Ghibelline stronghold at Poggibonsi, carried out principally, and eventually successfully, by his deputy Jean de Braiselve and the Florentines between June

---

[9] F. Baethgen, 'Der Anspruch des Papsttums auf das Reichsvikariat', *Medievalia* (Stuttgart, 1960), p. 140; Davidsohn, *Storia*, 11. i, pp. 841–7; idem, *Forschungen*, iv, pp. 188–90.

[10] Martène and Durand, ii, cols 288, 315–16.

[11] F. Tempesti, 'Provenzan Salvani', *Bullettino senese di storia patria*, n.s., vii, 1936; Davidsohn, *Storia*, 11. i, pp. 813–14; G. Tommasi, *Dell'historie di Siena* (Venice, 1625; reprint Bologna, 1973), pp. 36–42; G. Martini, 'Siena da Montaperti alla caduta dei nove', *Bullettino senese di storia patria*, lxviii, 1961, pp. 93–5.

and November. He then moved over to the north-west, destroying, it was claimed, the important Pisan harbour at Porto Pisano, and taking Motrone, further up the Riviera coast.[12] The last moves were presumably intended to make it difficult for Conradin to come south into Tuscany with the help of Pisa. But this activity did not alter the facts of political life. Among the principal cities, Charles had the support of Florence, Pistoia, and Lucca. The position was described by the pope in a letter written in November 1267:

The king of Sicily has been a long time in Tuscany and is still detained in the siege of Poggibonsi. He has been made *podestà* of Florence, Pistoia, and Lucca, and by us peacemaker of Tuscany. Against him are the Sienese and the Pisans and many Ghibellines with whom the Romans are inclined to make an alliance together with the Senator Henry of Castille.[13]

Henry of Castille, whom Charles had allowed to become senator of Rome, had gone over to Conradin.

When Charles left Tuscany in April 1268 Conradin was already at Pisa. Rebellions in Sicily and Naples made it essential for Charles to go south to conserve his kingdom. He left Jean Braiselve with French troops in Tuscany. Pisa and Siena welcomed Conradin enthusiastically and gave him considerable sums of money. Florence remained loyal to the Guelf side and the pope praised its constancy, ending the excommunication imposed for refusing to accept Jacopo di Collemezzo as *podestà*.[14] It was by no means clear that the Guelfs were going to win. The worst moment came on the day Conradin made his grand entry into Siena, 24 June. Braiselve's French force, leaving Florence, went south by a parallel route up the Arno Valley, hoping to join in the resistance to Conradin further south. Near Laterina they were set upon by Conradin's Germans, coming out of Siena, and the greater part of them killed or taken prisoner.[15] Conradin and his army went on in a triumphant march from Siena to Rome and thence to the edge of the kingdom of Naples. But Charles and his commanders were in the end too clever for them, as they had been for Manfred. Conradin was ingeniously defeated on 23 August 1268 at the Battle of Tagliacozzo, in the Abruzzi hills to the east of Rome.[16] He was captured while trying to escape by sea, tortured, and finally executed on 29 October. The cruelties inflicted on Conradin and some of his supporters, made the name of King Charles hated and feared, but there could be no doubt

---

[12] Davidsohn, *Forschungen*, iv, pp. 188, 197–200; Baethgen, 'Der Anspruch', p. 140; Davidsohn, *Storia*, 11. ii, pp. 10–12, 26–29; R. Sternfeld and O. Schultz-Gora, 'Ein sirventes von 1268 gegen die Kirche und Karl von Anjou', *Mitteilungen des Instituts für österreichische Geschichtsforschung*, xxiv, 1903, p. 618.

[13] Martène and Durand, ii, cols 542–3.

[14] Ibid., col. 615.

[15] Davidsohn, *Storia*, ii. ii, pp. 45–6.

[16] The battle and the events leading to it have been elaborately investigated by P. Herde, 'Die Schlacht bei Tagliacozzo', *Zeitschrift für bayerische Landesgeschichte*, xxv, 1962.

now that the Hohenstaufen, with their claim to rule in Naples and Italy, were finally destroyed.

The most important political change in Tuscany which resulted from the Battle of Tagliacozzo was that Siena was forced to come over to the Guelf side. After Tagliacozzo the Sienese tried repeatedly, with the help of Guido Novello and his Ghibellines and Germans, to extend the territory which they controlled outside the city. In June 1269 a Sienese army led by Guido and Provenzan Salvani went against Colle val d'Elsa to the North. There it was met by a largely Florentine force led by Aldobrandino de' Pazzi and by Charles's vicar, Jean Britaud. The Sienese were heavily defeated, with great loss of life and booty. The head of Provenzan Salvani, the Ghibelline leader, was struck off by Carlino Tolomei, an enemy from one of the Sienese banking families. The Florentines could feel at last that the Sienese Ghibelline victory of Montaperti, nine years earlier, had been avenged, but Siena still did not submit. In December 1269 Guido Novello was appointed *podestà*. The end of the Ghibelline regime there came in 1270 by the agency of Charles's vicar, Guy de Montfort, whose pressure on the city brought about submission, the exodus of the Ghibellines, and the re-entry of the Guelfs on 15 August.[17] With the winning of Siena, Guelf power in Tuscany had advanced as far as was practical. Short of establishing control of Pisa, a great commercial city whose enmity with Lucca and Florence was based on disputes about territory and commerce as well as party feeling, not much more could be done.

During the period of warfare between Charles and the Hohenstaufen from 1265 to 1268, great strides were made in establishing links between the merchants and bankers of the Tuscan cities and the international alliance of pope, Naples, and France—links which were to make it from this time difficult for Florence, Siena, Pistoia, and Lucca to adopt anything but a Guelf position in international affairs. The leading commercial houses of these cities became so deeply dependent on the trade of Naples and the finances of the papal court that the loss of these connections would have been deeply harmful. These commercial links are not, however, easy to connect with the internal life of Florence; although they were certainly prominent we know little about the political actions of the great commercial houses there. We also have only limited indications of their commercial activity in the world outside: there are no central accounts of the papal chamber for this period, and there is little evidence about trade at Naples. We are dependent for information mainly on the letters of the pope and Charles relating to loans and granting privileges, which often referred to subordinate merchants whose links with the commercial houses may be obscure. What can be learned about this world?

¹⁷ Davidsohn, *Storia*, II. ii, pp. 63–6, 82–4; Tempesti, 'Provenzan Salvani', pp. 36–8.

The essence of Clement IV's scheme for the Angevin invasion was that the money should be eventually provided from the clerical tenths to be levied in France, but that Charles and his forces in Italy should be funded in the first instance by Italian bankers advancing cash which would be repaid to their agents in France.[18] A letter survives which was written from Tours on 29 November 1265 by a Sienese merchant, Andrea de' Tolomei, to his partners in Siena. Its author speculates about the effect that such large transactions in money will have on the currencies of Tours and Provins and brings to life the way in which the scheme depended on companies which had branches both in Italy and in France.[19] The pope, whose letters display a clear grasp of papal finance, was insistent, in writing to Cardinal Simon de Brie who was in charge of the collection of the taxes in France, that all the money must be used to repay Italian bankers, and none of it for raising troops in France.[20] At one stage the pope agreed that money might be raised from Roman merchants, who were not international financiers of the type common in Tuscany, by giving them the security of ecclesiastical property in Rome itself instead of assignments on taxes. It seems that about £60,000 was loaned on this basis between August 1265 and January 1266, the payments being made not in Rome but at Paris or St Maur-les-Fosses to agents of the Bonsignori who had taken over the debts.[21] This, however, was an uncharacteristic and exceptional part of the papal financial plan, which in general depended mainly on Tuscans. The Bonsignori of Siena appear to have been the main agents of papal and Angevin finance throughout the pontificate of Clement IV and through into the early 1270s. This is the company known later as the *Gran Tavola*, which was established by Orlando Bonsignori and his associates and began to fall into decay after his death in 1273.[22] It is impossible to estimate the total of the loans made by this or any other company, but we have evidence that they were owed £9,000 Tournois in February 1265 and lent another £20,000 in June 1265; and £10,550 between November 1265 and January 1266. In March 1266 they are said to have lent £50,000.[23] During the early 1270s they made many loans to Charles I, who expressed his love for them in a letter of 1273 in which

---

[18] The scheme and its execution are described by Jordan, *Domination angevine*, pp. 536–58; G. Martini, 'La politica finanziaria dei papi in Francia intorno alla metà del secolo XIII', *Atti d. Accademia Nazionale dei Lincei*, 1951, ser. 8, Memorie, Classe di Scienze Morali, iii; N. Housley, *The Italian Crusades* (Oxford, 1982), pp. 222–31.

[19] *Lettere volgari del secolo XIII scritte da Senesi*, ed. C. Paoli and E. Piccolomini (Bologna, 1871), pp. 55–6.

[20] Martène and Durand, ii, cols 178–80, 5 August 1265.

[21] Ibid., cols 176–7. The whole episode is described by F. Schneider, 'Zur älteren päpstlichen Finanzgeschichte', *Quellen und Forschungen aus italienischen Archiven und Bibliotheken*, ix, 1906, pp. 15–37.

[22] M. Chiaudano, 'I Rothschild del Duecento: la Gran Tavola di Orlando Bonsignori', *Bullettino senese di storia patria*, n.s., vi, 1935; idem, *Studi e documenti per la storia del diritto commerciale italiano nel sec. XIII* (R. Università di Torino, Memorie dell'Instituto Giuridico, ser. ii, Memoria viii, 1930).

[23] Martène and Durand, ii, cols 103–4, 125–6, 139–40, 149–50, 248, 258–9, 295–7.

he asked his representatives in France for investigation of the debts due to them.[24] In September 1275 they paid Charles's annual census of 8,000 *oncie* to the pope for him.[25] The cardinals, assembled at Viterbo during the long papal vacancy from the death of Clement IV in November 1268 to the election of Gregory X in September 1271, had to turn to the Bonsignori repeatedly for loans to pay for the defence of the papal lands between Orvieto and Lake Bolsena.[26] Among other Sienese companies we have much more limited evidence that the Tolomei and the Salimbeni companies were also involved in papal finance at this period, but they were apparently much less important.[27]

Among the Florentines lending to the pope and Charles I, the most prominent were the Frescobaldi company. They were said in June 1266 to have loaned various sums totalling £14,000. They also continued to deal with Charles later.[28] The Cerchi, whose representatives promised at Perugia to help the church on 2 May 1265, were recorded a few days earlier as having made a loan of £1,000.[29] We also find indications of loans from the Bardi and the Scali.[30] These are the only Florentines of whose prominent service to the papal–Angevin cause in the pontificate of Clement IV we can be sure. No doubt there were others who are now unrecorded. Different kinds of documents might well give us a different picture. We can also be sure that, whether or not they were involved in lending money to the pope and Charles, many other Florentines had to link themselves with the papal cause to some degree, openly or secretly, in order to take part in the ecclesiastical financial business of transferring money to Rome. It has been estimated that 146 members of Florentine companies are recorded as making oaths of obedience to the papacy between 1263 and 1265.[31] Many others who found obedience to the papacy essential for gaining their bread came from Siena, Pistoia, and Lucca, which also specialized in this sort of business. However, among all these mercantile companies, only the Bonsignori are referred to as *mercatores camere* or *mercatores pape*,[32] so they probably had a close association with the pope that was not shared by any rival company.

[24] S. Terlizzi, *Codice Diplomatico delle relazioni tra Carlo I d'Angiò e la Toscana*, Documenti di storia italiana, xii (Florence, 1950), no. 656; other references to Charles's relations with the Bonsignori, nos 201, 205, 208, 272, 273, 281, 358, 387, 429, 664, 740, 759.

[25] Terlizzi, no. 710.

[26] N. Kamp, 'Die Herrscherthrone im Schatz der Kardinale', *Festschrift Percy Ernst Schramm*, i (Wiesbaden, 1964).

[27] *Reg. Clément IV*, p. 285; Terlizzi, nos 313, 424.

[28] Martène and Durand, ii, col. 344. Other entries relating to Frescobaldi: cols 123, 177–8, 208, 300; *Reg. Clément IV*, p. 23; Terlizzi, nos 4, 212, 762.

[29] Davidsohn, *Forschungen*, iii, pp. 18–19; Martène and Durand, ii, col. 128; *Reg. Clément IV*, p. 22.

[30] Terlizzi, nos 9, 10, 180; and perhaps also Martène and Durand, ii, col. 152 and *Reg. Clément IV*, pp. 35, 455.

[31] Davidsohn, *Storia*, 11, i, p. 765.

[32] E. Jordan, *De Mercatoribus Camerae Apostolicae Saeculo XIII* (Condate Rhedonum, 1909), pp. 17–19.

After the period of the war with the Hohenstaufen, the next big papal financial effort was the sexennial tenth to be collected for use in a crusade, which was imposed by Gregory X at the Council of Lyons in 1274 and was to run for six years from that date. This was a quite different kind of effort from the triennial tenth of 1264: it was imposed all over Europe and administered in a leisurely fashion without pressure for the immediate production of sums of money in Italy. It has left documents of a different kind which, though very fragmentary, make it a little easier to estimate the relative part played by the different companies in the local management of the tax collection. Among the useful indications given by the records of this tax are the following. The proceeds of the taxation of North Italian dioceses were mostly handed over between 1274 and 1280 to a large number of different Lucchese merchants, principally it would seem the Ricciardi and the company of the sons of Paganello Dulce but also many others, to the Bonsignori of Siena, the Ammanati and Chiarenti of Pistoia, the Alfani of Florence, the Scotti of Piacenza, and some companies from Vercelli.[33] Money collected in Tuscany during the same period was deposited with the Battosi and Bettuli of Lucca, the Bonsignori of Siena, the Mozzi and the Pulci and Rimbertini of Florence.[34] In Latium half the proceeds of the first year were deposited with the Ricciardi of Lucca and the Mozzi of Florence. By 1281 most of the money raised seems to have been placed in the hands of the Ricciardi.[35]

In England, where the handling of the tax is rather well documented, there was considerable anxiety in the early days about placing the money in the hands of merchants who would be safe custodians if there were a Welsh invasion. Local ecclesiastical advice given to the collectors at the beginning of June 1277 was that they should trust the Ricciardi of Lucca and the Scotti of Piacenza, presumably because these merchants were employed by the king. But the collectors had also been instructed (in a letter sent a little earlier by Pope John XXI) to divide at least some of the money equally between the Ricciardi, the Scotti, the Chiarenti and Ammanati of Pistoia; the Bonsignori of Siena; and the Scali, the Pulci and Rimbertini, and the Mozzi of Florence. This they did. If we go on to the final statement of the placing of the moneys raised from this tax in England by 1283, we find that a very considerable sum, over £65,000 sterling, was held approximately in the following way: £11,000 by the Ricciardi, £7,000 by the Bettori of Lucca, smaller sums by the Cardelini, Squarcialuppi and Getti Honesti of Lucca; £9,000 by the Scotti of Piacenza; £5,000 by the Bonsignori of Siena; the rest by Florentine firms, of which the Scali with nearly £6,000, the Mozzi with £4,500, the Cerchi with

[33] M. H. Laurent, 'La Decime de 1274–1280 dans l'Italie septentrionale', *Miscellanea Pio Paschini*, i (Lateranum, n.s., xiv, 1948), esp. pp. 375–7.

[34] *Rationes Decimarum Italiae nei secoli XIII e XIV: Tuscia 1. la decima degli anni 1274–1280*, ed. P. Guidi (Studi e testi, 58, 1932), p. xxxix.

[35] *Rationes Decimarum Italiae nei secoli XIII e XIV: Latium*, ed. G. Battelli (Studi e testi, 128, 1946), p. 423.

£4,500, the Pulci-Rimbertini with nearly £4,000 are the most prominent, the rest being held by the Bardi, Frescobaldi, Falconieri, and Ardinghelli. The total Florentine share was larger than the Lucchese.[36]

Evidence of this kind shows us that the papacy and its collectors had dealings in various parts of Europe with a large number of bankers and merchants, chiefly Tuscan but drawn from various cities. It suggests that in the later 1270s the Lucchese share in this business was very large, possibly larger than that of the bankers of any other city. Florentines were similarly prominent, Sienese less so. What this kind of evidence does not tell us is which were the most important firms at the papal court itself—those most likely to be lenders to the popes and perhaps therefore most influential in papal politics. The kind of evidence which suggests that the Bonsignori had this crucial position from 1265 to 1271 is lacking for the rest of the 1270s because our information is principally about local collection and local deposit of funds. When therefore we come to the most dramatic episode in papal-Florentine relations in the 1270s—the visit of Gregory X to Florence in June–July 1273, when he stayed in the Mozzi palace on the Arno and attempted a reconciliation of Guelfs and Ghibellines—we lack the evidence to place it in the background of papal financial policies. We do not know precisely how important the Mozzi were to Gregory X. The probability in fact is that though they were important, Gregory X's only special link was with the Scotti from his own city of Piacenza.[37]

We happen to know that when the Bonsignori of Siena were the *mercatores pape* in December 1267, they were also managing the movement of money between two of the pope's chief enemies, the commune of Siena and Henry of Castile.[38] The victory of the Guelfs, however, made it much more difficult for merchants to be open Ghibellines if they wished to do ecclesiastical business. It also had the effect of ousting Ghibellines from Naples. Charles I, who had even more constant need for money than the pope did, attracted merchants as lenders by giving them the commercial advantage of a privileged trading position in his own kingdom. His enemies the Pisans were excluded, and this factor was extremely harmful to Pisan commerce in Southern Italy after 1265. The alliance of pope, Naples, and France therefore had the result of facilitating commercial activity by merchants from Tuscan Guelf cities in a wide area extending from Paris to Naples. During the 1260s and 1270s this area was occupied by a large number of Florentine, Sienese, and Lucchese firms: this was still the period of Guelf rather than Florentine dominance. But the new Guelf ascendancy provided the framework within which the Florentines would rise to a supreme position within the following twenty years.

[36] W. E. Lunt, 'A Papal Tenth Levied in The British Isles from 1274 to 1280', *English Historical Review*, xxxii, 1917, pp. 66, 74, 76–7, 79–80; idem, *Financial Relations of the Papacy with England to 1327* (Cambridge, Mass., 1939), Appendix vi. See also R. W. Kaeuper, *Bankers to the Crown: The Riccardi of Lucca and Edward I* (Princeton, 1973), pp. 46–8, etc.
[37] Jordan, *De Mercatoribus*, p. 21.   [38] Ibid.

The establishment of Guelf power in Florence at Easter 1267 was a military action carried out by some hundreds of French knights under the command of King Charles's representative Jourdain de l'Isle and by Guelf exiles under Count Guido Guerra.[39] The result of this intervention by the Angevin king was that Florence endured a social and political revolution which was acute and far-reaching, the kind of change that the pope had been trying to prevent and which Charles favoured: a dramatic substitution of Guelfs for Ghibellines. The Guelfs were compensated for the damage done to their property in years of exile, the Ghibellines were exiled. There are two major documents in the Florentine archives which illustrate this revolution in detail. The *Liber Extimationum* records the results of enquiries to discover damage done to the property of exiled Guelfs. It contains information about 626 heads of households, including many notable families famous in Guelf history before and after this period[40]—Cavalcanti, Scali, Adimari, Donati, Spini, Bardi, Mozzi, and Buondelmonti, for example. It tells us the names of the families who came back in 1267 and also of many, though by no means all, who were to be rich and prominent in the city in the next few decades. The *Libro del chiodo* (Book of the nail), on the other hand, contains lists of those Ghibellines who were to be punished. The punishment was in some cases exile beyond the Florentine *contado*, the external lands controlled by the city, in some a fixed exile within the *contado*, and in others a declaration of suspicion. The lists are incomplete and name heads of families only. Estimates of the persons actually moved out vary from three thousand to four thousand. Whatever the precise figures, a very large number were certainly banished, and in many cases the families remained permanently exiled after this period.[41] The exile of the Ghibellines in 1267 was the end of the oscillations of the middle of the thirteenth century, and had the result that many notable families (like the Uberti, whose famous head—Farinata—was interviewed by Dante in *Inferno*), were cut off for ever from their native soil.

The fierce hatred exhibited in the sentences of exile seems to have animated Florentine official policy throughout the next decade—with the assistance, of course, of King Charles. This hatred was apparent in Florentine action against Siena at the battle of Colle in June 1269, in the Florentine demolition of the stronghold of the Pazzi of Valdarno—one of the most important Ghibelline

---

[39] Events at Florence from November 1266 to April 1267 were examined long ago by G. Salvemini, *Magnati e popolani in Firenze dal 1280 al 1295* (Florence, 1899), pp. 194–231 and by Davidsohn, *Forschungen*, iv, pp. 174–97 (see also ! :s *Storia*, 11. i, pp. 829–49), and have not been much discussed since. The comments in S. Raveggi, M. Tarassi, D. Medici, and P. Parenti, *Ghibellini, Guelfi e popolo grasso* (Florence, 1978), pp. 80–90 give interesting analyses of the political position of many individual Florentines.

[40] *Liber Extimationum*, ed. A. Brattö (Göteborg, 1956).

[41] Lists from the *Libro del chiodo* partially printed in *Delizie degli eruditi toscani* ed. Ildefonso di San Luigi (Florence, 1770–89), viii, p. 221; discussed by Davidsohn, *Forschungen*, iv, pp. 190–1; I. Del Lungo, 'Una vendetta in Firenze il giorno di S. Giovanni del 1295', *Archivio storico italiano*, ser. 4, xviii, 1886 (separately published, slightly enlarged, Florence, 1887).

families in the *contado*—at Ostina in September 1269, in the execution of two sons of Farinata degli Uberti in May 1270, in the sending of envoys to Gregory X after his election urging continued resistance to Ghibellines, in continued attacks on the Ghibelline Ubaldini in the Mugello to the north of Florence,[42] and many other actions of the 1270s. There was one serious effort to impose peace between Guelfs and Ghibellines—Gregory X's attempted pacification during his visit to Florence in July 1273—but it showed only the impotence of the papacy in the face of Florentine and Angevin Guelfism. The years between the death of Clement IV in November 1268 and the election of Nicholas III in November 1277 were a period of weak papal policy in Central Italy. A three-year vacancy was followed by the pontificate of Gregory X (September 1271–January 1276) and then by the very brief pontificates of Innocent V (January–June 1276), Hadrian V (June–August 1276), and John XXI (September 1276–May 1277).

Gregory X was from the North of Italy and probably had little interest in Tuscany. He was principally concerned with the project of mounting a crusade, for which he spared no pains. He summoned the Council of Lyons and left Italy for two years, to die immediately after he returned. On the way to Lyons he visited Florence. He had already expressed his impatience with Florentine hostility to the Ghibellines and had tried to exert influence against it by sending first the Dominican General John of Vercelli, and then a Florentine guelf Dominican, Aldobrandino Cavalcanti, to the city with letters stating his view that great benefits would follow from peace.[43] An undated letter—not later than the spring of 1273—rebuked the Florentines sharply for their continued fostering of conflict. It also reprimanded them for attacking the properties of Cardinal Ottaviano degli Ubaldini, a great churchman with Ghibelline sympathies from an important Tuscan noble family who had, nevertheless, been an ally of Charles of Anjou at least in his original attack on Naples in 1265, and had ridden with him to the borders of the kingdom.

You, however, as your actions clearly make known, not only close your ears against us and against the sound advice of that master [the Dominican envoy of the pope] but daily kindle fires of greater iniquity as you inflict more frequently more spiteful attacks on your neighbours, killing them or destroying their property.[44]

When he came to Florence, however, Gregory came with Charles of Anjou and with Baldwin, claimant to the throne of Byzantium; and was also visited by delegates of King Philip III of France, anxious to press his bid for the empire against Rudolf of Habsburg, whom the pope favoured.[45] When he had

---

[42] Davidsohn, *Storia*, ii, pp. 68, 78, 101; idem, *Forschungen*, ii, p. 179.

[43] Davidsohn, *Forschungen*, iv, pp. 211–12.

[44] F. Kaltenbrunner, *Actenstücke zur Geschichte des deutschen Reiches unter den Königen Rudolf 1. und Albrecht 1.* (Vienna, 1889), p. 9.

[45] A report by the envoys of the king of France on their discussions with the pope and cardinals

to deal at the same time with these representatives of great powers and great interests, the domestic problems of Florence and Tuscany played a smaller part in the mind of Gregory than they do in accounts of his visit to the city given by Florentine chroniclers. This no doubt explains why the plan Gregory announced there was so feeble, and so much more favourable to the side of the Guelfs and Charles than to the Ghibellines. The Ghibellines were represented before Gregory by members of their leading families: Guglielmo de' Pazzi, Neri Boccalato degli Uberti, Gualterone de' Soldanieri, and others who were allowed to enter Florence for negotiations. There were also representatives of Count Guido Novello and Simone his brother. Much of the settlement,[46] which was announced ceremonially by the pope on 12 July 1273 by the Ponte di Rubaconte near the Mozzi palace before he laid the foundation stone of a new church on the same site, was concerned with the Conti Guidi of Poppi, the family of Guido Novello who had been the military leader of the Ghibellines for many years. For the ordinary Florentine exiles, the proposal was that their women and children should be allowed to return; the men themselves might return when allowed to do so by King Charles, to whom they were to provide hostages. The representatives of the Ghibellines were already complaining that their safety was threatened by Charles in Florence when the pope left the city four days after the reconciliation.[47] Thus the reconciliation came to nothing. When Gregory returned to Florence in December 1275, shortly before his death at Arezzo, it was a city under interdict for refusing to accept papal orders, and the sick pope would have refused to pass through it if heavy rain had not made it difficult for him to cross the Arno at any other point.[48]

Though we have a great deal of evidence about the persistently anti-Ghibelline external policy of Florence and about the exile of the Ghibellines, we have little information—in comparison with the period after 1280, from which the records of the city councils began to survive—about the internal political structure of Florence during the decade after 1267. The Guelf party, the organization of those who had won in 1267, probably exercised a considerable amount of power, mainly because they had recovered control of the city by force and ousted their enemies, and to a lesser extent because of the fate of the property which had been left behind by the Ghibellines. This was divided into three parts, one part of which had gone to the commune, one to compensate the Guelfs who had suffered during the Ghibelline dominance, and the third to the Guelf party, which therefore became an institution with

in Florence in July 1273 is printed in *Monumenta Germaniae Historica, Constitutiones,* iii, ed. I. Schwalm, 1904–6, p. 585.

[46] G. Lami, *Sanctae Ecclesiae Florentinae Monumenta* (Florence, 1758), i, pp. 499–502; *Les Registres de Grégoire X (1272–1276),* ed. J. Guiraud (Paris, 1892–1960), pp. 129–32.

[47] The episode of Gregory's visit to Florence and the reconciliation plan are covered in Davidsohn, *Forschungen,* iv, pp. 211–25 and *Storia,* II. ii, pp. 120–32.

[48] Davidsohn, *Storia,* II. ii, pp. 170–1.

financial strength. In December 1277 the Guelf party lent £6,000 to the commune, and we know also that it had accounts with the Scali, the Mozzi, Frescobaldi, Bardi, Acciaiuoli, and other important bankers.[49] The Florentine chronicler Villani reports Cardinal Ottaviano degli Ubaldini's comment on the fate of the Ghibelline lands and palaces: 'Since the Guelfs have turned them into movable property, the Ghibellines will never return'.[50] If these properties were sold rather than destroyed or wasted, there is sense in the remark. We may also imagine at this period that the six captains of the Guelf party, replaced at the beginning of 1275 by a single captain drawn from abroad, conveyed the wishes of their members in a way it would be difficult for the city to refuse. Their power may have been similar to the description of it by Villani:

By order of the pope and the king the Guelfs made three knights Captains [this should in fact be six] and called them first Consuls of the Knights and then Captains of the Party. Their office lasted two months, they were chosen alternately by the two groups of three *sesti* of the city and met for councils in the new church of Santa Maria Sopra Porta as the most public place of the city and where there are many Guelf houses around. They made their secret council of fourteen and the greater council of sixty great men and men of the people, by whose scrutiny the captains of the party and other officials were elected.[51]

The true situation is obscure but we can be sure that, however it was exercised, the Guelfs who had come back from exile had a dominant power.

A document dated 2 May 1273 gives us the names of some of the people important in the Guelf party. Count Alessandro degli Alberti granted that three of his holdings of land to the north of Florence should, if his sons died without male heirs, pass to the Guelf party of Florence, represented in the document by Cavalcante Cavalcanti and by Stoldo di Jacopo Rossi. Present at the making of the agreement were Buonaccorso Bellincioni, Bondelmonte de' Buondelmonti, Berto Frescobaldi, Guido Accolti de' Bardi, Tommaso de' Mozzi, Simone di Donato Donati, Chierico de' Pazzi, Vieri de' Cerchi, Rosso della Tosa, and Gherardo Ventraia de' Tornaquinci.[52] These are well-known names of men from great families, some are of ancient Guelf houses—the father of Guido Cavalcanti the poet; Rossi who had carried the flag of the Guelf Florentines at Benevento; one of the Buondelmonti whose quarrel was supposed to have started the Guelf–Ghibelline feud in 1215; famous representatives of the Donati, Tosinghi, and the Pazzi. Some are prominent members of families well known for their huge commercial interests: Tommaso de' Mozzi, Berto Frescobaldi, Guido Accolti de' Bardi, Vieri de' Cerchi. The

[49] Ibid., p. 162.
[50] Villani, VII. xvii.
[51] Ibid., see also Davidsohn, *Forschungen*, iv, p. 197.
[52] G. Mengozzi, 'Documenti danteschi del R. Archivio di Stato di Siena', *Bullettino senese di storia patria*, xxviii, 1921, p. 102. See also Davidsohn, *Storia*, 11. ii, pp. 145–6.

inclusion of Vieri de' Cerchi in the inner council of the Guelfs in 1273 in a deed that was of importance to Florence's foreign policy is interesting, because members of his family had been linked with the Ghibellines before 1267; and at the end of the century he failed catastrophically to dominate the Guelfs.[53] On the whole, however, these are the kind of men whom one would expect to be leading the Guelf party in 1273.

There are other fragments of information that can be used to fill out a little of our picture of the social groups controlling the Guelf party.[54] But the lack of suitable evidence makes us extremely ignorant about the political constitution of Florence at this period. It is not clear whether there was a typical communal organization of twelve 'good men' with councils, which consented to legislation, with a Guelf party existing within the commune and influencing it, as Davidsohn thought; or whether, as Ottokar thought, the Guelf party and the commune at this period were more closely identified, so that the Guelfs ran the city directly.[55] There can be no doubt, however, of the supremacy of Guelf power. During the period from 1267 to 1277, Charles of Anjou remained imperial vicar in Tuscany.[56] The revival of Ghibellinism in Northern Italy, and Gregory X's encouragement in 1273 of the election of Rudolf of Habsburg as king of the Romans, who might have been crowned emperor and might have intervened to re-establish imperial powers in Italy, were threats to Charles.[57] But Gregory was concerned with a pan-European crusading plan for which he wanted a German leader, not with Tuscany, and did not seriously interfere with Charles in Italy. The French (and pro-French) pope of 1276, Innocent V, confirmed explicitly (contradicting the original arrangement of 1265) that there was no objection to Charles being both senator of Rome and vicar of Tuscany.[58] Charles thus remained in possession of a political power to the north as well as the south of the papal state, similar to that held by the Hohenstaufen in the earlier part of the thirteenth century and potentially dangerous to the papacy.

What it meant in practice in Tuscany was that Charles replaced the Hohenstaufen. Instead of a German force, a principally French force of soldiers was maintained there at his disposal, administered by his officials but paid for by the Tuscan cities. This was the system of the *tallia*. A force of three hundred to five hundred mounted troops, quite a large army to be kept in existence for long periods in the thirteenth century, was regularly maintained

---

[53] Raveggi *et al.*, *Ghibellini, Guelfi*, pp. 84–6. There is a good account of the Cerchi by F. Cardini in *Enciclopedia Dantesca* (Rome, 1970–8), i, pp. 915–18.

[54] This has been done by N. Ottokar, *Il comune di Firenze alla fine del Dugento* (Florence, 1926), pp. 38–47, and by Tarassi in Raveggi *et al.*, *Ghibellini, Guelfi*.

[55] Davidsohn, *Forschungen*, iv, pp. 196–7; Ottokar, *Comune di Firenze*, p. 40.

[56] Baethgen, 'Der Anspruch des Papsttums auf das Reichsvikariat', pp. 141–53.

[57] Léonard, *Les Angevins de Naples*, pp. 110–24.

[58] A. Theiner, *Codex Diplomaticus Dominii Temporalis S. Sedis* (Rome, 1861–2), i, p. 197; cf. M.-H. Laurent, *Le Bienheureux Innocent V (Pierre de Tarentaise) et son temps* (Studi e testi 129, 1947), p. 333.

by the Guelf towns of Tuscany, which sent representatives to parliaments, usually held at Empoli, to discuss the response to Angevin pressure.[59] The *tallia* survived into the fourteenth century, long after Angevin power in Tuscany had declined, and later became to some degree a Florentine weapon. The regular meetings and payments by the Guelf towns—Florence, Siena, Prato, Lucca, Pistoia, S. Gimignano, Volterra—are an important part of the background to the long-term expansion of Florentine influence. In the 1270s, however, the *tallia* was dominated by the Angevin king and his officials who were the main centralizing power in Tuscany, and it must have seemed at that time that they had rudimentary institutions on which some kind of monarchy might eventually be built.

Charles had been appointed *podestà* of Florence and of other cities. Throughout this period the *podestà* of Florence was appointed with the king's approval and the incumbents were royal vicars; they were, however, mostly Italians.[60] The king's central authority in Tuscany, on the other hand, was run by three important Frenchmen: the vicar-general, the marshal and the treasurer. The vicars-general were considerable French noblemen. The first of them, Jean de Braiselve, was captured and killed by Conradin in June 1268.[61] He was succeeded by Rudolf Faiel, then by Jean Britaud de Nangis who had been a household official of the king of France, and then by a still more splendid person, Guy de Montfort, son of Simon de Montfort.[62] Montfort was at that time making his fortune in the service of Charles of Anjou. After being sent to Tuscany by the king in the Spring of 1270, he added to his new Neapolitan lands by marrying Margherita Aldobrandesca, the heiress of the Count of Pitigliano. On 13 March 1271 he met at Viterbo Henry of Almaine, son of Richard of Cornwall and nephew of Henry III of England, Simon de Montfort's enemy, visiting the cardinals on their way back from the crusade to Tunis with the kings of Naples and France. Inspired perhaps by the Italian custom of vendetta, which he would have observed since coming to Italy, Guy killed Henry in the church of San Silvestro.[63] This famous crime led to Guy's expulsion from the king's favour for a decade. Montfort was succeeded as vicar-general by Henry, Count of Vaudemont, who was followed by Jacques de Burson in 1272, by Gautier Appard in 1274, and by Raymond de Poncelles

[59] See, for example, the order by Charles to Tuscan towns to send sindics to discuss the *tallia*, dated 5 July 1273 (Terlizzi, *Codice diplomatico*, no. 584). There are many other references to the system in Terlizzi and in the San Gimignano documents in Davidsohn, *Forschungen*, ii. See also D. P. Waley, 'Condotte and Condottieri in the Thirteenth Century', *Proceedings of the British Academy*, lxi, 1975, pp. 349–51.

[60] They are listed in Davidsohn, *Forschungen*, iv, pp. 538–9; some of the titles applied to them are quoted there.

[61] Davidsohn, *Storia*, 11, ii, pp. 8–46.

[62] Ibid., p. 62; Terlizzi, no. 209.

[63] F. M. Powicke, 'Guy de Montfort (1265–71)', *Transactions of the Royal Historical Society*, ser. 4, xviii, 1935; Davidsohn, *Forschungen*, iv, pp. 201–11.

in 1275.[64] The vicar-general was assisted by a marshal who was also a French knight.[65] A French clerk was appointed as treasurer.[66] Apart from Guy de Montfort, these officials have in general left only the most formal information about their activities. But the French presence must have been prominent, especially in Florence. The fact that Braiselve was later remembered in Italy as an authority on courtly behaviour, and that Brunetto Latini—that great link between Florence and French literary culture—was employed as a notary by Britaud,[67] suggests that they may have had a literary as well as a political importance.

The great obstacle to Guelf control of the whole of Tuscany was Pisa, a city in some respects quite different in character from Florence, Siena, and Lucca because of its maritime situation, its seaborne trade with the eastern Mediterranean, and its empire across the water in Sardinia. Pisa remained the second or third city in Tuscany, independent in its Ghibellinism, to the end of the period covered by this book. In the 1270s it was still extremely powerful, and in general hostile to making terms either with King Charles or with the Tuscan Guelfs—including the rulers of its closest neighbour and rival, Lucca. Pisan politics were profoundly disturbed by the presence of two great magnates, both also holders of lands in Sardinia, who were more disposed to agreement with the Guelfs, Giovanni Visconti and Ugolino Gherardesca. These men were both exiled in 1274. Visconti died but Ugolino was in league with the Guelf forces which defeated Pisa heavily at Asciano, near the city, in 1275. The following year peace was made, with concessions to Lucca, and Ugolino returned to Pisa. But of course the peace was only an interlude in a continual battle.[68] In the rest of Tuscany, however, the years 1265 to 1277 saw a considerable change. Some parts of it—the establishment of Guelf control and involvement in a great Guelf axis running through France, Tuscany, the papal court, and Naples—were to be permanent. For the time being the Guelf families lived under an Angevin umbrella, which may have seemed to some

[64] Terlizzi, nos 267, 448, 670, 716. These men and also the marshals and treasurers mentioned below will be found in the index of Frenchmen in the kingdom of Naples in P. Durrieu, *Les Archives angevines de Naples*, ii (Paris, 1887).

[65] Jourdain de l'Isle 1267 (Davidsohn, *Forschungen*, iv, p. 188), Amiel d'Agoult c.1267–71 (ibid., p. 193, idem., *Storia*, III, pp. 113–14), 'Theobaldus de Ursemayo' 1271–2 (Terlizzi, no. 413), Louis d'Auvergne 1272 (ibid., no. 448), Eustache de Faiel 1272 (ibid., no. 451), Jacques de Senacourt 1274 (ibid., no. 672), Robert de Saint Serleau (?Saint-Sanz-Lieu) 1275 (ibid., no. 717), Roger de Ars 1276 (ibid., no. 730).

[66] Stephan de Picosis 1270 (Terlizzi no. 186), Henri Barat 1271 (ibid., no. 279), Jean le Noir 1272–3 (ibid., no. 432, 627), Magister Stephanus 1275 (ibid., no. 711), Bertaud de Courtlieu 1277 (ibid., no. 769).

[67] Davidsohn, *Storia*, II, ii, pp. 9, 62.

[68] An additional source (apart from Davidsohn) for the Pisan story is D. A. Winter, *Die Politik Pisas während der Jahre 1268–1282* (Halle, 1906) and the analytical works of E. Cristiani, *Nobiltà e popolo nel comune di Pisa* (Naples, 1962), and D. Herlihy, *Pisa in the Early Renaissance: A Study of Urban Growth* (New Haven, 1958). See also E. Cristiani, 'Gli avvenimenti pisani del periodo ugoliniano in una cronaca inedita', *Bollettino storico Pisano*, xxvi–xxvii, 1957–8.

extent to have merely replaced German by French dominance. That was to end very soon. As long as it lasted it provided Tuscany with a partly French protectorate, which probably facilitated the influence of French culture as well as encouraging the Guelfs of the cities to a continuous intransigent exclusion of their hated enemies.

2

The Supremacy of Florence, 1277–1294

IN the later years of the thirteenth century, after 1277, events tended to strengthen the independent power of the Guelf oligarchs of Florence in a way that might have been hoped for but could scarcely have been expected in the difficult years of the sixties. One reason for this was the sheer economic expansion of the city, which seems in this period to have substantially increased its wealth and influence in comparison with its neighbours. But there were also major political changes, which removed the limitations to the independent power of the Tuscan Guelf cities and opened a field for the free expansion of Florence. Angevin influence in Tuscany was cut back by Pope Nicholas III (1277–80) and largely removed by the Sicilian Vespers of 1282. Rudolf of Habsburg failed to replace it with German power. The power of the Ghibelline exiles was eroded by the campaigns of Martin IV (1281–5) in Romagna. Ghibelline Pisa suffered a terrible catastrophe in its defeat by the Genoese at the naval Battle of Meloria in 1284, which was exploited further by Florentine attacks. Arezzo was crippled by the Florentine victory at Campaldino in 1289. By the 1290s, Florentine Guelf influence was spreading out over Tuscany without meeting serious hindrances—that is until the new intervention of the papacy and the French during the pontificate of Boniface VIII, which will be recorded in a later chapter. In 1294 the power of the Florentine Guelfs was much stronger and better established than it had ever been before.

The election of Nicholas III on 25 November 1277 brought into the papal chair a remarkable and strictly Italian pope whose conception of his office was based on essentially Italian presuppositions. Gian Gaetano Orsini had been a cardinal for thirty-three years, and at times a prominent cardinal; he was a member of one of the greatest Roman families and cardinal protector of the Franciscan order.[1] He was imbued, as no other pope of the late thirteenth century, with a deep attachment to the two most prominent ingredients of the Italian church: the grandeur of the apostolic succession at Rome and the religious power of St Francis. His feeling about the Franciscans was graphically recorded in accounts of the emotional scene when, as a new pope, he handed over protection of the order to his nephew, Matteo Rosso Orsini (see p. 50). His enormous respect for the basilica of St Peter's was expressed in 1279 in a bull in which he granted indulgences to it:

[1] On Nicholas before his election, see R. Sternfeld, *Der Kardinal J. G. Orsini* (Berlin, 1905).

for the glorious prince of the apostles and his venerable basilica built by divine direction in the city of cities we have had a feeling of spiritual devotion from the time we attained an age of discretion, which, as we reached the honour of the cardinalate and obtained the office of archpriest in that basilica, was always increased by promotion and grew as we were advanced . . . this is the house of God built firmly on the rock . . . this is the divine tabernacle loved by celestial choirs, venerated eternally, this is the place specially annexed to the Roman pontiff.[2]

To Orsini's strongly Roman sensibility, the power of the Angevin house in Central Italy was unnecessary and offensive; and the conflict of Guelf and Ghibelline in Tuscany, on which that power partly depended, was an undesirable division in the Italian world. King Charles bitterly resented the election of Nicholas, as he showed in a letter he wrote after the event to Cardinal Guillaume de Braye, denouncing the cardinal's change of sides which had made the election possible.[3]

Nicholas's most remarkable political step was the ending of direct Angevin power in Rome and Tuscany. His constitution of 18 July 1278, *Fundamenta Militantis Ecclesie*, forbade the election of foreigners as senators of Rome and thus excluded the king of Naples. Charles gave up his vicariate in Tuscany when he made his oath of fealty to the pope on 24 May 1278.[4] In September of that year Charles ceased to have formal power to the north of his kingdom, though he retained a vicar in Florence for one more year. These changes involved a certain amount of sweeping back of Angevin power from the swollen limits it had reached at its climax in the earlier part of Charles's reign. The process was to go further as a result of the reduction of Charles's kingdom, following the Sicilian Vespers of 1282.

The intervention of Nicholas III in Florence, a less spectacular but quite important aspect of his policy, may have originated in a Florentine desire for external arbitration to repair the breakdown of relations within the Guelf party. In the late 1270s there appears to have been a division, at the highest level involving the greatest families, between the Adimari on one side and on the other the Della Tosa, Donati, and Pazzi, which may have been inspired partly by the Adimari marriage connection with the Ghibelline Conti Guidi and Ubaldini families outside Florence.[5] During the period between 1267 and 1301 it seems to have been in practice difficult to keep Guelf and Ghibelline families absolutely apart, so that Guelf–Ghibelline family connections provided an occasional cause for jealousy and hostility within the Guelfs. Intervention seems to have sprung from the appeal of the Florentine Guelfs to

[2] *Collectio Bullarum Sacrosanctae Basilicae Vaticanae*, i (Rome, 1747), pp. 202–3.

[3] F. Baethgen, 'Ein pamphlet Karls i. von Anjou zur Wahl Papst Nikolaus III', *Sitzungsberichte der Bayerischen Akademie, Philosophisch-Historische Klasse*, 1960.

[4] *Registres de Nicolas III*, ed. J. Gay (Paris, 1898–1932), p. 106. On Nicholas in general, see A. Demski, *Papst Nikolaus III: Eine Monographie* (Munster i. W., 1903); Baethgen, 'Der Anspruch', p. 153.

[5] Davidsohn, *Storia*, ii. ii, pp. 189–91.

the papal court for a peacemaker at the end of July 1278. The result was Nicholas's decision, announced on 28 August, to send Cardinal Latino Malabranca, a notable Dominican and a nephew.[6] Nicholas no doubt aimed to heal divisions both within the Guelf faction and between Guelf and Ghibelline, thus frustrating the Angevin policy of maintaining feuds in order to build power by supporting one side.

Latino arrived in Florence on 8 October 1279. He appears to have acted in close association with the Mozzi banking family. Andrea Mozzi, later to become bishop of Florence in 1287 and to be removed from that office in 1295 by Pope Boniface probably because of his quarrelsome and oppressive behaviour in the diocese, was appointed Latino's delegate. The cardinal resided in the palace of Tommaso Spigliati and Vanni de' Mozzi, and it was there that the oaths to support his peace were sworn in the following February.[7] He got power from the commune in November 1279. In January 1280 he made his proposals, which were accepted. Ghibellines were to be readmitted and the fruits of their possessions restored to them, except that the leading Ghibelline families—Uberti, Lamberti, Fifanti, Scolari, Bogolesi, and others—were to remain in exile. In February there was a general pacification and reconciliation of the leading families of the Guelf and Ghibelline sides, and a general acceptance of the peace by the Guelf oligarchy.

The period from 1280 to 1283 saw apparently important changes in the political constitution of Florence, but the probability is that they had little impact on the political structure. It saw the experiment instituted by Latino of a *signoria* of fourteen 'good men', including a mixture of Guelfs and Ghibellines to balance the parties. The Guelf *grandi* in practice tended to push out their Ghibelline colleagues over the next two years, and in any case the great Ghibellines were still exiled; the situation was still that a Guelf Florence refused to make peace with banished enemies scattered over Tuscany and Romagna. In June 1282 came the institution of the priorate, with three priors chosen from the guilds of Calimala (cloth traders), Lana (textile manufacturers), and Cambio (money changers). In the course of the 1280s the priorate, later extended to six members, increasingly became the real *signoria*. This probably had the effect of strengthening the mercantile element in Florentine politics because it was impossible to be a prior without being a member of a guild, and therefore to some extent involved in the commercial or industrial worlds. During the 1280s Florence appears to have been dominated by a combination of the old Guelf families without strong trading connections, such as the Donati or Della Tosa, and families of very strong mercantile

[6] Latino's embassy was fully investigated by Davidsohn, *Forschungen*, iv, pp. 226–58. Recently the documents of the peace have been published by I. L. Sanfilippo, 'La pace del Cardinale Latino a Firenze nel 1280: la sentenza e gli atti complimentari', *Bullettino dell' Istituto Storico Italiano per il medio evo*, lxxxix, 1980–1, and an account by M. Sanfilippo, 'Guelfi e ghibellini a Firenze: La "pace" del cardinal Latino', *Nuova rivista storica*, lxiv, 1980.

[7] Sanfilippo, 'La pace' p. 227.

power, such as the Mozzi, Bardi, Becchenugi, Spini, Cerchi, and Falconieri. It is dangerous to distinguish families into social groups in this way because the holders of a name were a clan embracing several or many nuclear families, which could also embrace individuals with very different economic and social positions. But the intrusion of the priors who had to be members of guilds into the political summit probably strengthened the representation of mercantile interests in politics. We must attribute this change in part (though the analysis is entirely hypothetical) to the growing industrial and commercial strength of Florence, in part to the political factor of the decline of Angevin influence, which deprived the Guelf aristocracy of an ally. The same period saw the beginning of legislation to make effective the overt distrust of those *magnati* in the city who were capable of using their physical power to oppress the less powerful members of the *popolo*. Magnates were obliged from 1280 to provide guarantors liable for substantial payments if they were guilty of offences against *popolani*.[8] We have then in the 1280s a modification in the government that gave a voice to commercial interests as well as to the old Guelf families, and the first hints of the hostility to magnate power which was to erupt in the next decade.

The disabused comments on the new system of priors made by Dino Compagni, the most knowledgeable and illuminating chronicler of late thirteenth-century Florence, suggest that we should not overemphasize its novelty.

The rules were that they, the priors, were to watch over the commune's property, that the magistrates should be answerable to everyone and that the small and weak should not be oppressed by the great and strong. This was useful to the people; but it soon changed because the citizens who entered that office aimed not to observe the laws but to corrupt them. If a friend or a relative suffered penalties they procured that the magistrates or officials should hide the fault so that they remained unpunished. They did not look after the commune's property but found the best way of robbing it and took much money out of the chamber to reward men who had served them. The weak were not helped, rather the great injured them and so did the rich men of the people who were in office and related to the great; and many were protected by money from the penalties of the commune to which they were liable. So the good citizens of the people were discontented and blamed the office of priors because the great Guelfs were the rulers.[9]

If we take Compagni at face value—he was an acute observer who played a part in political life in these years—we shall see the priorate as a rather minor diminution in the power of the Guelf leaders. The political structure of Florence in this period is one of the most seriously studied aspects of Florentine history. It was the subject of several substantial analyses earlier in

---

[8] N. Rubinstein, 'La lotta contro i magnati a Firenze—la prima legge sul "sodamento" e la pace del Cardinale Latino', *Archivio storico italiano*, ser. 5, cxv, 1935.

[9] *La Cronica di Dino Compagni*, ed. I. Del Lungo, Rerum Italicarum Scriptores, IX. ii, p. 18.

this century by Davidsohn, Salvemini, and Ottakar.[10] They based their interpretations upon the very large quantities of information about city politics to be found in the published and unpublished records of the city councils, which start in the 1280s.[11] These give a vast amount of information about the names of the holders of offices, about the views they expressed in council meetings, and about the decisions of those councils. They make the Florentine politics of the period from about 1280 exceptional at such an early period in the richness of its documentation. The debate which has been built on these documents, however, has limitations. We know a great deal about political actions, very little about the actors. There have been exquisite discussions of the class and factional basis of government drawn from the council records, based on very little accurate knowledge of the social position of politicians; much less discussion of equally important topics for which the documentation is harder to find—for example the geographical expansion of the Florentine state, or the genealogy and economic interests of the politicians. The overworked problem of the class structure of Florentine government should be kept in perspective. Compagni reminds us that it probably did not change very much, apart from the explosive period dominated by Giano della Bella between 1293 and 1295. Ancient landed wealth and more modern commercial wealth were very closely involved with each other. We should imagine the ruling groups as changing very gradually in character rather than as changed suddenly by constitutional innovation.

Nicholas III lived less than three years as pope, to die on 22 August 1280. His successor, Martin IV, who was to provide a boost for the Guelfs, was a French pope with political conceptions recalling those of Clement IV and a very strong contrast to the Italianate style of Nicholas.

Martin IV's election to the papacy was an example of the paradoxical way in which the destinies of an institution with such profound European significance could be redirected by the most trivial events of local Italian politics.[12] The conclave was again at Viterbo, where in 1278 the commune had done its best to persuade Nicholas to spend time in the town by making lavish offers of free accommodation and stable government,[13] but where the Orsini government of the town, introduced by Nicholas, was now upset by an uprising. This led to an intrusion into the cardinals' meeting and the removal of the members of the Orsini family from the assembly. Hence the election on

---

[10] Davidsohn, *Storia*, II. ii, *passim*; Salvemini, *Magnati e popolani*; Ottokar, *Il comune di Firenze*. There are modern analyses in Raveggi *et at.*, *Ghibellini, Guelfi*, pp. 165–237, and J. M. Najemy, *Corporatism and Consensus in Florentine Electoral Politics, 1280–1400* (Chapel Hill, 1982), pp. 17–42.

[11] *Le Consulte della Repubblica Fiorentina dall 'anno* MCCLXXX *al* MCCCXCVIII, ed. A. Gherardi (Florence 1896–8); *Consigli della repubblica fiorentina*, ed. B. Barbadoro (Bologna 1921–30); unpublished provvisioni in the Archivio di Stato, Florence.

[12] J. Haller, *Das Papsttum: Idea und Wirklichkeit*, v (Esslingen am Neckar, 1962); p. 58 provides a summary of the election.

[13] P. M. Baumgarten, *Aus Kanzlei und Kammer* (Freiburg in B., 1907), p. 48.

22 February 1281 of Simon de Brie, a Frenchman who was acceptable to Charles of Naples, had played a large part in making the political efforts of Clement IV successful, and was ready to revive on a large scale the system of using French money to strengthen the power of the papacy and the Guelfs in Italy.

Whereas Nicholas III had made serious attempts to extend papal authority by taking control of Romagna (a dangerous power-vacuum where the towns, free from any imperial control, were tending to fall under the sway of the great Ghibelline captain, Guido da Montefeltro, lord of Urbino) but made no lasting progress, Martin was rather more successful: 'not craftily as his predecessor had done but trembling with Gallic fury be sought publicly to destroy our memory. He sent wild Frenchmen against us . . .' This is the complaint of a writer presenting the grievances of Guido.[14] The troops, gathered from various parts of Italy and France, led by a French rector, paid for with French money, did succeed in taking Faenza, Cesena and Forlì and seriously defeating Guido.[15] Ironically, however, this extension of papal and Guelf power in Romagna, with French and Angevin help, was accompanied by the most serious of all blows to Angevin power in the south, the Sicilian Vespers: the popular anti-French rebellion, which broke out at Palermo on 30 March 1282, led rapidly to the expulsion of Neapolitan authority from Sicily and the substitution of the government of Peter of Aragon. This was an event of great importance for the rest of Italy. It meant that the Angevin state was permanently crippled by the amputation of Sicily; that, at least until 1302, the king of Naples (Charles I who died in 1285 and then his son Charles II), was constantly diverted from intervention on the Guelf side in Northern Italy by the compulsion to devote his resources to attempt to reconquer a lost part of his own kingdom; and that he became a permanent pensioner, dependent on any help that he could get in men and money from his allies the pope and the Tuscan Guelfs.

The effect of these events in Tuscany was probably to strengthen the Guelf sentiments and Guelf defiance of the rulers of Florence. Ghibelline powers in Sicily, in Forlì, and in Pisa represented fairly distant threats, but nevertheless made it important to allow no Ghibellines political standing at home. At Siena, nearer to Florence, an attempted Ghibelline *coup d'état* failed in July 1281.[16] In Florentine politics these years are strongly marked with Guelf assertions. There was no longer any external papal support for a place for the Ghibellines in the principal political offices in the city, so they disappeared from political office in 1282. Florence sent a substantial force of 600 men to

---

[14] H. M. Schaller, 'Ein Manifest des Grafen Guido von Montefeltro nach der Schlacht von Forlì (1 Mai 1282)', *Storiografia e storia: studi in onore di Eugenio Duprè Theseider* (Rome, 1974), ii, p. 684.
[15] D. Waley, *The Papal State in the Thirteenth Century* (London, 1961), pp. 193–204.
[16] Martini, 'Siena da Montaperti', p. 101.

help Charles of Naples in June 1282 after the Sicilian Vespers. The condemnation of Farinata degli Uberti and his two dead wives for Cathar heresy by the Franciscan inquisitors in October 1283 must have been encouraged by the Guelf desire to deal firmly with the memory of the great Ghibelline leader of 1260 and with his property. We find Corso Donati, Dante's enemy in 1301, already prominent as an outspoken and aggressive exponent of Guelf views, arguing in a deliberation in February 1285 that all imperial lands on the borders of Florence should be taken into Florentine jurisdiction and their owners made to pay taxes.[17] The substitution of a clearly Guelf pope for the ambivalent Orsini and the consciousness of serious, but not actually dangerous, Ghibelline movements elsewhere in Italy stimulated the Guelf leaders to assertive reiterations of their interests.

Giacomo Savelli, who succeeded Martin IV as Pope Honorius IV was, like Nicholas III, a member of a great Roman noble family with extensive property around the city and a keen native interest in its politics. His brother Pandolfo Savelli had been appointed by the Romans as one of their senators when they rebelled against the vicars of the now enfeebled Charles of Naples in January 1284. He was related to the Orsini, and might have been expected to revive some of the policies of Nicholas III. In Villani's prejudiced view he did indeed sustain the Ghibellines more than the Guelfs.[18] The fact is that he was an old man so crippled by gout that he could not consecrate the host without mechanical aids; he made no very distinct move in Italian politics, though he did try to raise more money from the church for Charles's recovery of Sicily. He died after exactly two years in office, on 3 April 1287.[19]

The same essential character—the lack of a distinct contribution to Italian politics and the failure to make a new initiative—also marked the pontificate of his successor, Nicholas IV. He survived for a longer period, February 1288 to April 1292, but he did not make a much more deliberate contribution to papal Italian policies or to Tuscan politics. Nicholas IV was Jerome of Ascoli, who had been minister-general of the Franciscan order, and he was now the first member of that order to become pope. That was of course an interesting sign of the position the order had reached at the heart of the church sixty years after Francis's death. But Nicholas was a man without distinct political aims, who again lacked the capacity shown by Nicholas III and Martin IV for original initiatives.

When Nicholas IV died on 4 April 1292 there were twelve cardinals. One of these, the Frenchman Jean Cholet, died soon after, leaving eleven, nearly all Italian. Two, Pietro and Jacopo, were members of the greatest of all the Roman noble families, the Colonna. Their elevation, produced by the rather

[17] Davidsohn, *Storia*, 11. ii, 238–9, 322; N. Ottokar 'La condanna postuma di Farinata degli Uberti', *Archivio storico italiano*, ser. 5, lxxvii, 1919; *Consulte*, i, pp. 169–70.
[18] Villani, VII. cxiii.
[19] Biography by M. Prou in *Registres de Honorius IV* (Paris, 1888).

accidental connection between their house and Jerome of Ascoli, was perhaps the most important result of his pontificate. With them was associated Giovanni Boccamazza, who had been elevated by his relation, Honorius IV. Opposed to the Colonna were two Orsini: the aged Matteo Rosso, who had been a cardinal since 1262; and a young man Napoleone who was to live on into the 1340s. With them was associated their relation Latino Malabranca, the favourite of the Orsini Pope Nicholas III. Outside these two groups were two other cardinals with powerful personalities. One of them was Benedetto Caetani, later Boniface VIII, a member of another Roman family who also had behind him a considerable career as an ecclesiastical politician which gave him a knowledge of the wider church. He had been promoted by the great architect of European papalism, Martin IV. He was a canon lawyer and he had experience of England and of France, where he had remarkable success in 1290 in imposing on the French clergy the decretal of Martin IV *Ad fructus uberes* allowing confession by mendicants.[20] Benedetto Caetani united in himself two rather different types of motivation common among cardinals: the Roman ambition to use the office for promotion of one's own family, and the ecclesiastical politician's desire to assert Roman supremacy over the church in Europe. The other notable cardinal was Mathew of Acquasparta, an Umbrian who was a Franciscan with a considerable scholastic reputation, a former minister-general of the order, who had been promoted by the Franciscan Pope Nicholas IV. He kept apart, however, from Nicholas's beloved Colonna. The college was completed by two cardinals from Lombardy—Gerard of Parma, and Petrus Peregrossus of Milan, both old curial officials—and a Frenchman, Hugues Aycelin.

In this almost entirely Italian college, the powers of the Colonna and Orsini factions were prominent and evenly balanced. It was impossible to get a majority for any internal candidate, and the vacancy dragged on for two years.[21] It was ended on 5 July 1294 by the election of the most extraordinary pope of the later Middle Ages, Peter Murrone, Celestine V. Peter was an aged hermit, probably eighty-four years old, from near Sulmona, in the mountains of the northern part of the kingdom of Naples, far to the east of Rome, near the Adriatic. He had had great success as a religious leader, and had created a congregation of hermits within the Benedictine order in that part of Italy. He was well known, of unquestionable saintliness and religious zeal, a model of success within the church in utterly selfless, religious terms, and could indeed be regarded as the kind of man who would make a true pope if only the papal curia were not a battleground for Roman nobles and French administrators. But he was also an old and tired man who wanted only to die as a hermit. If he had ever been capable of maintaining the papal office, which is improbable,

---

[20] H. Finke, *Aus den Tagen Bonifaz VIII.* (Münster i. W., 1902), p. vi.
[21] Good accounts of it are to be found in G. Digard, *Philippe le Bel et le Saint-Siège de 1285 à 1304* (Paris, 1936), i, pp. 140–71 and P. Herde, *Cölestin V. (1294)* (Stuttgart, 1981), pp. 31–83.

that time was long past. It is astonishing that he should have been elected.[22]

The election of Celestine V was prompted by a mixture of spiritual hope and political calculation. The papal curia was not at this time in the kind of desperate political situation, at the mercy of German and French invaders, in which it had been in the 1260s; but the absence of a pope was extremely dangerous. One manifestation of this was the independent policy pursued by Benedetto Caetani in encouraging the expansion of Orvieto towards Lake Bolsena in return for support for his attempt to gain control of the nearby Aldobrandeschine lands, a policy directly opposed to the wish of most of the cardinals to restrict Orvieto.[23] By the spring of 1294 the cardinals, now at Perugia, were becoming fairly desperate in their desire for a pope, in spite of the impossibility of reaching agreement. A pope was also very much desired by King Charles II of Naples, because he needed papal approval of his treaty of La Junquera with Aragon which he hoped would isolate Frederick of Sicily and permit Neapolitan reconquest of the island. The candidature of Peter Murrone was certainly promoted by Charles II, but there were also cardinals with spiritual ideals—notably Latino Malabranca, who had had dealings with Peter earlier—for whom the hermit was a genuinely attractive figure. It is impossible to uncover the strands of political and spiritual calculation which led to the choice.

The pontificate of Celestine V was an unqualified disaster. The pope was unable to resist powerful selfish interests which came to bear on him especially from two quarters. His own order was outrageously favoured; he even tried to add to it the greatest of all Benedictine abbeys, Monte Cassino, situated not very far away on Neapolitan soil. The interests of the king of Naples were favoured with similar extravagance. The twelve new cardinals (an increase of more than a hundred per cent) whom Celestine created in September 1294 were all either Neapolitan or French, and several were councillors of Charles II. This was a devastating transformation of the college. In November the papal curia moved to Naples, and it was obvious that it would soon become a mere appendage of the Angevin monarchy. Celestine quickly began to realize, as did the cardinals, that his position was absurd. He resigned on 13 December 1294, five months after his election, and Benedetto Caetani, the cardinal who most obviously had the force of character to save the papacy, was elected on 24 December.

Between 1292 and 1294, when papal policy was in abeyance because of the vacancy, Florentine politics were disturbed by an extremely interesting upheaval, probably made easier by the impossibility of papal intervention, in which the main factor was an attempt to reduce the influence of the *magnati*

[22] His election and his pontificate have been fully investigated by Herde, *Cölestin V.*
[23] P. Herde 'Das Kardinalskollegium und der Feldzug von Orvieto im Val del Lago (1294)', *Miscellanea Historiae Pontificiae*, xlv, 1979.

and to widen the social basis of the priorate.[24] *Magnati*, magnates, are difficult to define. The word was evidently used in a rather imprecise way to describe those great families whose material power constituted a potential danger to lesser men and to peace in the city. *Potentes, nobiles vel magnates* were defined in Florentine legislation as those 'in whose houses or family (*domibus vel casato*) there is or has been within twenty years a knight or whom common opinion names and holds to be *potentes, nobiles* or *magnates*'. The vagueness is evident, but the connection with knighthood shows that what people feared was the use of physical power by the great; and indeed there had for some years been legislation designed to limit arbitrary physical action by such people. The economic and demographic expansion of the thirteenth century had brought to the fore in Florence (and indeed in many other cities, for this was by no means a Florentine peculiarity) the distinction between the magnates and the *popolo*, the people, an even vaguer word, which is very frequently to be found in the chronicles. The importance and danger of the magnates in city life were clearly connected with the customs of family feud, which were very imperfectly controlled by the commune. The danger of arbitrary physical action, we must assume, was more effectively resented by the growing classes of traders and artisans, whose way of life disposed them less to physical defence and who found in the commune and in the growing power of the guilds a way of imposing their wishes on the relatively small number of dangerous families.

The political changes made at the beginning of 1293 were connected with the leadership of a man from a prominent family, Giano della Bella. The changes were partly the result of new rules for the election of priors, whose term of office lasted only two months, laying down that no guild was to have more than one member in the priorate, and that no one who had been a prior was to be re-elected for three years. This had the effect of spreading the elections so that between the years 1292 and 1295 the social composition of the priorate was transformed by the inclusion of many new priors from families of a somewhat lower social level. In January 1293 the priors introduced one of the most important constitutional innovations in the history of Florence, the Ordinances of Justice, which laid down that priors must be members of guilds and not knights, and that there was to be a new office of 'standard-bearer of justice' with a guard of one thousand men to enforce decisions against magnates summarily without a formal trial. Later in the year magnates were excluded from the priorate and the councils.

The period of intense popular action was temporary. In 1295, Giano della Bella fled from the city and some of the constitutional limitations on magnates

---

[24] Interest in the period 1293–5 was aroused by Salvemini's *Magnati e popolani*. There is a full account of it in Davidsohn, *Storia*, 11. ii, ch. 10. Recent discussions in Raveggi *et al.*, *Ghibellini, Guelfi*, pp. 239–321, and Najemy, *Corporatism and Consensus*, ch. 2.

were modified. In the early years of the fourteenth century the political system was to swing back in favour of oligarchic power, especially after the expulsion of the Whites in 1302. But the standard-bearer of justice remained as a member of the priorate and the exclusion of magnates, a list of seventy-two families, from some constitutional positions remained as an embodiment of continued belief in the importance of the distinction between great men and *popolo*. The period from 1293 to 1295 saw a considerable upheaval in politics which left marks in succeeding years, and the later distinction between Blacks and Whites, the two parties who divided political power in Florence in 1300, was probably affected by suspicions between those members of the old oligarchy, like Corso Donati, who were offended by the ordinances, and those, like Vieri de' Cerchi, who had been more sympathetic to them. The *magnati–popolo* division, which approximates to a 'class' division, cut across and complicated the traditional conflicts between Guelfs and Ghibellines and between families.

An interesting indication of the feelings aroused by the dispute is contained in one of Dante's early philosophical poems, *Le dolci rime d'amor*, which literary scholars place in the evolution of his style at about 1295. Developing the old poetic theme that nobility is derived from the virtue of a man not from his lineage, Dante rejected the definition of nobility as 'long-standing possession of wealth together with pleasing manners' in favour of a definition drawn from some acquaintance with Aristotle's *Ethics* as 'the seed of happiness placed by God in a well-disposed soul'. Beginning his involvement in politics—the first records of his participation in city councils are from 1295 and 1296—Dante seems to have expressed a philosophical point of view which was intended as a criticism of magnate conservatism and to have left a faint record of a young intellectual's dislike of the oligarchs' claim to superiority.

According to legend, Dante had earlier been in the Florentine army that won the great victory against Arezzo at Campaldino in June 1289. During the ten years between the death of Martin IV in March 1285 and the resignation of Celestine V in December 1294, there was little papal or foreign intervention in Tuscany and the cities managed their affairs in their own way. The most marked feature of this period was Florentine aggressiveness and expansion. The wars against Arezzo and Pisa, which lasted intermittently but involved the raising of large armies and considerable taxation in the years from 1288 to 1292, were probably a cause of the popular discontent in 1293. Florence may not have done lasting harm to Pisa, but the other great Ghibelline foe, Arezzo, was dealt a devastating blow from which it never recovered. Giano della Bella, the popular leader in Florence, was *podestà* of Pistoia in 1294, an early stage in Florence's long-continued campaign to subject that independent commune. In spite of being a period of political upheaval in Florence, the early 1290s are also a period in which the city's external political power stretched further than ever before.

In 1300, after a display put on for him in Rome by a group of Florentine *grandi*, Boniface VIII is reported to have said that the Florentines were the fifth element in nature: 'Since the Florentines rule and govern the whole world it seems to me that they are the fifth element. There are four elements which rule the whole world; earth, water, air and fire. But I add the fifth element, namely the Florentines, who seem to rule the world.'[25] The idea, which he was supposed to have uttered earlier in the same conversation, that the Florentines 'nourish, rule, and govern the Roman court' has a particular appropriateness to that year in which, as we shall see later, Boniface was both heavily dependent on the Florentines for money, and extremely anxious to ensure the commune's political dependence on the papacy. Boniface was however less complimentary a year later: now less pleased with the Florentines he said they were 'usurers and lived at the pleasure of the Church and from commercial deals'.[26] But behind both comments lay a general awareness of the over-whelming economic importance of Florentine money and commercial power at the end of the thirteenth century.

The parade of Florentines before Boniface VIII, which probably took place in the early part of 1300, is reported in two accounts.[27] Each names twelve Florentines who took part in a grand procession before the pope. Eight of the names are the same in both accounts, and most can be identified. The eight are Musciatto de' Franzesi, appropriately representing the king of France; Vermiglio Alfani, representing the king of Germany, a notable banker who did indeed have relations with that King;[28] Simone de' Rossi, said to represent the Byzantine emperor; Guicciardo de' Bastori, said to represent the Great Tartar, the name of a man who did in fact bring news from Asia to the pope in 1300;[29] Manno degli Adimari, representing the King of Naples, who did hold a fief of that king in 1292;[30] Lapo di Farinata degli Uberti, representing Pisa, a well-known son of the great Ghibelline;[31] Cino Diotisalvi representing Gherardo da Camino, mentioned as lending money for the Capponi firm to the patriarch of Aquileia in 1302;[32] and Bencivenne Fulchi, representing the Hospital of St John, recorded in 1298 as receiving money

---

[25] F. Sarri, 'Frate Tebaldo della Casa e le sue trascrizioni petrarchesche', *Convegno petrarch-esco tenuto in Arezzo nei giorni 11–13 ott. 1931, Supplementa agli Annali della Cattedra Petrarchesca, Arezzo*, p. 82. See also A. Frugoni, 'Il Giubileo di Bonifacio VIII', *Bullettino dell'Istituto Storico Italiano*, lxii, 1950. I am indebted to Professor Richard C. Trexler for pointing out the importance of this episode which was, curiously, ignored by Davidsohn.

[26] Finke, *Bonifaz VIII.*, p. xxv

[27] The other is in *Giunta di M. Francesco Serdonati al Libro de Casi degl'Huomini Illustri di Messer Giovanni Boccaccio* (Florence, 1598), pp. 807–10.

[28] Davidsohn, *Storia*, IV. ii, p. 596.

[29] L. Petech, 'Les marchands italiens dans l'empire Mongol', *Journal asiatique*, ccl 1962, pp. 563–6.

[30] Davidsohn, *Storia*, IV. ii, p. 806

[31] Ibid., II, ii, p. 466.

[32] *Registres de Boniface VIII*, ed. G. Digard, M. Faucon, A. Thomas, and R. Fawtier (Paris, 1884–1935) no. 4690.

from that order on behalf of the Peruzzi family.[33] The other eight names in the two accounts are more obscure.[34] The event is associated with Boniface's proclamation of the Jubilee and, though no other record of it survives, it is evidently not a legend. Since some of the actors are known to have been connected with the rulers they are said to have represented, it is reasonable to suppose that others were too. The difficulty of identifying individual merchants who did great business for great princes, when we already know the names of so many Florentine firms, and their partners, is itself a testimony to the profusion and world-wide sweep of Florence's business interests.

It is a curious fact that the state of the Florentine economy at this particular period, which historians commonly suppose—no doubt in some general sense correctly, but without precision—to have been exceptionally rich and flourishing, is difficult to document with evidence about the state of families, firms, or industries within the city. There is very little material of this kind from the thirteenth century. The first account-books of great commercial firms all date from the fourteenth century: those of the Alberti from 1304, the Peruzzi from 1308, the Frescobaldi from 1312, the Del Bene from 1318, the Gianfigliazzi from 1320.[35] In fact some of these early account books help very little in explaining the internal economy of the great families even in the fourteenth century. The Alberti and Peruzzi books are not accounts of commercial operations but the personal accounts of wealthy men; they give little indication of the ultimate sources of their money. The only documents useful for analysing the sources of commercial wealth are the Frescobaldi book, which contains accounts of the firm at the papal court in 1312; and the Del Bene records, which show how Francesco Del Bene and Co. carried on the Calimala trade in North European cloth in 1318. They both date from well after 1300.

For the period before 1300 we have virtually no systematic evidence from within Florence itself: no customs accounts, no accounts of industrial or substantial commercial enterprises. A long financial account covering the period from 1273 to 1278, the most substantial document of this kind and a good example of its class, is in fact an account of guardians of under-age children; it tells us little about manufacturing or commerce, though it does reveal that companies we know from other sources (such as the Peruzzi,

---

[33] Ibid., no. 2827.

[34] Sarri's document has Ugolinus de Vicchio (King of England), Raynerius Langra (King of Bohemia), Bernardus Ernaj (Alberto Della Scala), Guido Talanche (Frederick of Sicily). Serdonati's document has Ugolino de' Cerchi (King of Castile), Rinieri dei Fighinaldi (King of Hungary), Benedetto de' Nerli (Master of St John), Pera di Pera Baldovinetti (Lords of Camerino).

[35] All published or described by Armando Sapori, *I libri degli Alberti del Giudice* (Milan, 1952); *I libri di commercio dei Peruzzi* (Milan, 1934) (the *libri segreti* of Arnoldo and Giotto dei Peruzzi, pp. 395–512); *La compagnia dei Frescobaldi in Inghilterra* (Florence, 1947) (accounts at papal court, pp. 85–136); *Una compagnia di Calimala ai primi del Trecento* (Florence, 1932) (the Del Bene company); *I libri della ragione bancaria dei Gianfigliazzi* (Milan, 1943).

Antella, Davizzini, Falconieri, and Compagni) accepted money on deposit for use in commercial operations.[36] We have to judge the development of the Florentine economy almost entirely by the use of records from other places: the records of the papal curia, which tell us about the movement of papal money and loans to the popes; English customs accounts and other royal records, which tell us about the movement of goods, and financial relations with the crown; documents from Northern France and the low countries, which record similar information for those areas; a few records of the Champagne fairs; a very few survivals from the destroyed Neapolitan archives; scattered customs accounts from many parts of Italy and Europe.

Our knowledge of the Florentine commercial economy is thus almost entirely non-Florentine. It is difficult to decide how much our impressions are distorted by this circumstance: it tends to highlight the families engaged in large-scale international trade—such as the Mozzi, Cerchi, Frescobaldi, Bardi, and Peruzzi—and to leave in obscurity the small cloth manufacturers in Florence itself. We are left with a very limited picture of the total economic scene in the city. It also has the still more frustrating effect of making it impossible to detect the factors in the process of economic change that in the late thirteenth century lifted Florence into the first rank and made it superior to the other Tuscan cities. We cannot judge the extent of or reasons for the expansion of trade within the city. We can only guess how far the success of Florentine firms in international finance was due to the creation of larger reserves of cash by industrial expansion. It is conceivable that intensive reading of the many registers of notarial documents surviving from the thirteenth century may one day make it possible to express opinions about these matters. At present they are largely obscure.[37]

One of the economic circumstances clearly related to the primacy of Florence indicated by Boniface VIII is the success of the Florentine currency. In 1296, payments of papal taxation in Tuscany were made far more frequently in gold florins, minted in Florence since 1252, than in any other coin; £8,691 out of £21,047 was paid in this way, the next most important coins being the silver ones of Volterra and Tours.[38] This is an indication of dominance whose origins can be explained only hypothetically. It is probable that by the late thirteenth century, Florence had a very substantial cloth

---

[36] C. Vesine, 'Il libro della tavola di Riccomano Jacopi', *Archivio storico italiano*, ser. 3, xviii, 1873; M. Chiaudano, *Studi e documenti*, pp. 64ff.

[37] One notarial register has been published: *Biagio Boccadibue (1298–1314)*, i, fasc. 1 and 2, ed. L. De Angelis, E. Gigli, and F. Sznura (*Università degli Studi di Firenze, Fonti di storia medievale e umanistica, I notai fiorentini dell'età de Dante*, Pisa, 1978, 1983). Biagio was used by members of the Mozzi family but the documents tell us about landholding, not commercial business. Aspects of the physical expansion of the city are discussed by F. Sznura, *L'espansione urbana di Firenze nel Dugento* (Florence, 1975). There is an interesting general discussion of Florentine growth by P. Malanima, 'La formazione di un regione economica: la Toscana nei secoli XIII–XV', *Società e storia*, vi, 1983.

[38] J. Day, 'La circulation monétaire en Toscane en 1296', *Annales*, xxiii, 1968.

industry that produced goods of relatively low quality for sale chiefly in the Mediterranean. Although the Florentines were great exporters of wool from England most of it probably did not go to Florence, where the textile industry relied principally on the wool of the western Mediterranean. But the production of cheaper cloths must have been considerable. A Pisan galley shipwrecked near Corfu in 1280 or 1281 was carrying more cloths made in Florence than in Lombardy or Flanders. In 1299 more Florentine than Lombard or Flemish cloths were being sold at Orvieto for distribution in Umbria.[39] Occasional evidence of this kind is the only basis we have for judging the size and character of cloth production, which must have been the most important Florentine industry. The probability is that it had shot ahead since the early thirteenth century, when it was not prominent in the records, to become much larger than similar trades at Siena and Pisa—not a centre of high-quality production exporting on a vast scale to Asia, but a major supplier of cloth nearer home. Florence was a more suitable centre for a large cloth industry than hilly Siena or malaria-ridden Pisa.[40] By the late thirteenth century, we may suspect, these advantages had produced their effect, and the superior Florentine industry helped to produce the large sums of cash for investment in commercial enterprises in Naples, France, Flanders, England, and the papal court that gave the Florentines their reputation as Europe's greatest financiers.

The most interesting piece of evidence about international trade by Florentines in the late thirteenth century is contained in two letters sent by Consiglio de' Cerchi and company in Florence to their partners in England in March and June 1291, containing comments and instructions about the business they were carrying on.[41] They were exporting wool and cloth from England and selling letters of exchange for making payments in Italy. Their business involved much contact with the Champagne fairs. In addition, although they had no representatives at the papal court at this time—an important fact in view of their later quarrel with the pope in 1300—they were helping the Abbey of Kirkstead, probably a supplier of wool, with business there. The letters show us, like the letters of international merchants from other Italian cities in the thirteenth century, how much trade was dependent on having correspondents in several places, and also on a constant awareness of political and economic factors that would influence prices, and must therefore be taken account of in making plans. The first letter tells how the cloth trade was to be carried on in accordance with the regulations made by the Calimala, the guild of cloth importers in Florence. Two hundred sacks of wool were to be exported to meet the scarcity overseas caused by the murrain in England and by the war between England and Flanders, which would prevent Flemings

[39] H. Hoshino, *L'Arte della lana in Firenze nel Basso Medioevo* (Florence, 1980), pp. 68–130.
[40] Herlihy, *Pisa in the Early Renaissance*, pp. 48–51.
[41] *Nuovi testi fiorentini*, ed. A. Castellani (Florence, 1952), ii, pp. 593–603.

crossing the Channel; although it was pointed out that money for buying it would be scarce in England because of the tenths granted by the pope to Edward I, which would probably have to be paid in fact by loans from Italians.

The second letter was written after news arrived of Philip I V's arrest of Italians, which moved the commune of Florence to send an embassy to him and the pope to plead for release of representatives of a number of Italian firms with influence at the papal court: the Bonsignori of Siena, Ricciardi of Lucca, Chiarenti of Pistoia, and the Mozzi, Spini, Pulci-Rimbertini and Frescobaldi of Florence.[42] The Cerchi were not at this time important papal bankers and seem not to have been active in France, but they were worried by the news because it would mean that money due to them in Flanders and Champagne might not be paid.

English records are a good source of information about Italians. They supply, for example, a considerable amount of information about wool exports by Florentines: Bardi, Cerchi, Frescobaldi, and Falconieri in the 1270s; Bardi, Cerchi, Frescobaldi, Pulci-Rimbertini, Mozzi, and Spini in the mid 1290s.[43] At the other end of Europe, the kingdom of Naples was certainly an important field of Florentine activity. Most of the records have been lost, but we know that in the 1290s the Bardi, Acciaiuoli, and Mozzi were heavily engaged in the export trade in wheat, using privileges they gained by making loans of money to the hard-pressed King Charles I I.[44] An account-book of Renieri Fini de' Benzi and brothers of Figline at the Champagne fairs shows them dealing with other Tuscan companies in those parts from 1296.[45] A few surviving letters show the Cerchi, Mozzi, Spini, and Scali engaged in the trade in wool and cloth at Marseilles in 1295 and after.[46] It appears that the Florentines had exploited the natural advantages given them by their trading capacity and by their Guelf connections to become especially prominent in the sea trade to Naples and Rome from Aigues Mortes and Marseilles in Charles of Naples' county of Provence. The Bardi were especially prominent here.[47] The Provence–Italy route was particularly important, but this kind of evidence could be multiplied to show Florentine activity in many parts of Europe in the 1290s. It is clear that the Florentines had become immensely

[42] Davidsohn, *Storia*, ii. ii, p. 508; *Registres de Nicolas I V*, ed. E. Langlois (Paris, 1886–1905), p. 1000.

[43] T. H. Lloyd, *The English Wool Trade in the Middle Ages* (Cambridge, 1977), pp. 72–3.

[44] D. Abulafia, 'Southern Italy and the Florentine Economy, 1265–1370', *Economic History Review*, ser. 2, xxxiv, 1981, p. 380; G. de Blasiis, 'La dimora di Giovanni Boccaccio a Napoli', *Archivio storico per le provincie napoletane*, xvii, 1892, pp. 87 ff.

[45] *Nuovi testi fiorentini*, ii, pp. 674–96; F. Carabellese 'Un nuovo libro di mercanti italiani alle fiere di Sciampagna', *Archivio storico italiano*, ser. 5, xiii, 1894.

[46] P. Berti, 'Documenti reguardanti il commercio dei Fiorentini in Francia nei secoli XIII e XIV e singolarmente il loro concorso alle fiere di Sciampagna', *Giornale storico degli Archivi Toscani*, 1857, p. 173, etc.

[47] E. Baratier and F. Reynaud, *Histoire du commerce de Marseille*, ii (Paris, 1951), pp. 164–70.

active as traders and exchangers of money on a vast scale. The Sienese, the Lucchese, and the Pistoiese could be found in the same business, and the Pisans of course had a maritime sphere of operations in the Mediterranean in which the Florentines were not serious competitors; but from Scotland to Sicily the Florentines were the most prominent in the international commercial business of Europe.

For most of the period from 1277 to 1294, the position of Florentine companies in the business of papal finance remained very much what it had been earlier, or at least changed rather slowly. That is to say that the papacy used a large number of bankers from several Tuscan cities to collect the money due to it in various parts of Europe, and also used a smaller number of bankers, partly but not entirely Florentine, as *mercatores camere* (merchants of the chamber) to provide money for the papal court itself, often as loans. Nicholas III used the Alfani and Frescobaldi of Florence and the Battosi, Caccianimici, and Ricciardi of Lucca, but his favoured *mercatores camere* were the Bonsignori of Siena and the Pulci and Rimbertini of Florence.[48] From the time of Martin IV we have records of the taxes collected in the papal states showing that most of the money went to the Ricciardi of Lucca, and records of collection in Tuscany showing that it went to various Lucchese firms as well as to the Bonsignori of Siena and the Mozzi and Pulci-Rimbertini of Florence.[49] Thus Pope Martin IV seems to have used four firms as *mercatores camere*: Pulci-Rimbertini, Mozzi-Spini, Bonsignori, and (after May 1283) Ricciardi—that is, two Florentine, one Sienese, and one Lucchese. These were the companies that among other things made him a loan of £20,000 on 27 April 1283.[50] Honorius IV seems to have followed much the same pattern.[51]

It is during the pontificate of Nicholas IV, between 1288 and 1292, that we see the pattern beginning to change in a way that was to lead eventually to the complete domination of papal finances by Florentine companies in the pontificate of Boniface VIII. Nicholas began by using as his cameral merchants the same four companies Honorius had used, but he made two significant changes. In 1288 he added the Chiarenti of Pistoia, and in 1291 the Frescobaldi of Florence.[52] The Frescobaldi did not remain in that position for long, but the Chiarenti were important throughout Boniface's pontificate. The reason for their addition is obscure—it has been suggested it was because they had a connection with Nicholas's favourite Colonna cardinals—but the

[48] Jordan, *De Mercatoribus*, p. 23; G. Arias, *Studi e documenti di storia del diritto* (Florence, 1902), pp. 86–8. They use information now printed in *Reg. Nicolas III*.

[49] *Rationes Decimarum Italiae nei secoli XIII e XIV, Latium*, p. 423; *Tuscia, I. La decima degli anni 1274–1280*, pp. xxxix, 235, 237.

[50] Jordan, *De Meratoribus*, pp. 24–6; Arias, pp. 88–96; *Registres de Martin IV* (Paris, 1901–45); Theiner, *Codex Diplomaticus Dominii Temporalis Sanctae Sedis* (Rome, 1861–2), i, p. 262.

[51] Jordan, ibid., p. 26; Arias, pp. 96–9; *Reg. Honorius IV*; Housley, *Italian Crusades*, p. 232.

[52] *Reg. Nicolas IV*, pp. 961, 1000; Jordan, ibid., pp. 26–8.

smallness of Pistoia and its condition of semi-subjection to Florence meant they could not be very serious rivals to the Florentines.

Still more important were the beginnings of the decline of the Bonsignori and the Ricciardi, the two non-Florentine companies. This started before the pontificate of Boniface. In July 1294, the Ricciardi—an extremely active company on a European scale—suffered a very severe blow from which they did not recover: King Edward I of England, at the beginning of his great war with France, deprived them of control of the English customs, leaving them with a debt they were incapable of paying. This was also the end of their usefulness to the papacy. The reasons for their collapse are not clear but it may have been that, as holders of papal money, they had failed to pay over to the English king the proceeds of taxes for the Holy Land granted to him in 1291.[53]

The Bonsignori also disappeared from the heart of the papal financial system at the end of the century. Their inability to pay their debts was the cause of considerable scandal during the pontificate of Boniface VIII, but it is probable that their usefulness to the Chamber was declining by the end of Nicholas IV's pontificate.[54] The earliest document giving an indication of their difficulties is a letter sent by the representatives of the firm at the papal court to their colleagues in Siena on 12 September 1291. This letter says that the Bonsignori owe the papal chamber 10,500 marks sterling received from the proceeds of the sexennial tenth in England imposed in 1274. Similar sums are owed by the Mozzi (10,000 marks), the Ricciardi (14,000 marks) and the Pulci (3,000 marks). The letter writers compare their position with the more favourable treatment granted to the Chiarenti, whom they call the pope's 'special merchants', who were granted control of the very large debts of the king of France; and the Frescobaldi, who were granted the handling of large sums expected from a tenth imposed on the Cistercians.[55] These favours meant that they could expect to handle sums which would enable them to meet the debts for which they were immediately due, while the Bonsignori lacked such resources. The Bonsignori company had been reorganized in 1289 after some years of declining fortunes, but it was affected by disputes between the partners and did not recover respect. It may be also that it suffered from being entirely a finance company without interests in industry or in the trade in commodities.

[53] Kaeuper, *Bankers to the Crown*, pp. 209–20.

[54] Chiaudano, 'I Rothschild del Duecento'; idem, *Studi e documenti*; E. Jordan, 'La Faillite des Buonsignori', *Mélanges Paul Fabre* (Paris, 1902).

[55] Jordan, 'Faillite', pp. 428–30. An undated payment (Archivio di Stato, Florence, Diplomatico, Strozziane-Uguccioni, 13..) records the debts of the company of Lambertuccio de' Frescobaldi to the papacy arising from their receipts of money for the 'decimae terre sancte'. The company had received 37,295½ florins, £1,116.6s.8d of Tours gross, £7,449.14s.3d of Tours paru., 182 marks 8/6 sterling, £600 of Padua and 6 marks *gracen* of which they had paid out some '*pro negotio terre sancte*', some '*pro defensione Regni Sicilie*' and some to the bishop of Riete. This account may refer to any period between the 1280s and 1305 when Lambertuccio died (Davidsohn, *Storia*, IV. ii, p. 369).

The troubles of the Bonsignori and the Ricciardi, both arising from the collection of money in England, sprang out of the dependence of these big international enterprises on balancing large sums of money received from several different businesses. It was possible for them to fall into serious difficulties if payment were suddenly demanded and not compensated by some new source of money or credit; they were susceptible to lack of confidence from their creditors. The Florentine firms, probably having larger and more varied sources of money, were ousting their competitors. Probably the reason which lay at the root of this Florentine superiority and dominance in financial matters was the greater size of the city and its cloth industry, which gave Florentine companies a greater capacity to take risks because the risks in one trade could be offset by profits from other branches of trade. This made them particularly attractive to the papal chamber, which was constantly demanding large loans of money ahead of the collection of the taxes which were to pay for them, and therefore had to have bankers with an immediate command over large supplies of cash.

In the late thirteenth century, Florence emerged into a new position of independence and dominance. On the political side the character of this development is fairly clear. The German and French military intervention which had marked the period before 1282 had been brought to an end, and the expulsion of the Ghibellines—a surgical operation of terrible rigour—did in the end allow the existence of a more placid political organization. On the economic and social side the picture is obscure. We cannot see the character of Florentine life in its everyday reality apart from the few intimate glimpses allowed by Compagni (and to a lesser extent Villani), and the generally rather abstract evidence of politics provided by the records of the city councils. Our impression, however, is of a city growing rapidly in population and in industrial and commercial strength, which had for the first time come clearly to the forefront of the Tuscan communes and into world-wide financial importance. If we could see the world in which Dante spent the first thirty-five years of his life we should see immense activity, building, expectation of ever greater profit, and the vigorous and corrupt political life of an expanding industrial city.

3

Religion: the Model of Francis of Assisi

THE most prominent figure in the Italian imagination in the thirteenth century was not a pope or a politician but a saint: Francis of Assisi. There are few cases in European history of individuals whose lives have been so generally accepted as an inspiration by the people of a whole country; perhaps in the religious field only the greatest of the sixteenth-century reformers are comparable, and they were the objects of much more controversy. Francis's life appeared to have a perfection which gave him a unique position in Christian history. He could be regarded, according to inclination, either as the supreme case of a man following the example of Jesus and the Apostles, or, to carry his importance to a still higher level, as the herald of a new age in the history of the world. But, in addition to that, the particular form his life took had a special appropriateness to the local conditions of Italian society. He was a preacher who embraced complete poverty but expressed a delighted love of the physical world, a man of superhuman power who attracted simple brothers to establish a new way of life which would excite the enthusiasm of ordinary people in a strife-torn society lacking religious or political authority. He was exactly what the Italian world needed. He provided a model which was absolute in both its total orthodoxy and its total radicalism, and provoked a constant imitation which gave a distinct colour to Italian religious life.

In the late thirteenth century, Francis's life was known chiefly from the account given of it by St Bonaventure, the minister-general of the Franciscans, in the *Legenda Maior Sancti Francisci*,[1] which he presented to the chapter-general of the order at Pisa in 1263, and which immediately became the official biography. Boniface's *Legenda* was intended to be a work of compromise, to present an acceptable view, and the earlier lives were to be destroyed. In spite of its political purpose, however, it is a work with freshness and charm by an author who had spiritual and literary powers. To read it is perhaps the best way to understand the impact which the memory of St Francis had on most people in succeeding generations. Bonaventure begins by saying that Francis was raised up by God as 'professor, leader and herald of evangelical perfection'. His devotion to poverty and the grace infused into him made him the fulfilment of the vision of St John in the Apocalypse of the 'angel ascending from the rising sun having the sign of the living God. That this messenger of

---

[1] Published in *Analecta Franciscana*, x, 1926; English translation by E. G. Salter (London, 1904).

God lovable to Christ, to be imitated by us, admirable to the world was Francis, God's servant, we conclude with indubitable faith'. Bonaventure then devoted fourteen short chapters to aspects of Francis's life which revealed the character of his saintliness; he paid no attention to the chronology of Francis's life, which has to be put together from other sources. Beginning as the son of a merchant at Assisi, Francis started his mission by giving away his clothes to the poor and kissing the lepers. His way forward was shown by the divine order he received to rebuild the ruined church of San Damiano outside Assisi. After stripping himself of his worldly possessions he settled at the Portiuncula on the plain below Assisi; other refugees from conventional society joined him, forming the beginnings of the Franciscan order. The essence of his rule for the order was inspired by Christ's command to his disciples to have no property. Francis took the rule to Rome and eventually acquired the approval of Pope Innocent III. Many experiences, like the vision of the chariot of fire in a garden at Assisi, confirmed his aims. He himself travelled and also sent out his Franciscan brothers, whose number was increasing. He established a mendicant order for women, the Clarisses and the 'third order' for laymen (third after the mendicant orders for men and women). Eventually the point was reached at which five thousand brothers could assemble at the Portiuncula. Francis was distinguished by austerity: refusal of pillows, jumping into snow to cool tempted flesh, endurance of painful treatment for an infected eye. He cultivated humility, preaching about his own sins, rejecting authority in the order. He insisted on absolute poverty and mendicancy; he would beg for bread in the streets before accepting a cardinal's invitation to dinner. He had a great love of animals and a capacity for friendship with them. He longed for martyrdom, travelling to the lands of the Saracens and offering to walk through fire to prove his faith to the Sultan. He had a great capacity for immersing himself in prayer. He set the value of prayer higher than that of reading holy books. He had the gift of prophecy and of reading the hidden thoughts of other people. He was convinced of the value of preaching and preached even to the birds. He performed many miracles. He loved to pray in solitude and it was in that position at the hermitage of La Verna, high up in the Apennines, that he received the vision in which the marks of the stigmata were impressed upon him. During the months of sickness and desolation of the body which preceded his death, he called his sufferings his sisters and lay naked on the earth to lift his face up towards heaven.

The first establishment of a rule probably took place in 1209. After much wandering in Central Italy and abroad, Francis was in Rome during the Fourth Lateran Council of 1215. By 1217 when the brothers met at the Portiuncula, the order was already large and international. By this time the Clarisses, the women's order, already existed. The tradition of official ecclesiastical protection of the Franciscans from the highest level began when

Cardinal Ugolino became protector in 1217. Some years before Francis died in 1226 control of the order had already slipped from his hands, a result of the very large numbers that flocked into it and of the able and ambitious men among them. The First Rule of 1221 was not all Francis's work; still less was the Second and final Rule of 1223. He had appointed as head of the order Brother Elias, who came to be regarded by the later rigorists as a traitor responsible for the beginning of its degradation. In the testament he composed shortly before his death, Francis told his followers to behave 'like strangers and pilgrims' without property, but he also thought he had to insist on absolute obedience to the ministers of the order.[2] The early and in a sense carefree days in which Francis and his disciples had given away their clothes had vanished utterly in less than twenty years, replaced by a vast and complex organization often subject to political disputes. Bonaventure's *Legenda* of 1263 was a result of his reaction to the process of conflict and stabilization which had taken place in the previous half century.[3] He was minister-general from 1257 to 1273. During that period he established the character of the order more firmly along lines which were no doubt preferred by the vast majority of friars. It had become an organization based on convents, in which the friars lived and ate without having personal property; they were encouraged to undertake scholarly work; and their main functions were preaching and leading an exemplary religious life. This generally accepted interpretation of the rule marked a fundamental change from the ideals of poverty and mendicancy originally adopted by Francis. The change had been caused by two main factors. The first was the sheer growth of the order. In 1282 there were said to have been forty-eight friaries in Tuscany and fifty-five in Umbria, where the order had started, and many hundreds in other parts of Italy and elsewhere in Europe—in total over 1,200, with many thousands of friars.[4] The ideals of the order had been extremely attractive to the young intelligentsia of the church so that by this time many of the most prominent theologians in the universities had joined it. Bonaventure himself was one of the most important scholastic thinkers of the century. In these circumstances it was impossible to maintain the original ideals of simple mendicancy. The second factor behind the change was the wish of the papacy to give the order a secure position within the church. Ever since Francis's first appeal to Innocent III, the friars had been dependent on papal support: as a world-wide organization, they were exempt from control by bishops in the ordinary way and were an increasingly important part of the centralized organization of the church that

[2] *Opuscula sancti Patris Francisci Assisiensis*, Bibliotheca Franciscana Ascetica Medii Aevi, i, 2nd edn (Quaracchi, 1941), pp. 77–82.

[3] The developments of this period are set out by R. B. Brooke, *Early Franciscan Government: Elias to Bonaventure* (Cambridge, 1959), and J. Moorman, *A History of the Franciscan Order from its Origins to the Year 1517* (Oxford, 1968).

[4] D. Cresi, 'Statistica dell'ordine minoritico all'anno 1282', *Archivum Franciscanum Historicum*, lvi, 1963.

was characteristic of the thirteenth century. Popes had intervened by legislation in bulls to allow the friars to use property held for them by others (*Quo Elongati*, 1230; *Ordinem Vestrum*, 1245) and also to exercise the functions of preaching, confessing and burial which superseded rights jealously guarded by the ordinary clergy (*Nimis Iniqua*, 1231; *Cum a Nobis*, 1250). By the time of Bonaventure's generalate the Franciscans were numerous, wealthy in the corporate sense, and often learned. They were a great and powerful organization. They had built or were building large churches in many cities; St Francis himself was buried beneath the great double basilica that rises magnificently at the west end of Assisi, which made the simple town where the Franciscans had originated a centre of pilgrimage and an ecclesiastical capital.

Bonaventure's life stands at the extreme distance from some of those aspects of Francis which have excited modern romanticism and were no doubt of great importance in Francis's own evolution—that is to say, his attachment to romance legend—'I am the herald of the great king'[5]—and his exultation in the enjoyment of the physical world expressed in the canticle that thanks God for Brother Sun, Sister Moon, Brother Wind, Sister Water, Brother Fire, Mother Earth, and Sister Bodily Death.[6] It is difficult to know how important these strictly non-ecclesiastical aspects of Francis were to the men of the later part of that century. Although it presents well enough the main points which probably stood out in the popular picture of Francis, Bonaventure's *Legenda* could also be regarded as a rather cloudy presentation of the original story, designed to hide rather than to illuminate the contrasts between Francis's original wishes and the form the order had taken in the next fifty years. Bonaventure was a statesman who had to compromise between presenting the essence of the Franciscan message, in which he was a true believer, and defending the existing condition of the order. He had consulted those old men who knew most about the real Francis, but he also ordered the destruction of the other evidence not contained in his life. The General Chapter at Paris in 1266 laid down

that all earlier lives of the blessed Francis should be destroyed, and where they can be found outside the order brothers should attempt to remove them since that life which is made by the Minister General was compiled in accordance with what he had from the mouths of those who were nearly always with Francis and know everything for certain.[7]

During the late thirteenth century, dissidents in the order were subjected to long and brutal imprisonment. The General Chapter at Padua in 1277 ordered

[5] 'Praeco Sum Magni Regis' (Thomas de Celano, 'Vita Prima Sancti Francisci Assisiensis', *Analecta Franciscana*, x, 1926, p. 15).

[6] The 'Cantico di Frate Sole' is in G. Contini ed., *Poeti del Duecento*, i (Milan–Naples, 1960), p. 33.

[7] A. G. Little, 'Decrees of the General Chapters of the Friars Minor 1268–1282', *English Historical Review*, xiii, 1898, p. 705.

the provision of 'many strong prisons';[8] the order was not a band of united enthusiasts. The authoritarian destruction of evidence which provided an alternative picture to that given by Bonaventure was a mark of the great tensions within the order, principally between the ambitions of those who accepted its present condition and those who wished to revive the original extreme wishes of Francis, and to condemn the adaptations to which they had been subjected during the growth of the order. Bonaventure adapted the stories to play down Francis's insistence on total mendicancy and his suspicion of the life of the scholarly cleric. As a result of this censorship, modern scholars have had to carry out elaborate investigations to recover the evidence on which to build a realistic historical life of Francis. The real Francis, as distinct from Bonaventure's Francis, does not matter greatly to students of the age of Dante, but the tenuous preservation of the original documents about his life does. It provided the rigorists of the early fourteenth century with a body of information to which they could refer when criticizing contemporary practice. There were the two earlier lives by Thomas of Celano,[9] composed in 1228 and 1247, which had provided the standard account before Bonaventure composed his. Still more important were the stories preserved by Francis's companions, Leo, Angelo, and Rufino, who survived into the mid-thirteenth century. These were apparently preserved in writing at Assisi, and in the fourteenth century many of them were copied into manuscripts which still survive, including the *Speculum Perfectionis* written in 1318.[10] Bonaventure's attempt at suppression of evidence was a failure to the extent that enough survived to provide his rigorist opponents with a comparatively little known but useful body of traditions to support their opinions and the two views of Francis and his order which were represented by his *Legenda Maior* and by the *Scripta Leonis* may be seen as supporting two somewhat different views of the order in the late thirteenth and early fourteenth centuries.

When we are concerned principally with the significance of the Franciscans for Italian life, it is important to remember that we are talking of an organization founded in Italy, growing out of the Italian scene, but which by the late thirteenth century must have been more North European than Italian in its total membership. The whole order met in general chapters and had one minister-general; it was a single, world-wide body. So the Italian roots were inseparable from powers within the order issuing from other parts of Europe. 'Paris, Paris, why do you destroy the order of St Francis?' the companion of

---

[8] *Archiv für Literatur- und Kirchengeschichte des Mittelalters*, vi, 1892, p. 47.

[9] Printed in *Analecta Franciscana*, x, 1926.

[10] The *Speculum Perfectionis*, ed. Paul Sabatier, publications of the British Society of Franciscan Studies, xiii, xvii, 1928 and 1931. This material has been investigated by R. B. Brooke, *Scripta Leonis, Rufini et Angeli Sociorum S. Francisci* (Oxford, 1970), and R. Manselli, *Nos Qui cum Eo Fuimus* (Rome, 1980).

Francis, Giles of Assisi, is supposed to have cried.[11] The papacy could not ignore the behaviour of an order with such power and influence. In 1279 Gian Gaetano Orsini, whose father is supposed to have been a member of the third order and to have received a prophecy about Gian Gaetano from the lips of Francis himself, became Pope Nicholas III. He had been cardinal protector of the Franciscans, but on becoming pope he handed the position over to his nephew cardinal Matteo Rosso Orsini. 'We give you', he said according to one writer, 'the desire of our own heart, the pupil of our eyes'. His words were stopped by tears in which others present at the assembly joined. After handing over the charge of the order, according to the same author, he abandoned other business (to the surprise of the curia) to devote two months to the study of its rule in preparation for the bull *Exiit qui Seminat*.[12] This was the high point of papal connections with the Franciscans. They were linked with a Roman clan which understood them in their Italian setting, which could respond to them with the emotion and tears appropriate to an order of men based on the inspiration of such deep feeling. Nicholas III was the most Italian of popes, a man whose ambitions were dominated by his conceptions of what the papacy could do for Italian religion and politics. By 1288 there was a Franciscan pope, Jerome of Ascoli, Nicholas IV. But this was not a permanent relationship. Nicholas III and IV were separated by Martin IV, a French pope with much less interest in the Italian scene. In the long run, popes were to be more concerned with the Franciscans as part of a European power game, and conversely the Italian friars were to be deeply affected by aspects of their order outside Italy.

The local significance of the Franciscans within Italian society was affected not only by wide social variations between the lonely hermitages of the Apennines and the populous cities, but also by the impact of European movements of thought and European politics in which the order inevitably became entangled. The gothic architecture of the upper basilica at Assisi, built during the pontificate of Innocent IV in a style of building which was still rather unusual in Italy at that time, and the scholastic theology of Bonaventure and Mathew of Acquasparta, two ministers-general who were Italian and important in Italian affairs but also Parisian scholars, are examples of the Northern world influencing Italy because the Franciscan order was a European and not merely an Italian organization.

In considering the role of the Franciscan order at the end of the thirteenth and beginning of the fourteenth centuries, we have to distinguish between two things. First there is the order in general, which remained a well established, ubiquitous and prominent feature of Italian life, developing gradually along

---

[11] *Analecta Franciscana*, iii, 1897, p. 86.

[12] 'Philippi de Perusio Epistola de Cardinalibus Protectoribus Ordinis Fratrum Minorum', ed. O. Holder-Egger, *Monumenta Germaniae Historica, Scriptores*, xxxii, pp. 681–3; Chronica XXIV Generalium, *Analecta Franciscana*, iii, 1897, p. 368.

the lines laid down by the time of Bonaventure and promoted by Bonaventure himself. This is the Franciscan order that matters as part of the general background of Italian society and thought, the order for which the walls of Assisi and Santa Croce were painted, and which provided much of the religious inspiration for Italian writing. It was promoted by Nicholas III's bull *Exiit qui Seminat* (1279), which defended the moderate poverty, the ownership of property on behalf of the friars by the pope, and the acceptance of scholarship along Bonaventuran lines. It was still more promoted by Martin IV's *Ad fructus uberes* (1281), which gave friars full power to act as confessors as long as each man confessed once a year to the parish priest; by *Exultantes in Domino* (1283), which allowed Franciscan ministers themselves to appoint the custodians of their property; and by Nicholas IV's privileges for the decoration of the basilica at Assisi. Boniface VIII in *Super Cathedram* (1300) tried to limit Franciscan intrusions into the world of the ordinary clergy by preaching, confessing, and burying; and Clement V in *Exivi de paradiso* (1312) tried to deal with abuses of the rules allowing friars to handle property and money. But these were fairly superficial trimmings of a highly developed and stabilized part of society.

There was on the other hand the dissident Spiritual wing of the Franciscan order, which was never very numerous in Italy but made a great deal of noise, influenced papal attitudes to the order—*Exivi de paradiso* was partly an attempt to give weight to spiritual interpretations of the rule—and has considerable literary importance because of its influence on Dante in his later years. The separate and critical ideas of the Spirituals were really based on two important influences: first, on the survival of primitive Franciscan attitudes to poverty (chiefly in smaller country centres in Umbria and the March of Ancona); and second on the adoption of the philosophy of history derived from the writings of Joachim of Fiore.[13] These two factors combined into a powerful set of radical attitudes that shook the government of the order quite seriously in the period between 1294 and 1312. The defence of absolute poverty was represented in the late thirteenth century most strongly by the group of zealots including Peter of Macerata (later Brother Liberato), and Peter of Fossombrone (later Angelo da Clareno), who were persecuted and imprisoned by the authorities of the order in the March of Ancona in the 1270s. In 1289 they were sent to Armenia by the minister-general. When they returned to Italy in 1294 they came back to a political situation which was temporarily transformed by the election of a pope, Celestine V, who was naturally sympathetic to them. Peter Murrone was himself the founder of an order of hermits. He believed in a life of obscurity and extreme austerity that

---

[13] The history of these movements can be read in D. L. Douie, *The Nature and the Effect of the Heresy of the Fraticelli* (Manchester, 1932); M. Reeves, *The Influence of Prophecy in the Later Middle Ages: A Study in Joachimism* (Oxford, 1969); M. D. Lambert, *Franciscan Poverty* (London, 1961).

was in some ways essentially similar to that longed for by the Franciscan Spirituals, and he allowed them to found a new order in which they would be removed from the heavy hand of the Franciscan establishment under the generalate of Liberato and the protection of Cardinal Napoleone Orsini. This release was very short. The accession of Boniface VIII made them refugees again, this time in Greece. They returned after the death of Boniface, and soon after this Liberato died. In the easier atmosphere of the papal curia of Clement V (1305–14) and with the support of Napoleone Orsini the zealots found more tolerance. Clement attempted a genuine compromise between the two wings after hearing both sides, stated in *Exivi de paradiso* (1312). Angelo survived into the 1320s and wrote the *Historia Septem Tribulationum*, which contains the most important account of the history of the rigorists.

The idea of seeing the trials of the Franciscan enthusiasts as a succession of 'seven tribulations' implies of course that they are regarded as conforming to a providential historical pattern. Angelo was not, however, a particularly enthusiastic historical interpreter; he appears to have had a conventional and orthodox view of the church. The most interesting and prominent of the historical analysts was a Piedmontese friar, Ubertino da Casale, who played a substantial part in the ecclesiastical politics of Central Italy in the early years of the fourteenth century. The writer from whom the radical historical theology of this period was ultimately derived, Joachim of Fiore, was a Cistercian abbot in Calabria who died in 1202. He left various works which attempted an application of fundamental religious number patterns to history, particularly the dualism of the two testaments, the Holy Trinity, and the twelve Apostles. From his writings it was possible to derive the view that the history of the world was divided into three ages, corresponding to the Father, Son and Holy Ghost; that the thirteenth century would see the transition to the third age; and that this would be marked by great upheaval, including the coming of Antichrist. It was also possible to interpret the history of the world in such a way as to give supreme importance to St Francis and his most faithful followers.

It is not very easy to distinguish the influence of Joachim from the influence of the Book of Revelation, with its obscure visions of future great events and a symbolism which could also be applied easily to actual events of the contemporary or future world. The interpretation of the Book of Revelation was common in the most orthodox circles. That and the highly symbolic tendencies of the writings of Bonaventure encouraged speculation along those lines that found an extreme embodiment in Ubertino's *Arbor Vitae Cruci-fixae*, composed in 1305 or soon after.[14] Ubertino came to central Italy after

---

[14] There are accounts of Ubertino in F. Callaey, *L'idealisme franciscain spirituel au XIVᵉ siècle: étude sur Ubertin de Casale* (Louvain, 1911), and G. L. Potestà, *Storia ed escatologia in Ubertino da Casale* (Milan, 1980). His *Arbor Vitae Crucifixae* has been reprinted in facsimile: Ubertinus de Casali, *Arbor Vitae Crucifixae Jesu*, ed. C. T. Davis (Turin, 1961).

some years of study at Paris, and after an important encounter with the great French Franciscan theologian Pierre Jean Olivi who was lecturing at Florence in 1287. Olivi was a learned and careful scholar who had been consulted by Nicholas III about the future of the Franciscans, but he took over from Joachim the idea that the world was approaching the beginning of the third age in which Antichrist would have to be overcome, and thought that Francis—the specially successful imitator of Christ—and his order had a special role in present and future history.[15] Olivi seems also to have carried forward the assimilation of the life of Francis to the life of Jesus. Not only did he have the stigmata and twelve disciples, but it seemed possible to Olivi that there might be a resurrection of Francis in the course of the troubles about to befall the church.[16] Ubertino was profoundly influenced as well by meeting several of the simple holy men and women of Central Italy: Angela da Foligno, Clare of Montefalco, Margaret of Cortona, and Peter the Combmaker of Siena. When he was dismissed to the hermitage of La Verna because his preaching was disapproved of and began to write the *Arbor Vitae Crucifixae*, he was very much under the double influence of Italian local pietism and of sophisticated theological reactions to the theology of Joachim.

The general structure of the *Arbor* is influenced by imitation of Bonaventure's *Lignum Vitae* (Tree of life), a short book in which the minister-general, following the hint given by 'the tree of life, which bare twelve manner of fruits' in Revelation 22, had set out meditations on the life of Christ in the likeness of parts of a tree, the branches representing his virtues. Ubertino took over this idea and blew it up into a vast work, many times as long, with a profuse elaboration of detail, arranging the gospel story in memorable patterns to draw out the wealth of significance hidden in each of its episodes. For example, the events of the day of Jesus's entry into Jerusalem mystically signify divine wisdom, and they figure and exemplify the manner of the ultimate victory of Jesus over the world. The events of the day show the three attributes of God: his power, his wisdom, and his goodness. Each of these attributes is shown by three points in the story: power by the fact that the owners of the ass and foal gave them up for Jesus to ride on, by the attraction of people flocking to meet them, and by the ability to clear the temple of the money-changers; wisdom because Jesus knew where the ass was to be found, because he foretold the destruction of Jerusalem, and because he could reply wisely to the Pharisees. Why did Jesus send two disciples to fetch the ass and the foal? Because of the two testaments, the two aspects of scripture—letter and spirit, the two precepts of charity, the two kinds of perfection of earthly life—active and contemplative, the two peoples to be converted.[17]

[15] Reeves, *Prophecy*, pp. 194–201.
[16] R. Manselli, 'La resurrezione di San Francesco dalla teologia di Petro di Giovanni Olivi ad una testmonianza di pietà popolare', *Collectanea Francescana*, xlvi, 1976.
[17] Ubertino da Casale, *Arbor*, IV. i, pp. 275–7.

Book V of the *Arbor* follows a different line from this harmless pursuit of symbol and figure; it applies the method to the Book of Revelation and to contemporary history, assuming a prophetic insight of a kind not sanctioned by the orthodox church. It has three prominent elements: figural interpretation, the Joachist historical scheme, and number symbolism. The life of Christ prefigured the life of Francis. Elijah, filled with angelic ardour and seeming to set the world on fire, prefigured Francis's similar characteristics. Adam's creation after the fifth day prefigured Francis's life at the end of the fifth age of the world. The beast in Revelation 13 prefigured Pope Boniface VIII. This kind of interpretation is put within the framework of the seven ages of Joachim's second *status*, the second of three *status* into which he divided the whole history of the world. The age of the government of the Spirit on earth, Joachim's third *status*, disappears, at least in the fullness of Joachist interpretation, though the whole plan is intended to reach its culmination in a victorious coming of Christ to earth. Thus the historical plan becomes realistically concrete. Ubertino was well informed about Church history and used his knowledge subtly. The result resembles some kinds of Marxist interpretation in its attempt to fit events into a meaningful pattern. There are seven ages after the birth of Christ. Age One starts with Jesus and his preaching. Age Six begins with St Francis and includes the struggle against the Whore of Babylon. Age Seven is to see the coming of Antichrist and the final victory of the returned Christ.

If Francis was the angel of the sixth seal, as Bonaventure had also allowed him to be without following out the Joachist implications of this view, he had a crucial importance in the whole scheme of history. His precepts and wishes were forces of good in the fight against evil, and they were to be obeyed implicitly. Ubertino was thus able to quote from the *Scripta Leonis* passages, which he could claim embodied the truth about Francis's opinions, including emphases on the dangers of wealth and learning, which fitted the rigorist view and were inconvenient for the contemporary government of the order, and which must be obeyed because of Francis's importance in the battle against evil. Ubertino argued also that clerks in his day were threatened by a particularly subtle philosophical temptation because they could be seduced by Aristotle and appear to be defending the Gospel when they were actually destroying it. There were clerks at Paris who as a result of this insidious influence in fact rejected all articles of faith; they were merely theists believing, under the influence of Aristotle and Averroes, that pagan philosophy was a sufficient basis for ethics, that the world was eternal, and that free will was limited. But still worse dangers were to be faced in the government of the church. Boniface VIII was identified with the beast who came out of the sea in Revelation 13. The other beast that followed him and had 'two horns like a lamb and spoke as a dragon' was the worldly clergy which supported Boniface, its two horns being the two mendicant orders, Franciscans and

Dominicans. The wounding of the beast, Revelation 13: 3, corresponds to the blow given to Boniface when the Colonna cardinals announced he was not canonically elected because Celestine V was still the real pope. The beast's war against the saints is Boniface's persecution of the spiritual Franciscans. Benedict XI, Boniface's successor, seems to become the second beast, and the two popes together appear to be identified by Ubertino with the Joachist 'mystical Antichrist' who is to precede the 'open Antichrist'. Like all millenarians Ubertino believed the final struggle was about to begin.[18]

In 1308 Ubertino left Italy with Cardinal Napoleone and later played a prominent part in the discussions which led to *Exivi de paradiso*. He was a learned man. His historical theology is a line of thought which may not have had much importance among the crowds of mendicants, the members of third orders, and the holy men and women who stand out among them in Central Italy. For example, in 1312 there was a rebellion of Franciscan spirituals in Tuscany,[19] who were probably mainly enthusiasts for rigour in the application of the rule rather than disciples of Olivi and Ubertino. Ubertino also provides us, however, with a link between the learned world and the world of common saintliness which is parallel to the link provided by Dante's *Comedy* and may have influenced the great poem. One of the men Ubertino met in Tuscany was Peter, *vir deo plenus petrus de senis pectenarius*,[20] the Sienese comb-maker and member of the Franciscan third order whose prayers, according to Dante, opened Purgatory (xiii. 128) to Sapia Provenzano after she had thanked God for the defeat of her Sienese relatives at the Battle of Colle in 1269. A commentator on Dante tells us

Piero Pettinaro had a comb shop at Siena in Camollia and was a citizen of Siena, and it is said that he went to Pisa to buy combs and bought by the dozen; then he went to the Ponte Vecchio in Pisa and sorted them out. If one of them was broken he threw it into the Arno. He was often told that even if it was broken a comb was worth something and should be sold. Piero replied: I do not want anyone to have bad goods from me. When he saw someone going with the rectors' men to execution, he went on his knees and said: God be praised who has kept one from that danger. For such things the Sienese, a very remarkable people, said he was holy.[21]

Peter was presumably a somewhat more impressive pietist than this report suggests, and Dante and Ubertino must have heard stranger reports of his virtues; but he stands as an example of the simple religiosity of ordinary people that ran alongside the extravagant utterances of learned enthusiasts.

Ubertino also met an otherwise unknown *devotissima virgo Cecilia de*

---

[18] Ubertino da Casale, *Arbor*, V. viii, pp. 465–7.
[19] A. M. Ini, 'Nuovi documenti sugli spirituali di Toscana', *Archivum Franciscanum Historicum*, lxvi, 1973.
[20] Ubertino da Casale, *Arbor*, Prologue, p. 4.
[21] *Commento alla divina Commedia d'anonimo fiorentino*, ed. P. Fanfani (Bologna, 1866–74), ii, p. 217.

Florentia, probably a Franciscan tertiary who 'instructed me in the whole
process of the superior contemplation of the life of Jesus and the secrets of my
heart and many other things'.[22] He met Angela da Foligno, 'to whom Jesus so
revealed the defects of my heart and His secret benefits that I cannot doubt He
spoke in her and she restored all my gifts lost by my malice immensely
multiplied so that I was no longer what I had been'.[23] Angela, another
Franciscan tertiary, has become famous because of her dictated autobiography. We know also from the life of Margaret of Cortona that Ubertino was
present one day when she rebuked her son for sleeping instead of going to
matins.[24] These people whom Ubertino met represent the real and popular
religious enthusiasm of Italy, which we have to take account of in trying to
explain its thought.

By 1300 the religious life of the Italian cities had long been dominated by
religious organizations that imitated the pattern set up by St Francis for his
order. They were not Benedictine, nor did they follow an order derived from
the Benedictine rule; they lived in convents but were devoted to poverty; they
were centralized and depended on papal privileges. When it was decided in
Florence in 1291 to release prisoners from the city gaols, the choice of persons
appropriate to receive this grace was entrusted to the prior of the Dominicans,
the warden of the Franciscans, the provost of the Humiliati, the prior of the
Augustinian hermits of Santo Spirito, the prior of the Carmelites and the prior
of the Servites of St Mary.[25] These ministers were chosen of course because
they belonged to orders for whom, unlike Benedictines or Cistercians, public
business outside the convent was not an inappropriate activity. Nevertheless
it is interesting that they should all be orders that had developed in the
thirteenth century and were very much influenced by the Franciscan model.
The dominant position of the mendicant orders in urban life in the thirteenth
century is often still visible in the size of their buildings, placed on the
outskirts of the medieval city where there was room for expansion; for
instance at Siena, where the big churches of San Francesco, San Domenico,
Sant Agostino and Santa Maria dei Servi still very obviously hold this position
at four corners of the town. At Florence the mendicant churches—Santa
Croce (Franciscans), Santa Maria Novella (Dominicans), Ognissanti
(Humiliati), Santissima Annunziata (Servites), Sant Egidio (Friars of the
Sack), and Santo Spirito (Augustinians)—were all, except for Santo Spirito in
Oltr'Arno, built in the suburban areas into which the population was
expanding in the thirteenth century and where it was easier to find space from
which to dominate the life of the old centre.[26] The mendicant orders all owed

[22] Ubertino da Casale, *Arbor*, Prologue, p. 4.
[23] Ibid., p. 5; cf. Callaey, *L'Idealisme franciscain*, p. 19.
[24] Callaey, op. cit., pp. 9–10.
[25] *Consulte della Repubblica fiorentina*, ii, p. 86.
[26] A. Benvenuto Papi, 'L'impianto mendicante in Firenze, un problema aperto', *Mélanges de l'École Française de Rome*, lxxxix, 1977.

much to the example of the Franciscan model, and they all succeeded in adapting themselves to the needs of Italian cities, building large churches and convents occupying a prominent place in the urban landscape. They combined the interior pursuit of devotion and study with the external offering of preaching, teaching, and sacramental ministration which brought them into contact with the surrounding lay world. They gave the city a spiritual and intellectual leadership which could not be provided by the older religious orders, and which was symptomatically expressed by the great scale of their buildings.

There were of course substantial differences between the various mendicant orders. If we look at their different roles within Florence we shall be struck by the greater prominence of the Franciscan and Dominican convents of Santa Croce and Santa Maria Novella and the relatively modest position of the Humiliati and the Augustinians. The order of Augustinian hermits was a creation of the mid-thirteenth century; it was largely the work of Cardinal Riccardo Annibaldi, who had succeeded in welding together in one organization a large number of eremetical houses—mostly in the countryside of Tuscany, Umbria and the March—and procuring the bull of Alexander IV of 1256 which gave them a single rule combining the old rule of St Augustine and the new ideals of mendicancy.[27] The Augustinians did not achieve great historical prominence in Florence until the appearance of Simone Fidati da Cascia, a popular preacher who had been influenced by the Franciscan Spirituals, advocating mendicant poverty and denouncing Florentine licentiousness in the 1320s and 1330s. The eremitical background of the Augustinian order and the fact that it had been made up out of a number of houses in the country whose instincts were for withdrawal probably made it less able to adapt to the city. But the church and convent in Oltr'Arno were being built through the second half of the thirteenth century and the order must have been a familiar part of city life.[28] The Dominicans, on the other hand, were clearly wealthy and prominent by the middle of the thirteenth century, and they are extremely well recorded in the register of deaths in the convent—a splendidly maintained record with brief biographical entries about each of the friars. This gives us a social conspectus which shows clearly that the brothers included members of important Florentine families and men remarkable for learning. Filippo domini Rigaletti, who died in 1283, drew his origin 'ex nobilibus parentibus', a Soldanieri brother died in 1287, a son of a judge in 1296, an Adimari in 1299, a priest who was said to know the Decretals

---

[27] F. Roth, 'Cardinal Richard Annibaldi, First Protector of the Augustinian Order 1243–1276', *Augustiniana*, ii, 1952–iv, 1954; B. van Luijk, *Gli eremiti neri nel Dugento con particolare riguardo al territorio pisano e toscano*, Biblioteca del bollettino storico pisano, 7 (Pisa, 1968); K. Elm, 'Gli eremiti nel Dugento', *Quellen und Forschungen*, l, 1971.

[28] M. G. McNeil, *Simone Fidati and his De Gestis Domini Salvatoris* (Washington, 1951); Davidsohn, *Forschungen*, iv, pp. 491–2.

by heart in 1304.[29] Many of the brothers were said to have procured gifts of land to the convent from their relations. Santa Maria Novella, the Dominican convent, was the first to be built on a very large scale. The foundation stone of the present church was laid by Cardinal Latino on his visit to Florence in 1279.[30] In the late thirteenth century, it must already have been a comfortable place in which a well-endowed body of friars lived a superior life. The most famous Florentine Dominican of this period was the preacher and lecturer Remigio de' Girolami who died in 1319, a member of a good Florentine family, notable for his sermons about city politics, a graduate of Paris who was honoured for his learning by Pope Benedict XI in 1304.[31]

The community of Servites have the distinction of being the only substantial order founded in Florence itself. Their early history is the clearest case of the interrelationship between religious life and the commercial city. The Servites originated in the 1230s and 1240s in the mobilization of orthodox lay opinion during the highly successful battle waged by the Dominican St Peter Martyr against the Cathar dualists in 1244–5, which ended the serious history of heresy in Florence. Their devotion to Mary was doubtless originally an assertion of orthodoxy against the Cathar denial of goodness in the created world. The Servites later traced their origin to a semi-mythical group of seven lay penitents who made an agreement to live piously. An early fourteenth-century account of the foundation of the order emphasizes its links with lay commercial life and with Florence:

The city and the citizens find physical usefulness [*utilitas corporalis*] in the mutual exchange of earthly goods so that various businesses and trades are found in the city to carry this exchange on more usefully. Before they joined together these seven men were involved in this earthly business and in exchange in the merchant guild [*secundum mercantie artem*].

They became instead 'dealers in celestial goods' (*celestium negotiatores*). The author emphasizes that the order is especially connected with Florence; as the Franciscans have a particular connection with Assisi and the Dominicans with Bologna, so the Servites are linked with Florence.[32] Although the number of Servite convents grew quickly and very soon spread across the Alps into Germany, they did in fact remain a primarily Italian order with strong roots in Tuscany. The most important convent was the house at Cafaggio in the suburbs of Florence, the site of the present Santissima Annunziata, where the

---

[29] S. Orlandi, *Necrologio di Santa Maria Novella* (Florence, 1955), i, pp. 131, 139, 156, 172, 187.

[30] Davidsohn, *Forschungen*, iv, 466–82; J. White, *Art and Architecture in Italy: 1250–1400* (Harmondsworth, 1966), pp. 7–8.

[31] Orlandi, *Necrologio*, p. 220.

[32] 'Legenda de origine Ordinis Fratrum Servorum Virginis Mariae Auctore Incerto 1317', *Monumenta Ordinis Servorum Sanctae Mariae*, i, 1897, pp. 72–4. The early history of the Servites has been fully recounted by F. A. Dal Pino, *I Frati Servi di S. Maria dalle origini all'approvazione (c.1233–1304)* (Louvain, 1972).

community was established in the 1250s; and the most notable figure in the early history of the order was a Florentine, St Filippo Benizzi, who was prior-general from 1267 to 1285. The connection with the Guelf party in Florence also seems to have been strong. In 1280 the Guelfs decided to put the party's archives into a box to be looked after by the brothers at Cafaggio.[33] The lucky survival of a financial account of the house at Cafaggio for the years 1286–9 enables us to see close connections between the Servites and some of the most prominent Florentine families of the period, particularly those who were associated a few years later with the White faction. The Falconieri were closely connected, and so were the Cavalcanti. The account mentions the receipt of money for the saying of masses for Jacopo, brother of Guido Cavalcanti, who was a canon of the Cathedral, and money for the funeral of Guido's father, the sceptic of *Inferno* X. The Cerchi were prominent—Vieri de' Cerchi gave 26s. 8d. for the convent to buy land—so were the Adimari, the Alfani and Folco Portinari, father of Dante's Beatrice. The Servites of Cafaggio also played a part in the battle of Campaldino: three brothers from the convent, including Gherardo Adimari and Benedetto Beati, went with the army, and the third—who presumably had not taken the oath—was made a knight before going. After the battle six brothers attended the funeral of one Tici de' Visdomini, who had died in it, and his commune presented the convent with a gift of £20.[34] This account provides us with a slight but exceptional glimpse of the connection between an order and the ruling elite of Florence at a particular moment for which we have no parallels from the other orders. We see the Servites of Cafaggio exulting in their connection with the triumphant Guelf elite at the time of Campaldino. We should assume that the mendicant houses, though their religious purposes may have been directed towards poverty and the poor, depended on the support of the wealthy as members and as patrons. Ubertino da Casale denounced modern Franciscan neglect of the simple life of prayer, tears, and work as ordained by the founder in favour of the trivialities of city life; 'luxuriousness, wandering through the squares and the forum, frequent and useless visits of women, laughing and jokes . . . It is not enough to have left the deserts, even the suburbs do not please us, we are not happy except in those places where there is the greatest number of people.'[35] He was probably thinking of Santa Croce at Florence.

We can imagine the mendicant orders as the heart of the religious move-ment of the thirteenth century. Attached to them were other organizations whose members were either half lay or entirely lay but were committed to religious work and the devout life. The closest were the tertiaries, members of the so-called 'third orders' who enjoyed an ambiguous existence half lay and

---

[33] Dal Pino, *Frati Servi*, ii, p. 321.

[34] E.-M. Casalini, 'Il convento di S. Maria di Cafaggio nella cerchia delle amicizie di Dante', *Studi storici dell'ordine dei Servi di Maria*, xvi, 1966, pp. 178–82.

[35] *Archiv für Literatur- und Kirchengeschichte des Mittelalters*, iii, 1887, p. 77.

half spiritual that presented problems to city authorities because there were serious questions about their ability to perform military service, swear oaths, or submit to lay courts.[36] All the mendicant orders eventually acquired separate bodies of tertiaries attached to them, but this condition of life was particularly connected in the popular mind with Francis's call to penitents to join in an abstemious life of devotion to religious purposes. For most of the thirteenth century—the 'third order' terminology was commoner after the Franciscan Pope Nicholas IV proclaimed a rule for penitents in 1289—these people were commonly known as *frati e suore della penitenza* (brothers and sisters of penitence), *continenti* or *pinzocheri*. They wore religious habits that set them apart from the laity and, though they could be married, they followed fairly strict rules.

In the 1280s and 1290s the penitent groups of Florence became prominent as a result of Bishop Andrea Mozzi's attempt to free the Dominican penitents from union with the Franciscans.[37] The documents produced in the course of this affair make certain facts about the tertiaries fairly clear. They were not very numerous; the total number of both Dominican and Franciscan tertiaries was probably under eighty. They often belonged to superior families; the Dominican tertiaries included a member of the Mozzi family—perhaps the reason for the bishop's interest in them—who was a relation of Giano della Bella and a Soldanieri. And they held quite a lot of property, much of which was devoted to the social work of supporting the hospitals of Santa Maria Nuova and San Paolo, so there is no reason to doubt the sincere religious purposes of the third orders; but their ability to interest bishops, popes, and legates in producing documents about their disputes was probably a result of their high status and the social and political importance of their members.

A further step away from the strictly religious life of the mendicant orders and the semi-religious status of the third orders were the confraternities of laymen. These were societies established to encourage men and women to lead a strictly religious life without leaving the lay world. Their rules included abstinence, regular attendance at religious services, often centring on a particular church, the singing of *laude* or hymns, sometimes the carrying out of regular penitential flagellation.[38] An early description of their activities is

---

[36] C. Piana, 'Silloge di documenti dell'antico archivio di S. Francesco di Bologna. VI: la posizione giuridica del Terz'Ordine della penitenza a Firenze nel secolo XIV', *Archivum Franciscanum Historicum*, l, 1957.

[37] G. G. Meersseman, *Dossier de l'Ordre de la Pénitence au XIIIe siècle* (Spicilegium Friburgense, 7, 1961), pp. 28–36. This book contains the best account of the history of the third orders.

[38] Idem, *Ordo fraternitatis: confraternità e pietà dei laici nel mondo medioevo* (Rome, 1977); idem, 'Études sur les anciennes confréries dominicaines', *Archivum Fratrum Praedicatorum*, xx, 1950–xxiii, 1953; G. Monti, *Le confraternità medievali dell'alta e media Italia* (Venice, 1927); J. Henderson, 'The Flagellant Movement and Flagellant Confraternities in Central Italy 1260–1400', *Studies in Church History*, 15, 1978; R. F. E. Weissman, *Ritual Brotherhood in Renaissance Florence* (New York, 1982).

contained in the contemporary life of Ambrogio Sansedoni (d. 1268), where we are told that in Siena there were

> various movements of the spirit of God and congregations of good men, including laymen, of which some were organized for divine *laudes* which were sung every day in the places of the religious and first at the Dominican church, even by children who were trained to *laudes* of this kind with wonderful devotion that spread to other cities. Others were for raising alms that they obtained with wonderful fervour and gave out to the poor. Others scourged their bodies publicly as they went through the city with veiled faces and they included great men and sometimes famous sinners.[39]

The popularity of confraternities sprang out of the penitential movements common in the Italian world in the early thirteenth century and the antiheretical efforts of these years. Some aspects of their life received a stimulus from the extraordinary flagellant movement that arose suddenly in Perugia in 1260 under the leadership of Ranieri Fasani, perhaps inspired partly by the belief of some Joachists that the world would end in that year, and by the shattering defeat of the pro-papal Guelfs at Montaperti.[40] Though that was a local outburst of fervour, it appears to have had an effect outside Perugia by encouraging *disciplina* (flagellation), which remained a fairly common practice in Renaissance Italy.

The confraternity movement was widespread in the late thirteenth century. By that time the survival of rules regulating the lines of confraternity members—their observance of fast, their attendance at services with candles, their processions, their charities—enables one to see the movement as a well-established expression of lay piety. By 1300 about fifteen confraternities are known to have existed in Florence, often linked with mendicant churches.[41] It was the confraternity of St Mary the Virgin which commissioned Duccio to paint the *Rucellai Madonna* for Santa Maria Novella in 1285.

The confraternities are the most substantial expression of the widespread religious enthusiasm, the regular expression of penitential devotion in attendance at churches, ceremonial procession, alms giving, hospital work, and individual self-denial which was common and highly organized in the Italian cities of the thirteenth century. If we could visit Florence in 1300 we should find not only a large number of small religious houses, but also, around the great convents of mendicants, many tertiaries and confraternity members living in fairly close connection with their churches.[42] Some of the tertiaries lived close to the convents; women are described in 1277 as 'ladies who live by

---

[39] Meersseman, *Ordo Fraternitatis*, ii, p. 955.

[40] *Il movimento dei Disciplinati nel settimo centenario del suo inizio (Perugia–1260)* (Deputazione di storia patria per l'Umbria, Appendici al Bollettino, 9, 1962).

[41] M. D. Papi, 'Confraternite ed ordini mendicanti a Firenze. Aspetti di una ricerca quantitativa', *Mélanges de l'Ecole Française de Rome*, lxxxix, 1977, p. 724.

[42] Evidence of the many small religious houses is set out in Davidsohn, *Forschungen*, iv, pp. 401–22.

the church of Santa Croce and who are garbed with the cord of the friars
minor'.[43] Many more members of confraternities built their religious lives
around the mendicant churches. We should also find a great variety of lay
religious devotion. The Militia of the blessed Virgin Mary, commonly known
as the *Frati Gaudenti*, the 'cheerful brothers', a military order for laymen
established at Bologna in 1261, included several members of good Florentine
families in 1289.[44] The company of Or San Michele, which became rich in the
fourteenth century, grew out of assemblies in the 1290s to sing hymns before a
miracle-working image of the Virgin painted on a column outside the city
grain store.[45] It led to competition for honours between the Dominicans and
Franciscans at which Guido Cavalcanti jeered in a poem.[46] But the cool
scepticism of an occasional educated aristocrat was a lonely voice in the flood
of popular religious emotion to which many members of his family
contributed.

The scepticism of Cavalcanti has become the normality of civilized
enlightenment. It is extremely difficult to achieve an understanding sympathy
with the emotions of crowds in a medieval town. The rules and deeds of
property which provide most of the surviving evidence for the orders and
confraternities leave nearly everything to the imagination. We approach
closer to real religious feeling in reading the outpourings of Angelo Clareno or
Ubertino da Casale, but the best source of information about the character of
strong religious emotion is to be found in the lives of saints. Fortunately a
significant group of lives of Central Italian saintly women survives from the
period around 1300.

The important saints for whom we have useful contemporary sources are
the following: St Angela da Foligno (1248–1309), a Franciscan tertiary, an
account of whose life was set down by Arnold of Foligno OFM and approved
by Cardinal Jacopo Colonna in 1309–10;[47] St Clare of Montefalco (1268–
1308), the story of whose life was written immediately after her death by
Berengario da Sant' Africano, the vicar of the Bishop of Spoleto, in expectation of the move towards canonization made in 1309;[48] St Margaret of
Cortona (1247–97), immortalized soon after her death by the pen of her
Franciscan confessor;[49] the Blessed Oringa Menabuoi (1240–1310), another
Franciscan tertiary commemorated in an apparently contemporary

---

[43] Davidsohn, *Forschungen*, iv, p. 78.

[44] D. M. Federici, *Istoria de' Cavalieri Gaudenti* (Venice, 1787), ii, p. 127; Davidsohn, op. cit.,
p. 495.

[45] Villani, vii. clv; Davidsohn, op. cit., pp. 435–9.

[46] *Poeti del Duecento*, ii, pp. 558–9.

[47] *Le Livre de la bienheureuse Angèle de Foligno*, ed. P. Doncoeur (Paris, 1927); cf. *Acta
Sanctorum Bollandiana* (Antwerp, etc., 1643–) January, i, p. 186.

[48] M. Faloci Pulignani, 'Vita di S. Chiara da Montefalco scritta da Berengario di S. Africano',
Archivio storico per le Marche e per l'Umbria, i, 1884; ii, 1885.

[49] *Acta Sanctorum*, February, iii, p. 300.

account;[50] and the Blessed Margaret of Faenza (1230–1330), founder of a Vallombrosan abbey at Florence also apparently recorded in a contemporary life.[51] These saints are all from Central Italy, and all women. There are no parallel lives surviving for men, though a number of men who lived in Central Italy in this period, more men than women in fact, were reputed to have saintly qualities.[52] Three of the women, the subjects of the more interesting lives—Angela da Foligno, Clare of Montefalco, and Margaret of Cortona— came from places not very far apart and are known to have had links with Ubertino da Casale. Ubertino himself reports his meeting with Angela.[53] He is mentioned in Margaret's legend, and her expectation of a future struggle between the Friars Minor and Antichrist, a view easily connected with the radical historical theology, is also reported in the same source.[54] Clare is said in her legend to have been in danger because of her association with Cardinal Jacopo Colonna when he was in dispute with Boniface VIII,[55] and the cardinal is also said to have approved the life of Angela.[56] The general connection of this group with radical religious enthusiasts is clear.

Are we dealing with a literary school rather than a social phenomenon? The possibility should not be ignored. However, only two of these women had their lives written by Franciscans. Ubertino probably came into contact with them because they were already remarkable, and the lives do not have much literary similarity. Why the prominence of women? The probability is that we are dealing here with a genuine social phenomenon that was to some extent permitted by St Francis's remarkable association with St Clare and the foundation of the Clarisses. The combination of religious and sexual energy in female mystics probably produced more violent manifestations than were observable in men, manifestations more deserving of literary record. Without the association of Francis and Clare, however, and the licence it gave for the practice of the independent female religious life, and without the association of this female licence with the third order, whose members (unlike the enclosed Clarisses) could live in the world, it is possible that Renaissance Italy would not have seen the remarkable series of female saints stretching through to St Catherine of Siena in the fourteenth century and St Catherine Ricci in the sixteenth. The difficulty encountered by women of superior rank in taking an independent religious life is shown by the story of Clare's desperate and determined escape from her family at the beginning of the century. It is also

---

[50] G. Lami, *Deliciae Eruditorum* (Florence, 1736–69), xviii, p. 189.

[51] *Acta Sanctorum*, August, v, p. 845.

[52] A rough calculation of the *santi* and *beati* of central Italy in the late thirteenth and very early fourteenth centuries recorded in *Bibliotheca Sanctorum*, ed. F. Caraffa (Rome, 1961–9) produces far more men than women: 42 to 12.

[53] Ubertino da Casale, *Arbor Vitae*, Prologue, p. 5.

[54] Callaey, *L'Idéalisme franciscain*, pp. 9–10; *Acta Sanctorum*, February, iii, p. 346.

[55] Faloci Pulignani, 'Vita di S. Chiara', i, p. 618.

[56] *La Bienheurense Angèle*, ed. Doncoeur, p. 5.

shown by the life of the most famous Florentine saint of the thirteenth century, Umiliana de' Cerchi (1219–46), who belonged to an already prominent family. She was frustrated in her attempt to join the Clarisses and forced to marry, and after her husband's death was forced to return to her father's family. The best she could do in pursuit of her religious aspirations was to retire to a life of seclusion in a tower of the family house, where she adopted the habit of a penitent.[57] There is some parallel between her life and that of Piccarda Donati, also a member of a great Florentine family; dragged out of a convent by her brothers to be married, her bitter experiences were celebrated by Dante in *Paradiso*. It must have been almost impossibly difficult for a woman of high social status to adopt a completely independent religious vocation like Margaret of Cortona. The most striking example of the upper-class saintly woman in the thirteenth century is Margherita Colonna (1254–80). She had the advantage of help from her strongly pro-Franciscan brothers, one of whom was Cardinal Jacopo Colonna, and her mother was the aunt of Pope Nicholas III.[58] The period around 1300 happens, however, to have produced a particularly outstanding group of writings about saintly women which provide us with an unusual body of information about the character of religious life in the society pervaded by the mendicants and the tertiaries.

The most impressive features emphasized in these lives are the constant familiar discussion which some of these women had with God, and their capacity for ecstatic raptures. Angela recalled visions in which she had taken her clothes off to offer herself to Christ, the constant appearance of Christ to her in sleeping and waking, that he made her drink the blood from the wound in his side. She was so overpowered by looking at pictures of the Passion that a friend tried to hide them from her.[59] Margaret had long conversations discussing all sorts of matters with God; by her account he frequently referred her to the Friars Minor and gave her a long list of wicked people which constitutes an analysis of wickedness in contemporary society; adulterers, people devoted to finery, false *podestà*, dishonest notaries, false merchants, envoys of courts, sellers of bread and wine, cheese and oil, and so on.[60]

What must have impressed contemporaries most powerfully was the capacity of these women to produce physical manifestations of rapture.

[57] Article by A. Benvenuto Papi, 'Umiliana Cerchi' in *Dizionario biografico degli Italiani*, xxiii, 1979. Idem., 'Umiliana dei Cerchi: nascita di un culto nella Firenze del Dugento', *Studi francescani*, lxxvii, 1980; *Acta Sanctorum*, May, iv, pp. 385–418. The articles in *Movimento religioso femminile e francescanesimo nel secolo XIII*, Società Internazionale di Studi Francescani. Atti del VII Convegno Internazionale, Assisi, 11–13 ottobre 1979 (Assisi, 1980), though interesting on the period of St Clare, have little to say on the later part of the century. The contributions by R. Rusconi ('L'espansione del Francescanesimo femminile nel Secolo XIII') and A. Vauchez ('L'Idéal de sainteté dans le movement féminin franciscain aux XIIIe et XIVe siècles') contain comments on Umiliana.

[58] L. Oliger, *B. Margherita Colonna (†1280) le due vite*, Lateranum, n.s. 1 (no. 2), 1935.

[59] *La Bienheureuse Angèle*, ed. Doncoeur, pp. 9–15.

[60] *Acta Sanctorum*, February, iii, pp. 311, 348.

Angela reported that at times of inspiration she stood silent in her cell, incapable of speech—so much so that her friend thought she was dying, and interfered with her period of consolation.[61] Clare would be taken with rapture while speaking to people about religious matters: 'suddenly she lost the powers of the body and remained sitting like a stiff statue often with a rosy colour and thus speaking she remained in that absorbed fervour'.[62] Margaret would lose sense and motion—*sensum perdidit atque motum*—in ecstasy while speaking with her confessor and other Franciscans. Her behaviour at communion in the Franciscan church was an overpowering sight:

They saw Margaret not by the cross but almost in the cross consumed with dire miseries whose signs were so wonderful that we thought her at the point of death. Through her excessive suffering she ground her teeth, she twisted like a worm or a collar, she became ashen-pale, her pulse ceased, speech ceased, she froze, her throat was so affected by hoarseness that she could scarcely be understood when she returned to her senses.[63]

The impact of these women on the people around them was powerful. The people of Cortona flocked to see the spectacle of Margaret in church 'leaving their workplaces and trades, men and women, the babes and sick left lying in their beds, filled the oratory of our house, built to the honour of St Francis, with crying and wailing'. She reported that God had revealed to her in prayer that the Cortonesi should make peace with the Bishop of Arezzo—we do not know how much notice was taken of this advice, but it was at least remembered. The people of Cortona arranged for her to be embalmed and buried at her death.[64] People from Spoleto and Montefiascone, some distance away, we are told, were aware of Clare's powers. A notarial document dated immediately after her death recorded a visit to her body by many local people, including the *podestà* and rector of Montefalco, who witnessed that she had a separate cross attached to the flesh of her heart. When the heart was taken to cardinals Jacopo Colonna and Napoleone Orsini in Rome, some people thought the claims were fictitious.[65] As news of Margaret of Faenza's sanctity spread, crowds of people visited her, including 'counts, barons, prelates and members of religious orders', seeking the consolation of speech with her.[66] Oringa Menabuoi was helped in the building of her monastery by the men of Castelfranco and Santa Croce sull'Arno because 'each one avidly desired her presence'. She tried to prevent fighting between the men of Santa Croce and Fucécchio:

[61] *La Bienheureuse Angèle*, ed. Doncoeur, p. 16.
[62] Faloci Pulignani, 'Vita di S. Chiara', i, p. 606.
[63] *Acta Sanctorum*, February, iii, pp. 304, 316.
[64] Ibid., pp. 316, 310, 356.
[65] Faloci Pulignani, op. cit., ii, pp. 214, 243–51.
[66] *Acta Sanctorum*, August, v, p. 850.

When she heard [after uttering warnings] that one morning they had entered the enemies' territory armed, she summoned a council of the village and tried to dissuade them from doing what they had decided, otherwise they would suffer the evils of death or prison. When they spurned her warnings, all she predicted happened.

She was also appealed to as a peacemaker when two clans of Santa Croce were fighting.[67]

Austerity, prayer, visions, and rapture are features of the personal life of all these women; a certain social pre-eminence as objects of wonder and devotion is also common to them all. Otherwise, the recorded stories of their lives are not very similar. Oringa Menabuoi was a simple, precociously pious girl from near Lucca who fled from home when her brothers tried to marry her off. She was accepted into a virtuous household at Lucca, and was then taken to Rome and Assisi where a lawyer from her own country tried to win her love. The same man is also said to have pursued her into St Peter's at Rome. At Assisi she fled from him into the basilica of San Francesco, where she had a remarkable vision of the city of God. Eventually she returned to her own village to found a community of tertiaries; this seems to have happened in 1279, and the house was recognized at least by 1296.[68] Margaret of Faenza was also the co-founder of a monastery, the Vallombrosan St John the Evangelist at Florence, founded in 1282. Margaret came to Florence from Faenza, already a nun, together with Umiltà, also a woman who left a reputation of beatitude.[69] After Umiltà's death she took on the laborious work of searching for money and food so that the work of establishing the new community could be continued.

In contrast to these two, Angela was a woman whose conversion took place in her late thirties, after the death of her family, and the story connected with her is entirely personal, not associated with any attempt at founding a religious group. A central part in her imagination is played again by St Francis and by Assisi. The friar who wrote the story down was at the convent at Assisi. One day, perhaps in 1291, she arrived at the basilica and shouted, sitting at the entrance to the garden. She had with her a group of companions who waited for her reverently inside the church. Her confessor came out and sent her away. She said later that she had received a promise of grace on the road from Spello to Assisi. Kneeling in the entrance to the church, she had seen 'St Francis depicted in the bosom of Christ [presumably the image of Christ and St Francis in one of the stained glass windows of the nave of the upper basilica]. He said to me: "thus bound I shall hold you." She was shouting. "I do not know love. Why do you abandon me?" '[70] This scene of her desolation is almost all the definite information the account of her contains. It does at

---

[67] Lami, *Deliciae*, xviii, pp. 205, 227–9.
[68] Ibid., pp. 285–317.
[69] Davidsohn, *Forschungen*, iv, p. 418; *Acta Sanctorum*, May, v, p. 205.
[70] *La Bienheureuse Angèle*, ed. Doncoeur, pp. 21–7; M.-J. Ferré, 'Les principales dates de la vie d'Angèle de Foligno', *Revue d'histoire franciscaine*, ii, 1925.

least bring out something of her character, and it shows the importance for her of St Francis, who appears of course elsewhere in her autobiography.

Clare of Montefalco started her religious life as a child of six in a house of religious women presided over by her sister. It received the Augustinian rule from the Bishop of Spoleto in 1290, and she became abbess after her sister's death. The outward story of her life, in one community, as reported in the written story contains very little in the way of external events. On the other hand there is the emphasized link with Cardinal Jacopo Colonna, and also the extremely interesting fact that Clare had conversations, probably in 1307, with heretics of the 'Free Spirit' in the Franciscan order in Umbria. She was asked by the Franciscans of Gubbio whether a man can do what he will, whether it is true that there is no hell, whether a soul can lose desire in this life, and replied emphasizing the dangers in such propositions.[71]

Margaret of Cortona on the other hand, had had a fairly turbulent early life. She had been driven out by her parents from her home on Lake Trasimene and was seduced by a well-to-do young man from Montepulciano, with whom she lived for nine years and bore children; then he was murdered, and she fled to join the Franciscan tertiaries at Cortona. She now showed what seems a striking indifference to her children, expressing no emotion when told by an enemy that her son had drowned himself in a well at Arezzo. But she showed the most extravagant penitence for her past sins: she went back to Montepulciano, where she had once been richly dressed, to be led around the town, veiled, drawn by a rope around her neck by a woman who cried out: 'This is that Margaret who once made her clothes her pride and wounded many souls in this land by her vain glory and bad examples'.[72]

The female biographies of the period around 1300 provide us, then, with a survey of popular religious behaviour. This could be enlarged by information of a less detailed kind which survives for other holy men and women in Central Italy at that period, and by more elaborate but less reliable information contained in lives written longer after the deaths of their subjects, like Raymond of Capua's life of Agnes of Montepulciano (c.1274–1317),[73] but such information would not alter very much the deductions we are able to draw. The first is that the establishment of new religious communities was common and fairly easy. They were not in fact prevented by ecclesiastical authority and often found popular financial support. The second is that the homeland of the Franciscan order, Umbria, remained in some sense the powerhouse of Italian spirituality. Assisi and its great basilica continued to have a special place in the Italian imagination; it could be described as the capital of popular religious life, and Francis had a supreme role as the inspirer

---

[71] Faloci-Pulignani, 'Vita di S. Chiara', ii, pp. 204–8, 220; L. Oliger, *De Secta Spiritus Libertatis in Umbria Saec. XIV* (Rome, 1943).

[72] *Acta Sanctorum*, February, iii, p. 307.

[73] Ibid., April, ii, p. 793.

of religious emotion and the intermediary between God and men whose innovations provided a model for many new enthusiasts. The third is that the psychological power of popular religious leaders easily won encouragement and respect from laymen as well as from clergy. This wide acceptance of the value of individual religious enthusiasm resulted in part from the fact that central Italy was a region in which higher authority was weak in both church and state. The pope was largely irrelevant at the local level; bishops were numerous, and dioceses were not in general rich or powerful; the fragmentation of lay political authority was so extreme that there were no individual despots to whom common people could look for accepted political control, and warfare and faction were the constant realities of life. It was said of one of the Franciscans admitted to the order by Francis, Benedetto Sinigardi of Arezzo, that when he returned to his home town in 1268 he 'laboured especially to extinguish the enmities which cruelly flourished between the powerful and the magnates of the city', and cured one of the great men on condition that he would live in peace.[74] This was what many hoped the saintly would achieve.

The early fourteenth-century chronicle of San Miniato, a small, independent state in the Arno Valley between Florence and Pisa, presents a particularly graphic record of the continual bloodshed resulting in part from a small community's inability to resist external marauders, in part from the continuous feuds of its own citizens which were often linked with one or other of the external armies. This was what political life was like for the majority of Umbrians and Tuscans outside the larger cities. The chronicle also shows us the natural connections between devotion to religion and the hope of remedy against constant political upheaval. In 1311, we are told some

men of Pisa, Lucca, San Miniato and almost all Tuscany, inspired by God and the Virgin Mary, went about almost naked, beating themselves, visiting churches, calling for penitence, peace and mercy in high voices. Because of this many people pardoned injuries and made peace with their enemies so that God should have mercy on their sins. The whole country was in such a good disposition that the commune of San Miniato made a law to restrain the iniquity and malice of the wicked, who would not pardon for love of God and the Virgin, that whoever did not make peace with his enemies during the month of June should be compelled to do so by the *podestà*. As a result of this all the men of San Miniato and nearly all those of the district came into peace and concord.[75]

This happy state of affairs did not of course last very long, but it showed the connection between piety and the thirst for peace. It was natural that the saints should command respect in a world in which there was no political stability

---

[74] G. Golubovich, *Biblioteca bio-bibliografia della Terra Santa e dell'oriente francescano*, i (Quaracchi, 1906), p. 146.
[75] 'Diario di Ser Giovanni di Lemmo da Comugnori', ed. L. Passerini, *Documenti di storia italiana*, vi (Florence, 1876), p. 175.

and the only assurance could be provided by the spiritual authority of religious devotion and austerity which was easily visible within a small community.

Umbria—that is Perugia, Assisi, and the surrounding region—produced profound novelties in religious life whose influences rippled out over the rest of Italy. Umbria gave birth to Francis, to the flagellants, to the female saints. We cannot imagine thirteenth-century Italian religion without these influences. The commercial centres of Tuscany were some distance from the centres of religion in Umbria (Pisa, the furthest, was about a hundred miles from Assisi). The conditions of political life there were rather more stable as a result of their wealth and their protecting *contadi*. Tuscany was an area of larger and more successful states. But the internal political lives of these cities were also deeply ridden by faction, and they lacked the control of stable aristocratic hierarchies or despots. Ecclesiastical authority in them was almost equally weak. They were therefore open to influences from Umbria. Although they could not match the brilliance of its religious expression they were equally pervaded by the proliferation of religious communities and willing to accept the authenticity of holy men and women and the supremacy of the Franciscan ideal.

4

Lay Thought at Florence

IN previous chapters we have looked at two contrasting worlds—material ambition in politics and economics, and spiritual devotion in religion. In both these areas of Italian life we have seen an intensity of feeling which would be difficult to parallel in Europe to the north of the Alps. We must now turn to a third aspect—the world of lay thought, which was less extensive, more tentative, but also in some respects still more peculiarly characteristic of the Tuscan mind.

In the North in the thirteenth century, the world of thought was sharply divided into lay and clerical sectors. Laymen enjoyed a vernacular poetry in French, German, and English which exploited the themes of Provençal lyricism, Arthurian legend, and chivalric romance which were related to the lives of knights and gentry. Christian theology and philosophy were increasingly dominated by the great movement of scholasticism springing from the study of Aristotle and the church fathers at Paris. By 1300 this had created an overwhelming proliferation of Latin treatises which attempted to set out religious beliefs and philosophical explanations of man and nature in terms derived ultimately from Greek and Judaic thought, and which were generally unintelligible to those who had not had a university education. These two worlds of thought overlapped and intermingled to some extent: it is difficult to disentangle the secular and philosophical elements in the writings of Andreas Capellanus, the theorist of courtly poetry; or to decide how much contemporary views of love and warfare depended on the love of God and the crusade. But between the writings of the philosophical theologians such as Aquinas and Scotus and the poetry of Chrétien de Troyes and Wolfram von Eschenbach there is an essential distinctness of thought worlds that arose from the social division between clergy devoted to the sacraments and contemplation, and laymen devoted to the family and the battlefield. During the thirteenth century this division was intensified by the economic success of the clergy in enlarging and strengthening their separate ecclesiastical landed power.

Tuscany was greatly influenced by movements of thought and art derived from Northern Europe. Several of the greatest scholastics—St Bonaventure and St Thomas Aquinas are the most notable cases—were Italian, and carried into their homeland ideas derived from the debates at Paris; Italian poetry in its early evolution was almost entirely dependent on borrowing Provençal conventions. But Italian society was not suitable for the complete acceptance of the fundamentally divided world of ideas which was appropriate in the North. There are two main reasons for this. One is the relative weakness of ecclesiastical society in Italy. Italy was not dominated to the same extent as England, France and Germany by bishops, dioceses, and universities devoted, like Oxford, essentially to the preparation of ecclesiastical careers. The great Italian universities of Bologna and Padua were more concerned with the secular studies of medicine and Roman law. The Italian church was also more influenced by the mendicant orders, which were in closer contact with the laity. The other reason is the strength of independent secular life in the cities. The commercial cities of Tuscany contained educated laymen who, though they would have been baffled by the treatises of modern logicians and meta-physicians, were capable of reading the Latin literary classics for themselves; unlike the gentry of the North, they were not totally devoted to the pursuits of chivalric warfare and the chase. They were important enough to create an incipient world of thinkers to which the North at this time had no parallel.

The most clearly distinctive feature of the intellectual life of the Tuscan cities was the existence of a large class of laymen whose professional work involved them in the study of Latin. This class was comprehended at Florence in a major guild of lawyers and notaries, the *giudici e notai*. The *giudice* was a superior person designated, like the knight with the title of 'lord' (*messer* or *dominus*), and he would very likely have had a university education at Bologna. The notary received the lesser title *ser*. His profession involved not the judicial knowledge proper to the lawyer but the more rudimentary ability to compose documents, letters, conveyances, wills, and agreements. They often had to have a binding force, and for this some knowledge of law was essential. No doubt this is why the two professions were contained within the same guild. From the point of view of their civilizing influence, however, the important thing about the lawyers and notaries was that they had to have a good command of Latin in order to set out their arguments. It is the role of Latin in Italian lay society which is of primary importance. Tuscany in the thirteenth century contained a large number of independent communes. Each one of these had to maintain diplomatic relations by sending letters to its neighbours. Each had an internal republican organization whose meetings and decisions had to be recorded. Each had a complex life involving land conveyancing and commercial agreements, all of which had to be set out in Latin documents. The quantity of documents was enormous and the range of expertise required, extending fom simple receipts to diplomatic arguments, was very large. Most of these documents have long ago perished in fire, flood, and decay, but the surviving records of some smaller communes—Prato for instance, which still has a very large number of thirteenth-century records—gives one some idea of the sheer quantity of expert Latin composition that Tuscan society required. Most of this was done by laymen.

This situation was radically different from that which obtained for example—to take a case from the opposite end of the spectrum—in England, where the opportunities for serious Latin composition by laymen in the course of ordinary business were much fewer, and the elaborate study of Latin must have been almost entirely confined to clergy. The equivalence of *clericus* and *literatus*, still accepted in England in 1300, should not be taken to mean that only the ordained were literate; many laymen were *clerici* in that sense, foreshadowing the meaning of *clerk*. But it would still have been very unusual for a layman to have a serious interest in the classics or in writing Latin. The existence of the notarial class in the Italian cities led to the possession of exactly that interest by a large lay group. The role of the notary at all levels of society, up to the political level with its mass of intricate and elegant correspondence, was the main social reason for the intellectual peculiarity of the Italian cities. It is the existence of the notaries, not the existence of the merchants, which made the Italian cities the precursors of the essentially lay culture of the modern world.

In 1291, the Florentine guild included 65 *giudici* and 376 *notai*, a substantial number in a city of less than a hundred thousand people.[1] They included people who are individually important in the background to Dante, like Lapo Gianni the poet, Brunetto Latini, or Lapo Saltarelli the turncoat lawyer. But it is the general diffusion of a lay knowledge of Latin and the classics which the profession assumed that is of primary importance. Beside the class of literary men we must also place the general literacy which was encouraged by the demands of city politics and diplomacy, and by commerce. Politics required an ability to speak elegantly and to understand Latin documents—these duties were not in any sense entrusted to the clergy as they were in some Northern-European states—and commerce over long distances had to be conducted through the constant interchange of letters and accounts. It is characteristic of Florence before 1321 that there are no institutions of higher education apart from the religious *studia* in the monasteries. In this sense, education was weaker at Florence than it was at Arezzo and Siena.[2] Indeed, the isolation of Florentine society—the richest and most innovative in Tuscany, one of the richest in Europe—from the European tradition of higher education must be regarded as one of the reasons for the exceptional originality of the Florentine intellect throughout the fourteenth and fifteenth centuries. Only a society

---

[1] The best account of Florentine lawyers and notaries in the late thirteenth and early fourteenth centuries is by Davidsohn, *Storia*, IV, ii, pp. 221–51. There is a full account of them in the period after 1380 in L. Martines, *Lawyers and Statecraft in Renaissance Florence* (Princeton, 1968).

[2] C. T. Davis, 'Education in Dante's Florence', in his *Dante's Italy and Other Essays* (Philadelphia, 1984). On higher education in Tuscany at this period, see also H. Wieruszowski's essays, 'Mino da Colle di Val d'Elsa rimatore e dettatore al tempo di Dante', ' "Ars Dictaminis" in the time of Dante' and 'Rhetoric and the Classics in Italian Education of the Thirteenth Century' in her *Politics and Culture in Medieval Spain and Italy* (Rome, 1971).

which was both highly literate and also preserved from the straightjacket of the university world could be so unexpectedly creative. But we must also assume that at a fairly low level, the opportunities for education were considerable; there were many *doctores puerorum* and masters of grammar. Very little record of them has survived, but when Dante tells us that he could struggle through Boethius and Cicero on first becoming attracted to philosophy (*Convivio*, xii, 12), and when he shows his considerable grasp of rhetorical skill in his letters, we must be seeing evidence of the results of general education outside the notarial class.

The world of Renaissance thought that grew up in Italy was dependent on this distinct character of the urban civilization of Tuscany. It was a more unified world than that of the medieval North. It was not dominated by the distinction between the priest and the knight. The culture of the cities was a matrix which was strong enough to create an outlook of its own, to receive the gifts of Northern poetry and Northern scholasticism, to mingle them with native reminiscences of ancient politics and ancient writings, and to make a new amalgam of great power which would eventually be transmitted to the European world. We must imagine Tuscan society in the thirteenth century as being in one sense extremely provincial, lacking the universities and courts which created medieval culture, but also as having a new and distinctive social strength which was enough to create a new vision of the world and of man. The extreme political confusion of Tuscan society which we have observed in earlier chapters brought terrible disasters into the lives of individuals. The mass of intellectual and aesthetic influences from Rome and Paris which crisscrossed the Tuscan landscape give it an appearance, if we look at it at any time before 1300, of provincial disorder, of feeble acceptance of whatever thoughts happened to come that way. But if we look at it twenty years later, when the masterpieces of Dante, Giotto, and Duccio have come into existence, it is clear that the Tuscan cities have suddenly created out of this mass of influences their own new world visions.

To understand the intellectual background of Dante—the materials out of which he created the *Comedy*—we must attempt to imagine the world of thought available to an educated Florentine layman before 1300. One element, the most important, was vernacular poetry, which will be discussed in the next chapter. But before turning to poetry we must take into account the prose world of ideas. In Dante's lifetime Florence, without a university, was essentially, as Petrarch described it half a century later, a 'commercial and cloth-making' city.[3] The nearest university of any note was at Bologna, fifty miles away. It was often attended by Florentines, but the culture available to Florentines in Florence itself was that which could be attracted by commercial wealth in a place without a university. This was a peculiar state of affairs, and

. [3] Petrarch, *Familiari*, xviii. 9.

its peculiarity is fundamental to the development of the Florentine vision. We must imagine the ideas available to the Florentine as being of two kinds. First there was the native lay culture of the notaries, based on widespread literacy and the ability to read Latin books—a culture of low status but with its own particular sets of ideas. Secondly there was the culture introduced into Tuscany by clerics who were familiar with the scholasticism of Paris and able to produce vernacular versions intelligible to laymen. Florence's wealth gave it a strong ability to attract this kind of second-rate scholasticism because its wealthy mendicant convents were convenient centres of preaching and lecturing for friars who had been abroad. We must imagine Dante as growing up, like the other Florentine poets, surrounded by the immediate culture of the notaries but aware at the same time of the more distant voice of scholasticism which came to him in books and lectures and in the conversation of acquaintances. The two elements are there from the beginning but the power of scholasticism became greater: it dominates his later writings in *Paradiso* and *Monarchia*. If we turn back from them to the earlier writings in *Vita nuova* and *Inferno* we find him much closer to the preoccupations of the notaries and the poets which surrounded him from his adolescence.

The world of ideas of the Florentine notaries has survived best in the writings of two men of that class, Brunetto Latini and Bono Giamboni, the first of them a master presented with veneration in *Inferno*, the second a more obscure figure, unmentioned by Dante, known to us only from his own works. Brunetto was also mentioned in a famous passage by Villani the Florentine chronicler and disciple of Dante:

In the year 1294 died in Florence a splendid citizen who had the name Ser Brunetto Latini, who was a great philosopher and a high master of rhetoric, both in speech and in the written word. It was he who expounded Cicero's *Rhetoric* and made the good and useful book called the *Tesoro* and the *Tesoretto* and the key to the *Tesoro* and other books of philosophy and about vices and virtues and was the rhetorician (*dittatore*) of our commune. He was a worldly man but we mention him because he began the process of civilizing (*digrossare*) the Florentines and making them expert in speaking well and knowing how to guide and govern our republic according to political science.[4]

Brunetto was exiled during the period of Ghibelline rule in Florence from 1260 to 1266, when he stayed in France. He then returned to Florence, and from 1266 to 1292 was a fairly prominent person, not only as official notary of the commune but also as an ambassador and a politician. His opinions are often mentioned in the records of City councils.[5]

Brunetto's exile in France and his later deeply rooted position in the city

[4] Villani, VIII. x.
[5] The best account of his life is T. Sundby, *Della vita e delle opere di Brunetto Latini* (Florence, 1884), with additions by R. Renier, I. Del Lungo, and A. Mussafia.

gave him the best opportunity to act for Florentines, both as an enricher of native culture and as a reporter of French cultural developments. His principal works, which must have been well known in late thirteenth-century Florence, are *Li livres dou Tresor*, written in French during his exile and later translated into Italian as the *Tesoro*, an encyclopaedic work of natural science, history, rhetoric, morals, and politics; *Il tesoretto*, a didactic poem also written in France; and *La rettorica*, a translation with explanations of part of Cicero's *De inventione*.[6] An illustration in a manuscript of one of Brunetto's works shows him lecturing to an audience.[7] The combination of wide learning conveyed in the vernacular, poetry, and political activity at the heart of the city, which impressed Dante and Villani, made Brunetto, a man of no philosophical originality and no political importance outside Florence, the obscure har-binger of a whole new culture which was to spring into towering achievement a few years after his death. The text of the *Tresor* is probably the best source of information about the spread of learned information available to a lay Florentine.

The *Tresor* is conceived in the manner of thirteenth-century encyclopaedias and attempts to introduce the reader to a very wide range of subjects. It is divided into three books. Book I, the most miscellaneous, tells us about biblical, Roman, and medieval history, but also about natural science, the basic theory of the complexions and elements, and the structure of the heavens. Book II is mostly about ethics and is derived from Aristotle's *Ethics*, but also deals with virtues and vices. Book III is about rhetoric, derived from Cicero's *De inventione*, and about government. The most interesting thing about the structure of the whole work is the prominence given to the subjects of the second and third books—ethics, rhetoric, and politics—the 'practical' side of philosophy: 'the science of speaking well and governing people is more noble than any art in the world'.[8] The importance given to these aspects of learning is no doubt the result of Brunetto's own professional concern with them as a notary and city counsellor. Put in its thirteenth-century context against the background of the theological and philosophical treatises of the universities it might seem an eccentricity. Put in the context of later Renais-sance ideas, on the other hand, it appears as a primitive first statement of a set of assumptions which will later become a highly developed tradition of thought, giving supreme importance to the literary skill of the imitator of

---

[6] *Li livres dou Tresor de Brunetto latini*, ed. F. J. Carmody (Berkeley–Los Angeles, 1948), *Il Tesoro di Brunetto Latini* ed. L. Gaiter (Bologna, 1878); *Tesoretto* in *Poeti del Duecento*, ii, pp. 175–277, bilingual edition by J. B. Holloway (New York and London, 1981); *La Rettorica*, ed. F. Maggini (Florence, 1968). On other translations see *Volgarizzamenti del Due e Trecento*, ed. C. Segre (Turin, 1953).
[7] Reproduced in H. Wieruszowski, 'Brunetto Latini als Lehrer Dantes und der Florentiner', *Archivio italiano per la storia della pietà*, ii, 1957, but not in the reprint of the article in her *Politics and Culture*.
[8] Brunetto Latini, *Trèsor*, i. 1.

Cicero and to the science of politics. Brunetto starts this tradition appropriately, writing on the basis of experience within the republican city-state as a
member of the class of notaries, the most characteristic city-state profession,
to which so many of the leading Italian writers of the next two centuries down
to Machiavelli were to belong. Brunetto, rather than the classicists of the late
fourteenth century, is the true founder of the tradition.[9]

The reader of Dante will not find it difficult to recognize in Brunetto's book
I sketches of topics that reappear later in the *Comedy*, often of course
strengthened by Dante's additional knowledge of other sources. In *Convivio*
(ii. 6), Dante has an account of the hierarchies of angels in the order angels,
archangels, thrones, dominations, virtues, principalities, powers, cherubim,
and seraphim, the order in which they appear in the *Tresor* (i. 12), which he
changed later in *Paradiso* (xxviii) to an order he learned from Dionysius the
Areopagite. Many writers discussed angels, but it is quite likely that Dante's
interest was aroused and informed originally by Brunetto. Dante could have
read in Brunetto the fact, which became important to him in *Convivio* (iv. 5),
that Aeneas founded Rome 'at the time of King David, at the beginning of the
fourth age of the world' (*Tresor* i. 34), showing the parallel providential
development of the Jewish and Roman worlds. It is possible that Dante's
attribution to Brunetto in *Inferno* (xv. 61) of the idea that the quarrelsome
element in the Florentine population came down from Fiesole derives from a
recollection of Brunetto's chapter (*Tresor* i. 37) in which he made the
foundation of Florence a result of the defeat of Catiline's army beseiged in
Fiesole.[10] At the end of this chapter Brunetto adds a sentence in which he says
that he knew from the experience of his own exile the quarrelsomeness of the
Florentines, which Dante may have remembered when he was in exile himself.
It is conceivable that when Dante in *Inferno* (xv. 85) thanked Brunetto for
teaching him 'how man may make himself eternal'—obviously a reference to
the power of either great actions or literary success to make a man's reputation
live on—he had in mind Brunetto's remark in the *Tresor* (ii. 120) that 'those
who treat of great things show that glory gives the good man a second life, . . .
after his death the renown which his good works have make him seem to be
still alive.'

It is not, however, the precise echoes of particular passages that are
important in Brunetto's influence on Dante, but the general scope of the
information he supplied and the direction of interest he encouraged. Brunetto
links the history of the thirteenth century as far as the Guelf victory of Charles
of Naples at Tagliacozzo with the history of empire and papacy stretching

[9] A point also made by C. T. Davis, 'Brunetto Latini and Dante', in *Dante's Italy*, p. 173.
[10] On this tradition, see N. Rubinstein, 'The Beginnings of Political Thought in Florence',
Journal of the Warburg and Courtauld Institutes, v, 1942. In *Tresor*, i. 37 Brunetto attributes
Florentine faction to the fact that the site of Florence had previously been named after Mars, the
God of Battles, not to the Fiesolans.

back to the Romans, to the primitive church, the Trojans, and the Old Testament. Brunetto then jumps suddenly from history to explain the theory of the four complexions—hot, cold, dry, wet—that determine the character of men and beasts. Then he moves to the four elements—air, fire, water, earth. From this he goes to the heavenly circles, the geography of the world, the building of houses, finally to a long list of animals and birds. Except for the building of houses, these are all topics in which Dante was interested, and it is easy to imagine that the continuity linking modern Guelfism and Ghibellinism with the history of Rome and the Jews in the ancient world, which plays such a large part in his political thought, or the fascination of the movement of the heavenly circles around the earth, which becomes increasingly prominent in *Convivio* and *Paradiso*, owed something to the early awakening of interest in these matters by the reading of the *Tresor*.

The second book of the *Tresor* is concerned with moral philosophy. It is made up of two sections, the first drawn from Aristotle's *Ethics*, the second a list of virtues that owes much to the *Summa de Virtutibus* of the early thirteenth-century French bishop, Guillaume de Perrault. The combination is significant. The *Ethics*, the only work of Aristotle with which Dante quite clearly had a close acquaintance, exercised immense importance in the Italian world both in Latin and in Italian versions.[11] But the combination of Aristotle's philosophical foundation of the ethical life with a more trivial cataloguing of the virtues as observable in everyday life is even more suggestive of the direction which thought was to take in Dante's *Convivio* and *Inferno* and in later Renaissance ideas. Edward Moore identified more than a hundred and fifty quotations from the *Ethics* in Dante's works.[12] The general importance of a book which taught that men had a natural tendency to strive towards the good and that there was a distinction between the practical and contemplative virtues must have been very great. If we look at Brunetto's rendering, we can also see the importance of the attempt to turn Aristotle's ideas into Italian. The pursuit of *eudaimonia* in the *Ethics* becomes the pursuit of 'beatitude' in the *Tresor* (ii. 7) as 'the thing in the world that is best and most joyful and delightful', an aim that comes, with the use of the Italian word, to hover between the happiness of this world and the eternal felicity of the saints. Aristotle's *megalopsychia* becomes not 'pride' but 'magnanimity' (*Tresor* ii. 23), a grand virtue for the great-spirited, implying the pursuit of honour and contempt for meanness which was to influence Dante's conception of the great spirits in Limbo and of Farinata degli Uberti who was too great-spirited to destroy his fellow citizens even if they belonged to the opposing party.[13]

[11] C. Marchesi, 'Il compendio volgare dell'etica aristotelica e le fonti del VI libro del "Tresor" ', *Giornale storico della letteratura italiana*, xlii, 1903; idem, *L'etica nicomachea nella tradizione latina medievale* (Messina, 1904).

[12] E. Moore, *Studies in Dante*, i (Oxford, 1896), pp. 339–42.

[13] M. Corti, *La felicità mentale* (Turin, 1983), pp. 44–53.

The concern with different types of virtue transmitted into Italian from Aristotle and Guillaume de Perrault encouraged a psychology in which the classification of kinds of virtue and vice in their external manifestations was supremely important. The influence of this approach on Dante can be seen in *Convivio* IV and in *Inferno*.

Brunetto's third book is the most distinctive part of his work. It is divided into two parts: an account of rhetoric, derived from Cicero's *De inventione*; and an account of the government of cities, derived from John of Viterbo's *De Regimine Civitatum*[14]—a book designed to give guidance to the *podestà* of Italian communes, again emphasizing the virtues they should cultivate and the vices they should avoid. This is the section of the *Tresor* most completely rooted in the city-state. Its teaching depends on the fact that 'Cicero said that the highest science of governing a city is rhetoric, that is the science of speech because without speech cities could not be establishments of justice and human companionship' (*Tresor* iii. 1). This was a view that appealed to the inhabitant of a city-state in which political decisions resulted not from the orders of a prince but from the exchange of opinion in assemblies, like those Florentine councils whose records survive from the 1280s onwards, still conveying to us the opinions of citizens like Brunetto Latini. The supremacy of rhetoric was the natural assumption of a republican, best expressed by a notary who was supposed to be expert in that art. The immediacy of the art of rhetoric for the Florentine is still better expressed in Brunetto's *Rettorica*, where he goes through Cicero sentence by sentence, expounding his meaning with reference to imaginary cases of debate in court or council—sometimes in interchanges involving Ajax, Catiline, or Caesar, sometimes in illustrations, taken directly from contemporary life:

Florentine merchants took ship to go overseas. There came a cruel misfortune of weather, which put them in fearful fright so that they decided that if they escaped and reached a port they would offer their goods to whatever God was there and worship him. Finally they arrived at a port in which Mahomet was worshipped and held to be god. These merchants worshipped him like a god and made him a great offering. So they were accused of breaking the law . . .

Or, again:

the commune of Florence whose ambassadors had commanded them to take payment from the chamberlain and go immediately to the lord pope to prevent the passage of knights coming from Sicily into Tuscany against Florence.[15]

These passages convince one of the genuine acceptability of Cicero to the thirteenth-century Florentine, and the ease with which he could regard the life of the present as a direct continuation of the life of Rome. If one wants to see

[14] *Iohannis Viterbiensis Liber de Regimine Civitatum*, ed. G. Salvemini, Bibliotheca Iuridica Medii Aevi, iii (Bologna, 1901).
[15] *La rettorica*, ed. Maggini, pp. 109–10, 114.

the study of rhetoric within a compendium of human knowledge which was interesting to the Florentine, however, the *Tresor*'s juxtaposition of science, history, philosophy, and rhetoric is probably the most instructive guide.

The *Tresor* is a plain and extensive book of learning. It conveyed valuable information to the ordinary man, and it is easy to see why Villani regarded Brunetto as the great civilizer. But it is not typical. If we look at lay writing in Florence at this period we are struck, not by the extent of attempts to convey plain learning to the common man, but by the intermingling of philosophical doctrine and literary fancy. Plain learning remains very largely the sphere of the clerics and the university experts; that is why the *Tresor* is peculiar and important. Laymen, on the other hand, go in for literature, story-telling, allegory, and conceit, although doctrine may be seriously involved in the literary fancy. A good example of this genre is the main surviving work of Brunetto's notarial colleague and contemporary, Bono Giamboni, *Il libro de'vizî e delle virtudi* (The Book of vices and virtues). Like Brunetto, Bono is known to have been working in Florence from the 1260s to the 1290s.[16] Not much is known about him except that he was an active translator from Latin to Italian—another important way of feeding the lay world—but *The Book of vices and virtues* is an original composition. Its purpose is to give the reader a conspectus of virtues and vices and to encourage him to join the right side in the battle between them; it has therefore a partly philosophical and partly theological aim. The method Bono adopts for putting his message across, however, is a mixture of Boethian and Prudentian allegory. The book begins with the writer in despair and rescued from this condition by a figure of Philosophy (drawn from Boethius) who explains that heaven can only be reached by alliance with the virtues, and takes him off on a journey to meet them. After a preliminary encounter with Christian Faith they observe a great battle between the vices—Pride leading Vainglory, Envy, Anger, Melancholy, Avarice, Gluttony and Lust—and the virtues—Faith leading Prudence, Justice, Fortitude, and Temperance. The battle evolves into a curious reworking of providential world history in which Faith is attacked by a series of heresies and then by Muhammedan paganism which conquers Italy, leaving only France free as a Christian centre from which the world can be reconquered.

The import of this odd piece of imaginary history, following the enumeration of real heresies, is not clear. Was it intended as a criticism of contemporary Rome, or an exaltation of contemporary France? What is clear, however, is that Bono is presenting the battle of the virtues and the vices as an allegorical story, with a certain amount of literary ornamentation, which merges into a partly imaginary world history. It is in a sense a very primitive kind of literature, but at the same time it is very complex because it calls on a

---

[16] S. Debenedetti, 'Bono Giamboni', *Studi medievali*, iv, 1913; *Il libro de' vizî e delle virtudi*, ed. C. Segre (Turin, 1968).

considerable amount of reading and involves an elaborate adaptation of the story to the moral demands of the various virtues and vices.

Another work which has some of the same characteristics is Brunetto Latini's *Tesoretto*. This is in part a rendering in verse of a compressed version of some of the information contained in the *Tresor*: natural science, geography, and morals. But the information and counsel are presented in the course of a story in which the wandering Brunetto meets Nature, hears advice being given to a knight by Courtesy, Generosity, Loyalty, and Prowess, and encounters a figure of Cupid from which he turns to Ovid to receive help in dealing with the pains of love. The poem has a tailpiece addressed to another Florentine poet, Rustico Filippi. The vision of Cupid—'standing naked, a bright boy with a bow and arrows and wings and feathers'—is slightly unexpected after the rather measured tone of the poem before that. Does the reference to Ovid imply that Brunetto is aware of Ovid's flippancy? It is difficult to be sure, but it is at any rate clear that Brunetto is purveying a confection of charm and information quite different from the *Tresor*. The *Tesoretto* is a mixture of genuine learning, allegory, poetic romanticism, and humour. In the Florentine lay world, as opposed to the world of the clergy, the writing of poetry, which was a fairly common occupation for gentlemen, was much more normal than the writing of philosophy or science, which were primarily clerical subjects. Hence the peculiarity of the *Tresor*'s generous presentation of philosophy and science in the vernacular, a peculiarity really so striking as to be the foundation of a new culture. If one were an educated man in Florence, however, one would be familiar with the writing of poetry in Italian (the main tradition of Italian poetry will be the subject of the next chapter), and familiar also with translations from French Romance literature and from Latin literature. One would assume that the literary and philosophical worlds—not the technical, philosophical world of Albertus Magnus and Aquinas, which belonged to the clergy, but the simpler philosophical essays of Boethius and Cicero—were quite closely bound up with each other, and both accessible to the layman with literary ambitions. One would have the embryo of what later becomes the world of ideas of the Renaissance gentleman.

Next door to the sophisticated lay world, geographically very close to it indeed but theoretically quite separate, was the world of ecclesiastical learning. This was imported into Florence chiefly by the Dominicans, the preaching order which set up the great house of Santa Maria Novella. It may well have been promoted by the Franciscans and other orders in Florence also, but it is the Dominicans who have left substantial evidence of the existence of this kind of thinking in Florence; and we should anyway expect the Dominicans, with their specialization in preaching and learning, to be the most enthusiastic students of the sciences.

The manuscript writings of one of the Dominicans of this period, Remigio de' Girolami, have been resurrected from oblivion during the twentieth century, and they provide a very striking illustration of the way in which a friar could represent the learning of the university world within the city. The Girolami were an important Florentine family. Remigio's brother Salvo de' Girolami, a member of the Lana guild was one of the first priors in 1282[17] and several of his relations were exiled as Whites in 1302. Remigio was a Paris-trained philosopher and theologian, probably a pupil of Aquinas at Paris in the late 1260s[18] but in Florence most of the time from 1260 to his death in 1319.[19] For some of that period he was both *lector* in the *studium* at Santa Maria Novella and a prominent preacher in the city. His sermons, delivered on occasions like the deaths of cardinals, the visits of kings, and also such internal events as the entry of Charles of Valois in 1301, provide an exceptional contemporary Florentine commentary on some of the notable occasions and people of the period between 1280 and 1319.[20] He evidently had a lively interest in politics as well as a substantial grasp of scholastic philosophy and theology, so that he was well placed to act as a reporter of the university learning of Paris to the Florentine upper class to which he belonged.

In recent years several of Remigio's Latin treatises have been published.[21] Scholastics were prolific writers and nobody in the immediate background to Dante is now so extensively documented as Remigio. There is even a danger that the abundant printed materials might lead to his being given a position of exaggerated importance. It is important to remember that he is not mentioned by Dante, and his historical personality is almost entirely a creation of modern research. The only direct evidence that Dante is likely to have had contact with him is provided by his vague remark that he attended the 'schools of the religious and the disputations of the philosophers' (*Conv.* II. 12) in the years after the death of Beatrice, the 1290s. This probably refers to visits to Santa Maria Novella and Santa Croce. The likelihood that Dante was in some sense a pupil of Remigio or his colleagues is quite strong, but it cannot be more than a hypothesis.

What would he have learnt? Two things may be said about Remigio's

---

[17] Davidsohn, *Storia*, II, ii, p. 287.

[18] E. Panella, 'I quodlibeti di Remigio dei Girolami', *Memorie domenicane*, n.s., xiv, 1983, p. 35.

[19] Idem, 'Per lo studio di fra Remigio dei Girolami (†1319)' *Memorie domenicane*, n.s., x, 1979, pp. 206–33; idem, 'Remigiana: note biografiche e filologiche', *Memorie domenicane*, n.s., xiii, 1982.

[20] The identifiable historical references are usefully collected by G. Salvadori and V. Federici, 'I sermoni d'occasione, le sequenze e i ritmi di Remigio Girolami Fiorentino', *Scritti vari di filologia a Ernesto Monaci* (Rome, 1901).

[21] C. T. Davis, 'Remigio de' Girolami and Dante', *Studi danteschi*, xxxvi, 1959; M. C. De Matteis, *La 'teologia politica communale' di Remigio de' Girolami* (Bologna, 1977); *Contra Falsos Ecclesie Professores*, ed. F. Tamburrini (Rome, 1981); E. Panella, 'Un introduzione alla filosofia in uno "studium" dei Frati Predicatori del xiii seculo. "Divisio scientie" di Remigio de' Girolami', *Memorie domenicane*, n.s., xii, 1981; idem, 'I Quodlibeti di Remigio de' Girolami', ibid., n.s., xiv, 1983. For other publications see *Contra Falsos Ecclesie Professores*, pp. 342–4.

writings. The first is that he was an expert scholastic, well versed in the materials of the arts and theology faculties in the universities. *Contra Falsos Ecclesie Professores*, the largest work by him that has been published, is a chain of texts on the theme that the church reflects and embodies all the liberal and mechanical arts. Its most obvious purpose was to serve as a handbook for preachers, and the abundant evidence of Remigio's own important preaching role in Florence does perhaps mean that preaching rather than teaching or research was his main concern. It is, however, a learned work which displays much knowledge, for example, of the writings of St Augustine and St Thomas Aquinas. Remigio's writings also include *Quodlibete*, discussions of theological questions, which were part of the normal activity of the schools. He would certainly have been able to give students an authoritative account of the theories of Aquinas, and to represent the contemporary Dominican school of thought.

Remigio may have been a failure in the scholastic world; he did not stay in Paris. In one of his manuscripts there is a Latin poem composed on a sleepless night: 'When I was lying in bed on the night after Christmas I spent some of the time without sleep and suddenly came into my mind a comparison [*cogitatio comparativa*] of my condition with that of successful people known to me.' The poem is a direct revelation of the inner mind of a kind unusual in the thirteenth century.

> Everyone does well except me. Out of Florence
> I live weeping, not denying that is just, but asking for pity.
> I turn over books, read many of them, try to make
> my mind rule me, cover my shame,
> think and rethink.
> Many enemies attack me, the undeserving blush
> with honours, the fathers spurn me, laugh in revenge,
> no friend remembers me.
> My opponents are well supported, under-age they are
> already adult, they make the people in authority
> silly, no one is hostile to them.[22]

The poem ends with acceptance of God's will. Perhaps Remigio had to accept the Florentine backwater as a poor alternative to Paris. The second feature of his thought is a peculiarity, the result of his stay in Florence: a keen interest in the problems of city politics and an application to them of the fruits of philosophical learning.[23] He composed at least two political treatises, *De Bono Communi* and *De Bono Pacis*, while *Contra Falsos Ecclesie Professores* contains a long passage about the relations between papal power and temporal powers, which is rather out of place in that work. Remigio is a significant

[22] Salvadori and Federici, 'I sermoni d'occasione', pp. 502–3.
[23] This aspect is well analysed by C. T. Davis, 'An Early Florentine Political Theorist: Fra Remigio de' Girolami', in *Dante's Italy*.

figure in the history of political thought because he was the first properly educated student of classical philosophy—Brunetto was a dilettante who cannot deserve this description—to attempt to apply what he had learnt from Aristotle and Cicero to the problems of Florence seen from the inside.

De Bono Communi[24] and *De Bono Pacis*[25] were both probably composed in the aftermath of the Florentine Revolution of 1301. They are the works of a man appalled by the evidence of faction and greed exhibited by these events, and who turned to the ancient writers for arguments that would show the citizens they were conducting politics in the wrong fashion. *De Bono Pacis* answers the question 'whether for the good of peace within cities and villages there should be remission of injuries and damages without the assent of all individual persons and even against the wish of some, including clergy', a question highly appropriate to the situation in 1302 and after, when bitterness had been so much increased by exile and confiscation. It is an attempt to provide a theoretical basis for the healing of wounds in Florence. The answer that both these treatises supplied was the political theory of Aristotle's *Ethics* and *Politics*: the good of the whole community matters more than the advancement of any individual within it, because no individual can live a full life independently without the facilities provided by the community. Therefore the advancement of communal well-being is always to be preferred as a political object. It is interesting to note that Remigio also makes use of heroic figures from Roman history, such as Cincinnatus or Fabritius, as examples of the placing of community before personal interest; and one of his important sources is Cicero. Like other critics of factional vindictiveness, Remigio probably made little difference to the actions of his audience; but it is extremely interesting that the revolution of 1301 should have been the occasion for the first attempt that we know of to create a political thought which adapted Aristotle and Cicero to Florentine needs. The application of the ideas of classical authors who wrote about the politics of the ancient city to the similar circumstances of the Renaissance city is the central theme of Florentine political thought as it will be seen, more fully developed, a century and two centuries later in Bruni and Machiavelli. This line of thought starts with Remigio; Brunetto had recommended and vulgarized Aristotle and Cicero, but Remigio is the first to introduce them into a political theory for the modern city. We know less about Remigio's teaching in Florence before 1301, but it is reasonable to suppose that he presented himself long before that date as an expert on classical and Christian learning, anxious to relate it to the needs of a Florentine audience, so that the layman who had the energy and interest for it could have got something beyond the reading of Cicero and Boethius for which lay education prepared him.

[24] Ed. M. C. De Matteis, *La 'teologia politica communale'*; analysed by Minio-Paluello, 'Remigio Girolami's De Bono Communi', *Italian Studies*, xi, 1956.
[25] Ed. De Matteis, op. cit., and by C. T. Davis, *Studi danteschi*, xxxvi, 1959.

At the time of the revolution of 1301, the prior of Santa Maria Novella was, as it happens, another important figure in the early history of Italian political thought, Ptolemy of Lucca. Ptolemy was chiefly an annalist, but he had a large role in the development of political thought because of two of his more theoretical works: *Determinatio Compendiosa de Iurisdictione Imperii*, probably composed in 1277–8 in defence of Nicholas III's attitude to imperial power in Italy;[26] and the later part (Book II, Chapter 5 to Book IV, Chapter 28) of Aquinas's *De Regimine Principum*, left incomplete at its author's death in 1274,[27] which was probably written at some time close to 1300. Ptolemy's principal political interest was the defence of papal supremacy over the empire and other lay regimes, and a substantial part of both these books is devoted to that theme. But he was also clearly aware of the difference between princely and republican political systems, and of the importance of the latter in Italy. He distinguishes from princely government the *regimen politicum*, the word being derived, he says 'from *polis* which is plurality or city, because this government belongs properly to cities as we see especially in parts of Italy and it once ruled at Athens' (*De Regimine Principum*, iv. 1). Ptolemy had lived with St Thomas Aquinas in his last years;[28] he was a messenger from the very heart of Thomism. He did not spend very much of his life in Florence—until he became bishop of Torcello at the end of his life he lived mostly at Lucca—and there is no evidence that he influenced any particular Florentine; but he is a good example of the opportunities that the convents of the friars provided for contact with authentic exponents of scholasticism who had an interest in questions then topical in Florence.

Another case of a scholastic migrant is the radical Franciscan theorist Pierre Jean Olivi who was sent from France to be *lector* at Santa Croce from 1287 to 1289.[29] The only influence exerted by Olivi at Florence that we know of is the effect he had on the Franciscan spirituals, particularly Ubertino da Casale; but a noted Parisian theologian at Santa Croce very likely made some impression on the lay audience, though he would presumably not have been able to speak to them in Italian. On the other hand, an important Italian-speaking visitor was the Dominican Giordano da Pisa, who had studied at Bologna and Paris and was in Florence from 1303 to 1306. Texts or reports of many of his sermons have survived and their use of the vernacular makes them an interesting parallel and contrast to the Latin sermons of Remigio de'

[26] Ed. by M. Krammer (M. G. H. Fontes Iuris Germanici Antiqui in Usum Scholarum, 1909); analysed and dated by C. T. Davis, in 'Roman Patriotism and Republican Propaganda: Ptolemy of Lucca and Pope Nicholas III', in *Dante's Italy*.

[27] R. M. Spiazzi ed., *Divi Thome Aquinatis . . . Opuscula Philosophica* (Rome, 1954); analysis by N. Rubinstein, 'Marsilius of Padua and Italian Political Thought of his time', *Europe in the Late Middle Ages*, ed. J. R. Hale, J. R. L. Highfield and B. Smalley (London, 1965), pp. 51–4, 60–5; C. T. Davis, 'Ptolemy of Lucca and the Roman Republic', in *Dante's Italy*.

[28] A. Dondaine, 'Les "Opuscula Fratris Thomae" chez Ptolémée de Lucques', *Archivum Franciscanum Historicum*, xxxi, 1961.

[29] Douie, *Heresy of the Fraticelli*, pp. 89–90.

Girolami. Giordano was a homely preacher. His usual aim was to reach the
heart of the average citizen by using illustrations drawn from everyday life.
But he was also capable of trying to explain scholastic concepts to a lay
audience. On 17 February 1305, for example, he tried to explain the
Aristotelian concept of form to a Florentine congregation:

Charity is a form in the soul. Form: perhaps you do not understand that. It is not the
form of a shoe or a cap. Certainly they are a kind of form but the learned call 'form' that
virtue which is in things by which they operate. So that the form of the sun is the light
by which it works; the form of trees is their virtue by which they bear fruit.[30]

Giordano was a famous preacher and his are the earliest Italian sermons
delivered in Florence to survive. Others must have been delivered in the
thirteenth century with similar messages.

Mendicant intellectual links were often with Paris. We must also allow for a
considerable intellectual interchange between Florence and the university of
Bologna, which was probably more important for the lay world because it
particularly affected the professions of law and medicine. In this case the
messengers in the interchange were themselves laymen. We know, for
example, of two notable Bolognese doctors who were active in such intellectual interchanges. Taddeo Alderotti, who was the most famous thirteenth-
century professor of medicine at Bologna and was also referred to by Dante as
a translator of Aristotle's *Ethics* from Latin into Italian, was a Florentine by
birth who spent the greater part of his later life in Bologna. He died in 1295
after being a prolific writer on medical matters in the previous thirty years.
But he also kept up relations with his native city. In 1274 he married a young
wife of the Florentine Rigaletti family, whose brother was a canon lawyer at
Bologna who was left a house near Santa Croce in Taddeo's will. Having no
legitimate son he left the rest of his property to a bastard son, a nephew, and a
half-sister who married into the Florentine Pulci family. One of his most
successful publications was a short treatise on hygiene dedicated to the
Florentine magnate leader Corso Donati.[31] Among Taddeo's most notable
pupils was another Florentine, Dino del Garbo, who died in Florence in 1327
shortly after being involved in the famous case against Cecco d'Ascoli, who
was burned because of his heretical views about astrology. Dino was the son
of a Florentine physician. Although he spent much of his later life in Bologna
and Siena, he kept up his links with Florence, and was listed among the
members of the guild of physicians and apothecaries in 1297. He was also the
author of the most famous commentary on the poem *Donna me prega*,[32]
written by Dante's friend Guido Cavalcanti.

There are two documents containing interesting evidence about the intel-

[30] Giordano da Pisa, *Quaresimale fiorentino 1305–1306*, ed. C. Delcorno (Florence, 1974). Cf.
C. Delcorno, *Giordano da Pisa e l'antica predicazione volgare* (Florence, 1975).
[31] N. G. Siraisi, *Taddeo Alderotti and his Pupils* (Princeton, 1981), pp. 27–42, 77–82.
[32] Ibid., pp. 55–64, 82–6.

lectual impact of Bologna on Florence, both connected with Guido Cavalcanti. The first is a short treatise written by a Tuscan philosopher at Bologna, *Magister Jacobus de Pistorio* (Master James of Pistoia), and dedicated to Guido. It is about *felicitas*, happiness. The argument is that happiness is the result of rational activity, the highest felicity being the contemplation of 'the separate substances and especially God himself' by the speculative intellect. 'Separate substances' are purely rational entities, so this is an exaltation of the contemplative life. It is not, however, a typically Christian view of the question; that would emphasize the inadequacy of the experience of happiness in temporal life, and the superiority of knowledge of God attainable only after death. The treatise is almost entirely dependent on Aristotle and belongs to the school of Latin Averroism, which interpreted Aristotle without trying to make him compatible with Christianity.[33] Little else is known about James of Pistoia so, apart from the fact that it was probably written between 1290 and 1300,[34] we cannot place the treatise in a precise setting. The other document is Dino del Garbo's commentary on Cavalcanti's *Donna me prega*, which could have been written either at the end of the thirteenth or, more likely, the beginning of the fourteenth century.[35] Cavalcanti's poem, which is very obscure and will be examined in the next chapter, is about the psychology and physiology of love. Dino's commentary is a gloss by a learned expert on medicine, attempting to explain the meaning partly by adducing references to Aristotle's books on the natural sciences.

It is difficult to make a case about the Florence–Bologna relationship out of the fragments of information which survive.[36] Even in the very prominent cases of Taddeo and Dino the evidence is slight, and our estimate of their significance must be largely speculative. What can be said speculatively is this. The number of Florentines trained as doctors and lawyers at Bologna in the late thirteenth century must have run into hundreds. They were laymen, many of whom had relations of marriage and friendship with other Florentines. Because of their intimacy with lay society it is probable that their influence on the attitudes of laymen to intellectual matters was at least as important as that of the mendicant orders. Florence had a lay intelligentsia fed by the notaries, the lawyers, and the doctors. When we try to imagine its intellectual quality we should think of Brunetto Latini and Dino del Garbo, not Remigio de' Girolami.

The link between Cavalcanti and Aristotelianism is not necessarily typical of the intellectual relations between Bologna and Florence. It is, however,

---

[33] P. O. Kristeller, 'A Philosophical Treatise from Bologna Dedicated to Guido Cavalcanti: Magister Jacobus de Pistorio and his "Quaestio de Felicitate"', in *Medioevo e rinascimento studi in onore di Bruno Nardi* (Florence, 1955), i.

[34] Corti, *La felicità mentale*, p. 7.

[35] Guido Cavalcanti, *Rime*, ed. G. Favati (Milan–Naples, 1957), pp. 359–78.

[36] There is a useful survey by Davidsohn, *Storia*, I, pp. 1209–16; IV. iii, 244–52.

extremely interesting because physicians like Dino who used Aristotle for scientific information had a natural opportunity to see him outside the Christian context. The higher levels of medicine in Florence must have been strongly influenced by Bologna, and it may be that Bolognese interests in Aristotle were extensively conveyed to Florentines. The peculiar conditions of the Florence–Bologna relationship may have produced something similar to Jean de Meung's lay interest in philosophy shown in the *Roman de la Rose*. We have the possibility of a genuinely lay reaction to scholasticism that is rare in Europe at this period but obviously extremely important.

This is what we know of the more prosaic aspects of the Florentine world of lay intellectuals, among whom Dante lived until 1301. There is no doubt that the reflection of Brunetto's interests is prominent among Dante's. There are less clear, but nevertheless probable, indications that he was influenced by the scholastics of Santa Maria Novella and the Bolognese Aristotelians. The Florentine lay world is perceptibly, if we include the poets in it, the intellectual context in which Dante was nurtured and began to piece together the elements of his own outlook that was soon to blossom in *Inferno*. The study of Dante in relation to medieval thought conceived more generally, which sometimes attracts Dante scholars, is to a large extent a futile pursuit. His origins must be seen in their relationship with one particular, exceptional, and rather undeveloped sector of medieval thought: the world of the Florentine intelligentsia with their interest in Latin literature, their slight knowledge of Aristotle, and their fascinated pursuit of the virtues and vices as modes of human behaviour. Great poetry grows in hothouses of competitive poetic endeavour. This particular hothouse existed in the milieu of rudimentary philosophical interests appropriate to the educational level of the Florentine layman.

5

The Beginning of Dante's Poetic Revolution

IN the thirteenth century, Italian was a new literary language. It had none of
the tradition of versification and highly developed literary forms that in
English, French, and German stretched back into the early Middle Ages: no
Beowulf, Nieberlungenlied, or *Chanson de Roland.* The intellectual and
aesthetic revival of the twelfth century, which enlightened both Northern
Europe and Italy, had little impact on Italian as an instrument of aesthetic
expression. There was nothing comparable with the poetic romances of
Chrétien de Troyes, with the lyrics of the Provençal troubadours, with
Parzival or even with English poetry laboriously creeping out of the devas-
tation of the Norman Conquest.

The establishment of the *volgare* as a great literary tongue was the most
fundamental act of Italian self-assertion in the medieval and Renaissance
period. It was done with great speed. At the beginning of the thirteenth
century there was nothing. A century later there was Dante's *Comedy.* Most
of the credit for this must go to Dante himself; no other individual writer in
any literature can have done so much to mould and elevate the languages of
both poetry and prose and at the same time to create a sense of a native literary
tradition as Dante did in the poetry of the *Comedy,* the prose of *Vita nuova*
and the critical framework of *De Vulgari Eloquentia.* Dante, however,
thought of himself as writing in the *dolce stil nuovo,* the 'sweet new style'—a
new phrase introduced by him in *Purgatorio* xxiv, 57—which he shared with a
group of contemporary writers, notably Guido Cavalcanti and Cino da
Pistoia. There are reasons, to which we shall come later, for doubting whether
the poets of the *dolce stil* did in fact constitute a school having common aims.
What they undoubtedly did have in common, however, was the ability to
write better than their predecessors. Their combined efforts had the effect of
lifting Italian very quickly onto a level appropriate to the civilization of the
Tuscan cities in which they wrote. In spite of Dante's overwhelming superiority it is necessary to look, before discussing him, at the other major poets of his
place and time in order to see the evolution of ideas and styles out of which his
writing developed, both in sympathy and in reaction, when he was still a
young man.

The poetry of late thirteenth-century Tuscany was consciously derived
from the conventions used by two previous schools of poets. The first of these
was the school of Provençal troubadours, which flourished mainly in the

twelfth and early thirteenth centuries. Dante showed his familiarity with Provençal by composing a passage of eight lines in that language which he inserted at the end of *Purgatorio* xxvi. The speaker is the poet of the Dordogne, Arnaut Daniel (*c.*1180–1220), whom Dante, like Petrarch, regarded as a supreme poet. In the early part of *Purgatorio* there are three cantos dominated by Sordello (*c.*1200–69), an Italian from near Mantua who wrote in Provençal at a time when Italian poetry was still in its infancy. Dante admired Sordello partly for his remarkable personal detachment from the social and political circumstances of the time—he survived the abduction of the noble Cunizza da Romano and travelled widely between the courts from Castile to Naples, where he ended his life as a client of King Charles of Anjou—and also found him a convenient partner for the other Mantuan Virgil; but Provençal was still for Dante a live and important literary tongue, and Sordello represented that too. Lines from several other troubadours are quoted in *De Vulgari Eloquentia*. This view of the poetic past was normal among the earlier Italian poets, many of whom showed in their poetry a close familiarity with the language and the techniques of the troubadours.

The Provençal conventions were grafted onto the Italian language by a group of poets associated with the court of the Hohenstaufen Emperor Frederick II in Southern Italy in the first half of the thirteenth century. The poets of this school are somewhat less prominent in the *Comedy*. Dante makes much of one of them, Pier della Vigna, in *Inferno* xiii, but because of his suicide not because of his poetry; and the reference to another, Giacomo da Lentini 'the Notary', in *Purgatorio* xxiv, is intended only to associate him with the later Guittone d'Arezzo and Bonagiunta Orbicciani da Lucca as one of the poets who failed to achieve the *dolce stil*. In *De Vulgari Eloquentia* I. xii, however, Dante makes it clear that he regards the Sicilians of the time of Frederick II as the main school of Italian poets that preceded the Tuscans, and in that work he quotes Guido delle Colonne, Rinaldo d'Aquino, and Cielo d'Alcamo. Italian poetry really begins with Giacomo da Lentini.

The Sicilian school did not survive the extinction of the Hohenstaufen court of Frederick II and Manfred. The court of Naples set up by Charles of Anjou after Benevento in 1266 was for a long time principally French, and did not become an important centre of Italian letters. The cultivation of poetry moved from the South to the towns of Tuscany. The poets who are important between the battle of Benevento and the composition of the *Comedy* in the period 1266–1310 come from Arezzo, Siena, Pisa, Lucca, Pistoia, Bologna, and Florence. A large amount of poetry survives from the work of the practitioners of that half-century, many hundreds of *canzoni, ballate*, and *sonetti*.

The Provençal poets had often been noblemen and country gentlemen, and their poetry was largely intended for a world of country nobility; the Sicilians had been mostly officials connected in some way with the imperial court. The

Tuscan poets, in contrast, were gentlemen of the cities. Many of them are fairly obscure figures, but enough is known to place them clearly enough among the city élites. The Florentines include, for example, two members of the Frescobaldi banking family (Lambertuccio and Dino), one of the prominent Guelf Cavalcanti (Guido), one of the ancient Alighieri (Dante), at least one other banker (Monte Andrea), a notary (Lapo Gianni), two doctors (Maestro Rinuccino and Maestro Torrigiano). As the Florentine physician Dino del Garbo wrote when glossing Guido Cavalcanti's poem about love, *Donna me prega*, in the early fourteenth century:

This passion of love is most found among gentlemen [*hominibus nobilibus*] . . . great and powerful either because of their progeny or because of much wealth or virtue of the soul . . . other men of the people [*homines alii populares*] are more given up to thoughts about civic works which are necessary in life . . . Noble and powerful men, because they are not concerned with such labours, are more likely to be involved in thoughts centring on this passion.[1]

The writing of poetry was not in any financial sense a profession. Though it may have become for some writers, as we may judge from the extensiveness and seriousness of their compositions, something like a full-time occupation—the obvious cases are Guittone d'Arezzo and Dante—it must have been in most cases a polite occupation for gentlemen with taste and education and also leisure.

Beside the serious and high-minded, or fairly high-minded, poetry of the famous practitioners, there is also a considerable body of 'realistic' and 'comic' verse from this period.[2] These little poems tell us far more about the realities of marriage, shortage of money, dice-playing, and the tavern than do the poems of courtly love. Too little is known about the poets for us to be able to guess how far their real lives were mirrored in their verses. We do not know how far the savage and burlesque attacks on marriage or the grossly insulting descriptions of friends are to be taken as representing real views, as exaggeration for entertainment, or as material quite distinct from reality set out in obedience to the rules of a literary game. For example, there is a famous exchange of poems between Dante and Forese Donati, probably written in the mid-1290s when Dante was already a famous poet, which begins with a poem from Dante describing with obvious malicious humour how cold Forese's wife was in bed:

Anyone who heard the coughing of the luckless wife of Bicci called Forese might say that maybe she'd passed the winter in the land where crystal is made. You'll find her frozen in mid-August—so guess how she must fare in any other month! And it's no use her keeping her stockings on—the bedclothes are too short . . .

The coughing and cold and other troubles—these don't come to her from ageing

---

[1] Cavalcanti, *Rime*, ed. Favati, p. 373. *Donna me prega* is printed below, pp. 105–7.
[2] Collected in *Poeti giocosi del tempo di Dante*, ed. M. Marti (Milan, 1956).

humours, but from the gap she feels in the nest. Her mother, who has more than one affliction, weeps saying: 'Alas, for dried figs I could have married her to Count Guido!'[3]

We have no means of knowing whether Forese's wife could have been married to one of the Conti Guidi, nor do we know what sort of relationship between Dante and Forese lay behind this blistering poem.

The ambiguous relation of the comic poems to social reality gives us a problem of interpretation which is repeated in a more acute form in the love poems of serious poetry. What was Dante's real relationship with Beatrice? Did she know of his love? What did other people think about it? The same questions may be asked of course of all other thirteenth-century lyric poets: of Cavalcanti about Giovanna, of Cino da Pistoia about Selvaggia. The Italians took over from the Provençals the tradition of poetry in which the Lady was normally inaccessible. It is often difficult to know whether there was a real Lady at all. The constant cultivation of public love poetry exchanged between poets but separate from their real sexual relations presents us with a double poetic and real world, a dualism that does not exist in modern poetry. We are forced to assume that poetry is a world of largely idealistic structures, created with a separate poetic rigour and overlapping only narrowly the world of real personal contacts. The degree of overlap is something about which we can only conjecture. Most of the serious poetry of the late thirteenth century is of this kind. What makes the *Comedy* such an explosion is partly the fact that it breaks out of this world of poetry as elegant formal structure-making to present us with a poetic world of real people and situations.

In the thirteenth century, serious poetry was generally quite sharply distinguished from comic verse, following the principle stated later by Dante in *De Vulgari Eloquentia* that the 'illustrious vulgar tongue' (*illustre volgare*) was adapted for use in poems about superior material, especially the three great topics of 'prowess in arms, ardent love, and the direction of the will'.[4] The poets who are famous writers of comic verse at this period, such as Rustico di Filippo of Florence, or Cecco Angiolieri and Meo de' Tolomei of Siena, wrote principally in the comic style.

On the other hand, Dante occasionally descended into the comic style (as in the exchange with Forese Donati), but wrote principally in the traditional high style of courtly love poetry. The composition of *Inferno* was a sudden change because the styles of comedy and high seriousness were mingled in it; the real, named people were in some cases treated humorously—a notable example was cantos xxi to xxiii about political corruption, for which Dante had been condemned—in the midst of passages which were serious in the

[3] *Dante's Lyric Poetry*, ed. K. Foster and P. Boyde (Oxford, 1967), i, p. 148.
[4] 'Armorum probitas, amoris accensio et directio voluntatis' (*De Vulgari Eloquentia*, II. i; Dante Alighieri, *Opere minori*, ii, ed. P. V. Mengaldo *et al.* (Milan–Naples, 1979), p. 152).

highest degree. But this is looking ahead to the later part of the first decade of the fourteenth century. Down to 1300 the accepted convention distinguished poetry of the serious kind, mostly about love, from poetry about money, marriage, and other such coarse matters.

Most of the serious poetry which survives from the late thirteenth century is unadventurous elaboration of standard themes of the 'courtly love' inheritance, which the Tuscans took over from the Provençals and the Sicilians. The Tuscans also took over from their predecessors the custom of the *tenzone*—a series of poems on the same theme, replying to each other, composed by two or more poets. The popularity of the *tenzone* indicates more clearly than anything else the social basis of ordinary poetic composition at this period. Consciousness of the existence of the community of poets in Tuscany was strong. Poems were written for circulation, or at least for other poets to read. The interaction between poets is frequently evident both in the address of poems to other writers and in the signs of influence. Dante's adhesion to his friends Guido Cavalcanti and Cino da Pistoia (as opposed to Bonagiunta da Lucca and Guittone d'Arezzo) in *De Vulgari Eloquentia* and *Purgatorio*, and his strong consciousness of the traditions behind him, result from the character of the Tuscan poetic community. As a light-hearted example of the productions of the poetic world from which Dante sprang we may take this example of a *tenzone*, which includes one of the earliest poems that Dante wrote, composed in about 1283 when he was eighteen. The exchange begins with a poem issued by another Dante, Dante da Maiano, in which he describes a love vision about a woman with whom he was in love and asks for an explanation of it:

> Provedi, saggio, ad esta visïone,
> e per mercé ne trai vera sentenza.
> Dico: una donna di bella fazone,
> Di cu' el meo cor gradir molto s'agenza,
>
> mi fé d'una ghirlanda donagione,
> verde, fronzuta, con bella accoglienza:
> appresso mi trovai per vestigione
> camicia di suo dosso, a mia parvenza.
>
> Allor di tanto, amico, mi francai,
> che dolcemente presila abbracciare:
> non si contese, ma ridea la bella.
>
> Così ridendo, molto la baciai:
> del più non dico, ché mi fé giurare.
> E morta, ch'è mia madre, era con ella.

You who are intelligent, consider this vision and please show its true meaning. It was like this: a fair woman, in gaining whose favour my heart takes much pleasure, made me a gift of a green leafy garland; and charmingly she did so. And then I seemed to find myself clothed in a shift that she had worn.

Then I made so bold as gently to embrace her. The fair one did not resist but smiled; and as she smiled I kissed her repeatedly. I will not say what followed—she made me swear not to. And a dead woman—my mother—was with her.

Dante Alighieri replied with a poem in which he answered the question, giving an interpretation of the gift given by the lady in the vision, of the lady's shift which Dante da Maiano thought he was wearing, and of the presence of his mother:

> Savete giudicar vostra ragione,
> o om che pregio di saver portate;
> per che, vitando aver con voi quistione,
> com so rispondo a le parole ornate.
>
> Disio verace, u' rado fin si pone,
> che mosse di valore o di bieltate,
> imagina l'amica oppinïone
> significasse il don che pria narrate.
>
> Lo vestimento, aggiate vera spene
> che fia, da lei cui desïate, amore;
> e'n ciò provide vostro spirto bene:
>
> dico, pensando l'ovra sua d' allore.
> La figura che già morta sorvene
> è la fermeza ch'averà nel core.

You know how to interpret your theme, intelligent as you are; so I will not enter into any dispute with you, but only answer as best I can your elegantly phrased question. My view—speaking as a friend—is that the gift you first mention signified true desire, proceeding from merit or beauty, a desire that seldom comes to an end.

As for the garment, be confident that this will be love, given by her whom you desire, as indeed your spirit well divined—I say this in view of the act that followed. The dead figure that came on the scene is the constancy that she'll now bear in her heart.[5]

The poetry is not particularly good on either side. It is the product of writing to show off an acquaintance with the rules of composition, not to express a profound or original inspiration.

There were, however, a few men who took writing more seriously and wanted to use poetry for the expression of real ideas. Religious idealism was, as we have seen, a powerful force in Tuscany. Poetry could not escape its influence. The rudimentary scholasticism of the lay intelligentsia also impinged on poetry written in the same milieu. We shall see poetry incorporating sections of these other thought-worlds. The process of creating

---

[5] Foster and Boyde, i, pp. 2–5.

a 'religious' or 'philosophical' poetry took place, however, not by a straight-forward change of subject—which Guittone, the first poet we shall consider, attempted—but by an elaborate crisis of inspiration that forced· Dante to revolutionize the poetic imagination.

The most prominent poet in Tuscany in the 1260s and 1270s was an Aretine, Guittone d'Arezzo. Arezzo plays a smaller part in intellectual and artistic life after this period, but in the generation before the severe shock administered by the Florentine defeat in the battle of Campaldino in 1289 it may well have been the city in Tuscany best supplied with teachers of academic subjects. It had the earliest university in Central Italy outside Bologna; founded early in the century, and was frequented by many teachers of rhetoric, philosophy and medicine.[6] This background is probably important for the intellectual and moral ingredients in Guittone's writings. He is thought to have been born in the 1230s and died in 1294,[7] a well-to-do non-noble citizen of Arezzo. He left a considerable number of poems and also a number of prose letters—an unusual combination of works from a poet of the thirteenth century. His life and work were sharply divided in about 1265, when he was converted to the recently founded order of the *Frati Gaudenti*. Until that time he had been a 'courtly love' poet.[8] Membership of the order involved the adoption of an austere mode of life and a habit and could lead to living in a convent—for Guittone it seems to have led to the abandonment of three children—but it did not involve total withdrawal from the ordinary activities of laymen. The purposes of the order were good works within lay society, and social improvement as well as religion. One of Guittone's political *canzoni* was addressed to the *Frati Gaudenti* leader, Loderingo degli Andalò, in the period in 1266–7 when Loderingo and Catalano de' Malavolti were trying, not very successfully, to govern Florence on behalf of Pope Clement IV. Guittone consoles Loderingo for his trials and urges him to suffer them as do 'Christian knights'.[9] The position given to Loderingo and Catalano in Florence, ineffec-tive as it was, was a striking example of the hope of political benefits resulting from the devoted social and political activity of the *Frati Gaudenti*. Guittone associated himself fully with this well-meaning hope of improving the secular world by applying Christian principles of action.

Guittone maintained a wide correspondence with important people all over Tuscany. We have compositions addressed, for example, apart from the poets, to Count Guido Novello, the Ghibelline leader; to the bishop of Arezzo; to

---

[6] H. Wieruszowski, 'Arezzo as a Center of Learning and Letters in the Thirteenth Century', *Traditio*, ix, 1953, reprinted in her *Politics and Culture*.

[7] C. Margueron, *Recherches sur Guittone d'Arezzo* (Paris, 1966); A. Tartaro, *Il manifesto di Guittone e altri studi fra Due e Quattrocento* (Rome, 1974). The poetry is printed in *Le rime di Guittone d'Arezzo*, ed. F. Egidi (Bari, 1941), the prose in *Le lettere di frate Guittone d'Arezzo*, ed. F. Meriano (Bologna, 1922).

[8] V. Moleta, *The Early Poetry of Guittone d'Arezzo* (London, 1976).

[9] *Rime*, ed. Egidi, pp. 108–10. Cf. Margueron, *Recherches*, p. 224.

Corso Donati of Florence; to Count Aldobrandino di Santa Fiore; to Cavalcante Cavalcanti, Guido's father; to Pietro da Massa, papal rector in Massa Trabaria; to the secretary of the bishop of Volterra; and to the Pisan politicians Nino Visconti Giudice di Gallura and Count Ugolino della Gherardesca. He kept up a high moral commentary on events, ethical problems, and people in Tuscany as a whole. His letter to the Florentines after the battle of Campaldino—unfortunately lost—is mentioned in a Florentine chronicle; his poem addressed to the Florentines thirty years earlier, after the battle of Montaperti, commenting on the sad decline of their fortunes, survives.[10] Throughout the period from 1265 to 1294, Guittone seems to have been a poetic moralist, disapproving strongly of the poetry of sexual love (of which he had once been a notable practitioner) and ready with advice for a remarkable range of people.

Much of Guittone's good poetry comes from the earlier, 'courtly love' period of his life. After the conversion of 1265, the poetry of love disappears. Love is rejected as not merely painful but also wicked, and incompatible with the proper business of life. In a canzone probably datable to soon after his conversion, he expresses his intention to escape from love poetry:

> Ora parrà s'eo saverò cantare
> e s'eo varrò quanto valer già soglio,
> poi che del tutto Amor fuggh' e disvoglio,
> e più che cosa mai forte mi spare:
>   ch'a om tenuto saggio audo contare
> che trovare—non sa né valer punto
> omo d'Amor non punto;
> ma' che digiunto—da vertà mi pare,
> se lo pensare—a lo parlare—sembra,
> ché 'n tutte parte ove distringe Amore
> regge follore—in loco di savere.[11]

Now it will appear whether I can sing and if I am worth as much as I used to be now that I completely flee from and reject Love and more than anything it is odious to me: for to a man held to be wise I dare to relate that a man not stung by Love does not know how to make poetry or how to be worthy, but that he seems to me to be far removed from the truth if the thought and the language are in agreement, for in all parts where Love presses folly rules in place of knowledge . . .

Serious political comment is fairly prominent in Guittone's later poetry. We have a denunciation of the decay of the 'sweet land of Arezzo' written in a period of exile, perhaps 1265, perhaps 1261–2.[12] A respectful canzone addressed to Guido Novello, perhaps a few months or years before the Battle

---

[10] *Poeti del Duecento*, i, pp. 206–9.
[11] Ibid., p. 214.
[12] Ibid., pp. 222–6; cf. Margueron, *Recherches*, p. 93; Tartaro, *Il manifesto*, p. 23.

of Benevento, when Guido was the most powerful man in Tuscany, worthy (according to Guittone) to bear a crown, urges him to follow honour and moderation, and ends by saying that there is no honour without God.[13] Many years later, in the aftermath of the Pisan disaster at the hands of Genoa at Meloria, Guittone sent a powerful canzone to the great Pisan nobles Ugolino della Gherardesca and Nino Visconti 'certainly great barons and almost kings', pointing out that Pisa with 'its dear sons in death and in prison', its wealth turned into poverty, was in need of the help that the great men could give if they were aiming at goodness rather than mere greatness.[14]

More numerous however among Guittone's poems are straightforward statements of moral or religious belief that use the traditional literary language to make a moral point wholly opposed to the set of values for which the language was originally developed, as for instance in this attack on love:

> O tu, de nome Amor, guerra de fatto,
> segondo i toi cortesi eo villaneggio,
> ma segondo ragion cortesia veggio
> s'eo blasmo te, o chi tec' ha contratto.[15]

O you, Love by name, in fact war, according to your courteous followers I behave like a villain, but according to reason I see courtesy if I blame you and those who have links with you.

This is the substitution of reason for love, but in other poems the content is fully religious. For example in this *ballata* summoning to the dance, but to a dance in honour of Jesus, which depends for its effect on the strong, dance-like rhythm:

> Vegna,—vegna—chi vole giocundare,
> e la danza se tegna.
>
> Vegna, vegna, giocundi e gioia faccia
> chi ama Te, da cui sol' onni gioia;
> e chi non T'ama, Amor, non aggia faccia
> di giocundare in matera de noia.
>
> degna,—degna;—non pò che reo portare
> chi Te, gioioso, disdegna.[16]

Come, come whoever wants to rejoice and hold to the dance. Come, come, rejoice and make joy whoever loves Thee from whom all joy comes; and who does not love Thee, Love, let him not make a pretence of rejoicing in something that is wearisome.
   Disdain, disdain—who disdains Thee, joyous one, must be guilty.

---

[13] *Rime*, ed. Egidi, pp. 112–15; cf. Margueron, op. cit., pp. 208–12.
[14] *Poeti del Duecento*, i, pp. 235–40; cf. Margueron, op. cit., pp. 188–90.
[15] *Poeti del Duecento*, i, p. 218.
[16] Ibid., i, p. 230.

Dante's rejection of Guittone in *De Vulgari Eloquentia* (II. vi) for 'plebeian language and construction' does not really seem to hit the mark when one thinks of his ingenious use of words, his elaborate schemes of rhythm and repetition, his frequent reminiscences of the Provençals. Guido Guinizelli, whom Dante did approve and included among the *stilnovisti*, addressed an extremely complimentary sonnet to Guittone, probably at a fairly early date, perhaps the mid-1260s.

O my dear father, there is no need for anyone to attempt to praise you because no vice dares to enter into your mind without being thrown out by your understanding with arrows. To all vices, it closes its door, vices which seem commoner than marks in Venice: your soul rejoices among the Gaudenti who it seems to me have joys in abundance.

Accept the song which I present to your understanding to be grasped and clipped, I entrust it to you alone as a master. Because it is joined with such weak links: so look at each edge to clean the weak parts by your correction.[17]

The idea that Guittone could repel all vices because of his understanding is appropriate to his poetry. Equally appropriate was Guittone's reply, which ingeniously took up and echoed the words and rhymes of Guinizelli's poem and graciously accepted the title of 'father', replying with the familiar 'tu' to the more respectful 'voi'.[18] Looking at Guittone's work in the perspective of what came after it, however, his adaptation of old techniques to the new Tuscan subject-matter seems a laborious and largely unsuccessful enterprise. He lacked the originality or the sparkle to produce anything new. The religious and moral statements were conventional; the verse expression, ingenious in itself, was applied to them without life-giving passion. He wrote as a pontifical *dévot*. His approach is interesting for its expression of contemporary cultural assumptions, popularized by the universities and the new orders. It shows that Tuscan society needed a new kind of poetry, but his heavy moralism was absurdly inappropriate for a poet.

If Guido Guinizelli has been correctly identified by modern scholars, his poetic life did not extend to much more than a decade, from the mid-1260s to his death in 1276.[19] He was a lawyer described in the records as *judex*. Perhaps the learned elements criticized in his verse are connected with this profession and with his native city's university. His Bolognese family belonged to the Ghibellines in politics and, like all the major poets considered here—it is a remarkable symptom of the ubiquity and extremity of faction in the cities of Central Italy—he suffered severely for his allegiance since he was dispatched into exile with the Lambertazzi faction in 1274, and died in exile. The poems which survive, however, though they are not very many, are adventurous and were at the time controversial. They invited attacks from contemporaries and

---

[17] *Poeti del Duecento*, ii, p. 484.

[18] Ibid., p. 485.

[19] G. Zaccagnini, *I rimatori bolognesi del secolo XIII* (Milan, 1933), pp. 6–23.

a generation later the outstanding approval of Dante, who greeted Guinizelli, when he met him among the lustful in *Purgatorio* xxvi, as the father of the poets of the *dolce stil nuovo* and praised his 'sweet and light' verses.

It seems probable that Guinizelli began as an imitator of Guittone. This is indicated by the exchange of sonnets already mentioned, and by some of his other surviving verses.[20] He then turned his attention to nature, under the influence of the Sicilians, particularly Giacomo da Lentini, and composed a number of poems in which the use of natural objects for comparison with the beauties of the Lady is very marked.

> Io voglio del ver la mia donna laudare
> ed asembrarli la rosa e lo giglio:
> più che stella dïana splende e pare,
> e ciò ch'è lassù bello a lei somiglio.
>
> Verde river' a lei rasembro e l'âre,
> tutti color di fior', giano e vermiglio,
> oro ed azzurro e ricche gioi per dare:
> medesmo Amor per lei rafina meglio.[21]

I wish truly to praise my Lady and to compare her with the rose and the lily: she sparkles and appears more than the morning star and what is beautiful here below I compare to her. The green bank I compare to her and the air, all the colours of flowers, yellow and crimson, gold and blue and rich pleasures ready to be given. Love itself is made purer by her.

It has been suggested that this kind of poetry may have called forth a critical sonnet from Guittone which, if the connection is true, somewhat raises one's appreciation of Guittone's wit.

If I were such as could remain corrector without correcting myself I think I would certainly make a man change what seems to me an ugly error: for when he wants to praise his lady he says that she is beautiful as a flower or like a gem or a star or that she has the colour of carmine in her face. Now is it praise to extol for the lady what according to good sense is present in whatever the man can see or touch?[22]

Guido may also have inspired a sonnet by Chiaro Davanzati in which Giacomo da Lentini's poetry is likened to the crow who went to court with peacock feathers stuck to him.[23]

Guinizelli's importance depends chiefly, however, on one great poem, which seems to come from a still later stage of his evolution:

> Al cor gentil rempaira sempre amore
> come l'ausello in selva a la verdura;
> né fe' amor anti che gentil core,

---

[20] e.g. *Poeti del Duecento*, ii, p. 478, apparently addressed to someone entering a religious order.

[21] Ibid., p. 472.   [22] Ibid., p. 255.   [23] Ibid., p. 430.

né gentil core anti ch'amor, natura:
ch'adesso con' fu 'l sole,
sì tosto lo splendore fu lucente,
né fu davanti 'l sole;
e prende amore in gentilezza loco
così propïamente
come calore in clarità di foco.

Foco d'amore in gentil cor s'aprende
come vertute in petra prezïosa,
che da la stella valor no i discende
anti che 'l sol la faccia gentil cosa;
poi che n'ha tratto fòre
per sua forza lo sol ciò che li è vile,
stella li dà valore:
così lo cor ch'è fatto da natura
asletto, pur, gentile,
donna a guisa di stella lo 'nnamora.

Amor per tal ragion sta 'n cor gentile
per qual lo foco in cima del doplero:
splendeli al su' diletto, clar, sottile;
no li stari' altra guisa, tant' è fero.
Così prava natura
recontra amor come fa l'aigua il foco
caldo, per la freddura.
Amore in gentil cor prende rivera
per suo consimel loco
com' adamàs del ferro in la minera.

Fere lo sol lo fango tutto 'l giorno:
vile reman, né 'l sol perde calore;
dis' omo alter: 'Gentil per sclatta torno';
lui semblo al fango, al sol gentil valore:
ché non dé dar om fé
che gentilezza sia fòr di coraggio
in degnità d'ere'
sed a vertute non ha gentil core,
com' aigua porta raggio
e 'l ciel riten le stelle e lo splendore.

Splende 'n la 'ntelligenzia del cielo
Deo criator piu che ('n) nostr'occhi 'l sole:
ella intende suo fattor oltra 'l cielo,
e 'l ciel volgiando, a Lui obedir tole;
e con' segue, al primero,

del giusto Deo beato compimento,
così dar dovria, al vero,
la bella donna, poi che ('n) gli occhi splende
del suo gentil, talento
che mai di lei obedir non si disprende.
Donna, Deo mi dirà: 'Che presomisti?',
siando l'alma mia a lui davanti.
'Lo ciel passasti e 'nfin a Me venisti
e desti in vano amor Me per semblanti:
ch'a Me conven le laude
e a la reina del regname degno
per cui cessa onne fraude'.
Dir Li porò: 'Tenne d'angel sembianza
che fosse del Tuo regno;
non me fu fallo, s'in lei posi amanza'.[24]

Love always returns to the noble heart like the bird in the wood to the foliage; nor did nature make love before the noble heart or the noble heart before love; as soon as the sun came into being there was the splendour of light, nor did it exist before the sun; and love takes its place in nobility as properly as the heat in the clarity of the fire.

The flame of love catches fire in the noble heart like virtue in a precious stone which can take no value from the star before the sun makes it noble; when the sun has drawn out by its power that which is bad in it, the star gives it value; the lady, like the star, enamours the heart made chosen, pure and noble by nature.

Love stays in the noble heart for the same reason as flame in the tip of the torch: it illuminates it for its pleasure, clear and subtle; it is so proud that it cannot exist in any other way. So a low nature meets love as water does hot fire, because of the cold. Love stops for its appropriate place in a noble heart as diamond does in the iron of a mineral.

The sun beats on the mud throughout the day: it remains vile but the sun does not lose heat; a proud man says, 'I am noble by birth'; I compare him to the mud, the sun to noble valour: no one should believe that nobility is independent of the heart in the dignity of inheritance if it does not have a noble heart disposed to virtue, for the water bears the rays as the sun retains the stars and the brightness.

God the creator shines in the intelligence of the heavens more than the sun in our eyes: the intelligence understands its maker from out of the heavens and, turning the heavens, obeys Him; and in the way that instantly the perfection of the act disposed by a just God is carried out so in truth the beautiful lady, when she shines in the eyes of her nobleman ought to give him the will never to give up obedience to her.

Lady, God will say to me, 'Why do you presume?' when my soul is before him. 'You have passed the heavens and come to Me and compared Me to the objects of your vain love: but the praises belong to Me and to the proper queen of the kingdom, so let the deception end'. I shall say to Him, 'she had the appearance of an angel of your kingdom; it was not my fault if I loved her'.

Guinizelli's best verse is love poetry which has advanced beyond that

[24] *Poeti del Duecento*, ii, pp. 460–4.

ingenious exploitation of tight, formal patterns he found in his masters into a richer, flowing, enthusiastic celebration of love. The flow of the pattern of words and sounds is the most obvious characteristic. But the enthusiastic assertion of love in highly dramatic figures of speech is also important. There are several cases of the effective use of thunder. The identification of love with the intense beauty of the stars fills his poems with light.

> Vedut' ho la lucente stella diana,
> ch'apare anzi che 'l giorno rend' albore,
> c'ha preso forma di figura umana;
> sovr' ogn' altra me par che dea splendore:[25]

I have seen the shining morning star that appears before day gives us the dawn, which has taken the form of a human figure; I think she gives more splendour than any other.

The new fluency allowed the language for the first time to assume the quality of a fully developed modern poetic tongue, exhibiting the magical brightness and facility which we associate with Renaissance poetry in various languages, derived from the Italian exemplar.

In *Al cor gentil,* the toughness of the thought also looks forward to later poets. The main point expressed is that the brightness of love can animate only a noble heart. Here Guinizelli revives an old Provençal theme, that nobility is a matter of a man's quality independent of birth and wealth. The final development of the love–nobility argument, in the difficult fifth stanza, is that the effect of love on a noble heart is the same as the effect of God on those intelligent beings the angels, who move the heavens around the world in instant response to His will. It may be this passage or something like it in a lost poem that called forth the famous rebuke to Guinizelli from a more conventional writer, Bonagiunta Orbicciani da Lucca:

You who have changed the style of the elegant amorous compositions from the form of being which they used to have, in order to surpass every other troubadour . . . it is held to be a great strangeness, even if the sense comes from Bologna, to draw a song by force out of written authorities.[26]

The reference to Bologna implies that Guinizelli was thought to be writing poetry intelligible only to the university student. The poetry we have by him does not in fact contain any very difficult thought. But the fifth stanza of *Al cor gentil* introduces a combination of ideas that is important in Dante's verse and may have seemed original in 1276. There are two ideas. One is the use of the purely intellectual angels moving the heavenly spheres—the sun, moon, stars, and planets—about earth, which is at the centre of the universe. A full understanding of this idea would require a knowledge of thirteenth-century thinking about angels and about cosmology. The second idea is the equivalence of the angels' instant appreciation and transmission of God's

---

[25] *Poeti del Duecento*, ii, p. 469.   [26] Ibid., p. 481.

will—instant because they are purely rational beings—with the effect of the sudden awareness of love in the noble heart. This beautiful combination of cosmology and erotic metaphor is important in later poetry.

The closest to Dante among the Tuscan poets, Guido Cavalcanti, can be given a somewhat more substantial figure than the others, partly because a brief indication of his character was included by both Compagni and Villani in their chronicles. Compagni tells us that he had a feud with the great Florentine Guelf leader Corso Donati:

A young gentleman, son of Messer Cavalcante Cavalcanti, a noble knight called Guido, courteous and bold but disdainful and solitary and intent on study, who was an enemy of Messer Corso, had several times deliberately offended him. Messer Corso greatly feared him because he knew him to be of great soul and tried to assassinate him when Guido was going on pilgrimage to Santiago; but it did not come off. When Guido came back to Florence and heard about it he encouraged a number of young men who promised to help him against Corso. When he was on horseback one day with some of the Cerchi house, with an arrow in his hand, he spurred the horse against Messer Corso, thinking that he was followed by the Cerchi and hoping to get them to come over into the fight. While he was bringing the horse forward he threw the arrow which missed. With Messer Corso were Simone his son, a strong and bold young man, and Cecchino dei Bardi and many others with swords: failing to catch him they threw stones and some were also thrown from windows so that he was wounded in the hand.[27]

Guido died in 1300 after he had been sent out of Florence to Sarzana as one of the White Guelfs, exiled temporarily in the hope of calming party strife, and had returned sick. Villani comments that this was 'a great loss because he was like a philosopher, a virtuous man in various ways, though he was too soft and irascible.'[28]

The picture of the proud and intellectual noble individualist is not difficult to connect with the surviving poetry, which speaks with scorn of inferiors and includes a poem, addressed to Guittone d'Arezzo, parading the rudest criticisms: Guittone cannot construct a syllogism, his use of words is *barbarismo*, he cannot use literary figures, and he gets worse.[29] Guido himself came from the top of Florentine society. The earliest reference to him relates to 1267 when, probably in his teens, he was betrothed to a daughter of Farinata degli Uberti as part of the plan for pacifying Florence.[30] The great mystery about Guido is whether, and if so how far, his studiousness had involved him in heretical doctrine. Guido's father Cavalcante Cavalcanti was later placed in *Inferno* x among the Epicureans 'who make the soul die with

[27] *Cronica di Dino Compagni*, ed. I. Del Lungo, pp. 59–60.
[28] Villani, VIII. xlii.
[29] *Poeti del Duecento*, ii, p. 557. All Cavalcanti's surviving poems are printed in this volume. Other complete editions are *Rime*, ed. G. Favati (Milan–Naples, 1957) and *Rime*, ed. M. Ciccuto (Milan, 1978).
[30] Villani, VII. xv.

the body' and whom Dante was anxious to distinguish from his own beliefs. As mentioned in the last chapter, a recently discovered philosophical essay by a Bolognese scholar, dedicated to Guido, treats of human happiness in terms that are consistent with the views of Latin followers of Averroes' interpretation of Aristotle, which originated in Paris in the mid-thirteenth century and later spread to Bologna.[31] The highest human capacity, according to this treatise, is the pursuit of reason in this life, not the vision of God attainable only after death. After Cavalcanti's death, Dino del Garbo—the great Florentine physician who had been trained at Bologna—wrote a commentary on his difficult *Donna me prega*, interpreting it, rightly or wrongly, in Averroist terms.[32] It therefore seems likely that there were in Florence strands of aristocratic and learned free-thinking that denied the normal Christian doctrine of the soul as a unit that retained its faculties, including reason, independently after death, and that Cavalcanti is the clearest representative of this tradition. It also seems likely that these intellectual tendencies were linked with university scholasticism at Bologna, where there were many students and teachers from Tuscany. There is no reason to suppose that this unorthodox tendency of thought had any serious social importance, or that it was thought to present a problem to the ecclesiastical authorities. But the suggestion of a rather improper scepticism about religious matters is also conveyed by the jab at the Franciscans in a sonnet, already mentioned in Chapter 3, which Cavalcanti composed about the miracles associated with the painting of the Virgin at Or San Michele in 1292, which, according to Villani, attracted crowds from the country. The sonnet ends, 'The news goes through distant streets but the Friars Minor say that it is idolatry through envy because it is not near them'. The sonnet was addressed to a more conventional versifier, Guido Orlandi, who replied rather piously.[33] Cavalcanti's philosophical and religious opinions are likely to have been indefinite, and were perhaps not widely known. Their importance lies in the interest they held for a small group of friends, and in particular for Dante. Cavalcanti may have been the person whose example encouraged Dante at a fairly early point in his life on the path of serious philosophical enquiry. *Vita nuova*, however, was in part directed against Cavalcanti's ideas, and in *Inferno* ix–x Dante takes pains to reject those ideas he associated with Guido's father; Guido himself was not yet dead at Easter 1300, and therefore could not appear in the *Comedy*. It is likely that Dante's first steps in abstract thought were taken first in association with and then in opposition to the younger Cavalcanti, whose own intellectual evolution thus acquires the greatest interest.

Cavalcanti left a small number of satirical and pastoral poems and *tenzoni*.

---

[31] P. O. Kristeller, 'A Philosophical Treatise from Bologna Dedicated to Guido Cavalcanti, Magister Jacobus de Pistorio and his "Quaestio de felicitate" '; above, p. 87.

[32] Printed in Cavalcanti, *Rime*, ed. Favati, pp. 359–78.

[33] *Poeti del Duecento*, ii, pp. 558–60; Villani, VII, clv.

His commonest type of poem was an anguished lament about the devastating effects of love. Cavalcanti's ladies are grand and powerful, but his attention is most commonly concentrated not on them but on their destructive effects on him. It is the capacity of the lady to wound and kill which fills his poems. From this results the marked attention which he pays to the various parts of the body as they are affected by the deplorable strokes of love: the eyes, the heart, the mind, and the 'spirits', which are in scholastic physiology the materials which carry the commands of the brain and the pulsations of the heart to other parts of the body. Cavalcanti composed a sonnet, no doubt in self-parody, containing 'spirits' or some derivative of that word in each line.[34]

This attitude to love and natural philosophy was given its fullest expression, though not one which appeals to most of the emotions normally aroused by poetry, in *Donna me prega*, an elaborate analysis of the effect of love written largely in the technical language of scholastic philosophy.

> Donna me prega,—per ch'eo voglio dire
> d'un accidente—che sovente—è fero
> ed è si altero—ch'è chiamato amore:
>   sì chi lo nega—possa 'l ver sentire:
> Ed a presente—conoscente—chero,
> perch'io no spero—ch'om di basso core
>   a tal ragione porti canoscenza:
> ché senza—natural dimostramento
> non ho talento—di voler provare
> là dove posa, e chi lo fa creare,
>   e qual sia sua vertute e sua potenza,
> l'essenza—poi e ciascun suo movimento,
> e 'l piacimento—che 'l fa dire amare,
> e s'omo per veder lo pò mostrare.
>
>   In quella parte—dove sta memora
> prende suo stato,—sì formato,—come
> diaffan da lume,—d'una scuritate
>   la qual da Marte—vène, e fa demora;
> elli è creato—ed ha sensato—nome,
> d'alma costume—e di cor volontate.
>   Vèn da veduta forma che s'intende,
> che prende—nel possibile intelletto,
> come in subietto,—loco e dimoranza.
> In quella parte mai non ha possanza
>   perché da qualitate non descende:
> resplende—in sé perpetüal effetto;
> non ha diletto—ma consideranza;

[34] Ibid., ii, p. 530.

sì che non pote largir simiglianza.

Non è vertute,—ma da quella vène
ch'è perfezione—(ché si pone—tale),
non razionale,—ma che sente, dico;
 for di salute—giudicar mantene,
ché la 'ntenzione—per ragione—vale:
discerne male—in cui è vizio amico.

 Di sua potenza segue spesso morte,
se forte—la vertù fosse impedita,
la quale aita—la contraria via:
non perché oppost' a naturale sia;
 ma quanto che da buon perfetto tort'è
per sorte,—non pò dire om ch'aggia vita,
ché stabilita—non ha segnoria.
A simil pò valer quand' om l'oblia.

 L'essere è quando—lo voler è tanto
ch'oltra misura—di natura—torna,
poi non s'adorna—di riposo mai.
 Move, cangiando—color, riso in pianto,
e la figura—con paura—storna;
poco soggiorna;—ancor di lui vedrai
 che 'n gente di valor lo più si trova.
La nova—qualità move sospiri,
e vol ch'om miri—'n non formato loco,
destandos' ira la qual manda foco
 (imaginar nol pote om che nol prova),
né mova—già però ch'a lui si tiri,
e non si giri—per trovarvi gioco:
né cert' ha mente gran saver né poco.

De simil tragge—complessione sguardo
che fa parere—lo piacere—certo:
non pò coverto—star, quand' è sì giunto.
 Non già selvagge—le bieltà son dardo,
ché tal volere—per temere—è sperto:
consiegue merto—spirito ch'è punto.
 E non si pò conoscer per lo viso:
compriso—bianco in tale obietto cade;
e, chi ben aude,—forma non si vede:
dunqu' elli meno, che da lei procede.
 For di colore, d'essere diviso,
assiso—'n mezzo scuro, luce rade.
For d'ogne fraude—dico, degno in fede,
che solo di costui nasce mercede.

Tu puoi sicuramente gir, canzone,
là 've ti piace, ch'io t'ho sì adornata
ch'assai laudata—sarà tua ragione
da le persone—c'hanno intendimento:
di star con l'altre tu non hai talento.[35]

A lady prays me to tell her of an accident that is often proud and is so arrogant that it is called love: if anyone denies it let him hear the truth! And now I want a knowledgeable man because I do not expect a man of inferior heart to bring understanding to such a matter: For without natural science I have no wish to show where it is and who makes it, and what is its virtue and its potency, the essence and all the movement it causes and the pleasure which causes it to be called love, and whether a man can point it out to be seen. In that part where memory is—love resides, formed, as something transparent is by light by obscurity which comes from Mars and stays; it is created and has a sensible name, the custom of the soul and the will of the heart. It comes from a seen form, which is intelligible and takes its place in the possible intellect as in a subject. In that part it never has power because it does not derive from quality: in it there shines a perpetual effect, it has no delight but only contemplation; so that it cannot give an image of itself.

Love is not a virtue but comes from that which is perfection (which defines itself thus), not rational I say, but sensitive; it keeps the power of judging, away from the right path, for the intention takes the place of reason: it lacks discernment in him to whom vice is a friend. From its power death follows often, if by chance the virtue should have been impeded which helps the contrary way: not because it is opposed to nature; but in so far as he may happen to be removed from the perfect good a man cannot say that he is alive, for he has no stable control of himself. The same happens when a man forgets.

Its being is when desire is so great that it goes beyond natural limits and is never at rest. It changes the colour of the face, smiles into tears and turns the head away through fear; it stays for a short while in one place; also you will see that it is to be found most in people of noble nature. The new quality causes sighs and makes a man look at an unformed place, arousing anger which sends fire (a man who has not experienced it cannot imagine it), it stops him from moving, whatever else may attract him, and from turning to find relief: and certainly the mind has neither great understanding nor little.

From a similar temperament love draws a look which makes pleasure appear certain at this point: it cannot remain covered when it has arrived. Beauties, but not coarse ones, provide the dart because such desire is dissipated by fear: those struck by the dart get their reward. It cannot be known by sight, even the falling of white into such an object; and he who understands sees no form: and thus all the less those which proceed from it. Without colour, without being divided, fixed in a dark place, it drives out light. Without fraud I say, worthy of faith, that only from it is merit born.

You may go round with assurance, song, wherever you like, for I have so adorned you that your argument will be praised greatly by people who have understanding: you have no desire to be dealing with the others.

Cavalcanti is saying in this poem that the love which enters a man's bodily system as a result of seeing the woman he loves is an experience which has a

---

[35] *Poeti del Duecento*, ii, pp. 522–9.

profound effect on the sensitive part of his nature, but not much effect on the rational part. It has great physical results and it gives plesure; but it does not provide the lover with something which can be absorbed by his reason, and it is primarily destructive. This very brief recapitulation does no justice to the detailed movement of ideas in the poem, which is exceptionally obscure because the words Cavalcanti uses have a relationship with the language of contemporary science or natural philosophy—*natural dimostramento* is invoked as essential to the exposition in line 8—but a relationship which is not clear because the technical terms have been adapted for use in a poem. He refers to love as an 'accident' as opposed to a 'substance'; it comes to the part of the human body 'where memory stands', that is, the sensitive soul in scholastic terminology; it takes its place in the 'possible intellect', as opposed to the 'agent intellect', but does not establish itself there. These passages indicate the non-rational potentialities of love, and there is no doubt that Cavalcanti's purpose in the poem was to express his sense of the strongly non-rational effects of falling in love by analysing the passage of love with reference to textbook terminology. Thus he thinks of love as being a *species* introduced into the body through the eyes, transformed into a *phantasma*, which is lodged in the memory and understood by the intellect.

Lines 29–31 (love is not a virtue ... sensitive) present the problem of interpretation more acutely than the rest of the poem. Was Cavalcanti saying that the perfection of the human being is the sensitive part of his nature, the *anima sensitiva*, as opposed to the rational? If so he placed himself with the Averroists, who believed that the possible intellect—the part of the soul essential to rational understanding—was not individual to each man but was a share in universal intellect, detachable from each human being at death.

During the 1950s a bitter controversy raged about this last point, chiefly between two scholars, Bruno Nardi and Guido Favati.[36] Nardi argued that Dino del Garbo's interpretation of Cavalcanti's meaning was essentially correct: he *was* an Averroist. Favati argued that the meaning of *Donna me prega* could be worked out by using the language of orthodox Aristotelianism to be found in Thomas Aquinas's *Summa* and *Contra Gentiles*: the concepts of the poem were those generally used by scholastic thinkers of the time and contained nothing specifically Averroist, so Dino was expressing his own Averroism, not Cavalcanti's. Favati was probably right in saying that Averroism could not be proved from the very succinct and often mysterious language of the poem. On the other hand Dino del Garbo was a Florentine, writing only a few years after Cavalcanti's death; he knew far more about Cavalcanti

---

[36] The main stages were: Nardi, 'L'averroismo del primo amico di Dante', *Dante e la cultura medievale*, 2nd edn (Bari, 1949); Favati, 'La canzone d'amore del Cavalcanti', *Letterature Moderne*, iii, 1952; Nardi, 'Noterella polemica sull'averroismo di Guido Cavalcanti', *Rassegna di Filosofia*, iii, 1954; Favati, 'Guido Cavalcanti, Dino del Garbo e l'averroismo di Bruno Nardi', *Filologia Romanza*, ii, 1955; Favati, *Inchiesta sul dolce stil nuovo* (Florence, 1975), pp. 197–225. There is a new analysis of *Donna me prega* by Corti, *La felicità mentale*, pp. 16–37.

and his world than any modern analyst can know, and his ideas deserve to be taken seriously. It is on the whole likely that people of the time who knew about him did think of Cavalcanti as leaning consciously towards unorthodox views. The common view is recorded in Boccaccio's story in *Decameron* (vi. 9), in which Guido leans towards epicureanism.

It is necessary to draw particular attention to *Donna me prega* and the poems of suffering in love because these are written in the style against which Dante reacted in *Vita nuova*. Cavalcanti was also, however, a poet capable of expressing with great felicity, the sensual pleasure given by beauty. His poems of this type, somewhat closer to the style of Guinizelli, made an important addition to the development of the fluency characteristic of the *dolce stil* writers.

> Avete 'n vo' li fior' e la verdura
> e ciò che luce od è bello a vedere;
> risplende più che sol vostra figura:
> chi vo' non vede, ma' non pò valere.
>
> In questo mondo non ha creatura
> sì piena di bieltà né di piacere;
> e chi d'amor si teme, lu' assicura
> vostro bel vis' a tanto 'n sé volere.
>
> Le donne che vi fanno compagnia
> assa' mi piaccion per lo vostro amore;
> ed i' le prego per lor cortesia
> che qual più può più vi faccia onore
> ed aggia cara vostra segnoria,
> perché di tutte siete la migliore.[37]

You have the flowers and the foliage in you and whatever lightens and is beautiful to see; your face shines more than the sun: he who does not see you can never have value. In this world there is no creature so full of beauty and pleasure; he who fears love is reassured as much as he wants by your beautiful face. The ladies who keep you company please me greatly through your love; and I pray them for their courtesy that they do as much honour to you as they can and hold your lordship dear because you are the best of all.

Guinizelli and Cavalcanti are two of the poets of whom Dante later, in *De Vulgari Eloquentia* and the *Comedy*, expressed approval, and have been regarded as members of the school of *dolce stil nuovo*. The other writers normally connected with the *dolce stil* are the Florentines Lapo Gianni, Dino Frescobaldi, and Gianni degli Alfani, who are minor poets;[38] and above all the Pistoiese Cino da Pistoia. Cino was a charming poet who has left us far more

---

[37] *Poeti del Duecento*, ii, p. 493.
[38] Some of their poetry can be read in *Poeti del Duecento*, ii.

lyrics than any of the other *stilnovisti*, including Dante. He is also important in the history of literature because of the part his poems played in the transmission of the language of the *stil nuovo* to Petrarch and the fourteenth century. Cino must have been associated by others with the new poetry, at least of Cavalcanti, because it is that kind of writing that is lampooned in a sonnet directed to him by an old-fashioned poet Onesto da Bologna: ' "Mind" and "humble" and more than a thousand bags full of "spirits" make me think that in no other way can one make sense of your poetry writing. I don't know who makes you do it, life or death, for by your going philosophizing . . .'[39] Though not mentioned in the *Comedy*, Cino was greatly elevated by Dante in *De Vulgari Eloquentia* II. ii, where he is named as the Italian representing the poetry of love, as against Arnaut Daniel among the Provençals; while Dante himself represents the poetry of rectitude, as against Gerard da Bornelh, and is therefore named as one of the great modern poets. *De Vulgari Eloquentia*, however, was written about the same time as Dante's letter to Cino 'to the Pistoiese in exile'[40] and the verse correspondence between Cino, Dante, and Marchese Moroello Malaspina[41] (that is, during the early part of Dante's exile, about 1302–5), and at that time his poetic affection for Cino was probably strengthened by the political misfortune they shared.

The 'philosophizing' picked out by Onesto da Bologna appears in Cino only as something borrowed. This is perhaps why we have a sonnet by Cino which apparently replies to an accusation of plagiary made against him by Cavalcanti.[42] In one sense this is curious because Cino, who probably lived from about 1270 to 1327, was the only one of the great poets to have an undoubtedly considerable intellectual stature which he acquired by a conventional university career. He probably spent the 1290s, after he had entered the magic circle with a poem to Dante on the death of Beatrice, reading law at Bologna and in France, and then embarked on a distinguished career, which included being professor of law at Siena, Perugia and Naples and an important writer of legal textbooks.[43] His limited importance in the intellectual history of poetry emphasizes, in contrast, the dependence of Dante's evolution on the world of ideas in Florence.

It now seems probable that the most important document about the very young Dante is a long, allegorical poem consisting of 232 sonnets, unnamed but called for convenience *Il fiore* (The flower), which was found in a

---

[39] M. Marti, *Poeti del dolce stil novo* (Florence, 1968), pp. 752–3.

[40] Dante, *Opere minore*, ii, pp. 532–5.

[41] Foster and Boyde, ii, pp. 311–30.

[42] *Poeti del Duecento*, ii, p. 639.

[43] Cino's poetry is most fully printed in Marti, *Poeti del dolce stil novo*. For his life: L. Chiapelli, *Vita e opere giuridiche di Cino da Pistoia* (Pistoia, 1881), *Nuove ricerche su Cino da Pistoia* (Pistoia, 1911); G. Zaccagnini, *Cino da Pistoia: studio biografico* (Pisa, 1918); M. Barbi, 'Cino fu di parte bianca?', *Problemi di critica dantesca*, ii (Florence, 1941); G. M. Monti, *Cino da Pistoia giurista* (Citta di Castello, 1924); *Cino da Pistoia nel VI centenario della morte* (Pistoia, 1937).

manuscript in France in 1889.[44] *Il fiore* is based on the *Roman de la rose* and
tells parts of the story of that very long French poem in Tuscan and at much
reduced length. It retains the elaborate allegory of the *Roman* but leaves out
most of the philosophical aspects and presents an extremely tightly struc-
tured, elegant and amusing account of a seduction, ending with a graphic
description of the final deflowering. Attribution to Dante was long rejected
by most scholars, partly no doubt because such a scandalous poem was
thought inappropriate to the author of the *Comedy*. The strong advocacy of
Dante's authorship by the most respected student of the Italian poetry of the
thirteenth century, Gianfranco Contini, has changed the balance of opinions.
In addition to the indications of the place and time of the composition of the
Fiore, which suggests Tuscany in the late 1280s, and the naming of the author
as 'Durante', there is also a great deal of linguistic connection with Dante's
undoubted works, and it is mainly on this linguistic evidence that the
attribution depends.[45]

Apart from the language there is another aspect of *Il fiore* which is
important for an attempt to give it a meaningful position in Dante's work.
Most of the poem is taken up with debates between allegorical figures who are
either helpful or hostile to the enterprise of the 'Lover': Love, Jealousy,
Reason, Wealth, and so forth. The Lover's most prominent enemy, eventually
overcome, is Falsembiante (False-seeming), who is identified with the religious orders and whose companion is Madonna Costretta-Astinenza (Lady
Constrained-Abstinence), who is said to be sometimes a *pinzochera* (a woman
member of one of the third order). 'Those with whom I stand', says
Falsembiante at one point,

have so greatly confused the world that there is no prelate great enough to find a basis
against their power. With my deception I sink everyone but if any great man of letters
comes wanting to uncover my sin I confound him with the power I have. Master Siger
was not happy for long: he died with the sword in great suffering at the court of Rome
at Orvieto. Master Guillaume, the good man of St Amour was silenced in France and
banned from the kingdom with great upheaval.[46]

The two real men mentioned here were both enemies of the mendicant friars.
Guillaume de St Amour was the leader of the secular masters against the friars
at the university of Paris in the 1250s. Siger of Brabant was the leading
Averroist philosopher at Paris a little later. As a defender of Averroist ideas he
clashed with Aquinas who wished to emphasize that Aristotelian philosophy

---

[44] *Il Fiore e il Detto d'Amore attribuibili a Dante Alighieri*, ed. G. Contini (Milan, 1984); also
in *Opere minori*, I, i (Milan–Naples, 1984).
[45] Contini's arguments can be read in 'Un nodo della cultura medievale: la serie *Roman de la
rose—Fiore—divina Commedia*', *Saggi danteschi*, 2nd edn (Turin, 1976); in his article 'Fiore' in
the *Enciclopedia dantesca*, and in the introduction to his recent edition of *Il fiore*. Cf. the more
extended discussion by L. Vanossi, *Dante e il 'Roman de la rose' Saggio sul 'Fiore'* (Florence,
1979).
[46] Sonnet xcii.

was compatible with Christianity. This led to the condemnation of Averroist propositions by the bishop of Paris in 1277, and Siger left the university to make an appeal at the papal court where he died some time between 1280 and 1284. *Il fiore*'s reference to his end is one of the few mentions of it in Italian letters.[47]

The persistently anti-mendicant stance of *Il fiore* is in striking contrast with the glorious celebration of the mendicant orders and their most famous members, Aquinas and Bonaventure, in *Paradiso* x–xiii. Seen in the perspective of Dante's life, this contrast is one of the reasons for accepting *Il fiore* into the Dante canon. As will be explained later, *Paradiso* is so strongly marked by the correction of views presented in earlier works by Dante (for instance, views about free-will and judgement), that the critic naturally looks for some earlier statement about the mendicants. There is none—unless one allows *Il fiore* to provide it. The mendicant section of *Paradiso* also includes carefully placed references to Siger of Brabant and Joachim of Fiore, who was the author of works beloved by the spiritual Franciscans (which Guillaume de St Amour principally attacked), which may be intended to correct the impression given in *Il fiore*. It is not difficult to imagine *Il fiore* as being composed by the author of *Non mi poria già mai fare ammenda*, the playful sonnet in which Dante complains that his eyes were looking at the Garisanda tower in Bologna so that they missed a beautiful lady going by.[48] That was entered into a book at Bologna in 1287: somewhere about that date we must imagine *Il fiore* as being written by a very clever young man who shared Cavalcanti's flippant view of the mendicants and, even if he was not learned in university philosophy, very likely also shared his sympathy with the condemned Averroism of Paris and Bologna.

The existence of the *Comedy*, with its multifarious references to people and events in the thirteenth century, gives us an opportunity for tracking down hints about Dante's earlier life for which we have no parallel in the writings of other poets of the period. Dante's anguished concern about his own past frequently led him in later works to open doors into his early experiences. One example of this is in the Paolo and Francesca episode in *Inferno* V where Dante met two lovers condemned to be eternally near but separated in punishment for their adultery, which had begun when they were reading about Lancelot and Guinevere together. The episode is a tender rejection by Dante of the ethos of romantic eroticism in French literature. There are two points which connect the passage with Dante's earlier life. One is the male

---

[47] Another passage in *Il fiore* which helps to establish its date is the reference in Sonnet cxxvi to the mendicant persecution of Patarines in Prato, Arezzo and Florence. Evidence of this trial and torture of Cathars by Franciscans in Florence *c.*1280–6 is given by R. Manselli, 'Per la storia del l'eresia catara nella Firenze del tempo di Dante, il processo contro Saraceno Paganelli', *Bullettino dell'Istituto Storico Italiano*, lxii, 1950.

[48] Foster and Boyde, no. 14.

adulterer, Paolo Malatesta, Capitano del Comune at Florence in 1282–3,[49] and therefore almost certainly someone whom Dante, then seventeen, had seen if not known personally; he may also be recalling a liking for romance literature by Paolo, who was killed by his brother, Francesca's husband, a year or two later. The other is the French book, which can be identified, in which Dante read the story of how Lancelot took the first guilty kiss from Guinivere.[50] There are a few other Arthurian references in the *Comedy* but this episode makes clear to us, as they do not, that the 'exquisite wanderings of King Arthur' (*De Vulgari Eloquentia*, II. x—it is not clear whether the 'wanderings' refers to the prose or to the movements of the characters) were a branch of literature which had made a deep impression on Dante.

In other poets, the knowledge of French and Provençal literature is shown by their borrowing of words, figures of speech, and poetic forms; and the knowledge is clearly abundant. Only in Dante do we see the broader ideological effect of acquaintance with literature from the other side of the Alps. The eight-line imitation of the Provençal of Arnaut Daniel in *Purgatorio* xxvi, 140–7 is evidence of a command of ultramontane language which was probably not peculiar to Dante but which had implications which only he reveals. Italian literature could offer him only the lyric poems and a very derivative collection of prose. A serious writer, like a serious thinker, had to get inspiration from Northern Europe. We should therefore think of Dante, and probably of the other lyric poets whose poetry did not give them the opportunity to reveal their reading in the same way, as conscious of a European world of ideas and writing, of which they were situated on an outer edge. Dante should thus not be thought of like the great writers of modern England and France or of Italy in the fifteenth and sixteenth centuries, as drawing on a native tradition, but like Chaucer or the nineteenth-century Russians, as living self-consciously on the outside of the intellectual and artistic world which nourished them.

The Dante of the more amusing early poems was succeeded, or perhaps accompanied, by a Dante who wrote poems in something like the style of Cavalcanti, rather tragic expressions of the devastating effects of love. These include the first ten poems which were later put into *Vita nuova*, of which Dante probably wrote the prose commentary on the poems sometime between 1293 and 1295. An example of this style is the poem which contains the earliest mention of Beatrice in Dante's writings:

> Lo doloroso amor che mi conduce
> a fin di morte per piacer di quella
> che lo mio cor solea tener gioioso,
> m'ha tolto e toglie ciascun dì la luce

[49] Davidsohn, *Storia*, II. ii, p. 293.
[50] P. Toynbee, 'Dante and the Lancelot Romance' in *Dante Studies and Researches* (London, 1902).

che avëan li occhi miei di tale stella,
che non credea di lei mai star doglioso:
   e 'l colpo suo c'ho portato nascoso,
omai si scopre per soverchia pena,
   la qual nasce del foco
   che m'ha tratto di gioco,
sì ch'altro mai che male io non aspetto;
e 'l viver mio (omai esser de' poco),
   fin a la morte mia sospira e dice:
   'Per quella moto c'ha nome Beatrice.'

The sorrowful love that leads me to final death, at the will of her who used to keep my heart in joy, has withdrawn the light and daily withdraws it more—the light that once my eyes received from a star such that I never thought I would be sad on its account. And the wound I had from it I have kept concealed, but now it shows itself through excessive pain—pain caused by that fire which has drawn me away from happiness, so that now I can expect nothing but torment: and my life—which cannot last long now— sighs as it goes to death, and says: 'Through her I die, whose name is Beatrice.[51]

A more abrupt change came, presumably not long before the death of Beatrice in 1290, when Dante, in anticipation of her death, wrote the first of his new poems of praise, presenting her, more in the manner of Guinizelli, as a divinely beautiful woman whose presence was needed in heaven to complete its perfection, rather than as the cause of the misery of a lover without hope.

Donne ch'avete intelletto d'amore,
i' vo' con voi de la mia donna dire,
non perch'io creda sua laude finire,
ma ragionar per isfogar la mente.
   Io dico che pensando il suo valore,
Amor sì dolce mi si fa sentire,
che s'io allora non perdessi ardire,
farei parlando innamorar la gente.
   E io non vo' parlar sì altamente,
ch'io divenisse per temenza vile;
ma tratterò del suo stato gentile
a respetto di lei leggeramente,
donne e donzelle amorose, con vui,
ché non è cosa da parlarne altrui.
   Angelo clama in divino intelletto
e dice: 'Sire, nel mondo si vede
maraviglia ne l'atto che procede
d'un'anima che 'nfin qua su risplende.'
   Lo cielo, che non have altro difetto

[51] Foster and Boyde, no. 25.

che d'aver lei, al suo segnor la chiede,
e ciascun santo ne grida merzede.
Sola Pietà nostra parte difende,
   che parla Dio, che di madonna intende:
'Diletti miei, or sofferite in pace
che vostra spene sia quanto me piace
là 'v'è alcun che perder lei s'attende,
e che dirà ne lo inferno: "O mal nati,
io vidi la speranza de' beati".'

   Madonna è disïata in sommo cielo:
or vòi di sua virtù farvi savere.
Dico, qual vuol gentil donna parere
vada con lei, che quando va per via,
   gitta nei cor villani Amore un gelo,
per che onne lor pensero agghiaccia e pere;
e qual soffrisse di starla a vedere
diverria nobil cosa, o si morria.

   E quando trova alcun che degno sia
di veder lei, quei prova sua vertute,
ché li avvien, ciò che li dona, in salute,
e sì l'umilia, ch'ogni offesa oblia.
Ancor l'ha Dio per meggior grazia dato
che non pò mal finir chi l'ha parlato.

   Dice di lei Amor: 'Cosa mortale
come esser pò sì adorna e sì pura?'
Poi la reguarda, e fra se stesso giura
che Dio ne 'ntenda di far cosa nova.
   Color di perle ha quasi, in forma quale
convene a donna aver, non for misura:
ella è quanto de ben pò far natura;
per essemplo di lei bieltà si prova.
   De li occhi suoi, come ch'ella li mova,
escono spirti d'amore inflammati,
che feron li occhi a qual che allor la guati,
e passan sì che 'l cor ciascun retrova:
voi le vedete Amor pinto nel viso,
là 've non pote alcun mirarla fiso.

   Canzone, io so che tu girai parlando
a donne assai, quand'io t'avrò avanzata.
Or t'ammonisco, perch'io t'ho allevata
per figliuola d'Amor giovane e piana,
   che là 've giugni tu diche pregando:

'Insegnatemi gir, ch'io son mandata
a quella di cui laude so' adornata.'
E se non vuoli andar sì come vana,
    non restare ove sia gente villana:
ingegnati, se puoi, d'esser palese
solo con donne o con omo cortese,
che ti merranno là per via tostana.
Tu troverai Amor con esso lei;
raccomandami a lui come tu dei.

Ladies who have understanding of love, I wish to speak with you of my lady; not that I think I can exhaust her praises, but I want to speak to unburden my mind. I say that when I consider her perfection Love makes himself felt in me so sweetly that, did I not then lose courage, I would make people in love with her by speech alone. However, I will not attempt a style so lofty as to make me faint-hearted through fear; rather, I will speak of her excellence in a meagre style—compared with what she is—and to you, ladies and girls who know love; for it is not a thing to speak of to others.

An angel cries in the divine intellect, saying: 'Lord, in the world there appears a marvel in act, proceeding from a soul whose splendour reaches even here on high!' Heaven, whose only lack is the lack of her, begs her from its Lord, and every saint cries out for this favour. Pity alone defends our cause, so that God, his mind on my lady, says: 'My loved ones, bear it patiently that your hope remains as long as I please in the place where there is one who knows he will lose her, and who in hell will declare: "O ill-fated ones, I have seen the hope of the blessed".'

My lady is desired in highest heaven: and now I wish to show you something of her excellence. I say that any lady who would show she is noble should go in her company; for when she passes on her way Love casts a chill on base hearts, so that every thought in them freezes and dies; and were any such person able to stay and regard her, he would either become noble or die. And when she finds someone worthy to see her, he receives the full effect of her power; for what she then gives him turns to his good and happiness, and renders him so humble that he forgets every injury. Again, God has given her this greater grace, that no one who has spoken with her can come to an evil end.

Love says of her: 'How can a mortal creature be so lovely and so pure?' Then he looks at her and swears within himself that in making her God intends to make a marvel. Her colour is pearl-like, in a way befitting a lady, not to excess. She is the most perfect thing that Nature can produce: beauty is known as imaged in her. From her eyes, wherever she turns them, come fiery spirits of love that strike the eyes of whoever may be regarding her, and pass inward so that each one reaches the heart: you see Love depicted in her face, there where no one can fix his gaze.

Song, I know that when I've sent you forth you will go about speaking to many ladies. Now I charge you—having brought you up to be a modest young daughter of Love—that wherever you come you make this request: 'Tell me where I am to go, for I have been sent to her with whose praises I am adorned.' And if you don't wish to travel in vain, don't stop where there are base people; contrive, if you can, to show yourself only to ladies or men of courteous mind, who will lead you quickly to your destination. With her you will find Love; commend me to him, as is your duty.[52]

[52] Foster and Boyde, no. 33.

The prose parts of *Vita nuova* were written to accompany and explain a series of poems presented as being parts of the history of Dante's relationship with Beatrice. The story of *Vita nuova* is roughly this. Dante was first struck by love for Beatrice at the age of nine. Nine years later—this would be in 1283—he saw her again, and circulated to other poets a sonnet about a vision arising out of seeing her, which brought him into contact with Cavalcanti. After a long period of hopeless love for Beatrice, never expressed to her and often disguised by feigning a love for other women, Dante checked his despair by deciding to change his style and write in praise of her. Hence *Donne ch'avete intelletto d'amore*. The poems of praise of love and of the beloved continued, through the crises of the death of Beatrice's father and a serious illness of Dante, up to Beatrice's own death (in 1290). Some considerable time (more than a year) after that, Dante was attracted to another lady, whom he first saw at a window and who for a time seemed to him to be sent by Love as a replacement for Beatrice. A vision of Beatrice, however, restored her supremacy and the book apparently ends with Dante devoted to her memory but resolving not to write about her further 'until I can treat of her more worthily', a phrase which seems to be pointing forward to the reappearance of Beatrice in the *Comedy*.

At that time, Italian literature could show little prose writing of real quality. *Vita nuova* is a work of extraordinary originality and beauty that stands dramatically out of the historical sequence because it is difficult to point to anything from which it really derives or any existing category of literary works to which it belongs. Dante was no doubt affected by Cicero's accounts of friendship in *De Amicitia*; by Boethius's *Consolation of Philosophy*, in which there is also a lady, and which consists of poems interspersed with prose; and, nearer home, by *La rettorica* of the Florentine Brunetto Latini, which consists of translated passages of Cicero's *De Inventione* with exposition.[53] Other aspects of the work, though not the telling of a prose story, can be explained by considering Dante's reaction to the poetry of Guinizelli and Cavalcanti. Beatrice certainly owes much to the angelic ladies of Guinizelli; while the earlier part of the book can be read as a prose expression of Cavalcantian torments of love, the later part describes the exaltation of love in a manner which owes something to Guinizelli. The interests of Dante at this stage as a man concerned with both poetry and philosophy come out, for example, in this untypically theoretical passage in which he confronts the Cavalcanti of *Donna me prega*:

At this point someone whose objections are worthy of the fullest attention might be mystified by the way I speak of love as though it were a thing in itself, and not only a substance endowed with understanding but also a physical substance, which is

---

[53] These connections are discussed by D. de Robertis, *Il libro della 'Vita nuova'*, 2nd edn (Florence, 1970).

demonstrably false; for love is not in itself a substance at all, but an accident in a substance. That I speak of love as if it were a bodily thing, and even as if it were a man, appears from these three instances: I say that I saw him coming; now since 'to come' implies locomotion and, according to the Philosopher, only a body in its own power is capable of motion from place to place, it follows that I classify love as a body. I say also that he laughed and that he spoke, which things are appropriate to a man, especially the capacity to laugh; and so it follows that I make love out to be a man. To clarify this matter, in a manner that is useful to the present purpose, it should first be understood that in ancient times the theme of love was not taken as a subject for verses in the vernacular but there were authors who wrote on love, namely, certain poets who composed in Latin . . .

Thus if we see the ancient poets spoke of inanimate things as if they had sense and reason, and made them talk to each other, and that they did this not only with real things but also with things which are not real, making things which do not exist speak, and making accidents speak as if they were substances and men, then it is appropriate for someone writing in rhyme to do the same; not, of course, without some justification, but with a reason that can be later made clear in prose. And lest any uneducated person should assume too much, I will add that the Latin poets did not write in this manner without good reason, nor should those who compose in rhyme, if they cannot justify what they say; for it would be a disgrace if someone composing in rhyme introduced a figure of speech or rhetorical ornament, and then on being asked could not divest his words of such covering so as to reveal a true meaning. My most intimate friend [Cavalcanti] and I know quite a number who compose rhymes in this stupid manner.[54]

The interpretation of *Vita nuova* in relation to Dante's experiences of other poets does not however provide us with an explanation of some of the more strongly religious elements in the work, in particular the invention of the angelic Beatrice and her influence on those around her. Dante tells us that Beatrice so impressed people that 'when she passed through the street people ran to see her', 'when she was near to someone such uprightness possessed his heart that he did not dare to raise his eyes or to respond to her greeting', 'she went about crowned and clothed in humility' and many said of her 'this is not a woman but one of the most beautiful angels of heaven'. The impression Dante gives in these and other passages is that he is concerned not with the half-imaginary angelic lady of poetry but with a more real angelic person. When in another chapter Dante describes how he met Cavalcanti's lady, Giovanna, walking past followed by Beatrice and was inspired with the idea that Giovanna was 'Primavera', because she will come first (*prima verra*), and 'Giovanni', John who preceded the true light, it is difficult to decide whether this is a joke, a poetic fantasy, a serious indication of the religious or moral supremacy of Beatrice, or something of all three. The same difficulty is raised by the fairly extravagant use of the number symbolism of multiples of three to connect Beatrice with the Trinity.

[54] *La vita nuova*, trans. Barbara Reynolds (Harmondsworth, 1969), pp. 72–5. Editions of *Vita nuova* by M. Barbi (Florence, 1932), and in *Opere minori*, i, i, by de Robertis.

The real Beatrice Portinari, daughter of Folco Portinari, founder of the hospital of Santa Maria Nuova, and wife of Simone de' Bardi, whom, on the authority of Boccaccio, we believe to have been the person whom Dante loved and who inspired the Beatrice of *Vita nuova,* may or may not have been an angelic woman; we know nothing about her and have no way of anchoring the book in the realities of Dante's life. When we look at it from another literary point of view, however, we are struck by the resemblance of the book to a literary style which reflected a quite different aspect of real life from the one reflected in the love lyric. That is the style of Franciscan hagiography. Many of the numerous saints of Central Italy in the thirteenth century were women. Dante must have known about holy women of this kind and also of the lives sometimes written about them, which formed, as we have seen in Chapter 3, a remarkable branch of contemporary literature. Beatrice's sister Ravignana indeed married a brother of St Giuliana Falconieri (1270–1341) who founded a Servite tertiary order in 1305,[55] so the holy woman cannot have been an unknown figure in her circle.

But the written *leggende* of saints should perhaps be regarded as more important than the saints themselves as part of the background to *Vita nuova.* The legends of saints such as Clare, Francis's collaborator and the founder of the Clarisse, or Beatrice's contemporary St Margaret of Cortona (1247–97) contain literary conventions which seem to be echoed in *Vita nuova.*[56] Holy women were thought to lead lives marked by conformity with the life of Christ; they had the psychological power to inspire a following and to improve other people's moral lives, and their relationship with heaven in their mortal life anticipated the consummation of this relationship by their death. These characteristics are all present in the life of Beatrice. The story of *Vita nuova* is the story of Dante's movement from a love founded on the painful and negative aspects of the traditional 'courtly love' conception to a state of positive adoration of a dead woman for her moral and religious power. This kind of combination of distinct literary traditions—courtly love poetry and Franciscan biography—into a wholly unexpected new literary material has a characteristic originality similar to that to be found in some of Dante's other works. We do not have to suppose that *Vita nuova* records a conversion, though it may do so. What is proposed is that Dante's writing reveals a sensitivity to, an awareness of, one of the prominent features of life around him: the occurrence of women endowed with moral and religious authority who dominate the lives of the people who know them. The fragmentation of local religious and social life and the popularity of new religious groups gave women of this type, as we have seen, exceptional opportunities in Dante's Tuscany which are mirrored in the lady of *Vita nuova.*

[55] I. Del Lungo, *Beatrice nella vita e nella poesia del secolo XIII* (Milan, 1891), p. 113.

[56] V. Branca, 'Poetica del rinnovamento e tradizione agiographica nella "Vita nuova" ', *Studi in onore di I. Siciliano,* i (Florence, 1966).

Vita nuova ends with a sonnet in which Dante imagines himself linked by Love with a Beatrice who is now in heaven, beyond the outermost circles of the physical heavens which surround the earth as it was conceived by the astronomy of that time. At the end of 'New Life' he has a 'new understanding'.

> Oltre la spera che più larga gira
> passa 'l sospiro ch'esce del mio core:
> intelligenza nova, che l'Amore
> piangendo mette in lui, pur su lo tira.
>
> Quand'elli è giunto là dove disira,
> vede una donna, che riceve onore,
> e luce sì, che per lo suo splendore
> lo peregrino spirito la mira.
>
> Vedela tal, che quando 'l mi ridice,
> io no lo intendo, sì parla sottile
> al cor dolente, che lo fa parlare.
>
> So io che parla di quella gentile,
> però che spesso ricorda Beatrice,
> sì ch'io lo 'ntendo ben, donne mie care.

Beyond the sphere that circles widest passes the sigh that issues from my heart: a new understanding which Love, lamenting, imparts to him draws him ever upwards. When he arrives where he desires to be, he sees a lady who receives honour and who shines so that the pilgrim spirit contemplates her for her splendour.

He sees her such that when he repeats this to me I do not understand, so subtly does he speak to the sorrowing heart that makes him speak. I know he speaks of that noble one, for he often mentions Beatrice; so that I understand him well, my dear ladies.[57]

The link between love and the cosmology of the heavens which appears in this sonnet has an important future in Dante's poetry. He was moving out of his earlier interest in the poetry of erotic love into an interest in the structure of the mind and its capacity for thought, and the relationship of this with the structures of the universe.

In *Convivio*, which he wrote a decade later (1304–8), Dante told his readers how, after the death of Beatrice, he turned for consolation to works of philosophy:

I set myself to read that book of Boethius [*The Consolation of Philosophy*] in which he consoles himself for his anxiety and banishment. And then, hearing that Cicero had written another book dealing with *Friendship*, in which he had reported words of consolation of the excellent Laelius at the death of his friend Scipio, I set myself to read that too. And although I had difficulty in understanding them I finally made as much progress as I could with the aid of my knowledge of grammar and a little of my native

---

[57] Foster and Boyde, no. 57.

wit, by which I had already seen many things almost as if in dreaming, as may be read in the *Vita nuova*. And so, as it happens that a man goes looking for silver and unexpectedly finds gold, which a hidden cause presents not perhaps without divine command, I, looking for consolation, found not only a cure for my tears but words of sciences, authors and books which gave me the idea that Philosophy, the lady of these authors, sciences and books, was a supreme thing. I imagined her made like a noble lady and I could imagine her in no attitude save that of compassion so that the sense so wanted to look at her that I could scarcely turn away. As a result I began to go where she was truly revealed, in the schools of the religious and the disputations of the philosophers. So that in a short time, perhaps thirty months, I began to feel her sweetness so much that love of her drove out and destroyed every other thought.[58]

Dante's account of the origins of his philosophical studies is not entirely convincing because it is difficult to believe he was not familiar with Boethius and Cicero when he wrote *Vita nuova*. On the other hand, the importance given to Boethius is of the greatest interest because he may have been an inspiration and source for the neoplatonist philosophy which provided Dante with his later view of the nature of the physical universe, and also influenced him in other ways. The reference to the 'schools of the religious' is also, of course of great interest, because it seems to refer to Santa Croce and Santa Maria Novella, where there were friars who had been to the universities and books which contained the texts of scholastic philosophers.

Dante was probably correct in recalling that in the mid-1290s he had been actively pursuing philosophy and the mendicant philosophers who could expound it to him: this at any rate is consistent with the evolution of his poetry at that period, which shows a strong expansion of the interests suggested in *Oltre la spera*. *Vita nuova* was followed by a group of poems that can be regarded as a stage in Dante's poetic evolution.[59] They are all, at first sight, love poems. Two of them were elaborately discussed a decade later in *Convivio*, where Dante himself presented them as allegorical poems. We do not know for certain whether this was the truth,—that is, whether they had actually been written as allegorical poems—or a useful fiction which enabled Dante ten years later to use them as a way into the philosophical problems which he then wanted to discuss in the prose sections of *Convivio*. The poem which Dante discusses in Book III of *Convivio* is the one which appears to be the most 'philosophical' of the group, and it can be used as an example:

> Amor che ne la mente mi ragiona
> de la mia donna disïosamente,
> move cose di lei meco sovente,
> che lo 'ntelletto sovr'esse disvia.
> Lo suo parlar sì dolcemente sona,

[58] *Convivio*, II. xii. There is an annotated edition of *Convivio* by G. Busnelli and G. Vandelli, 2nd edn (Florence, 1964).
[59] Foster and Boyde, nos 59–68.

che l'anima ch'ascolta e che lo sente
dice: 'Oh me lassa, ch'io non son possente
di dir quel ch'odo de la donna mia!'
E certo e' mi conven lasciare in pria,
s'io vo' trattar di quel ch'odo di lei,
ciò che lo mio intelletto non comprende;
e di quel che s'intende
gran parte, perché dirlo non savrei.
Però, se le mie rime avran difetto
ch'entreran ne la loda di costei,
di ciò si biasmi il debole intelletto
e 'l parlar nostro, che non ha valore
di ritrar tutto ciò che dice Amore.

Non vede il sol, che tutto 'l mondo gira,
cosa tanto gentil, quanto in quell'ora
che luce ne la parte ove dimora
la donna, di cui dire Amor mi face.
Ogni Intelletto di là su la mira,
e quella gente che qui s'innamora
ne' lor pensieri la truovano ancora,
quando Amor fa sentir de la sua pace.
Suo esser tanto a Quei che lel dà piace,
che 'nfonde sempre in lei la sua vertute
oltre 'l dimando di nostra natura.
La sua anima pura,
che riceve da lui questa salute,
lo manifesta in quel ch'ella conduce:
ché 'n sue bellezze son cose vedute
che li occhi di color dov'ella luce
ne mandan messi al cor pien di desiri,
che prendon aire e diventan sospiri.

In lei discende la virtù divina
sì come face in angelo che 'l vede;
e qual donna gentil questo non crede,
vada con lei e miri li atti sui.
Quivi dov'ella parla, si dichina
un spirito da ciel, che reca fede
come l'alto valor ch'ella possiede
è oltre quel che si conviene a nui.
Li atti soavi ch'ella mostra altrui
vanno chiamando Amor ciascuno a prova
in quella voce che lo fa sentire.

Di costei si può dire:
gentile è in donna ciò che in lei si trova,
e bello è tanto quanto lei simiglia.
E puossi dir che 'l suo aspetto giova
a consentir ciò che par maraviglia;
onde la nostra fede è aiutata:
però fu tal da etterno ordinata.

   Cose appariscon ne lo suo aspetto
che mostran de' piacer di Paradiso,
dico ne li occhi e nel suo dolce riso,
che le vi reca Amor com'a suo loco.
   Elle soverchian lo nostro intelletto,
comme raggio di sole un frale viso:
e perch'io non le posso mirar fiso,
mi conven contentar di dirne poco.
   Sua bieltà piove fiammelle di foco,
animate d'un spirito gentile
ch'è creatore d'ogni pensier bono;
e rompon come trono
l'innati vizii che fanno altrui vile.
Però qual donna sente sua bieltate
biasmar per non parer queta e umile,
miri costei ch'è essemplo d'umiltate:
Questa è colei ch'umilia ogni perverso:
costei pensò chi mosse l'universo.

   Canzone, e' par che tu parli contraro
al dir d'una sorella che tu hai;
ché questa donna, che tanto umil fai,
ella la chiama fera e disdegnosa.
   Tu sai che 'l ciel sempr'è lucente e chiaro,
e quanto in sé non si turba già mai;
ma li nostri occhi per cagioni assai
chiaman la stella talor tenebrosa.
   Così, quand'ella la chiama orgogliosa,
non considera lei secondo il vero,
ma pur secondo quel ch'a lei parea:
ché l'anima temea,
e teme ancora, sì che mi par fero
quantunqu'io veggio là 'v'ella mi senta.
Così ti scusa, se ti fa mestero;
e quando pòi, a lei ti rappresenta:
dirai: 'Madonna, s'ello v'è a grato,
io parlerò di voi in ciascun lato.

Love, speaking fervently in my mind of my lady, often utters such things concerning her that my intellect is bewildered by them. His speech sounds so sweetly that the soul, as she attends and hears, says: 'Alas that I am unable to express what I hear of my lady!' And certainly, if I wish to treat of what I hear of her, I must first leave aside what my intellect does not grasp; and then, too, much of what it does understand, for I should not be able to express it. If then these words of mine which undertake her praise be found wanting, let the blame fall on the weak intellect, and on our faculty of speech which lacks the power to record all that Love says.

The sun that circles the whole world never sees anything so noble as when its light falls there where dwells the lady of whom Love makes me speak. All Intelligences on high gaze at her, and those who here below are in love still find her in their thoughts, when Love brings them to partake of his peace. So much does her being please Him who gives it her that He continually pours His power into her beyond the requirement of our nature. Her pure soul makes it clear through what she governs that she receives this perfection from Him; for among her beauties such things are seen that the eyes of those on whom her light falls send to the heart messengers full of longing, which gather air and turn into sighs.

The divine goodness descends into her in the same way as into an angel that sees Him; and let any noble lady who does not believe this keep her company and contemplate her bearing. Whenever she speaks a spirit comes down from heaven to testify that the high perfection she possesses transcends our measure. The gracious actions that she displays vie with each other in calling on Love with such a voice as must awaken him. Of her it can be said: nobility in woman is what is found in her, and beauty is all that resembles her. Further, it can be said that her aspect helps to induce belief in what seems miraculous; and so our faith is strengthened: and it was for this that she was established from eternity.

In her aspect things appear that show the joys of Paradise—I mean in her eyes and her lovely smile; for it is there, as to the place which belongs to him, that Love leads them. And they overpower our intellect as a ray of sunlight overpowers a weak sight; and since I cannot look steadily at them I must be content to write but little of them. Her beauty showers down flames of fire alive with a lofty spirit, the creator of all good thoughts; and like a lightning flash they shatter the inborn vices that debase one. Therefore let every woman who hears her beauty slighted for seeming to lack gentleness and humility, gaze at this lady, the very model of humility! She it is who brings back to humility whoever strays from it. She was in the mind of Him who set the universe in motion.

My son, it seems you speak in a sense contrary to one of your sisters, seeing that this lady, whom you declare so humble, she calls harsh and scornful. You know that the sky is always shining and clear and never itself grows dark; and yet our eyes, for a number of reasons, sometimes say the stars are dimmed. Similarly, when your sister calls this lady 'proud', she does not consider her as she really is, but only as the lady seemed to her. For my soul was afraid, and indeed it is still afraid, so that whatever I see, when this lady perceives me, seems harsh. Make your excuses thus, should the need arise; and when you can, present yourself to her and say: 'Lady, if it be your wish, I will speak of you everywhere.'[60]

---

[60] Foster and Boyde, no. 61.

In *Convivio* II. 2–15, Dante gave both a literal and an allegorical interpretation of this poem, both of which present it as being essentially philosophical in its meaning. The literal interpretation leads Dante to discuss the role of love in drawing beings towards their primal cause and the imperfection of the human mind, resulting from its place in the middle of the ascending scale of being, which makes the poet incapable of understanding the lady. He also tells us something about astrology and angels to explain the lady's place in the scale of being, which allows her more of the divine goodness than is accessible to men; and the final stanzas require a digression into optics. When he passes on to the allegorical interpretation, Dante reveals that the lady and the love which unites the poet with her really represent 'philosophy' and 'study'. The heavenly influences infused into her in the second stanza and the advantages to be gained from her company in the third represent the nature of philosophy as an activity which attracts men because of the divine light which is poured into it, and which unites love and wisdom.

The riddle about whether a poem which takes over so much of the traditional imagery of love poetry was really written to express a view of philosophy presents obstacles to one's enjoyment and understanding: it makes the reader fear that he is being tricked by a brilliant manipulator. It is clear, however, that the author of this and the other, similar poems was using a mixture of 'courtly love' and philosophical terminology in which the traditional language of love poetry was dominant but not exclusively in control. Maria Corti has pointed out, for example, that the famous first line of another poem in the same group, *Voi che 'ntendendo il terzo ciel movete*, appears to contain reminiscences of a sentence in Albertus Magnus's commentary on Aristotle's *Ethics—Preterea philosophi dicunt quod actiones omnes conveniunt in inferioribus ex motoris primis, sed non producunt actiones nisi intendendo eas*—in which movement (*movete, motoris*) and understanding (*intendendo*) are related in the same way.[61] The poet seems to have had three kinds of ideas in his mind at the same time: the traditional poetic praise of the beauty of the lady, the Boethian idea of the lady as an allegorical representation of philosophy, and the theory of the value of philosophy based on Boethius and Aristotle. It is difficult for a remote observer to sympathize with the aesthetic force of this overlapping group of apparently ill-fitting ideas but the incongruous mixture is inseparable from the power which enables Dante to reach a new level of elegance in a smooth, developing argument.

The new poetic sensibility in Dante's poetry and prose composed in the 1290s was the result of a movement from the traditional, imported forms of courtly love, which had a limited relevance to Tuscan life, to a confrontation with issues of love, religion, and philosophy that arose out of the world of ideas of the Florentine layman. This is not the world of the French courtier or

---

[61] Corti, *La felicità mentale*, p. 116.

of the university. It is the world of Florence with its particular mixture of Italian poetry, Latin classics, simplified philosophy, and mendicant piety. Dante's poetic exaltation of that world in the 1290s, in *Vita nuova* and the lyric poems, is a sudden creation of a new kind of literature, a new city literature springing out of an embryonic city culture. The change must have taken place at almost exactly the same time as the new painting in the *Life of St Francis* sequence at Assisi, whose origins will be investigated in the next chapter. The painting and the poetry do not rise from quite the same background, but there is a satisfying synchronism in their emergence.

The process through which Dante eventually arrived at his new type of philosophical poetry was fundamentally different from the process in which Guittone had attempted to apply the traditional styles of poetry to religious themes. Guittone's rather simple-minded campaign was a failure. Dante was in a sense moving in the same general direction: the development of a poetry which would deal with serious intellectual and religious themes. But his verse is the expression of a set of poetic reactions to real life and to literature, not of an abstract intellectual purpose. The poetry which finally results in, for example, *Amor che nella mente mi ragiona*, which has just been quoted, arises from a mingling of, amongst other things, the personification of philosophy in scholastic thinkers such as Albertus, the lady *Philosophia* in Boethius and the lady of courtly love poetry. This is the result of a troubled confrontation with Cavalcanti's materialist philosophy and with his poetry, a confrontation with the reality of feminine goodness observed in part within the framework of the Franciscan idea of saintliness, the inspiration of Guinizelli's poetry, the inspiration of ideas of Boethius and Aristotle. Dante's mind was composed of a confusion of poetic, philosophical, religious, and personal influences—a stew of incompatible ingredients, in very strong contrast to the simple, rational and moral purpose of Guittone.

The existence of a confusion of ideas and models out of which original poetry soars with unexpected beauty is a phenomenon with which it would be easy to find parallels elsewhere in literary history. In the case of Dante, lack of evidence makes the process much more obscure than it would be in, say, nineteenth-century Paris. But we are probably right to assume a fairly intense interaction between Dante and the society around him. As the anti-egalitarian forces in Florentine politics helped to produce the defence of an egalitarian definition of nobility in *Le dolci rime d'amor* in 1295–6,[62] the presence of defenders of Bolognese Averroism in Florence helped to provoke a poetry of idealized love used as a philosophical metaphor. All of this would, of course, have been useless if Dante had not been already a superbly competent poet. Given his poetic skill and his youth, however—Dante was still under thirty when all this happened—it was possible for the interaction of ideas arising

[62] Above, p. 35.

from several widely separate fields of thought to lead to the forging of a new kind of poetry. It was not the last kind of poetry Dante would write, but for the time being it was the greatest novelty in the Italian literary world. The breaking away from the courtly love tradition into Dante's novel allegorical poetry of the 1290s, which marked the establishment of true Italian city poetry, in contrast to the earlier derivative imitation of the Provençals, was necessary before Dante could take the further step into *Inferno*. In explaining the creation of the poetry of the 1290s we have to allow for a typically Florentine mingling of good poetry, religious idealism, and amateur philosophy, thrown together in a highly original mixture.

6

Classical Influence in the Visual Arts

IN a sermon to a Marian congregation at Imola delivered in 1286, the preacher presented a *questio* 'concerning the image of the Virgin in whose honour we are assembled here: "Whose is this image and inscription?" '[1] The question, he said, could be answered in four ways, relating to formation, possession, representation, and special devotion. The possession was God's, the representation of a mother and virgin, the special devotion of all Christians, especially those of the Dominican order. The answer placed under 'formation' is the most interesting part of the homily. It was made by the

holy spirit, because by that it was painted and formed and sanctified, and thus the holy spirit made it beautiful that it should please the eyes of God . . . And note that the holy spirit like the best craftsman made it beautiful, painting in it all the virtues and all the gifts and graces.

This sermon must have been delivered before a painting of the Virgin, but the preacher made no reference to the painter. The painting was a holy object containing spiritual virtues arising from its subject. The sermon expresses the idea of a painting as a statement of a religious conception to which time and place and the human creator were irrelevant. About twenty-five years later, Dante included in *Purgatorio* (xi. 94–6) his famous remark about Giotto superseding Cimabue as the most famous painter, with which the history of Renaissance adulation of the artist begins. The attribution of importance to the painter and his painting, instead of its subject ideally considered, was the result of the explosion of artistic invention which had already begun when the sermon at Imola was delivered.

The preacher was speaking in a provincial and backward setting remote from Rome, Assisi, and Siena, where by 1286 the work of Cavallini, Cimabue, and Giovanni Pisano—all of whom remained famous names in the Renaissance tradition—was already under way. Nevertheless it represents conveniently an ancient tradition from which Italian art was to break away rapidly. Nearly all the important art which has survived in Italy from the period before 1320 is religious. It consists of scenes and figures illustrating the bible or the lives of saints, and sepulchral monuments. The subject matter of serious art, though it went through many important changes of detail in the late thirteenth and early fourteenth centuries, was transformed very little in its

[1] Meersseman, *Ordo Fraternitatis*, iii, pp. 1136–7.

main character. But while the subject matter remained the same, the expectations of sophisticated artists and art lovers were transformed by their new interest in the effective representation of drama, space, and the human figure. These are the characteristics which appear to us valuable in the mature art of Giotto, Duccio, and Giovanni Pisano at the beginning of the fourteenth century, and which must have been in Dante's mind when he spoke of Giotto. Drama, space, and the human figure were used to give greater efficiency to the religious impact of art. They involved, however, an emphasis on the natural world of objects and people which has an interest in itself, and their use marks a significant step away from the pure evocation of beliefs and holy stories in scenes intended to impress the observer by their formal beauty and to remind him of the truths properly contained in the Bible and the legends of saints.

In a general way the development of the new art was due principally to two influences which were strong in the Italian world of this period. First to the influence of ancient painting and sculpture, of which there were many examples to hand especially in Rome, and whose impact was assisted by knowledge of the Northern French figure sculpture of the thirteenth century. Second to the influence of the rich societies of Siena and Florence, in which the wealth of patrons and the competition of city life provided an ideal setting for the refinement of artistic values. The first influence is easy to demonstrate by the comparison of ancient and modern art objects, the second is more difficult. We know a number of the patrons and we can see the connection between art and city religion, but the more general idea of the dependence of art on city life as a whole depends only on our knowledge of the physical presence of great artists in these societies, and the undocumented assumption that the life of the city was important for the visual artist as it certainly was for the poet. The origins of the revolution which lay behind Giotto's Arena chapel, if not more complicated, are in some ways more obscure than the background to Dante's *Comedy*.

Artists were craftsmen who worked for patrons, and who moved about between the places where work was offered to them. To understand the development of painting and sculpture we have to look at the connected influence of several centres of patronage, notably the papal court, Siena, Assisi, and Florence, where great projects were patronized. We have to take account of a variety of artistic influences imposed by the religious traditions of Italy, by the models of ancient art, and by knowledge of Northern Gothic art, which mingled in different proportions at various times and places.

The history of the visual arts in this period is complex, in part because of the interaction of several great centres of patronage, close enough to influence each other but economically separate as points from which commissions were issued. It is complicated also by the international character of the highest levels of Italian society. The papal court, which drew a large part of its wealth from Northern Europe, also included French cardinals as well as Italian, and provided an easy route by which Northern objects and ideas could enter Italy. The Franciscan order, whose capital was the great painted basilica at Assisi, was an international order. The wealth available for artistic work at Siena and Florence was heavily dependent on international trade: it is no accident that the two chapels Giotto painted at Santa Croce were patronized by the Bardi and Peruzzi, the chief Florentine families with commercial interests at Naples. The world of the great artistic patrons was therefore extremely international, in the sense that it depended on the movement of money into Italy from outside and the international movement of men. It consisted of a group of societies floating rather precariously on the European world and rather lightly rooted in Italy itself. To a limited extent, which must not be exaggerated, this encouraged the acceptance of alien artistic ideas.

The most important formative influences on art were, however, undoubtedly Italian. It is impossible to imagine the paintings of Giotto or the sculpture of the Pisani without the inspiration of Roman paintings and sculptured sarcophagi which lay behind them, or without the intense devotion of the mendicant orders which encouraged a like emotional intensity in the treatment of religious subjects. Distant influences from Northern Europe and Byzantium are probably also important. Architecture is not the field of art in which Italians made remarkable contributions, but it is the one in which the influence of the North is most clear because the Gothic style of building, foreign and incompatible with the Romanesque traditions of the Mediterranean, had already begun its influence (for instance, at Assisi) in the early thirteenth century and was to inspire a new Italian style during this period. Most sculpture was inseparable from architecture. Sculptors designed small structures, tombs, and tabernacles, in Gothic style, and were also undoubtedly influenced by the figure sculpture of Reims. This distant influence presents a problem. Except in cases where the patrons were Northerners, for example French cardinals, it is impossible to know how the influences were transmitted. There is no certain case of a major Italian artist crossing the Alps. We can only speculate. The problem of Byzantine influence, which has been seen for example in the painting of Duccio, is even more nebulous. What icons or manuscripts could the painters have seen? Could they have visited the East? We do not know. There are two avenues through which contacts between Byzantine and Western art could have been important: Venice with its eastern links, and the traffic with crusading states.[2] Specific knowledge of Byzantine art in Tuscany is rare. Finally our knowledge of the lives of all the Italian artists is extremely fragmentary, and theories about the art they had seen depend on speculation.

---

[2] H. Buchthal, *The 'Masterbuch' of Wolfenbüttel and its Position in the Art of the Thirteenth Century.* (Byzantina Vindobonensia, xii, 1979); K. Weitzmann, 'Crusader Icons and Maniera Greca' in *Byzanz und der Westen*, ed. I. Hutter (Österreichische Akademie der Wissenschaften, Philosophisch-Historische Klasse, Sitzungsberichte, Band 432, 1984).

It is clear, however, that art developed by the separate enrichment and interpenetration of a group of geographically distinct centres of patronage. The best way to approach it will be by examining them separately. Before doing that the reader may be helped if we set out the central point which will arise from this survey. The new art which emerged, particularly in Giotto's Arena frescos, was principally a result of interaction between an extremely vigorous but unrealistic native popular art in Tuscany and Umbria, and the external inspiration of observing the languid but realistic remains of classical painting in Rome and classical sculpture at Pisa. The popular art, which was obscurely painted in the mid-thirteenth century by the shadowy or invented figures who go under the names of Giunta Pisano, Guido da Siena, Coppo di Marcovaldo, the Master of St Francis and others, was produced for well-to-do communities by artists who displayed considerable power in the creation of dramatic images in which rich colours and sinuous patterns of the human form were important. It was an art notable for emotional power but not for realism of space or figure. Artists trained in these schools were affected at the end of the thirteenth century by the imitation of Roman paintings, probably inspired originally by the patronage of the Roman court, out of which a new form of painting arose in Rome and Assisi. Contemporaneously a new sculpture had been created at Pisa and Siena by the inspiration of Roman sarcophagi and French Gothic sculpture. All this happened while the papal court was still at Rome. After the collapse and departure of the court at the end of the pontificate of Boniface VIII, the movement was carried forward by the patronage of commercial communities at Florence and Siena and elsewhere. By the end of the first decade of the fourteenth century a new realistic art which combined religious power with an interest in physical and dramatic realism had been created.

Roman painting and mosaic in the late thirteenth century requires an exceptional exercise of the imagination because so much of it has been destroyed, has decayed, or is difficult to see. Old St Peter's has vanished in sixteenth-century rebuilding. Most of the work in St John Lateran is gone. San Paolo fuori le Mura was destroyed by fire in the nineteenth century. Only the Sancta Sanctorum, Santa Cecilia and Santa Maria in Trastevere, and Santa Maria Maggiore remain. The Roman art of this period has to be approached archeologically to a greater extent than any great artistic campaign of later centuries. We must imagine a group of buildings, partly rebuilt but more particularly adorned by a series of powerful popes, now largely destroyed or engulfed in the wealth of ancient and Renaissance buildings, which once constituted an original expression of Christian grandeur carried out by a great school of artists and paid for by the medieval papacy at its height. The paintings and mosaics are the source of several of the central characteristics of early Renaissance art.

Roman art was patronized by the popes of the period 1277 to 1305, several of whom, unlike their predecessors Clement IV and Gregory X, were attached to Rome, spent much time in the city, and were anxious to bolster its greatness by artistic adornment. The most important were the Orsini Nicholas III (1277–80); Nicholas IV (1288–92)—not a Roman but closely connected with the Colonna; and the Caetani Boniface VIII (1294–1303). The story begins with a great Maecenas, Nicholas III, whose aggressive policy of driving the king of Naples out of Rome and imposing peace on the Guelfs and Ghibellines of Tuscany was accompanied by a new attachment to the grandeur of the papal city. Nicholas's special interest in Rome, as a native Roman and as pope, is expressed in his letters. 'Within the walls of the city there dwells a great and sublime people whom God so blessed that the city was enlarged by celestial gifts and its people, fortified by divine aid, outdid other nations in magnificence and earthly power.' His political views were reflected by the Dominican Ptolemy of Lucca in the *Determinatio Compendiosa de Iurisdictione Imperii*, probably composed in the early part of the pontificate, which attacked imperial power but defended the divine concession of power to the Romans.[3] It is Ptolemy of Lucca also who in his *Historia Ecclesiastica Nova* included an unusual annalist's description of Nicholas's building schemes at St Peter's and the Lateran.

Nicholas III made many novelties, for at St Peter's he built a solemn pontifical palace in which he ordered the making of a house for all his officials, especially the penitentiaries who were enclosed behind one partition and where he had an orchard made, planted with many trees and of great size which he also surrounded with strong, high walls fortified with towers as if it were a city. He almost completely restored the church of St Peter's and had a number of popes painted, following the pictures in St Peter's, and restored St Paul's and St John Lateran . . . He completed the Lateran palace which Hadrian V had begun, and ordered that the holy basilica of the Sancta Sanctorum which was more obviously ruinous should be built up from ground level by uninterrupted work, the surfaces within lined with marble and adorned in the upper part of the vault with very beautiful paintings.

Another chronicler tells us that Nicholas's building at Rome was paid for with the proceeds of Gregory X's crusading tenths 'so that the assembly of the Roman court should be at the entrance to the houses of his kinsmen'—that is, the houses of the Orsini family.[4] Probably all the Roman building schemes of the popes of this period, like Nicholas's, depended on the money derived from European taxation rather than local revenues. Nicholas began this brief imperial tradition, and his face looks out with splendidly refined nobility from the painting he patronized at the Sancta Sanctorum. His work at St

---

[3] The *Determinatio*, ed. M. Krammer has been elucidated by C. T. Davis, 'Roman Patriotism and Republican Propaganda: Ptolemy of Lucca and Pope Nicholas III' in *Dante's Italy*.

[4] *Rerum Italicarum Scriptores*, ed. L. A. Muratori (Milan 1723–51), xi, cols 1180–1; ix col. 724.

Peter's—probably his biggest architectural and artistic enterprise and the one which most impressed contemporaries—can be reconstructed archeologically, but very little of the painting or sculpture survives.[5] If we want to see the character of his artistic influence we have to look first of all at the Sancta Sanctorum, the largely intact chapel for the housing of relics, which he constructed near the Lateran.

The Sancta Sanctorum is a compact building, fairly small with sides about seven metres long and an altar space projecting out from one of them.[6] The architecture is Gothic, a central pointed vault rising from columns in the corners. The four walls each have a narrow pointed window with the important mural paintings on either side of it, and below the window a shallow arcade. The general structure appears to be related to the transepts of the upper basilica at Assisi and belongs to the early attempts to import the Gothic architectural style into Italy. The ceiling of the altar space is decorated with a particularly fine mosaic of the bust of Christ within a circle upheld by four flying angels, which successfully conveys the impression of flight against a background of brilliant light. It is the successor of much earlier mosaic work at Rome, but has no immediate predecessor and was probably produced as a revival of the art of mosaic after a period of disuse, perhaps inspired by Byzantine mosaics or artists.

The painting on the upper surface of the walls consists of four pairs of scenes, each pair divided by a window, designed to glorify the religious traditions of Rome and the generosity of the pope. The east wall has on one side a large portrait of Nicholas III, kneeling but accompanied by St Peter and St Paul, whose figures are no larger than his, presenting a model of the Sancta Sanctorum. Beyond the window sits Christ enthroned, receiving it with outstretched hand. On the south wall are the *Martyrdoms of Peter* and *Paul*, Peter crucified upside down before a landscape of Roman buildings, Paul decapitated with the sword (Pl. 1). On the west wall are the *Martyrdoms of St Stephen* by stoning and *St Lawrence* attacked with rakes as he roasts on the gridiron. On the north wall is the *Martyrdom of St Agnes*, stabbed outside a tall doorway, and the *Miracle of St Nicholas*, shown in a double scene— inside a house in which he appears with a bag of gold to dower three maidens, and outside it being thanked by the father. Some of the scenes have lost complete authenticity through restoration but the stories of Agnes, Peter, and

[5] D. Redig de Campos, *I palazzi vaticani* (Bologna, 1967), pp. 25–33, figs 10–17; idem., 'Di alcune tracce del palazzo di Niccolo III', *Rendiconti della Pontificia Accademia Romana d'Archeologia*, xviii, 1941–2. On Nicholas's patronage in general, see M. D'Onofrio, 'Le committenze e il mecenatismo di papa Niccolò III' in *Roma Anno 1300*, ed. A. M. Romanini (Rome, 1983).

[6] J. Gardner, 'Nicholas III's Oratory of the Sancta Sanctorum and its Decoration', *Burlington Magazine*, cxv, 1973; J. T. Wollesen, 'Eine "vor-cavallineske" Mosaikdecoration in Sancta Sanctorum', *Römisches Jahrbuch für Kunstgeschichte*, xviii, 1979; idem, 'Die Fresken in Sancta Sanctorum', ibid. xix, 1981. Wollesen's articles have excellent photographs.

Paul are not badly overpainted, and enough remains in these and other parts of the decoration to indicate the design of the scenes and the general character of the painting.

The painted framing of the scenes is extremely rich with formal and semi-natural decoration, including acanthus plants rising from elaborate vases. The presentation of scenes including complex figures and landscape aiming at naturalism within frameworks of this type is an attempt to revive an ancient style of painting, familiar to us today chiefly from the work discovered at Pompeii but probably associated in the thirteenth century with early Christian paintings now vanished that then existed at St Peter's, San Lorenzo fuori le Mura, and elsewhere.

These Sancta Sanctorum murals provide us with the best opportunity to witness the reactions of artists at the very start of the Renaissance movement to the classical and early Christian past and to adapt the styles they found. We should notice first of all the attempt to spread the human figures through a deep space, which is a notable feature of the *St Paul martyrdom* (Pl. 1) and the *St Lawrence martyrdom*. The attempt to relate figures to buildings is particularly marked in the St Lawrence scene, where the saint's tormentors are underneath the arched portico of a building whose roof stretches back towards a distant tower, and in the St Nicholas miracle, where the gift of money inside the house is separate from the giving of thanks to the saint outside but the two scenes appear to be contained within the same space. These features may well have been improved by restorations in the late Renaissance, but it seems unlikely that the original structure of the paintings was altered. The faces of the figures are marked by a powerful roundness when they are seen head-on or obliquely. Several of the features which are valued in the more developed art of the early fourteenth century must have been present in embryo when the paintings were in their original condition.

Pope Nicholas III apparently had an interest also in the repainting of the interior of the basilica of the monastery of San Paolo fuori le Mura which was carried out in the 1270s and 1280s.[7] Four of the series of papal portraits he commissioned for that building have survived. The basilica of San Paolo was however destroyed by fire and subsequent restoration in 1823, and our knowledge of nearly all the large number of important paintings it contained is based on copies made in the seventeenth century. Lorenzo Ghiberti, the sculptor of fifteenth-century Florence, writing a century and a half after the work was done, connected the Old Testament series at San Paolo with Pietro Cavallini. It is the earliest work supposed to be by Cavallini, a Roman whose

[7] J. Gardner, 'S. Paolo fuori le Mura, Nicholas III, and Pietro Cavallini', *Zeitschrift für Kunstgeschichte*, xxxiv, 1971; J. White, 'Cavallini and the Lost Frescoes in S. Paolo', *Journal of the Warburg and Courtauld Institutes*, xix, 1956; P. Hetherington, *Pietro Cavallini: A Study in the Art of Late Medieval Rome* (London, 1979), pp. 81–106; S. Waetzoldt, *Die Kopien des 17. Jahrhunderts nach Mosaiken und Wandmalereien in Rom* (Vienna–Munich, 1964), with photographs of the copies.

name first appears in a document of 1273 as a member of the Cerroni family and who lived on well into the fourteenth century mostly, as far as we are concerned, in extreme obscurity, although his association with several important works has made him the most prominent name in the Roman school.

San Paolo had a large number of painted panels stemming ultimately from the fifth century, eighty-four in all, occurring in two rows along the walls of the nave above the arcade arches. On the right-hand side were scenes from the Old Testament, on the left-hand scenes from the Acts of the Apostles, mostly illustrating the life of Paul. Remains of inscriptions relating to the abbots of the monastery seem to indicate that the St Paul scenes were repainted in the years 1277–9, and the Old Testament panels in 1282–90. The form taken by the repainting seems to have involved a basic acceptance of the iconography and spatial arrangement of the classical scenes which were being re-worked. But the reason for the new enterprise was no doubt the decayed state of the old work. Interpretation to establish the degree of intervention of the thirteenth-century painters and the extent of the survival of fifth-century painting, on the basis of much later copies, which provide the only surviving record, is obviously difficult. We are dependent on the judgement of modern art historians. But it is at least clear that this large enterprise provided Cavallini and other Roman artists with an exceptional experience of enforced confrontation with the classical style and an opportunity to assimilate it and develop it along lines which interested them.

The St Paul series on the right-hand side presents simpler spatial forms. Normally the figures stand in a shallow space to the front of the scene, with a landscape including architecture behind. Occasionally, for instance in the scene of *Paul, Barnabas, and the Prison Keeper* (see Waetzoldt, Pl. 397), the figures are related in a more complicated way to space within a building, but this is unusual. Ghiberti did not connect Cavallini with the St Paul scenes, and it is possible that he had nothing to do with them. The Old Testament scenes, however, seem to reveal a clearer distinction between those left in their earlier form and those repainted in the thirteenth century, presumably by Cavallini. One of the subjects, the *Death of the Egyptian Firstborn*, is repeated: one version in the old form, one done by Cavallini, basically with the same structure of figures and landscape, but with a freer movement of figures and drapery. In some of the scenes which appear to be by Cavallini, for instance the *Appearance of Serpents before Pharaoh* (Pl. 2), we see him advancing to a more complicated disposition of figures in space. Pharaoh sits on a dais in front of a building. Eight other figures are ranged on either side of him, seven of them on the floor below the dais, receding from the front of the scene to a position equidistant with Pharaoh from the front. The seventeenth-century copies are too cursory to provide much information about the representation of emotion or drama. They do show, however, that Cavallini used the old paintings as a source of models of the arrangement of figures in a simple landscape with architecture, and used the opportunity to advance beyond them to paint figures with a less static appearance, a freer movement in relation to rather more complex architectural forms.

The artistic campaign of Nicholas III was followed ten years later by that of Nicholas IV, carried out in different circumstances and with a different purpose.[8] Nicholas IV was not a Roman noble but Jerome of Ascoli, the first Franciscan to reach the see of the apostle, and his artistic patronage was closely connected with the Roman Colonna family, which was devoted to the mendicant orders. The relative parts played by the Pope and the Colonna is not clear; but in the apse mosaic of Santa Maria Maggiore, Nicholas IV and Cardinal Jacopo Colonna kneel as equal donors on either side of the roundel containing the *Coronation of the Virgin*. The devotion of the donors to the Franciscan order is shown by the presence of St Francis and St Anthony of Padua in the same mosaic. Nicholas patronized work in two main Roman churches, St John Lateran and Santa Maria Maggiore, with which the Colonna were connected. In both cases the east end was rebuilt and decorated.

Only the Santa Maria Maggiore work survives. That however is extensive, and constitutes the most considerable specimen of mosaic to remain in Rome from this period. At the east end are the apse mosaic with scenes from the life of the Virgin below it and the patches of fresco in the north transept, both ascribed to Jacopo Torriti. At the west on the facade, now partially damaged or obscured by the building of the loggia in front of it, is a *Christ in Majesty* flanked by the Virgin and St John the Baptist, Apostles, and saints, and formerly the miniature figures of the two Colonna cardinals, Jacopo and Pietro, suggesting that, while the apse belongs to Nicholas IV's pontificate, the facade was done between his death in 1292 and the deposition of the Colonna by Boniface VIII in 1297. Below are four large scenes from the early history of the church. The facade is attributed by an inscription to Filippo Rusuti.

The *Coronation of the Virgin* is a large and splendid work, originally dated 1295 and presenting a subject only recently adopted in Italian art.[9] Below it are a series of seven scenes from the life of the Virgin. The finest of these is the central scene, the *Dormition of the Virgin*, in which the problem of filling a wide, flat space has been met by introducing a mosaic nearly three times as broad as its height with an extremely effectively elongated Virgin laid out on her bed and long rows of mourners stretching away into the distance on either side. This is a brilliant conception. The other scenes from the Virgin's life

[8] J. Gardner, 'Pope Nicholas IV and the Decoration of Santa Maria Maggiore', *Zeitschrift für Kunstgeschichte*, xxxvi, 1973; W. Oakeshott, *The Mosaics of Rome from the Third to the Fourteenth Centuries* (London, 1967), pp. 311–28 (with good photographs of the Santa Maria Maggiore mosaics).

[9] G. Coor-Achenbach, 'The Earliest Italian Representation of the Coronation of the Virgin', *Burlington Magazine*, xcix, 1957.

however are more remarkable for their bold clarity than for an interest in realism. At the other end of Santa Maria Maggiore the scenes by Rusuti display an advanced interest in the placing of figures in interior space which foreshadows developments in painting. The *Vision of John the Patrician* shows John in a complex building, reclining on a bed separated from the front of the picture by tall pillars with a vaulted ceiling rising behind him and a tall, castellated, and pillared structure on the roof. In the scene of *John the Patrician Visiting Pope Liberius* (Pl. 3), John and his three followers are placed within a church-like interior. Behind them rise columns supporting a complex group of vaults with gothic windows. These mosaics are not attempts to present interior space with any mathematical correctness, but they do show an interest in presenting it with considerable attention to the detail of the structure and with some movement towards spatial depth.

The Santa Maria Maggiore facade is probably work of the mid-1290s. About the same time, Cavallini was also working in two churches on the other side of the Tiber, Santa Maria and Santa Cecilia in Trastevere. The mosaics in Santa Maria in Trastevere, ascribed to Cavallini by Ghiberti, were done for Bertoldo Stefaneschi, a Roman nobleman and brother of Cardinal Francesco Stefaneschi, who appears kneeling below the Virgin and Child as donor in a separate mosaic panel.[10] Nothing is known about the date, and the supposition that the work was carried out in the 1290s is based on very general reasons. These mosaics are the best preserved of all Cavallini's works. They are set below an enthroned Virgin and Christ in the higher part of the apse of the church. Apart from the donor panel there are six scenes: *Nativity of the Virgin*, *Annunciation*, *Nativity of Christ*, *Adoration*, *Presentation*, and *Dormition*.

These mosaics were made at about the same time that Torriti was creating mosaics of the same subjects in the apse of Santa Maria Maggiore for a rival Roman family, and there must have been some competition between the two artists. Cavallini cannot in the circumstances of the 1290s be considered remarkable for his grasp of spatial realism or architectural forms. If we compare the figures in the work of the two artists, however, it is plain that Cavallini is more accomplished in his treatment of drapery, and also invests his people with a more definite appearance of action and intention. The angel in Torriti's *Annunciation* stands rather stiffly with hand raised, his drapery hanging in conventional patterned folds. Cavallini's angel (Pl. 4) is marching forward, leaning in the direction of his movement, arm outstretched, bringing a message of importance. The demurely seated Virgin establishes a true connection between the two figures. The folds of the angel's dress are drawn back in a complex and realistic fashion by the movement of his legs. It has been suggested that what we see in Cavallini's figures is the impact on an artist in

[10] J. Poeschke, 'Per la datazione dei mosaici di Cavallini in S Maria in Trastevere', *Roma Anno 1300*.

mosaic and paint of the new realism achieved, ahead of painting, by contemporary sculpture, and that the sculptor responsible for this influence may have been Arnolfo di Cambio, whom we shall meet later, and who had worked, as Cavallini had, in San Paolo fuori le Mura and also presumably worked at the same time as Cavallini in Santa Cecilia in Trastevere.

Mosaic is suitable for displays of great brilliance and splendour. It is not a medium for rapid experiments or for precise realism. The Roman revival of mosaic in the second half of the thirteenth century was inspired not only by recent Byzantine models but also by the long tradition of mosaic decoration in Rome itself, but the future in the West was in fact to be in painting. The Roman enterprises involved a mixture of the two, though the mosaics have survived better; Cavallini was in fact carrying out a major painting scheme at Santa Cecilia in Trastevere at about the same time as he did his mosaics at Santa Maria in Trastevere. The dates of the two campaigns are unknown and it is impossible to be sure which came first, though the Santa Cecilia work may be related to the year 1293 when Arnolfo di Cambio's ciborium in the same church was finished. Santa Cecilia may have been paid for by the wealthy French cardinal Jean Cholet, whose titular church it was. He died in 1293, but whether Cavallini painted before or after his death it is impossible to say.

The Santa Cecilia frescoes—or parts of them—were rediscovered in 1900 after being covered over for centuries and they are the finest surviving Roman painting of this period. What we have is a section of the *Last Judgement* painted inside the west end of the church: an enthroned Christ in a mandorla surrounded by angels, on either side the Virgin and John the Baptist and beyond each of them a horizontal row of six Apostles (Pl. 5) seated on two rows of choir stalls. Below Christ is an altar; on either side of that two angels blowing trumpets, on one side receiving St Lawrence and St Stephen and a crowd of the redeemed, on the other side driving the damned into hell. The painting is brilliantly coloured, mostly in red, blue, and green, and very impressive. Northern influence has been seen in the fact that the apostles bear the instruments of their martyrdom, which links the iconography with French cathedral sculpture. It may have been inspired by the taste of the French cardinal, like the Gothic ciborium by Arnolfo which was probably built in the church about the same time. Otherwise the roots of the painting are local. The faces of the apostles, rounded, powerful, definite and strongly coloured, depend on development of the tradition of painting faces in Rome. The sections that have survived do not provide much opportunity for spatial realism, but it is at least clear that the apostles are seated in very real stalls. The most important characteristics of the painting are in the figures of the apostles and their clothes. These are real, substantial men. Their figures have a rounded, powerful outline. Their togas hang from them not in simple lines but in realistic folds depicted in gradual shading with a very good use of light.

Boniface VIII, the last of the great papal patrons acquired an evil reputation for encouraging the making of sculptured portraits of himself. There are examples at Bologna, Florence, and Orvieto, paid for by communes which were grateful for the pope's political support and evidently aware that it was a kind of recognition which he valued.[11] They are portraits, but whether they signify the pope's devotion to his own grandeur or that of his office is doubtful. Unlike Nicholas III, whom he resembles in some respects, Boniface was not a great builder, but he was devoted to the enrichment of Roman churches and to the artistic glorification of the papacy within that setting. At St John Lateran he added a block of buildings with a loggia attached to it within which was painted a very grand fresco series celebrating the indulgence of 1300.[12] There were originally three frescoes depicting the *Baptism of Constantine*, the *Founding of the Lateran*, and *Boniface Blessing the People* from the loggia. The object was clearly to emphasize the connection of the papacy of 1300 with Constantine's grant of power by the Donation of Constantine to the pope's remote predecessor Sylvester, a cornerstone in Boniface's imperialist claims for the papacy. The prominence of the Caetani arms in the fresco also brought Boniface's family into prominence. The frescos relating to Constantine and the Lateran are totally lost. The form of the painting of Boniface's benediction can be seen in a seventeenth-century copy that shows him on the balcony of the loggia, under an imperial canopy, flanked by clerics and soldiers, with a crowd receiving his benediction below. A central fragment of the original, consisting of the pope and his two assistants (Pl. 6), survives in the Lateran church. It is painting of high quality with similarities to the painting in the St Francis cycle in the upper church at Assisi. It may or may not be by Giotto; at any rate it is one of the many links between painting at Assisi and Rome, and a relic of Boniface's discriminating patronage.

The pontificate of Boniface VIII may also have seen the erection in Rome of Giotto's *Navicella*, paid for not by the pope but by Cardinal Jacopo Caetani Stefaneschi.[13] This huge mosaic, probably about fifty feet broad and thirty feet high, was placed on a wall overlooking the atrium before St Peter's. It showed the Apostles' boat troubled by storm, with Christ walking on the water and rescuing St Peter from drowning. It was destroyed in the late Renaissance and is known only from copies. It was clearly, however, an extremely ambitious picture of ship and storm, with a marvellous presentation of natural and personal drama. Two heads of angels from the border—

[11] G. B. Ladner, *Die Papstbildnisse des Altertums und des Mittelalters* (Monumenti di Antichità Cristiana pubblicati dal Pontificio Istituto di Archeologia Cristiana, II Serie, iv), ii (Città del Vaticano, 1970), pp. 296–302, 322–36; J. Gardner, 'Boniface VIII as a patron of sculpture', *Roma Anno 1300*.

[12] C. Mitchell, 'The Lateran Fresco of Boniface VIII', *Journal of the Warburg and Courtauld Institutes*, xiv, 1951.

[13] W. Paeseler, 'Giotto's Navicella und ihr spätantikes vorbild', *Römisches Jahrbuch für Kunstgeschichte*, v, 1941.

all that survives of the original work—suggest that Giotto had taken great pains to copy the impressionistic style of faces in antique mosaics, abandoning the harder use of lines common in medieval work before him. Until it was destroyed the *Navicella* must have been the most prominent mosaic or painting to be seen anywhere in Rome. It is ironical that this work, in an ancient medium that had little future in serious art, may have served as an important stage in the evolution of Giotto's advanced style in fresco painting.

The series of papal artistic enterprises in Rome came to an abrupt end with the departure of the papal court to France in 1305. The period 1277–1305 in Rome is an exceptionally distinct episode in the history of art. Its importance is difficult to exaggerate because it provided painters inside and outside Rome with the original impulse to take up seriously the lessons of classical painting, and thus grafted a sophisticated naturalism on to the style of Italian religious art. Artists for the first time saw and benefited from the spatial and personal realism of classical art which had always been there for them to see. Why did they begin to take it seriously at this particular time? We can only guess. The consequences of thirteenth-century Roman painting are much clearer than its causes. We have no knowledge of the intentions of artists or the wishes of their patrons. The burst of patronage by Nicholas III was clearly important. Did his consciousness of the greatness of the Roman past and his wish to revive his own city lead him to encourage his craftsmen to revive its ancient artistic style? It is difficult to decide whether to attribute more importance to this ideological cause or to the more aesthetic experience of a group of well-paid and highly trained artists working in Rome and confronted by the relics of an art which inspired them, and which they were better able to imitate than their predecessors had been. Whichever kind of interpretation we adopt, the fact remains that it was Rome that provided the artists with the lesson that they should take nature (as opposed to religion and decoration) seriously, and launched them suddenly on a new career of artistic effort.

Long before the pontificate of Nicholas III, a striking adaptation of ancient art to modern needs had been made by an artist apparently unconnected with Rome, Nicola Pisano.[14] At the time of his greatest achievements Nicola worked mainly within the Ghibelline political world, which was hostile to the

---

[14] Account referring to earlier literature by J. W. Pope-Hennessy, *Italian Gothic Sculpture*, 2nd edn (London, 1972), pp. 169–80; A. Kosegarten, 'Die Skulpturen der Pisani am Baptisterium von Pisa: Zum Werk von Nicola und Giovanni Pisano', *Jahrbuch der Berliner Museen*, x, 1968; idem, 'Nicola und Giovanni Pisano 1268–1278', ibid., xi, 1969; M. Seidel, 'Die Verkundigungsgruppe der Sieneser Domkanzel', *Münchner Jahrbuch der Bildenden Kunst*, xxi, 1970; idem, 'Studien zur Antikenrezeption Nicola Pisanos', *Mitteilungen des Kunsthistorischen Instituts in Florenz*, xix, 1975; E. M. Angiola, 'Nicola Pisano, Federigo Visconti and the Classical Style in Pisa', *Art Bulletin*, lix, 1977; M. Seidel, 'Una nuova opera di Nicola Pisano', *Paragone*, 1978; A. Middeldorf-Kosegarten, 'Identifizierung eines Grabmals von Nicola Pisano', *Mitteilungen des Kunsthistorischen Instituts in Florenz*, xxii, 1978. Documents in G. N. Fasola, *Nicola Pisano* (Rome, 1941).

papacy. Though there is no reason to suppose that political division presented an impossible barrier to the movement of artists, it is interesting that rival papal and imperial allegiances might both provide incentives to turn to the Roman past which could have aesthetic results leading in the same general direction. Pisa, where Nicola worked around 1259 and later, was the most firmly Ghibelline of the Tuscan cities. It also had a strong sense of its own Roman ancestry, and far more sculptural survivals from the Roman period that artists could use as patterns than, for example, Florence or Siena had. Nicola may have worked in Frederick II's kingdom of Naples before he came north, but Pisa provided him with a fund of antique examples and an encouragement to use them. He completed the pulpit in the Baptistery at Pisa in 1259. Between 1265 and 1268 he constructed a larger pulpit for Siena cathedral. About 1264–7 his workshop was busy with the Arca di San Domenico in San Domenico, Bologna. In the late 1270s he worked on the Fontana Maggiore in the piazza at Perugia. At a period which is more difficult to define and may have been long, he worked on the now badly weathered sculpture for the exterior of the Pisa baptistery. By 1284 he was no longer alive. These works were all completed with the help of assistants, including his still greater son Giovanni and the Florentine sculptor Arnolfo di Cambio. The evidence of dramatic developments of style, which may reflect Nicola's taste or the effects of local ideology and his assistants' skill, is clear in the Pisa and Siena pulpits.

Like other Italian artists of this period, it is conceivable that Nicola may have visited Northern Europe and that he was inspired by the sculpture of Reims, but there is no conclusive evidence for it. The remarkable feature of Nicola's work was the use of figures copied from classical sculpture, which had a completely pagan significance, within new sculptures illustrating Christian stories and virtues for ecclesiastical settings. This encouraged him towards the evolution of more realistic figure designs and the more elaborate use of space in reliefs—innovations which had important artistic results. Nicola's adaptation of classical figures is clearest in the pulpit he made in Pisa, a city that had plenty of ancient sculpture to provide models and a long tradition of copying it. At Pisa there was nothing original about copying classical sculptures. Nicola's innovation was not the imitation of the antique but the fidelity of the imitation allowed by his sculptural skill and the ingenuity with which he constructed a new ecclesiastical style partly inspired by artistic lessons to be learnt from the Roman models.

The pulpit at Pisa is hexagonal. It rests on seven columns—six at the corners, one in the middle—some standing on animals representing the lower world. Above the capitals and in the spandrels above the vaults are figures representing prophets and evangelists and the virtues of Charity, Fortitude, Temperance, Prudence and Faith. Above these the pulpit proper is made up of five oblong reliefs showing the *Annunciation* and *Nativity*, the *Adoration of* the *Magi*, the *Presentation in the Temple*, the *Crucifixion* and the *Last Judgement*. The figures in the pulpit can in some cases be connected quite clearly with classical originals. At the right of the *Presentation* relief (Pl. 7) is an old, bearded man in heavy robes, staring at the Christ-child and supported by a boy behind him. This figure is copied from a relief on a neo-Attic krater which stood in a prominent place near the cathedral, and was popularly thought to have been presented to Pisa by a Roman emperor. The use of the figure as a suitable component of the scene was probably inspired by the phrase in the liturgy for the Presentation relating to Simeon: '*Senex puerum portabat puer autem senem regebat*' (The old man carried the boy [Jesus] but the boy ruled the old man).[15] Several of the faces in the *Presentation* relief, with emotions strongly marked by the muscular outlines of cheek and brow, were copied directly from faces in the Hippolytus sarcophagus, another ancient sculpture beloved of the Pisans, which was built into the outside of the cathedral.

Nicola's most famous classical borrowing is the male nude *Fortitude* (Pl. 8), standing in a swaggering posture above a capital with a lion cub on his right shoulder and another held down by his left hand, sometimes hailed as the first nude in Renaissance art. No direct model for this figure is known but it was undoubtedly copied from a classical Hercules. As the case of the patriarch in the *Presentation* relief shows, Nicola's borrowing might be inspired by a relationship between visual appearance and Christian texts, which would be difficult to track down. It would be assisted by the foreshortened and conflated view of the classical and Christian pasts, which was normal in the thirteenth century, expressed most sharply in ideas like Virgil's prophesy of the Coming of Christ, or at Pisa by the connection of the village of San Piero a Grado with the travels of St Peter. Historical confusion made the indifferent use of Christian and classical models easier. But, though the intellectual background might be confused, the aesthetic result of borrowing by a sculptor as skilled and imaginative as Nicola, was an enrichment of artistic reality. The figures on the Pisa pulpit, heavy as their forms are to the modern eye, exhibit a new capacity for rounded, deeply cut human forms, and an elaborate use of drapery folds. The reliefs also begin to show the possibilities of having a realistic background level of figures set behind the main participants in the foreground.

A consideration of Nicola's late style should take into account the Arca di San Domenico, and also the busts and heads for the upper level of the exterior of the Pisa baptistery. The former probably owes much to his pupil Arnolfo di Cambio. The latter are so badly worn that they do not display very well their original characteristics. The Siena pulpit of 1265–8, on the other hand, is largely intact since it has been preserved indoors; and though it is not entirely

---

[15] Seidel, 'Studien zur Antiken rezeption'.

the work of Nicola it was probably controlled by him, and shows marvellously an extension of the potentialities revealed at Pisa.

The Siena pulpit (Pl. 9) is bigger and more ambitious than the Pisan pulpit, although the general design is similar. It is octagonal, resting on eight outside columns and one central column, which has a group of figures representing the liberal arts around its base. Standing or sitting on the capitals are again figures of the virtues. The most important changes from the design at Pisa are that there are seven larger and more populated reliefs of the life of Christ, and that these are separated not by plain columns but by figures of the Annunciate Virgin, the writers of the Epistles, the Virgin and Child, Angels, the Christ of the Apocalypse, symbols of the Evangelists and Christ in Judgement dividing the Saved and the Damned in the reliefs on either side of him.

The sides of the pulpit are thus peopled with more than a hundred faces and bodies, a tremendously ambitious display of the population of the terrestrial and heavenly worlds. Only a close examination of the figures can show the extent of individualization and vigour in the extremely expressive bodies and faces. The advance in this respect beyond the style of the Pisa pulpit is remarkable. For example, both the *Crucifixion* reliefs have a centurion pointing up to Christ and there are some similarities between them in face and clothing. But while the Pisa centurion is a fairly stiff man, leaning slightly back with some awe expressed in his face, the Siena centurion (Pl. 10) is a terrified man, crouching, shoulders bent, clutching his robe, with a facial expression of anguished alarm.[16] At the other extreme of emotion, the faces of the Apocalyptic Christ and the Christ in Judgement are marvellously serene. The treatment of partially nude figures is sensitively realistic. Drapery is used elaborately to emphasize the forms of bodies imagined behind it. The limited individuality of the Pisa figures, derived at least in part from ancient relief carving, has been developed into a multitude of people expressing strong emotions realistically by the muscles of their faces and often by the intense curvature of their bodies. It is difficult to know to what influences we can attribute this sudden appearance of the crowd, the broad and detailed spectrum of human types and emotions. We should probably imagine a degree of competition between the workers on the pulpit, taking off from Nicola's earlier breakthrough at Pisa, and no doubt the influence of the crowd in the city streets. Sculpture changed in the hands of Nicola and his son Giovanni more precociously than painting in the development of facial individuality and bodily movement, and what painting achieved in these lines was due in part to imitation of sculpture. The pulpit relief apparently offered a field in which the recognition of human mobility was more easily accomplished than in other forms of art.

Nicola Pisano's son Giovanni is visible over a much longer period than his

---

[16] Seidel, 'Una nuova opera'.

father, from his early work on the Siena pulpit in 1265–8 to his monument for Margaret of Luxemburg at Genoa about 1313, and he has been described as the earliest visual artist whose development can be surveyed from youth to old age.[17] Between the Siena pulpit and the work at Genoa, the important commissions for which we have some evidence of time are the work on the facade of Siena cathedral (*circa* 1284–95), work on the outside of the Pisa baptistery, probably also in the 1280s and 1290s, the pulpit at Sant'Andrea, Pistoia, completed in 1301, and the pulpit in the cathedral at Pisa (*circa* 1302–10).

Giovanni shows very much more evidence than his father of French Gothic influence on his style. Whether the inscription on the Pisa pulpit—'Giovanni has encircled all the rivers and parts of the world endeavouring to learn much . . .'—actually refers to real travels is impossible to say, but the visible influence of French Gothic in his work is undoubted. We see it, for example, in the swing of the body and drapery in the small ivory *Madonna and Child* at Pisa cathedral, in the postures of the seated sibyls on the Pistoia pulpit, in the postures and facial types of his stone madonnas, seated and upright. Apart from the possibility of travel in France we must take account of the influence of workers at Siena cathedral who had been in France, and of objects brought from France to Italy. The ivory *Madonna and Child* (Pl. 11) is the most obviously direct echo of French Gothic in the Tuscan art of this age. The pushing forward of the Madonna's hips and the hanging of the drapery give it a clearly French appearance, which is probably dependent on the copying of some similar small, imported sculpture. Giovanni starts from the classicism of his father but he then develops in a quite different way from the other known pupil of Nicola, Arnolfo di Cambio, who was much more interested in the imitation of the antique. In the first place, Giovanni has a capacity for the expression of the strongest emotions in the faces of his figures. These range from the blissfully calm female faces of the standing sibyl from the facade of Siena cathedral or Margaret of Luxemburg at Genoa to the tortured endurance of the faces of Christ in the wooden crucifixions at S. Nicola, Pisa, and Sant'Andrea, Pistoia. Giovanni's people have at times a more delicate and complex realism in the faces than any other artist at the time could produce. Second, Giovanni has an interest in the complex twisting of the human figure, which derives from the North rather than the Mediterranean, and in the creation of patterns of bodies using this convolution. The result of the

[17] H. Keller, *Giovanni Pisano* (Vienna, 1942); early literature reported by Pope-Hennessy, *Italian Gothic Sculpture*, pp. 175–80. Modern works include M. Ayrton, *Giovanni Pisano Sculptor* (London, 1969); G. L. Mellini, *Giovanni Pisano* (Milan, 1970); A. Kosegarten, 'Skulpturen der Pisani'; A. Middeldorf-Kosegarten, 'Nicola und Giovanni Pisano'; M. Seidel, 'Die Rankensaulen der Sieneser Domfassade', *Jahrbuch der Berliner Museen*, xi, 1969; idem., 'Die Elfenbeinmadonna im Domschatz zu Pisa', *Mitteilungen des Kunsthistorischen Instituts in Florenz*, xvi, 1972; idem, ' "Opus heburneum", Die Entdeckung einer Elfenbeinskulptur von Giovanni Pisano', *Pantheon*, xlii, 1984.

combination of realism and twisting is most fully seen in reliefs which have a number of interrelated people rather than in individual figures, and in the work which Giovanni did in this form around 1300 he reaches a complexity of realistic emotion and movement which is reminiscent of the baroque. No other artist of the period achieves such an apparent pointing forward to the distant future.

The figures removed from the facade of the cathedral of Siena and placed in the cathedral museum (the top section of one of them, *Haggai* (Pl. 15), is in the Victoria and Albert Museum, London) now have a rather grotesque appearance due to bad weathering and to their necks, which extend forward so that the faces could be seen from the ground far below and so that the figures would appear to be communicating with one another. They were intended to be a collection of forerunners and prophets of the Virgin, the protectress of Siena; *Plato* and *Aristotle*; the rest from the Old Testament. The faces are marked by an intense expressiveness, strong, masculine emotions, for example, still visible in the faces of *Haggai* and *Isaiah*, which are in part imitated from ancient sculpture and must have determined the dramatic force of much Italian cathedral sculpture of the future, while the female faces of the *Sibyl* and the *Mary of Moses* have a more relaxed strength.

This sculptural skill was expressed in a more complicated fashion much later in the Pistoia pulpit, which, although it has been rearranged, is one of the best-preserved works of art of this age: the fresh detail of sculpture can still be enjoyed fully. It is hexagonal, with the same general shape as the Pisa and Siena pulpits; and though it is much smaller than the Siena example, Giovanni has also put figures between the reliefs. The most striking parts of the pulpit are the six figures of sibyls above the columns and the reliefs themselves. Take, for example, the *Seated Sibyl* (Pl. 13) in a natural but alert pose with crossed hands, voluminous drapery revealing the figure, looking slightly to the right with an expression of enigmatic charm; behind her an angel with outstretched hand touches her right shoulder, to her left a bearded prophet, leaning out of the spandrel, looks at her, while a parchment roll streams out of his left hand. These delightful exaggerations of the natural anticipate the figures in the Sistine Chapel. Or take the pattern of the first relief (Pl. 14). In the centre Mary reclines, stretching out a hand to reveal Jesus in his manger, creating an oval centre of the relief. To the top left the Annunciate Mary holds back her cloak in alarm as the angel with flying hair appears to her. At the bottom on the left the child is being washed. At the top right the Nativity is being announced by angels in a long swathe over the cattle in the Nativity scene to shepherds pressed into the right side. These figures are arranged in a complex, related series of flowing patterns which provides a striking example of the power to maximize the aesthetic pleasure given by the manipulation of the human body moving naturally.

The pulpit in the cathedral at Pisa is a much grander affair, no doubt a Pisan

1. *Martyrdom of St Paul.* Fresco, Sancta sanctorum, Rome.

2. *Appearance of Serpents before Pharaoh.* (Vatican Library, Barb. Lat. 4406, fol. 53, seventeenth-century copy of fresco, San Paolo fuori le mura, Rome).

3. *John the Patrician Visiting Pope Liberius.* Mosaic, Santa
Maria Maggiore, Rome.

4. Pietro Cavallini, *Annunciation.* Mosaic, Santa Maria in Trastevere, Rome.

5. Pietro Cavallini, *Seated Apostles.* Fresco, Santa Cecilia in Trastevere, Rome.

6. Giotto? Fresco fragment, St John Lateran, Rome.

7. Niccola Pisano, *Presentation*, Pisa baptistery pulpit.

8. Niccola Pisano, *Fortitude*, Pisa
baptistery pulpit.

9. Niccola Pisano, Siena cathedral pulpit.

10. Niccola Pisano, *Crucifixion*, Siena cathedral pulpit.

12. Arnolfo di Cambio, *Madonna and Child*,
Museo dell'Opera del Duomo, Florence.

11. Giovanni Pisano, ivory *Madonna and Child*,
Pisa cathedral treasury.

13. Giovanni Pisano, *Seated Sibyl*, Sant'Andrea, Pistoia pulpit.

14. Giovanni Pisano, *Nativity*, Sant'Andrea, Pistoia pulpit.

15. Giovanni Pisano, *Haggai*, Victoria and Albert
Museum, London.

16. Arnolfo di Cambio, 'Thirsty Woman' from Perugia Fountain, Galleria Nazionale
dell'Umbria, Perugia.

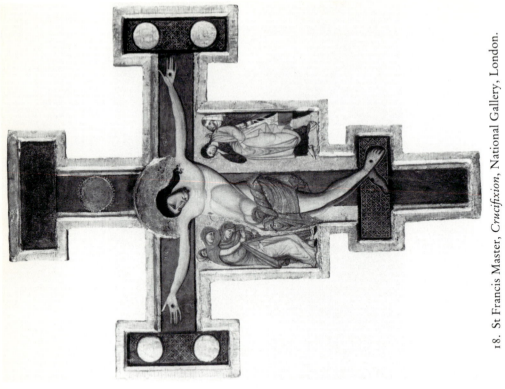

18. St Francis Master, *Crucifixion*, National Gallery, London.

17. Coppo di Marcovaldo, *Madonna and Child*, Santa Maria dei Servi, Orvieto.

19. Cimabue, *Crucifixion*, San Domenico, Arezzo.

20. Cimabue, *Crucifixion*, San Francesco, Assisi.

22. Duccio, *Rucellai Madonna*, Uffizi, Florence.

21. Duccio, *Crevole Madonna*, Museo dell'Opera del Duomo, Siena.

23. Duccio, Reconstruction of front of *Maestà*.

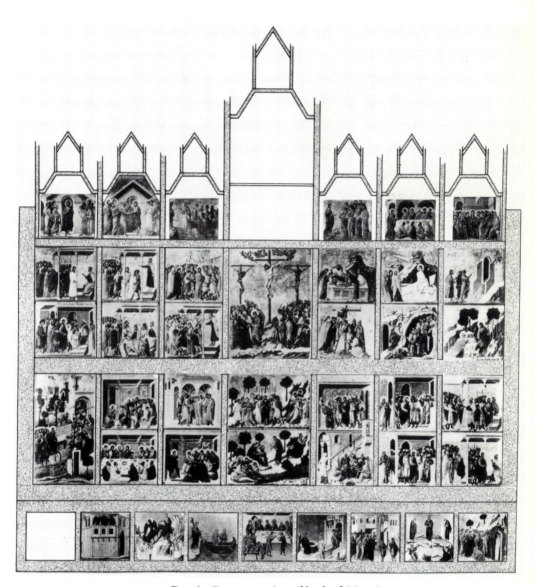

24. Duccio, Reconstruction of back of *Maestà*.

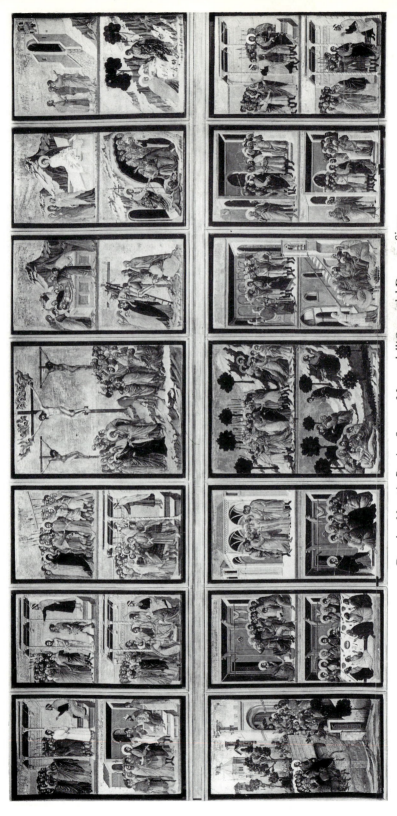

25. Duccio, *Maestà: Passion Scenes*, Museo dell'Opera del Duomo, Siena.

27. Duccio, *Maestà: Crucifixion.*

26. Duccio, *Maestà: Entry into Jerusalem.*

28. Duccio, *Maestà: Three Marys at the Tomb*.

29. Duccio, *Maestà: Jesus Teaching in the Temple*.

31. Giotto, *Ognissanti Madonna*, Uffizi, Florence.

30. Giotto, *Crucifix*, Santa Maria Novella, Florence.

32. *Life of St Francis*, scenes I–VI, north wall, San Francesco, Assisi.

33. *Life of St Francis*, scenes VII–XIII, north wall, San Francesco, Assisi.

34. *Life of St Francis*, scenes XIV–XV, east wall, San Francesco, Assisi.

35. *Life of St Francis*, scenes XVI–XXII, south wall, San Francesco, Assisi.

36. *Life of St Francis*, scenes XXIII–XXVIII, south wall, San Francesco, Assisi.

38. *Isaac and Esau*, San Francesco, Assisi.

37. Bardi and Peruzzi chapels, Santa Croce, Florence.

39. Giotto, east wall, Arena Chapel, Padua.

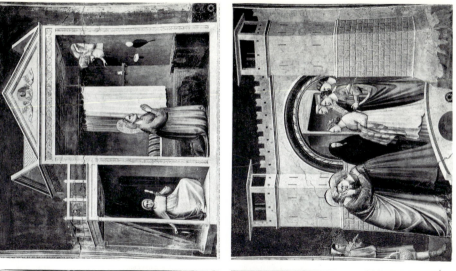

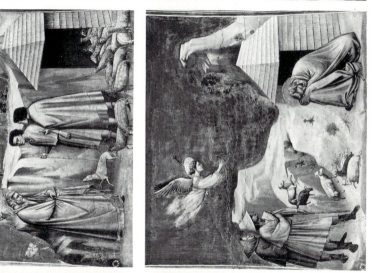

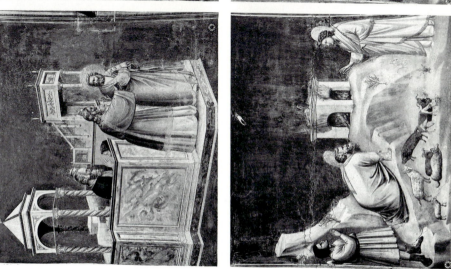

40. Giotto, south wall, top level, Arena Chapel, Padua.

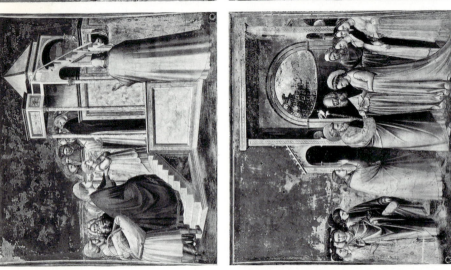

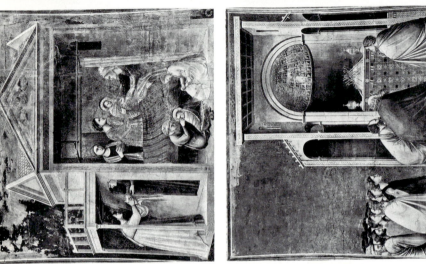

41. Giotto, north wall, top level, Arena Chapel, Padua.

42. Giotto, south wall, second level down, Arena Chapel, Padua.

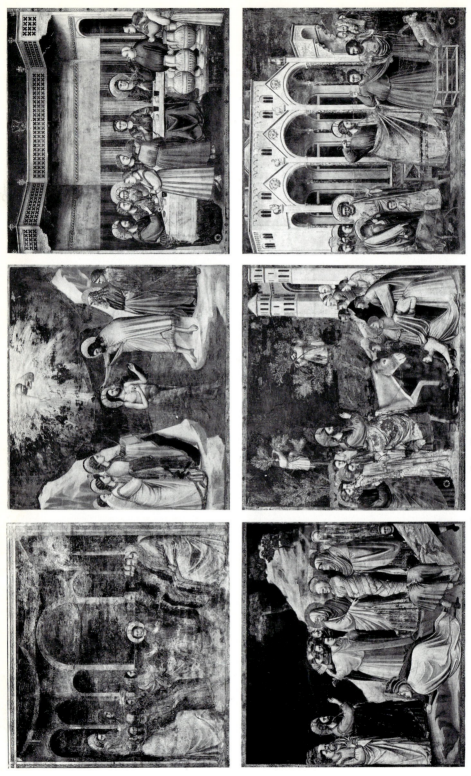

43. Giotto, north wall, second level down, Arena Chapel, Padua.

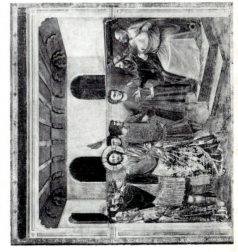

44. Giotto, south wall, third level down, Arena Chapel, Padua.

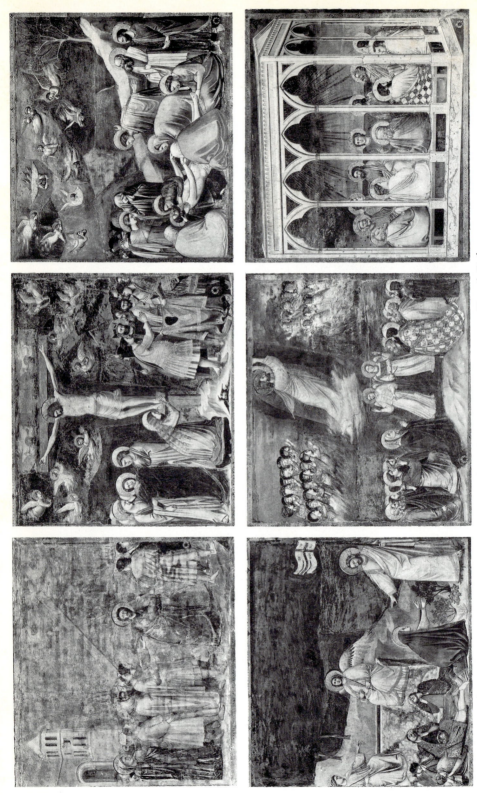

45. Giotto, north wall, third level down, Arena Chapel, Padua.

attempt to surpass the one at Siena, which takes up and elaborates the ideas and innovations of this school of pulpit design. There is an even larger number of figures than at Siena, including a less successful Herculean *Fortitude* (following Nicola's), and an early attempt at a female nude—a Venus Pudica representing *Temperance*, whose beautiful hair and face are spoilt by the awkwardness of her legs. But it cannot be said that the pulpit adds a great deal to the advances which had been made elsewhere. An inscription proclaims that Giovanni 'would not know how to sculpt ugly or base things if he wished to do so'. This praise of Giovanni surpasses that of his father on the Baptistery pulpit, and at Pistoia he had been described as 'son of Nicola, blessed with higher skill . . . endowed with mastery greater than any seen before.' The awareness—or self-awareness—of Nicola and Giovanni as artists endowed with individual skill is the earliest we can document in the Renaissance. There is nothing in the painting world to compare with the comments added by the sculptors to their work. This is not really surprising because the skill of sculptural creation must have seemed more remarkable. Paradoxical though it may appear, we must also accept that the three-dimensional realism which the sculptors acquired so early in stone was one of the sources of the grasp of the outlines of the human body and human drapery which Giotto and Duccio showed at their height.

Out of the world of Sienese sculpture emerged another artist, Arnolfo di Cambio, an extremely productive and wide-ranging sculptor and architect, who as a result of his geographical movements probably did a great deal to connect the centres of patronage at Siena, Rome, and Florence and to convey artistic influences between them.[18] He first appears, as an assistant contracted to work with Nicola Pisano on the Siena pulpit, in documents of 1267 and 1268. It has been thought, for stylistic reasons, that he may also have worked with Nicola on the Arca di San Domenico at Bologna. He then went to Rome. When the commune of Perugia wanted his services in 1277 for the construction of a fountain—which he completed between 1277 and 1281—they asked King Charles to release him. Charles did so, and also granted permission, interestingly, for 'marbles and other stones to be transferred from the City and its district for the same work',[19] which is presumably a direct indication of

---

[18] General accounts by H. Keller, 'Der Bildhauer Arnolfo di Cambio und seine Werkstatt', *Jahrbuch der preussischen Kunstsammlungen*, cv–cvi, 1934–5; A. M. Romanini, *Arnolfo di Cambio e lo 'stil novo' del gotico italiano* (Milan, 1969); M. Salmi, 'Arnolfo di Cambio', *Encyclopaedia of World Art*, i (New York–Toronto–London, 1959). On particular works J. Gardner, 'The Tomb of Cardinal Annibaldi by Arnolfo di Cambio', *Burlington Magazine*, cxiv, 1972; idem, 'Arnolfo di Cambio and Roman tomb design', *Burlington Magazine*, cxv, 1973; M. Seidel, 'Der Marientod des Arnolfo di Cambio', *Forschungen und Berichte, Staatliche Museen zu Berlin*, xv, 1973; F. K. B. Toker, 'Florence Cathedral: The Design Stage', *Art Bulletin*, cx, 1978; A. Reinle, 'Zum Programm des Brunnens von Arnolfo di Cambio in Perugia 1281', *Jahrbuch der Berliner Museen*, xxii, 1980; A. M. Romanini, 'Arnolfo e gli "Arnolfo" apocrifi', *Roma Anno 1300*.

[19] Romanini, Arnolfo di Cambio, p. 50.

the pillaging of ancient monuments to provide material for new ones at a quite considerable distance. At Rome Arnolfo had probably been responsible for the heavy statue of King Charles now in the Palazzo dei Conservatori, and possibly, at an earlier or later stage, for the great bronze statue of St Peter in St Peter's. In the 1270s and after, he and his workshop were responsible for a number of original and important works, incorporating in modern terms both sculpture and architecture, for the papal court and ecclesiastics associated with it. Arnolfo introduced major developments in tombs with horizontal effigies and elaborate canopies to be built into a wall, notably those of Cardinal Riccardo Annibaldi della Molara (d. 1276) in St John Lateran, Cardinal Guillaume de Braye (d. 1282) in San Domenico, Orvieto, and Boniface VIII at St Peter's, made during the early part of his pontificate. He also created the big new tabernacles of San Paolo fuori le Mura, dated 1285, and Santa Cecilia in Trastevere, 1293. These works are more important for the introduction of elaborate Gothic forms into Italian architecture, notably in the large and complex arches and pinnacles of the tabernacles. But of course they involved a considerable quantity of figure sculpture also. Since he was so actively in contact with the Roman world from the 1270s to the 1290s, Arnolfo must have been well informed about the developments in painting going on at the same time.

Arnolfo may have moved to Florence in the 1280s to begin work on the rebuilding of the Badia. He was certainly there from the mid 1290s at work on the rebuilding of the cathedral, which he presided over in its early stages up to his death some time between 1301 and 1310. In April 1300, in one of the rare documents relating to him, a tax exemption, he was described at Florence as a 'famous master more expert in the building of churches than anyone else known in neighbouring parts'. Tradition also credited him with work on the new city walls, begun in 1284, and the rebuilding of Santa Croce. Giotto must have known Arnolfo in the years around 1300, and his combination of skill in classicizing sculpture and Gothic architecture suggests him as a possible influence in the development of figure forms and of the keen interest in architecture characteristic of Giotto. There is no reason to associate him with Assisi, but it is very tempting and may be correct to imagine that he was one of the main sources of classicizing influences from Rome and Siena carried into Giotto's view in the ten or fifteen years before the painting of the Arena chapel.

The most powerful argument for this opinion is to be found in the sculptural fragments remaining from Arnolfo's work on the Perugia fountain and the facade of Florence cathedral. Neither of these works survives as a whole. The fountain, built in 1277–81, was dismantled in the early fourteenth century; the cathedral facade, the lower part of which received its sculptured surface before Arnolfo's death, was dismantled much later. Fragments of the sculpture from the fountain survive in the Galleria Nazionale at Perugia, while fragments from the facade survive in the Museo dell'opera del Duomo at Florence and elsewhere. These are the works which suggest Arnolfo's importance in the development of ideas about the human figure. There are three 'thirsty figures', cunningly designed with their mouths attached to the edge of the fountain. Two of them, a man and a woman, are reclining full-length with their backs to the viewer. They wear simple robes, close to the body, leaving one shoulder bare (Pl. 16). They are very beautiful examples of almost nude figure sculpture. The simple folds of the dresses both reveal the body and are arranged in satisfying curving and circular forms. The iconography of the fountain is not clear; whatever it was, Arnolfo cleverly adapted antique sculpture, perhaps an Etruscan model, to a naturalistic pose rather more freely than Nicola did at Siena.

A later development of Arnolfo's sculptural style, presumably around 1300, can be seen in three well-preserved figures from the cathedral facade, the enthroned *Madonna and Child* (Pl. 12), the standing *Santa Reparata*, and the reclining *Madonna of the Nativity*. These pieces must be roughly contemporaneous with Giovanni Pisano's advanced work on the Pistoia and Pisa pulpits, but Arnolfo has developed quite differently. He shows little interest in the baroque twisting of the figure beloved of Giovanni. He can be, as at Perugia, a rather close imitator of the antique—that is how the *Madonna of the Nativity* strikes one. The enthroned *Madonna* and the *Santa Reparata* have a weighty solidity of form which is different from Giovanni's lither figures. It is characteristic of Arnolfo to use rather uncomplicated drapery without much fantasy. These are human figures which have much in common, in their adaptation of naturalistic classical styles, with the figures in the Arena Chapel. They have the same solid weight and simplicity of clothes. It is quite possible to believe that Giotto developed his figure style partly by looking at Arnolfo's sculptures.

The apparently close connection between the figures of Giotto and those of Arnolfo and between Duccio's and Giovanni's suggests that sculptors invented the human forms which were eventually incorporated into story-painting on a flat surface. Behind this final stage we should imagine a half-century of fairly complex geographical interchange of influences: Nicola's classical models from Pisa followed by the French influence on Giovanni; heavy classical borrowings, probably stimulated by his long Roman period, by Arnolfo, who had already worked with the Pisani. We have no sources which would enable us to 'explain' these developments. We can only assume that the increasing expectations of rich communities, including Florence and Siena, encouraged the development of the sculptor's expertise. It is clear however that the results which we see were dependent on classical models, which were available in some places, notably Pisa and Rome, more than others. Florence was not rich in these remains, and the classicism adopted at the cathedral there must have been largely an importation. The influence of Rome in particular gave rise to a geographically broad community of artists scattered from Rome to Bologna, of which Arnolfo's career is the most striking evidence.

The important paintings which have survived from mid-thirteenth-century Tuscany and Umbria come from a totally different world from the Rome of Nicholas III and Boniface VIII. Not the world of the pontifical court, of learned cardinals and educated officials, not a world dominated by the relics of ancient Rome; this is the home of popular religion, of enthusiastic crowds of worshippers, of penitents intoxicated by the message of Francis and eager for the realities of devotion, not the ceremony of the ageless Roman see. The important paintings are pictures of Christ tortured on the cross, of the serene Madonna and Child and of the legend of Francis. The artists are expert painters and they are sometimes working for rich communities, but they paint objects of devotion for a primitive religion of city crowds interested in the central stories of the Christian faith. These are the schools of painters which were to give birth to the mature works of Giotto and Duccio after the Roman lesson had been learned and after the papacy had left Italy. But we must begin by looking at them briefly in their original primitive condition before they were transformed by the message of classical civilization. No Italian or Christian could of course be totally indifferent to the memory of Rome, and throughout the Middle Ages it had been an important force. But Italian painting in the mid-thirteenth century was rooted in local life in a way which made the demands of popular religion dominant, so that the message of the late antique panels of San Paolo fuori le Mura came from a quite different set of assumptions.

A brief look at some of the works of three of the masters active in Tuscany and Umbria in the mid-thirteenth century will give us a rough idea of the work which was current in the most ambitious centres before the Roman influence flooded in. Only one of these painters is a person to whom real identity can be given by documentary references. Coppo di Marcovaldo was a Florentine conscripted as a standard-bearer for the army which was defeated by the Sienese at Montaperti in 1260; there are also references to him and his son at work on frescos in the cathedral at Pistoia at various dates from 1265 to 1276.[20] Legend has it that he painted the panel of a Madonna and Child, the *Madonna del Bordone* in the Servite church at Siena, while in captivity after Montaperti and it is indeed signed and dated by inscription 1261. This, his most famous painting, is a panel largely filled by the Madonna seated on a wide throne with a back up to shoulder level. She is dressed in very elaborate drapery and bears the Child on her left arm. Behind are two small angels hanging behind the shoulders. The faces of the Virgin and Child were repainted in the fourteenth century, but the general design of the painting is doubtless genuine. It belongs to the class of large panel paintings, which

[20] G. Coor-Achenbach, 'A Visual Basis for the Documents Relating to Coppo di Marcovaldo and his son Salerno', *Art Bulletin*, xxviii, 1946.

became common in later thirteenth-century Tuscany, which aimed to present the Mother of Christ in a pose of regal grandeur indicated especially by her clothes and the representation of the attendant court of angels. There is another, rather less successful painting of the same kind, but less repainted, by Coppo in the Servite church at Orvieto (Pl. 17). Another painting probably by Coppo, of a quite different but equally typical kind, is a *Crucifix* probably painted for a church in San Gimignano and now in the town's museum. The body of Christ is marked firstly by its twisted condition, designed to indicate torture by the symbolism of a grotesquely projecting stomach with patterned muscles and ribs rather than by the most rudimentary attempt to render the hanging position realistically, and second by the simplified, patterned head, which serves to express tragic resignation. The *Crucifix* carries a powerful message, in a sense a powerfully depressing message, which is exaggerated by its considerable size and by the shape of the crucifix on which the body is painted. On either side of the torso of Christ is a series of panels containing episodes from the Passion.

The individuality of his approximate contemporary Guido da Siena is more obscure. The name is known only from a fourteenth-century addition to the *Madonna* in the Palazzo Pubblico at Siena, and has been applied to other works with an apparent stylistic similarity.[21] The large panel in the Palazzo Pubblico, although it bears the date 1221, was probably painted around 1270 for the Dominican church at Siena. It appears to contain novelties which result from new influences in Sienese art: the angels are separated from the Madonna by a cusped arch above her, which comes from the Gothic North—presumably via Nicola's Siena pulpit; the throne is more elaborate and slightly more realistic; the spread of the Madonna's knees gives her outline a broader shape. The crossing of the Child's legs, which provides an interesting linear pattern when taken in conjunction with the arms and hands, gives him a physically awkward shape. Above the main panel is a pediment with figures of the Redeemer and two angels. Guido may also be the painter of the earlier *Madonna del Voto*, made for the high altar after the victory of Montaperti in the 1260s and therefore an extremely important painting in the city devoted to the Virgin. Unfortunately this survives in a cut-down form, making it difficult to envisage its original appearance. Also associated with Guido is a splendid dossal (No. 7 in the Siena pinacoteca) with the Madonna and Child flanked by saints Francis, Peter, John the Evangelist, and the Magdalen, perhaps made for a Franciscan church. If there ever was a single painter Guido da Siena, which is by no means certain, he seems to have been an artist with a great deal of decorative liveliness rather than religious profundity, whose great surviving

[21] J. H. Stubblebine, *Guido da Siena* (Princeton, 1964); H. van Os, *Sienese Altarpieces 1215–1460: Form, Content, Function*, i (Groningen, 1984), pp. 16–30; J. Gardner, 'Guido da Siena 1221 and Tommaso da Modena', *Burlington Magazine*, cxxi, 1979; J. White, *Duccio* (London, 1979), pp. 25–32, 67–8.

works were created for Siena cathedral and for the city's Dominican and Franciscan churches.

Recent research has assigned to the early 1260s the two series of frescos painted on either side of the nave of the lower church of San Francesco at Assisi.[22] They are now in a poor state because the walls of the nave were broken to build side chapels in the fourteenth century, and they are also overshadowed by the more famous *Legend of St Francis* in the upper church. When they were painted, however, these frescos must have constituted an even more spectacular advance in the expression of the Franciscan message than the later paintings in the church above. They were the first presentation of Francis's life on such a large scale, and the bold step was taken of painting two parallel series to emphasize the connection between the life of Francis and the life of Christ. On the right-hand side of the nave the series is *Preparation for Crucifixion, Crucifixion, Deposition, Lamentation, Resurrection*; on the wall opposite we have Francis's *Renunciation of Worldly Goods*, the *Dream of Innocent III*, Francis's *Sermon to the birds*, the *Stigmatization* and the *Death of Francis*. The style of the painter, as far as we can now see it, is distinguished by considerable decorative skill, shown in the handling of the long draperies and the long, bent legs. Many years ago it was connected with the style of a cross in the gallery at Perugia which bears the date 1272, similar in some respects to the cross of Coppo di Marcovaldo at San Gimignano but without pictures of the passion and with a tiny St Francis kneeling at the feet of Christ—a cross in fact for a Franciscan church; and also with a rather unusual panel at the church of Santa Maria degli Angeli, Assisi, showing a very tall Francis in a long straight habit. Out of these paintings the entirely hypothetical Master of St Francis has been created. A well-preserved small crucifix attributed to him is in the National Gallery, London, and exhibits his skill in the decorative use of round, hanging poses of the body and of drapery (Pl. 18). Another, similar in some respects, is in the Louvre. He is also associated with an elaborate double-sided altarpiece which has been dismantled; when reconstructed it can be seen that one side had decorative paintings of the *Deposition* and *Lamentation*, flanked by Isaiah and the Franciscan St Anthony of Padua, the other a row of Francis, Simon with Bartholomew, James, John, Matthew, and Peter—again, a determined attempt from Perugia, near the Franciscan heartland, to push the Franciscan order into the circle of Christ and the Apostles.

[22] J. Cannon, 'Dating the frescoes by the Maestro di S. Francesco at Assisi', *Burlington Magazine*, cxxiv, 1982. On the St Francis Master see also D. Gordon, 'A Perugian provenance for the Franciscan double-sided altar-piece by the Maestro di S. Francesco', *Burlington Magazine*, cxxiv, 1982; B. Kleinschmidt, *Die Wandmalereien der Basilika San Francesco in Assisi* (Berlin, 1930), pp. 17–29; F. Santi, *Galleria nazionale dell'Umbria: dipinti, sculture e oggetti d'arte di età romanica e gotica* (Rome, 1969), pp. 26–31; M. Davies, 'An early Italian Crucifix at the National Gallery', *Burlington Magazine*, cvii, 1965; D. Gordon, 'Un crucifix du Maître de San Francesco', *La Revue du Louvre et des Musées de France*, xxxiv, 1984.

It has been shown that the design of one side of this altarpiece—saints placed under classical arches—was clearly a copy of the carving on a side of an early Christian sarcophagus in the building next door to the church in Perugia for which the altarpiece is now thought to have been made. The sarcophagus was used after it was discovered in 1262 to hold the remains of Giles, one of the companions of Francis, who died about that time. This interesting example of the indiscriminate use of ancient remains and the crude acceptance of ancient patterns by an artist who had comparatively little interest in the aesthetic characteristics of classical art has a parallel in a letter sent from the papal chancery to the Chamberlain of Rome after the death of Innocent V in 1276. He was to buy a container of porphyry 'or some other beautiful stone' to bury the pope in; if he could not find one he should commission a tomb similar to that recently made for the Countess of Arras which was a Gothic monument.[23] We are in a world where the veneration for antiquity is great but the copying of ancient art is accidental. The artists of the mid-thirteenth century were subject to a wide variety of occasional influences ranging from Byzantine to French art. But their achievements were principally determined by the need to supply objects for the veneration of the faithful, powerfully affected by the mendicant movement stemming from Francis. Hence the prominence within their work of the comfortingly serene Madonna and the unbearably tortured Christ on the cross. Within the problems raised by painting these works, the interests of the artists were principally directed towards the creation of effective decorative pattern rather than towards spatial or personal realism. The crucified Christ does not look like a real hanging body but the impression of torture and resignation is accentuated by the rounded patterns of lines in the face and the torso, and it is incorporated in a general artistic design that is both terrifying and aesthetically satisfying.

Central Italy in the later thirteenth century was rich in panel pictures, particularly of the Madonna and Child and the Crucifixion. In this it differed from most societies of medieval Western Europe in which the panel picture played a relatively small part. The explanation for the peculiarity[24] is to be found partly in the luxuriant growth of a mendicant religiosity in which both private contemplation of religious panels and the use of panels to excite the emotions of congregations were important. A manner of religious life in which it could be said that a congregation's weeping was more important than its words[25] had a force which found expression in paintings of great emotional power, perhaps now exhibited most strongly, since the almost total

---

[23] These two episodes are reported by Gordon, 'A Perugian Provenance', p. 75, and Gardner 'The Tomb of Cardinal Annibaldi', p. 141.

[24] Examined by H. Hager, *Die Anfänge des italienischen Altarbildes* (Munich, 1962) and H. Belting, *Das Bild und sein Publikum im Mittelalter* (Berlin, 1981).

[25] A recommendation to the *disciplinati* at Gubbio in the late thirteenth century, 'magis ad lacrimas attendentes quam ad verba' (V. de Bartholomaeis, *Origini della poesia drammatica italiana* (Turin, 1952), p. 278).

destruction of Cimabue's Santa Croce *Crucifixion*, in the similar though smaller work by him in San Domenico, Arezzo. The panel paintings of the mid-thirteenth century were also based on a long evolution of Mediterranean art and they had absorbed substantial features from the Byzantine icon, such as the hanging head of the *Imago Pietatis* in the Crucifixion. But they had not taken over much of Byzantine realism, and the individualistic strength that made them a great artistic movement was based on rather formal patterns.

This native Central Italian tradition and the Roman influence stemming from the patronage of Nicholas III met in the painting of the upper church at Assisi. The painting of this building was an enterprise of a new kind: the walls and vaults of a large and important church were entirely covered with frescos. The work was done by the finest masters and patronized by the pope, and was probably completed within a period of about twenty-five years extending from the late 1270s to the early years of the fourteenth century. The basilica of St Francis was of course a unique church, placed in a small Umbrian town but connected with the whole of Europe by its position in the Franciscan order and with Rome by the papal patronage of the order. The combination of great wealth, the Umbrian Franciscan setting and the link with Rome provided a specially favourable opportunity for the Umbrian–Tuscan and Roman traditions to mix and to produce a new collection of artistic models. The painting of the upper church is almost wholly without documentation: there is no contemporary written evidence for the names of the painters, and the only contemporary writing about the whole enterprise is contained in a small number of papal bulls granting indulgences for the decoration of the church which tell us nothing about the way the work was to be done. The church had been built mainly during the pontificate of Innocent IV (1243–54). The lower church was then decorated. The common modern opinion is that the painting of the upper church was carried out in two campaigns, following the grants of indulgences by Nicholas III in 1279 and Nicholas IV in 1288.[26] This is hypothesis based on the appropriateness of the styles of painting found in the church to the 1280s and 1290s. The assumption is, roughly speaking, that the apse, crossing, and transepts were painted in the 1280s, the nave in the 1290s. The link with the papacy, however, was much stronger than would be suggested merely by the papal grants of indulgences, which were made to many churches. The two popes were both men with a particularly strong connection with the Franciscan order: Nicholas III was Giangaetano Orsini, former cardinal protector of the order and certainly strongly devoted to it; Nicholas IV was Jerome of Ascoli, the first Franciscan pope. Both of them must have had a strong personal interest in Assisi. In addition to this there was the constant role of protection of the order and promotion of Assisi which the papacy had maintained throughout the thirteenth century, symbolized by the

---

[26] H. Belting, *Die Oberkirche von San Francesco in Assisi* (Berlin, 1977) is a valuable general study. Cf. the review by J. Gardner in *Kunstchronik*, xxxii, 1979.

existence of a mid-thirteenth-century papal throne in the church.[27] Attention
has often been drawn to the scene of Roman buildings in the painting of St
Mark above the crossing of the church certainly painted by someone familiar
with Rome, perhaps as an acknowledgement of papal patronage. Still more
important is the evidence of the influence of a Roman style, particularly in the
Old and New Testament sequences along the walls of the nave. Although we
are in total ignorance about the financial arrangements, apart from the papal
grants of indulgences, and about the identity of Roman artists who painted at
Assisi, it is probably right to think of this painting enterprise as one in which
the Roman influence was strong.

The scheme of subjects painted in the upper church is based on the fullest
possible development of the parallelism between Francis and Christ, already
exploited in the lower basilica, the Francis story ending with the saint's ascent
to heaven to parallel the Ascension of Christ.[28] Hence the famous scenes of the
Legend of St Francis along the nave have above them scenes from the Old and
New Testaments. The view of Francis and his order follows that presented by
St Bonaventure in his *Legenda Maior* so that the four Doctors, Ambrose,
Augustine, Gregory, and Jerome, attended by Franciscans in the nave vault
express the wish that the order should be learned, while the emphasis on the
Apocalypse at the east end of the church reflects Bonaventure's connection of
Francis with the Angel of the Sixth Seal, and the expectation that the order had
a part to play in the last days of the world. The east end presents much greater
difficulties of interpretation than the nave. The iconographical scheme should
probably be read partly as a combination of the objects of Francis's particular
devotion. The altars are to St Peter in the right transept, the Virgin at the high
altar, St Michael in the left transept. But it also provides a combination of the
Roman connection, with the martyrdoms of Peter and Paul in the right
transept, and the strong emphasis on the Apocalypse with St Michael, St John
and the angels of the Book of Revelation on the left.[29]

The identity of the painters of the nave is an insoluble puzzle, but it is
generally agreed that most of the east end was done by the Florentine
Cimabue.[30] Practically nothing is known about Cimabue outside the works
which are attributed to him. The documents indicate that he was in Rome in
1272, in Pisa in 1301 and dead in 1302, but give us no other help with the
influences on his early development. If he was, as is commonly believed, the

[27] B. Kleinschmidt, *Die Basilika San Francesco in Assisi* (Berlin, 1915), p. 144.
[28] C. Mitchell, 'The Imagery of the Upper Church at Assisi', *Giotto e il suo tempo* (Rome,
1971), p. 123; P. G. Ruf, *Franziskus und Bonaventura. Die Heilsgeschichtliche Deutung der
Fresken im Langhaus der Oberkirche von San Francesco in Assisi aus der Theologie des heiligen
Bonaventura* (Assisi, 1974).
[29] The relation between the scheme of the east end and the breviary is emphasized by I. Hueck,
'Cimabue und das Bildprogramm der Oberkirche von S. Francesco in Assisi', *Mitteilungen des
Kunsthistorischen Institutes in Florenz*, xxv, 1981.
[30] A. Nicholson, *Cimabue* (Princeton, 1932); E. Battisti, *Cimabue* (Milan, 1963; trans. R. and
C. Enggass, University Park–London, 1967); E. Sindona, *Cimabue* (Milan, 1975).

painter of the *Crucifixion* in S. Domenico, Arezzo (Pl. 19), he must have been trained in the school of Coppo di Marcovaldo and reached a high point of excellence in that style before he absorbed other influences. Two famous later works in Florence, the *Santa Trinità Madonna* and the Santa Croce *Crucifixion*, show that in the late 1280s or 1290s the stylized torso and face that make a profound impression at Arezzo had been superseded by a softer interest in anatomical realism.

The paintings by Cimabue in the east end of San Francesco, Assisi are nearly all ruined by damp and change of colour so that it is not easy to imagine their original appearance. If we look at the most famous, the *Crucifixion* in the left transept (Pl. 20), we find a painting which seems to depend on the drama of a crowded scene, filled with figures which convey a strong sense of solidity and movement, dominated by a Christ who is about one and a half times as large as the human beings below him. The figure on the cross is essentially in the style of the central Italian crucifixions like the one at Arezzo, a twisted symbolic figure. But this Christ has been placed in a tumultuous setting. The air about him is full of angels. Below his feet, apart from the kneeling St Francis, is a crowd of onlookers, many of them with highly individualistic faces, some of them with arms raised pointing towards the Saviour. This is the placing of the Crucifixion within a crowded conflict, a vision of the Crucifixion as an event in history rather than as an isolated expression of human suffering. If we look at the painting merely as a piece of art, the models with which it seems most obviously linked are the sculptured Crucifixions of Nicola Pisano on the pulpits at Pisa and Siena. They too have the enlarged Christ, and the crowds of figures against an unspecified background. Still more strongly they have in common the arrangement of crowds of robe-clad figures with carefully hanging drapery. Cimabue's *Crucifixion* is more powerful than either of these reliefs, but it looks as though he was a painter whose eyes had been opened to the possibilities of the human figure by observing the draped bodies set on the pulpit at Siena in the 1260s rather than someone who had been profoundly influenced by the art of contemporary or ancient Rome, in spite of his documented presence in Rome in 1272. This work impresses the observer as showing the possibilities of artistic development arising from the range of works and ideas available outside Rome.

The dependence of Assisi on Rome is shown most persistently by the decorative bands which run along the Gothic ribs and divide the wall paintings. These involve a great deal of use of peopled acanthus patterns, which are derived ultimately from classical patterns; it is most likely that the models for them would have been found in Rome, though they do exist in a different, sculptured form on the facade of Siena cathedral. Apart from this decorative feature, which exists in the east end as well as the west of the church, the dependence of the painting at Assisi on Rome is very much more obvious in the nave, which was probably painted later, in the 1290s. It is here that the union between the Tuscan style and the new Roman influence takes place.

The paintings on the walls of the nave are arranged in three levels. The two upper levels are stories from the Old and New Testaments. The Old Testament scenes, running from the Creation to Joseph, alternate with the windows on the right wall, starting from the crossing and running down to the entrance wall. The stories from the life of Christ run in the same way along the left wall but the two final scenes, *Ascension* and *Pentecost*, are on the upper level of the entrance wall above two scenes from the Francis legend—the *Miracle of the Spring* and the *Sermon to the Birds*—to emphasize the parallelism of Christ and Francis. Two of the vaults of the nave have decorations which make the same emphasis on the essential involvement of Francis and his order in the life of Christ and his Church: the figures in the *Deesis* are Christ, the Virgin, the Baptist, and Francis, while the four Doctors of the Church have each a Franciscan assistant. The whole of the lowest level of the nave, below the windows, is occupied by twenty-eight large, rectangular scenes from the life of Francis as told by Bonaventure. These are set within a very elaborate illusionistic framing system of painted architecture, made up of classical columns between the panels and a cornice above them. The scenes are arranged in groups of three, each within an architectural bay (with the exception of the scenes at the west end), and to emphasize their relationship the cornice above the panels is painted in perspective centred above each group of three as if they formed a single architectural unit. The ingenious use of the classical framing system for an important purpose, closely related to the subject matter of the painting, within the Gothic church, is very striking.

The hands of the Roman painters Jacopo Torriti and Filippo Rusuti have been seen in the painting of the *Deesis* and elsewhere.[31] Theirs are the only Roman names that can be connected with Assisi. But the influence of painting of the general style of Torriti, Rusuti and Cavallini, arising out of the study of classical and early Christian murals, is strong in the visible fragments of the badly decayed Old and New Testament scenes. Its strongest mark is in the two scenes of the story of the deception of Isaac by Esau, usually attributed to a hypothetical 'Isaac Master'. It is in the work of the 'Isaac Master', whoever he was, whose paintings precede the St Francis cycle below, that we first see characteristics which clearly point forward to the mature style of Giotto at Padua and Florence, and which seem to show the possibility of absorption of the Roman lessons in painting outside Rome.

The painting of the scenes of the *Legend of St Francis* which will be examined in more detail in a later chapter, was limited by the necessity to follow the legend of Bonaventure and to fit the episodes into a detailed pattern

[31] Belting, *Oberkirche*, p. 224; L. Bellosi, 'La decorazione della basilica superiore di Assisi e la pittura romana di fine Duecento', *Roma Anno 1300*.

designed to present a particular view of the significance of Francis and his order, which must have been imposed upon the painters. Within these limitations, the artist or artists followed the practice of embellishing the scenes with the most interesting and attractive technique available to them, advanced spatial realism and architectural inventiveness rather than the less acceptable or appropriate dramatic realism. The result is that the St Francis scenes have less human interest than either the Isaac scenes on the one hand or the frescos at the Arena in Padua on the other. But their wealth of scenic elaboration has given them their permanent attractiveness as the classic pictorial statement of the Francis story. The series appears to have been planned as a whole in order to give the fullest scope to the growing command of space, which had presumably become fashionable within this group of painters and patrons, without upsetting the unity of the meaning of the whole composition.

The St Francis cycle presented in a grand fashion, on a very large scale, a consolidation and advancement of the lessons about realistic space which had been learned at Rome in the short time between the accession of Nicholas III in 1277 and the painting of the nave at Assisi in the 1290s. It brought together the interest in the St Francis legend, which had been developed by native Umbrian and Tuscan painters, and the new technical skill which painters in Rome and sculptors at Siena had based on their study of classical models. The amalgamation of the two kinds of influence produced a powerful combination of religious emotion and artistic realism, a new balance of piety and art. Assisi thus provided the point of take-off for the adventurous advance of Tuscan artists at the beginning of the next century into narrative realism.

The Focus of the Investigation

THE object of this book, to which we can now point forward after the preparation in Part I, is to focus attention on a moment in the history of the Florentine mind: the first decade of the fourteenth century. We cannot be precise about the dating of either Dante's *Inferno* or Giotto's frescos in the Arena chapel at Padua, but the period 1304–10 would almost certainly include both of them. The points of inspiration at which steps towards a suddenly increased realism were taken in both painting and poetry must have been very close—near enough for the moment in time to stand out dramatically at a distance of nearly seven centuries.

In earlier chapters, different aspects of the background to the first decade of the fourteenth century have been followed through separately. By now some impression has been given of the political evolution of Tuscany, the economics and intellectual life of Florence, Tuscan poetry, and the evolution of painting and sculpture at Rome, Siena, and Assisi. These chapters have not been intended as parts of a general history of Tuscany in the late thirteenth century or as separate continuous narratives of painting, poetry and politics but were concerned entirely with events and movements selected from the world of the late thirteenth century which were to bear upon the lives of Dante and Giotto at the time, still in the future, when they would be composing their masterpieces. Our aim has been to identify the long-term forces which seem to have been responsible for a state of mind at a particular time.

What this book aims to achieve—only approximately, of course, because so much that we would like to know is unknown and so much that we know is irrelevant—is a picture of the influences which were important in creating a particular outburst of creativity of a revolutionary kind. In this case we are concerned with the imaginative inventiveness of two men, who may or may not have known each other. Legends of the meeting of Dante and Giotto in exile in Padua are striking and attractive, but lack any definite confirmation.[1] We can, however, as has been seen, present information about the previous history of painting and poetry which helps to explain the artistic advances they made in about 1304–10. As to why they were working in exile with those artistic ambitions, we can provide explanations which depend on the broader

[1] *Enciclopedia dantesca*, iv, pp. 245–6.

political and economic history of the Tuscan cities and Rome. Dante's *Vita nuova* and philosophical *canzoni* and the St Francis cycle at Assisi—works of the 1290s—are essential background to *Inferno* and the Arena chapel which are products of the same intellectual and aesthetic milieu but of a completely new political situation.

In Part II we shall move forward to the political events in the history of the papacy and Rome in the years 1300–05, which led to Dante's permanent exile and to the collapse of papal patronage. This political crisis is comprehensible only in the light of the background of papal and Florentine politics as described in Part I. The political crisis provides the immediate environment of two men who emerged from the Tuscan world of the thirteenth century but created their greatest masterpieces at some distance from their spiritual home. Part II, therefore, will aim to present the 'moment' of artistic creativity towards which the earlier chapters of the book have been moving.

Historical writing of this kind is of course easier if one is explaining a political event such as a rebellion, which takes place within a relatively simple series of social and political circumstances. Here we are concerned with major artistic innovations, which have to be set against the broad background of political, intellectual, and aesthetic movements which contributed to them in a world about which we have very imperfect information. The analysis is limited by many obscure and unresolved problems. It should, however, make some advance towards seeing an artistic development in the environment of the moment in which it was brought to birth.

PART II

The Age of the Papal Withdrawal

7

The Papal Revolution, 1294–1305

THE great and dramatic pontificate of Boniface VIII (1295–1303) led to two developments in the history of the papacy which had profound and immediate effects on the growth of the arts in Italy. The first was the intervention of the pope in the internal politics of Florence. This culminated in the *coup d'état* of Charles of Valois, carried out in November 1301, which was followed by the expulsion of the White Guelfs and the establishment of a Black hegemony in the city, which lasted far into the fourteenth century. The Black regime was not always on good terms with the papal court—in fact, the changed policies of the papacy under Benedict XI in 1304 and Clement V after 1305 produced violent conflict—but it remained the government of Florence and in the long run became again the chief papal ally in Central Italy. Among its opponents who were expelled was Dante Alighieri, whose *Comedy, Convivio,* and *Monarchy* were all written in exile; they could not have taken the form they did take without his permanent banishment. The *coup* of 1301 therefore had a great influence on Italian literary history.

The second series of events, which were far more important for papal history, was the pope's quarrel with the Colonna cardinals and Philip IV of France. The ultimate effect of these conflicts was the election in 1305 of a French pope, Clement V, who stayed in France and immediately transferred the papal court to that country. This involved the removal of the whole apparatus of the patronage of popes and cardinals from Rome and to a large extent from Italy. A great period in the history of architecture, painting, and sculpture in Rome came to an end. The financing of the visual arts in Italy after 1303 was therefore left very largely to patrons in the cities and to the Neapolitan court. The work of Giotto and Duccio and their followers in the Florentine and Sienese schools was largely patronized in this way, and took a course which was probably different from what it would have been if Rome had remained a centre of artistic activity.

These two developments will be described separately. This will involve a division of political history which is unnatural, and would be inappropriate for a historian concerned with either the history of the papacy or the history of Florence. Our concern here, however, is with the history of the Italian mind against the background provided by Florence and the papal court, and in this context it is convenient to separate and isolate the political events which had such dramatic cultural consequences.

When Dante looked back from exile on the catastrophe which expelled him from his native city, he saw it as a result of faction. In *Inferno* vi he meets Ciacco, an unimportant Florentine citizen famous for his gluttony, who begins by speaking of 'your city which is so full of envy that the sack overflows'. Dante, speaking as if the date were Easter 1300, asks him about the future of the 'divided city'. Ciacco replies with a slightly obscure prediction of the Cerchi–Donati riot on 1 May 1300, which was to intensify party divisions in Florence, the consequent expulsion of Black leaders in the summer of 1300, and the later expulsion of the Whites (including Dante) in 1302, with the help of Charles of Valois. In *Inferno* x Dante meets the shade of a great Florentine exile of an earlier generation, Farinata degli Uberti, who foretells Dante's future exile, which will arise from the hatred of other citizens. In *Inferno* xv he meets his old mentor, the humanist Brunetto Latini, who again foretells that he will be a victim of Florentine feuds, adducing the current legend that the population of the city was divided between the good strain descended originally from the Romans and the bad strain descended from the native Fiesolans.

In the political passages about Florence in *Inferno*, the responsibility for the crisis of 1301 is placed squarely on the Florentines themselves and on their disastrous tendency to engage in feud. This explanation is placed against a more general picture of a city affected by factional hatred. The crisis is seen as a repetition of the crisis of the 1260s which led to the expulsion of the Ghibellines. With Brunetto in *Inferno* xv are the decent Florentines, whose conduct had distinguished them from the rest forty years earlier: Guido Guerra, Tegghiaio Aldobrandi, and Jacopo Rusticucci. Among the traitors in *Inferno* xxxii are Carlino de' Pazzi, who betrayed the fortress of Piantravigne held by the Whites in 1302; and Bocca degli Abbati, who had notoriously betrayed the Guelfs at Montaperti in 1260. The two periods are linked personally by the Uberti family, still in exile and prominent in alliance with the Whites forty years after their original departure from the city, and thematically by the prevalence of faction, exile, and treachery. The 'divided city' (*Inf.* vi. 61), the 'city full of envy' (vi. 49), the 'nest of so much malice' (xv. 78), proud of its renown by land and sea, is widely represented also in hell (xxxv. 1–3).

Florentine faction sprang in part from the political disagreements and the quarrels of individuals found in every society; but it was greatly intensified by the tradition of family vendetta, which justified the desire for revenge and prolonged it from generation to generation among the large *consorterie*. This was a peculiarity of Italian society, resulting from the strength of blood relationships and the weakness of political control, which made it fundamentally different from the society of Northern Europe. Although the importance of class divisions was much emphasized by Florentine as by other city chroniclers, it is wrong to base on this characteristic an image of city politics divided by economic interest groups like those found in the bourgeois cities of other times and places. Political division within Florence was primarily a matter of family feud. In *Inferno* xxix Dante meets a second cousin, Geri del Bello, who had been killed many years earlier by a member of the Sacchetti family with whom he had a feud. The feud between the Alighieri and the Sacchetti was ended by a reconciliation only in 1342; it thus probably lasted for about eighty years. In *Inferno* Dante accepts the fact that the shade of Geri made a threatening gesture towards him because he was one of those who had failed to avenge the murder of one of his own kin.

The custom of avenging physical injury by private action, to which the family of the injured or murdered man were in honour bound as a group, was accepted in Florence. The Statute of the *Podestà* of 1325 contained detailed regulations about the management of blood feuds, in particular the important limitation that the revenge was to be exacted only from the perpetrator of the injury himself, but it did not attempt to outlaw the feud entirely.[1] The ramifications of the *consorteria*, the clan of people bearing the same name, were commonly so large that a blood dispute involving directly only two men could indirectly involve a very large number. When a pacification was arranged between the Cavalcanti and Pazzi in 1316 it involved eighty-one of the Cavalcanti and thirty of the Pazzi.[2] An incomplete document of 10 February 1296[3] records an agreement between a number of members of the Cerchi and Adimari families which was probably important for the composition of the Cerchi faction in succeeding years. Communal records tell us that in 1290 the commune had been willing to pay £2,000 for dowries in order to establish a matrimonial peace between the Lamberti and Della Tosa families, who asserted that they would not be able to find the money themselves, in order to prevent the disorder which might have resulted from their conflict.[4] The occasional documents of this kind which survive are indications of the power of wide family connections. The violence between powerful families which was sometimes ended by these agreements is often recorded in chronicles and sometimes in records. For instance an inquisition made probably in 1292 describes an attack by Giacotto Buchi de' Mozzi and a retainer of Vanni de' Mozzi on Betto di Bonaguida de' Bardi in which they threw him to the ground and struck him with lances and swords, making a great bleeding wound in his face.[5]

[1] The feud is examined by Del Lungo, 'Una vendetta in Firenze' and more generally by G. Masi, 'La struttura sociale delle fazioni politiche fiorentine ai tempi di Dante', *Giornale dantesco*, xxxi, 1930, and A. M. Enriquez, 'La vendetta nella vita e nella legislazione fiorentina', *Archivio storico italiano*, xci, 1933. See also J. Larner, *Italy in the Age of Dante* (London, 1980), pp. 123–4 etc.

[2] Enriquez, ibid., p. 127.

[3] Archivio di Stato, Florence, Diplomatico, Strozziane–Uguccioni.

[4] Archivio di Stato, Florence, Provvisioni 2, fos 84v, 87, 131–131v; Davidsohn, *Storia*, 11. ii, p. 488.

[5] Archivio di Stato, Florence, Diplomatico, Adespote Coperte dei Libri.

In the age of Dante, Florence's tradition of vendetta (a tradition shared with other Italians) acquired an enlarged political importance, because a number of the Florentine families which had local reasons for bitter hatred now also had world-wide connections as merchants and financiers which allowed them to call foreign powers into play on their behalf. This feature of the vendetta is of course already visible in the Guelf–Ghibelline disputes of the mid-thirteenth century, when enemies in Florence were able to link their disputes with the quarrels of the pope and the king of Naples. But the expansion of Florentine commerce in the later part of the century led to an extraordinary—and temporary—state of affairs in which some Florentine business firms had so great a world-wide standing that quarrels which originated in Tuscany could be transferred to distant parts of Europe, and occasionally they were so indispensable to the pope or the king of France that they could call substantial papal or French help to their aid in Florence. The custom of vendetta can be found in many societies, but the linking of the family vendetta with the rivalry of firms having a dominant importance in international commerce is a peculiarity of this time and place. It is difficult to think of other cases where vendetta, local political disorder, and international commerce were bound up in this way, and it must be regarded as a product of exceptional circumstances which gave a particular colour to the Florentine scene for a few decades.

One of the feuds surviving within Florence from the Guelf–Ghibelline quarrels of the 1260s was between the Velluti and Manelli families. Nearly thirty years later, in 1295, a gang of Velluti murdered a Manelli in the street near the Ponte Vecchio. The Velluti had to pay a fine of £7,000. They were influential at the time and the priors compelled the Manelli to exchange the kiss of peace with them. About the same time Donato Velluti

began to deal abroad with seigneurs in France and in England and to lend money to them and with Fenci and Duccio di Gherardo Malefici, with whom he was related through his mother, and certain others he began a trade in importing fine horses of high price from Padua into France, paying for them in cash and drawing letters of exchange, and assembled such a sum that he was more than 60,000 florins in credit. He himself had a particularly fine palfrey, one of the best in France, and the Franzesi, who at that time had a great position there, borrowed it from him and sent it back with its tail cut. At this he was so incensed that he killed the boy who had brought it back. He had to flee into a sanctuary and was in danger of his life because the Franzesi complained to the king of France and so did Giano della Bella who was there, wishing to revenge himself on us because Filippo my grandfather had been with Messer Oddo Altoviti and other citizens a leader in having him expelled from Florence. However, he got so much help that he did not die but it cost him 10,000 florins or more to save himself.[6]

This fairly trifling example of the transfer of a Florentine quarrel to France

[6] *La Cronica Domestica di Messer Donato Velluti*, ed. I. Del Lungo and G. Volpi (Florence, 1914), pp. 29–30. Ugo Altoviti is mentioned as a political opponent of Giano in *Cronica di Dino Compagni*, p. 43.

brings home the possibility of a connection between the main course of Florentine politics and the international influence which families could bring to bear on those politics. Giano della Bella was the exiled leader of the anti-magnate movement in Florence in 1293–4. The Franzesi were to be one of the main powers behind the expulsion of the Whites in 1302, and they were able to act effectively because their financial success in France had given them influence with the royal family.

The background to the expulsion of the Whites is explained in part by the Cerchi–Donati feud within Florence, to which we shall return, but also in part by the external influence of two great mercantile companies, the Spini at the papal court and the Franzesi in France, who were able to apply papal and French power to bring about Charles of Valois's entry into Florence in November 1301 and the consequent overthrow of the Cerchi faction.

Boniface's ambitious and expensive Italian policies, which made the Florentine bankers and the political support of Florence so important to him, were directed principally towards two ends: the settlement of the Sicilian question and the extension of the landed possessions of his own family, the Caetani.[7] Since the Sicilian Vespers of 1282, Sicily, in rebellion against the king of Naples, had been Aragonese. In June 1295, Boniface arranged the Treaty of Anagni by which James II of Aragon gave up his claim to Sicily and agreed to marry a daughter of Charles II of Naples. It was also intended that James's nephew Frederick should marry Catherine de Courtenay, heiress to a French claim to the Byzantine empire, and be subsidized by the papacy for an expedition to make good this claim. The treaty seemed at first to have secured a splendid settlement of the Sicilian question in the interests of Naples and the pope. The subsidiary arrangement, however, never took place because Catherine refused the marriage and the Sicilians made Frederick king of Sicily. Boniface spent his pontificate in unsuccessful attempts to procure Frederick's defeat and the restoration of Sicily to Charles II. Expeditions against Frederick were undertaken by Charles II with Boniface's help. James was induced to take part against his nephew and his fleet defeated the Sicilians at Capo Orlando in June 1299; but he then withdrew, and the Neapolitan army was defeated by the Sicilians at Falconaria in December. Boniface then turned for help to France. Charles of Valois, brother of King Philip IV, married Catherine de Courtenay and came into Italy in the summer of 1301. After spending the later part of that year and the early part of 1302 in restoring Florence to the Guelf cause, Charles went on to Sicily. But his troops were devastated by sickness, and in August 1302 he consented to the peace of Caltabellotta which left Sicily to Frederick for life. Boniface's policy, which

---

[7] Digard, *Philippe le Bel*, I, pp. 207–396, II, pp. 1–185; T. S. R. Boase, *Boniface VIII, passim*. Valuable accounts of aspects of the policies in Léonard, *Les Angevins de Naples*, ch. 3, and D. Waley, *The Papal State*, ch. 7.

the pope had generously supported with the church's money, was left finally in ruins.

Meanwhile Boniface had much more success in the extension of Caetani power nearer to Rome. In the earlier years of his pontificate he continued his policy of buying lands to the south of Rome, not far from the original family centre at Anagni. In the summer of 1297, this brought him into conflict with the Colonna cardinals, also landowners in that area. The result was the expulsion of the Colonna from the college of cardinals and a bitter war, lasting until 1299, during which the Colonna were defeated, their family centre at Palestrina razed to the ground, and a considerable amount of land transferred to the Caetani and the Orsini. To the north of Rome, Boniface had hoped to secure some of the inheritance of the Aldobrandeschi family by the marriage of his brother Roffred Gaetani to Margherita degli Aldobrandeschi. This marriage was dissolved in 1298 and from that time Boniface—in alliance with Siena, which was also trying to expand its territory at the expense of the Aldobrandeschi—was at war with the Aldobrandeschi.

The Italian wars consumed vast sums of money, to which must be added the pope's outlay in buying lands and in embellishing St Peter's and the Lateran. Boniface always required the active help of bankers in collecting taxes and in lending money to him. It is impossible to work out any complete figures for his income or expenditure: there are many financial documents,[8] far more than for any earlier pontificate, but they are not nearly complete enough to allow us even to guess at global sums; and for some sources of income, for example the profits of the Indulgence of 1300, we have no figures at all. It is possible, however, to get some impression from papal letters of the extent of borrowing for the wars. It seems probable, on the basis of this evidence, that Boniface was most hard pressed for money in 1299 when he had to pay for the Colonna war and also to support the efforts of Charles II and James II against Sicily. It was as a result of these efforts that Boniface became so dependent on the Florentine Spini bank in 1300.

At an earlier stage, the Spini had been business partners of the Mozzi. At some unknown date (perhaps after 1292, as one historian has suggested)[9] they were divided, and they appear to have been separate throughout the pontificate of Boniface VIII. Boniface normally entrusted the central management of his finances—that is the receipt of money, payments to cardinals, and the payment of the expenses of his household—to three companies: the Floren-

---

[8] They are usefully surveyed by F. Baethgen, 'Quellen und Untersuchungen zur Geschichte der päpstlichen Hof- und Finanzverwaltung unter Bonifaz VIII,' *Quellen und Forschungen aus Italienischen Archiven und Bibliotheken,* xx, 1928–9, reprinted in his *Medievalia* (Stuttgart, 1960). There is also a useful account of Boniface's finances in N. Housley, *Italian Crusades,* chs 6 and 7.

[9] G. Masi, 'I banchieri Fiorentini nella vita politica della città sulla fine del dugento', *Archivio giuridico,* cv, 1931, pp. 72–3.

tine Mozzi and Spini, and the Pistoiese Chiarenti.[10] If we are interested in the political importance of companies, however, we must look not to their regular day-to-day handling of small sums but to their loans. It was the ability to make large advances of cash to meet a critical need in advance of taxation, from which the money was eventually to be recovered, which distinguished the really useful firm and made it indispensable to the pope.

If we look at the evidence for advances of cash, we find the Spini drawing ahead to reach an apparently dominant position by the years 1299 and 1300. In the years 1295 to 1297 the Chiarenti and Franzesi were rather more prominent. The Chiarenti appear to have lent 25,000 marks for Charles II between July 1295 and February 1297, and in February 1297 they were commissioned to pay him the very large sum of 43,000 ounces,[11] equivalent to more than 200,000 florins, though it is not clear whether they paid it. In March 1299 they had paid 32,000 florins to James II.[12] The Franzesi were said in July 1296 to have paid Charles 5,000 ounces (25,000 florins) and 5,300 in January 1297 (perhaps the same sum). In September 1297 they were said to have paid him £1,000 Tours and 30,586 florins.[13] In February 1300 the Spini were said to have paid Charles 76,248 florins and they were ordered to pay him a further 4,000 ounces (20,000 florins). They had also apparently paid him 10,000 ounces (50,000 florins) in June 1299.[14]

The realities behind these entries in papal registers are uncertain. Orders to pay may not have been carried out, statements of payments made are repeated so that it is difficult to distinguish old payments from new ones, and no doubt the records of many loans have disappeared. But the implication of the surviving documents is that the Spini replaced the Chiarenti and Franzesi as the bankers principally responsible for payments for the Sicilian war, so that by the time the period of most extensive military activity in 1299 was over they remained for the time being the pope's largest creditors. A final statement of account made at the beginning of the pontificate of Clement V and covering dealings 'from the time at which you were admitted and received into the service of the said [papal] chamber both when your company and the company of the Mozzi was one and also later when your company was separated from the company of the Mozzi'—unfortunately there is no indication of when that separation took place—states that on 6 May 1300 the papal chamber owed the Spini 57,900 florins. After that date they had paid out further considerable sums, including 84,400 florins to Charles of Valois, but they had also received large sums from the papal tenths imposed in Italy and

[10] Baethgen, *Medievalia*, p. 235.

[11] 'Ounces' (*uncie*) were Neapolitan gold coins equivalent to about five florins. The papal chamber and bankers dealt in a variety of coins from various parts of Europe, including money of Tours in France and English sterling, whose exchange rates are not always known.

[12] *Reg. Boniface VIII*, nos 217, 1691, 2317, 2318, 3001; Housley, *Italian Crusades*, p. 235.

[13] *Reg. Boniface VIII*, nos 5465, 1515, 5477.

[14] *Reg. Boniface VIII*, nos 3469, 3116; Davidsohn, *Forschungen*, iii, p. 70, no. 318.

France so that by October 1306 they were finally in debt to the papacy.[15] In the later part of the pontificate the Bardi, not prominent before in this role, appear to have advanced money: in March 1302 they had paid 6,000 ounces (30,000 florins) to Charles II, and 4,200 ounces (21,000 florins) to Charles of Valois. It seems probable, nevertheless, that the Spini remained Boniface's chief creditors. The important point for the pope's relations with Florence, however, is the strong position of the Spini as creditors of the pope in the spring of 1300, the time at which he must have made the decision to intervene in Florence—presumably partly under their influence.

The Franzesi family—principally the three brothers Musciatto, Albizzo (the *Mouche et Biche* of French documents), and Niccolò—was apparently descended from a knight of Figline in the upper Val d'Arno which perhaps explains their interest in acquiring land at Staggia, just south of Poggibonsi.[16] In the early 1290s they attained an exceptional position as bankers working for the court of Philip IV of France. In 1295 they were collectors of the French tax on Italian merchants and in 1297 they made Philip a very large loan. During the subsequent decline in the French crown's use of Italians as financial agents, they appear to have retained at least personal links with the court.[17] Their links with the papal court were weaker, though not negligible since Boniface borrowed from them in his early years and in February 1297 gave them control of the profits of the Venaissin for five years.[18] In October of the same year, however, 'because of their many enormities and acts displeasing to us which it is not seemly or expedient to enumerate individually in this letter', the pope ordered that money from France which was to have been paid to them should go to the Mozzi, Spini, and Chiarenti.[19] We have no evidence of what these enormities may have been—perhaps involvement in diplomatic business of the King of France displeasing to the pope—but it is clear that their business with the papacy declined fairly sharply after this time.

The Franzesi were bankers from the Florentine *contado* who, although their sister was married to Simone de' Bardi, were probably rather detached from other main Florentine houses because of their close connection with the royal court in actions which were harmful to other Italians—Villani reports the stories that they inspired Philip IV's arrest of Italian merchants in 1291 and his later depreciation of French currency[20]—and also had a bad reputation at the papal court. Their close interest in the Italian policy of the French

[15] *Reg. Clementis V* (Rome, 1885–92), no. 1152. The 84,400 florins is also recorded as paid to Charles of Valois in June 1303 (*Reg. Boniface VIII*, no. 5266).
[16] The most useful accounts of the Franzesi are by Davidsohn, *Storia*, ii, ii, pp. 509–20; iii, pp. 85–90 and F. Bock, 'Musciatto dei Francesi', *Deutsches Archiv*, vi, 1943.
[17] J. R. Strayer, 'Italian Bankers and Philip the Fair', *Explorations in Economic History*, vii, 1969–70.
[18] *Reg. Boniface VIII*, no. 1659.
[19] *Reg. Boniface VIII*, no. 2091.
[20] Villani, vii. cxlvii; viii. lvi.

royal house in 1301 seems to have arisen from their desire to use the money they had made in France to buy themselves an estate in the northern part of the Sienese *contado*, probably because of their origins in a nearby part of the Florentine *contado* and the political sympathy of Siena. In April 1295 they applied for admission as citizens of Siena,[21] which was not granted until 1301. In 1297 and 1298 they acquired from Adolf of Nassau and Albert of Austria imperial rights over land around Poggibonsi, including Staggia;[22] the walls of the castle the Franzesi built at Staggia still exist. In April 1298 they submitted a petition for permission to buy land in the Florentine *contado*, which was granted only by a vote of thirty-one to thirty.[23] On 18 July 1301, when he had come to Tuscany with Charles of Valois, Musciatto's application for citizenship of Siena was granted.[24] In the years around 1300 they were deeply concerned with the transfer of their wealth to Tuscany and this was the reason why they came to Italy with Charles of Valois and supported his rough intrusion into Florence.

These commercial links are essential for the understanding of papal and French policy. To grasp the heart of the Florentine dilemma in 1301, however, we must return to Florence itself and to the Cerchi–Donati feud which split the city in two. The origins of this feud are obscure, but we should probably accept that among them are the enmities of two families living close together in the Sesto San Piero; and the dislike of Corso Donati (an aggressive and quarrelsome man nicknamed 'il barone' who was a central figure in the old Guelf oligarchy) for the much richer but socially inferior members of the Cerchi family who had not been staunch opponents of the anti-magnate movement of Giano della Bella in 1293–5. The dislike had probably been increased by Corso's marriage to a Cerchi who died in circumstances which aroused suspicion of poison, and by his subsequent marriage in 1296 to a rich heiress Tessa di Gaville. The Cerchi, to whom this second bride was also distantly related, opposed the marriage even though it had been permitted by the pope in May 1296. The quarrel appears to have become acute for the first time on a day in December 1296 when many members of great families were gathered at the funeral of a Frescobaldi. An innocent movement of one man excited others to reach for their swords, and the tumult resulted in an attack on the Donati house.[25] In December 1298 a Cerchi–Pazzi scuffle in the countryside led to the imprisonment of four young Cerchi and their subsequent death allegedly by poison.[26] These events led to a

[21] Archivio di Stato, Siena, Consiglio Generale 47, fo. 96v.
[22] Davidsohn, *Storia*, iii, p. 517; I. Moretti and R. Stopani, 'Il Palazzo Fortezza dei Franzesi a Staggia', *Antichità viva*, x, 1971; C. Talei-Franzesi, 'Frazesia Gens', *Miscellanea storica della Valdelsa*, xlvii, 1938–9.
[23] Archivio di Stato, Florence, Provvisioni, 7, fos 210, 212v–215.
[24] Archivio di Stato, Siena, Consiglio Generale, 60, fo. 108.
[25] Davidsohn, *Storia*, iii, pp. 31–43.
[26] Ibid., pp. 90–1.

widespread division of the great families into two factions. With the Cerchi were Adimari, Della Tosa, Mozzi; some of the Bardi, Rossi, and Frescobaldi; many of the Cavalcanti, Scali, and Falconieri; with the Donati—the Spini, Pazzi, Visdomini, Tornaquinci; most of the Bardi, the Buondelmonti, the Gianfigliazzi; and some Della Tosa. Many others less well known were also involved.[27] The reasons for the Spini support of Donati are not clear, but it was evidently their alliance which procured papal intervention in Florence.

A further stage in the intensification of the quarrel was provided when the *podestà* for the first half of 1299, Monfiorito da Coderta, allowed himself to be corrupted by Corso, who was carrying on a legal battle with his mother-in-law for his wife's property. In May 1299 a popular attack on the *podestà* led to his removal from office and the banishment of Corso. This left the Cerchi party fully in control of the government of Florence, where they were to remain until November 1301; and from December 1299 there was a clear majority of Whites in the priorate.[28] When their adversaries spoke in later years of Florence having been 'under the lordship of the Cerchi and their adherents'[29] it was not without foundation. But the exile of Corso drove him into alliance with the papal court. Papal patronage gave him the positions of *podestà* of Orvieto in the second half of 1299, and rector of Massa Trabaria in 1300. This happened to be just the time when the pope was most in need of Spini assistance. We therefore have a period of two years in which Florence was in the hands of the Cerchi, but Corso and the Spini also had their centre of power outside Florence at Rome.

It was probably in 1300 that the parties of the Cerchi and Donati came to be known as 'Whites' and 'Blacks', names which they retained thereafter. The origin of this nomenclature is to be found in the transfer to Florence of the names of factional parties in Pistoia.[30] Factional conflict in Pistoia was even more intense in the thirteenth century than it was in Florence. The division led in 1293 to the first imposition of a *podestà* by Florence, the beginning of the process which was to lead in the next sixty years to the complete absorption of the independent commune within the Florentine *contado*. Further interventions to suppress conflict led to the arrangement made in 1296 by which Florence took over control of Pistoia for a period of five years, to end on 1 July 1301. In 1300 the government of Pistoia was still in Florentine hands, and some of the leaders of the Whites and Blacks had been moved out of harm's way to Florence—the Whites staying with the Cerchi and the Blacks with the

[27] On the division of families, see Davidsohn, *Storia*, iii, pp. 35–6; G. Masi, 'La struttura sociale', pp. 24–6; Raveggi *et al.*, *Ghibellini, Guelfi*, pp. 317–19.

[28] Raveggi *et al.*, ibid., p. 309.

[29] Archivio di Stato, Florence, Provvisioni Protocolli, 2, fo. 66. '. . . tempore quo ciuitas Florentie sub dominio circulorum et adherentium eorum regebatur . . .'

[30] G. Masi, 'Sull'origine dei bianchi e dei neri', *Giornale dantesco*, xxx, 1927; idem, 'Il nome delle fazioni fiorentine de'bianchi e de'neri', *Studi medievali*, iii, 1926–7.

Frescobaldi. The Florentine parties became identified with the Pistoiese, and took over their names.[31]

Boniface was persuaded into direct intervention in Florence by a series of events which took place between March and May 1300. In the later part of March the commune sent a distinguished group of ambassadors to the papal court: Vanni de' Mozzi, Anastasio de' Bardi, Biligiardo Della Tosa, Guelfo de' Cavalcanti, Bindo di Pepo Adimari, and the lawyer Lapo Salterelli. The reasons for which the embassy was sent are unspecified.[32] It was made up of prominent Cerchi supporters, and was presumably intended to stop papal patronage of the Donati interest. It was evidently unsuccessful. On 18 April three Florentines at the papal court, Simone Gherardi degli Spini, the chief Spini representative there, Cambio da Sesto, a lawyer, and Noffo Quintavalle, another merchant, were condemned in Florence.[33] We do not know what they were accused of; we have only the report of Dino Compagni the chronicler, who tells us that they had influence with the pope and enlisted papal aid for some unspecified action against the Cerchi.[34] Boniface replied on 24 April with a letter to the bishop of Florence complaining of the condemnation, demanding cancellation of the sentences on pain of excommunication of the city officials, and summoning the accusers to appear before him within fifteen days.[35] Almost before anything could be done in reply to that, there was a new outburst of violence in the city. On the evening of May Day during a dance in the piazza of Santa Trinita, a Pazzi, an Adimari, a Donati, a Bardi, and a Spini attacked Ricoverino de' Cerchi and cut off his nose.[36] The commune reacted quite strongly. A general *balìa*, special power to deal with an emergency, was granted to the priors on 4 May.[37] In the next few days fines were inflicted, Corso was apparently sentenced to death, and balanced groups of the two parties were sentenced to exile at Castel della Pieve and Sarzana. The Cerchi supporters exiled included Dante's friend and mentor the poet Guido Cavalcanti, who died in August of the fever he caught at Sarzana.[38]

[31] Preface to *Storie pistoresi*, ed. S. A. Barbi, *Rerum Italicarum Scriptores*, xi, part v; Davidsohn, *Storia*, ii. ii, pp. 697–710; iii, pp. 49–52, 181–2; E. Cristiani, 'Cantino Cavalcanti e il consolidamento della parte bianca a Pistoia (novembre 1300–aprile 1301)', *Bullettino storico pistoiese*, ser. iii, iii, 1968.

[32] Archivio di Stato, Florence, Provvisioni Protocolli, 2, fo. 19v, 10 March 1299–1300: 'Infrascriptis sex ambaxiatoribus noviter electis pro comuni Florentie ad summi pontificis curiam ituris pro quibusdam utilibus et arduis negotiis in ipsa curia pro iamdicto comuni procurandis et peragendis.' Advance payment for twenty days. Cf. Davidsohn, *Storia*, iii, p. 138.

[33] *Codice diplomatico dantesco*, ed. R. Piattoli (Florence, 1950), pp. 82–3.

[34] *Cronica di Dino Compagni*, pp. 62–3.

[35] *Reg. Boniface VIII*, no. 3535; G. Levi 'Bonifazio VIII e le sue relazioni col comune di Firenze', *Archivio della Società Romana per Storia Patria*, v, 1882.

[36] Chierico de' Pazzi was fined £5,200 and £2,000 'propter vulnus in facie Richouerini de Circhulis sub anno domini millesimo CCC die Kallendorum Maij'. He was exonerated on 8 February 1303, and in December 1310 a petition by him and his father Giachinotto for repayment of the fines was granted (Archivio di Stato, Florence, Provvisioni, 14, fos 73–4v).

[37] Archivio di Stato, Florence, Provvisioni, 10, fo. 238.

[38] Davidsohn, *Storia*, iii, pp. 144–57.

But the decisive action was valueless. The city remained divided and papal interest grew. On 15 May, Boniface sent another letter to the bishop complaining that his actions had been misrepresented: it was untrue that he wished to diminish Florence's powers of jurisdiction and liberty; on the contrary, he wished to augment them. In particular, Lapo Saltarelli, the lawyer who had been on the embassy to Rome, had claimed publicly that the pope should not interfere in the judgements of the commune. In doing so he neglected the supreme powers of the pontiff: who should act as corrector of Tuscany if not the pope? Did not an earlier pope appoint King Charles of Naples vicar-general of Tuscany during the vacancy of the empire, and was not the empire now vacant since the pope had not recognized the newly elected king of the Romans, Albert of Austria? If the officials of the city and the offenders did not appear to answer a charge of heresy they would be under pain of excommunication.[39] Within a few days Boniface had decided on more direct intervention. On 23 May he appointed a legate to pacify Florence, Mathew of Acquasparta. Acquasparta was a man with immense prestige—cardinal, distinguished theologian, former minister-general of the Franciscans—and also a keen supporter of papal power. He had been papal legate to preach the crusade against the Colonna in Tuscany in 1297, and in January 1300 he had delivered a sermon at the Lateran on a theme dear to Boniface's heart, the superiority of papal to all temporal power. He left Rome for Florence on 26 May.[40]

Acquasparta was in Florence from the beginning of June to the end of September. His legation covered the priorate of Dante, which ran from 15 June to 15 August. In the lost letter written in exile, *Popule mee*, reported by Leonardo Bruni, Dante said that 'all my evils and troubles had their cause and beginning in the unlucky meetings of my priorate'.[41] The task of the priors at that moment was an impossible one. They had to defend the independence of Florence against a pope with whom the city had essentially no quarrel, but who was threatening them with intervention because of the influence of men at the papal court who represented a condemned faction anxious to recover control at all costs. They found themselves pushed into a position of apparent anti-papalism. On 27 June the commune, in response to Acquasparta's request, granted him a limited '*balìa* and the help of the secular arm for the reformation of peace between certain magnates and other magnates and between certain magnates and individual *populares* of the party [of the church] who have wars and enmities' for the length of his stay in the city, as long as he

[39] *Reg. Boniface VIII*, no. 3570; Levi, 'Bonifazio VIII', pp. 455–8.

[40] Davidsohn, *Storia*, iii, pp. 157–9; Archivio Vaticano, Obligationes et Solutiones, I, fo. 12v; Matthaei ab Acquasparta, *Sermones de S. Francisco de S. Antonio et de S. Clara*, ed. G. Gal, Bibliotheca Franciscana Ascetica Medii Aevi, x (Quaracchi, 1962), p. 18.

[41] *Leonardo Bruni Aretino Humanistisch-philosophische Schriften*, ed. H. Baron (Berlin, 1928), p. 54.

did not offend against the Ordinances of Justice.[42] The cardinal however achieved nothing; and perhaps felt very insecure, for an attempt was made by someone 'of not much sense'[43] to fire an arrow at him as he stood at the window of the episcopal palace. This perhaps stimulated a papal letter of 22 July, the most angry yet, which attributed Acquasparta's failure to the 'entries made by bad angels and of the presidents, rectors, friars, and other officials' in a city governed by 'souls hardened and obstinate in evil'. The pope gave his legate power to proceed against the persons and goods of the officials, as well as against the city.[44]

The legate left soon after issuing on 28 September an excommunication of the governors of Florence.[45] On 3 October a provision was issued stating that Florence had always been a staunch supporter of the papacy and of its fight against heretics. Its position had been misrepresented by 'sons of iniquity, supporters of falsity and detractors of the honour and status of their country wishing to sow tares between the holy mother and lady the Roman Church and the devoted sons the citizens of Florence and the commune and people', so that the legate had been given the impression that Florence had laws opposed to ecclesiastical liberty. There were no such laws, but in order to demonstrate the innocence of the commune they were hereby abolished.[46] But the damage was done. For the next twelve months, the city—still under the same government—remained in a curious state of suspense, condemned by the pope although still helping him in his Italian policy.

The quarrel of the city and the pope had little or nothing to do with anti-clericalism or anti-papal feeling. The pope's policy was probably caused by three things. First by the influence of Donati and the Spini, which may have given a false impression of the aims of the existing Florentine government and certainly gave him a worrying suspicion that Florence might cease to support him. Second by his concern at that time with events in southern Tuscany, an area in which Florence's power could be important. One of Boniface's main interests in 1300 was the war he was carrying on in alliance with Siena against the Aldobrandeschi with the aim of acquiring territory both for Siena and for his own Caetani family.[47] The war was to be successful, but in the summer of 1300 that was still unclear. At the beginning of July the pope was extremely worried by a Ghibelline rising at Gubbio, and at the same time things were going badly for the Sienese at Radicofani.[48]

[42] Archivio di Stato, Florence, Provvisioni, 10, fo. 260.
[43] *Cronica di Dino Compagni*, p. 65.
[44] *Reg. Boniface VIII*, no. 3899.
[45] Acquasparta's legation in Davidsohn, *Storia*, iii, pp. 157–86.
[46] Archivio di Stato, Florence, Provvisioni 10, fo. 280–280v.
[47] A. Lisini, 'La Margherita Aldobrandeschi e la dissoluzione della grande contea di S. Fiora e di Sovana', *Bulletino senese di storia patria*, new ser., iii, 1932.
[48] *Acta Aragonensia*, ed. H. Finke (Leipsig–Berlin, 1908–22), i, p. 60; Davidsohn, *Forschungen*, ii, p. 250.

The third cause, which is more obscure, is that the pope may have had plans for the extension of his power over Tuscany. The letter to the Bishop of Florence of 15 May had invoked his claim to exercise a vicariate over Tuscany during the imperial vacancy. That vacancy resulted from the election of Albert of Austria as king of the Romans, which Boniface did not like because in February 1300 Albert had concluded a marriage alliance with the king of France. The danger of the French and German kings acting together in Central Italian affairs was alarming. When Boniface received French and German ambassadors early in 1300 he said, according to the later report of one of the French envoys, Guillaume Nogaret, that he would not recognize the election of Albert unless the latter ceded Tuscany to the papacy.[49] On 13 May, two days before his letter to the bishop of Florence, Boniface wrote to the German electors saying that the Apostolic See, which had once transferred the empire to the Germans, intended to take back the province of Tuscany as part of its imperial inheritance, and was sending an envoy to discuss the matter.[50] Nothing came of these plans, but they had their place in the pope's choleric and intemperate diplomacy and may have affected his attitude to Florence.

There is no mention of the pope's general designs for Tuscany in the Florentine records, but they were probably known to some extent and may have increased the apprehension of the Cerchi, Dante, and their fellow Whites about papal intervention. The evidence of the records, however, is that Florence continued to support the pope and the king of Naples fairly enthusiastically with men and money. On 7 May 1300, Dante himself was at San Gimignano, where he appeared before the council of the commune as an envoy of Florence to present the case for a contribution to the *tallia*.[51] A papal envoy was sent, probably with the same message, later in the month, and San Gimignano eventually decided to take part in the *tallia*. On 18 May the king of Naples sent thanks to Florence for the financial help he was receiving from the commune via the Bardi merchants.[52] On 6 September the council of San Gimignano heard a representative of the king of Naples, asking for money, who came with a letter of recommendation from the commune of Florence.[53] There was no alteration therefore in Florentine foreign policy.

During the next year Boniface was waiting for his new agent, Charles of Valois, to come and carry out his intervention in Florence. Charles and Musciatto de' Franzesi were in Piedmont in July 1301 and reached the papal court at Anagni on 2 September. On the following day he was appointed captain-general of the states of the church and *paciarius*, peacemaker, of

[49] Digard, *Philippe le Bel*, ii, p. 26: 'nisi daret Ecclesiae Tusciam ex integro, intendebat quippe de Tuscia regnum disponere'.

[50] *Monumenta Germaniae Historica, Constitutiones*, IV, i, no. 105. On these issues see Levi, 'Bonifazio VIII', Baethgen 'Der Anspruch'.

[51] *Codice diplomatico dantesco*, pp. 80–1.

[52] Archivio di Stato, Florence, Capitoli 30, fo. 165.

[53] Davidsohn, *Forschungen*, ii, p. 251.

Tuscany. On 5 September Boniface held a public consistory in which he explained his intention of using Charles for the reconquest of Sicily and for making peace between Blacks and Whites in Tuscany, but denied that he intended to establish his government over that province.

When we called him it was our intention to call him for the Sicilian question. This was the principal reason and is still our intention. But since it is winter and he can now bring little fruit and because it is written 'first seek the kingdom of God' we wish him first to restore our sons of Tuscany to peace and to a good state. And so we have placed this burden on him and made him peacemaker of Tuscany so that he shall impose peace between our sons who call themselves blacks and whites. I do not say vicar because I do not want to introduce the vicariate although the false Florentines say that I want to occupy the rights of Tuscany and their rights. Certainly they lie. I do not interfere in the rights of Tuscany but I know their rights well and of what kind they are for they are usurers and live at the pleasure of the church and from commercial deals which they carry on throughout the lands.[54]

Boniface thus expressed his contempt for the Florentines, whose financial support was indispensable to him and whose political support, if not indispensable, had certainly continued to be useful. He confirmed his intention of imposing a peacemaking on Florence which was indeed in line with actions of earlier popes, such as Nicholas III's intervention through Cardinal Latino twenty years earlier. He denied the rumours of his intention to impose his rule on Tuscany, which had been aroused by his letters in May 1300. Charles of Valois then moved north, and in October was waiting in Siena for the right moment for entry into Florence.

Boniface had in fact lifted the interdict on Florence in November of the previous year. The Florentine government continued to behave in a generally friendly fashion to the pope and to his ally the king of Naples while waiting in an atmosphere of increasing tension for the blow which might befall it. The contrast between the insolent assumption of power by an aggressive pope and a strong member of the French royal house, and the timorous impotence of the wealthy city on whom both were financially dependent is extraordinary, though perhaps not very surprising in the context of deep division in the city and of traditional Italian fear of Northern European military power.

In the days before Charles's entry into the city, the Florentines had many discussions and established several committees, but they made no serious attempt at resistance. Dante's famous public statement, against helping the pope in June 1301, was a vain gesture by a bold individual against this policy of submission and compliance. In March of that year the commune had decided to make a grant of 5,000 florins to Charles of Naples in response to a request from the king's envoys.[55] On 17 April it was decided to pay for a hundred horsemen, *milites stipendiarii*, to serve the pope in the Marittima until the end

[54] Finke, *Bonifaz VIII*, p. xxv. The best account of these events is in Davidsohn, *Storia*, iii.
[55] Archivio di Stato, Florence, Provvisioni 10, fo. 310v.

of June.[56] On 19 June the priors put to the councils the question of whether this service should be continued. Knowing that they were making a controversial proposal and hoping to get it through, they linked it with an uncontentious issue about the commune of Colle and presented them together on the same day, first to the Council of One Hundred combined with a general and special council, then to a second meeting of the Council of One Hundred. Votes were cast in a public manner by standing up. At the first meeting Dante was the only opposition speaker recorded, though one other speaker advised postponement. At the second meeting only two speakers are recorded, of whom Dante was the only opposition speaker: 'Dante Alighieri advised that nothing should be done about service to the lord pope'. The proposal was passed by the rather small majorities of forty-nine votes to thirty-two, and forty-one to twenty-six, which shows the general state of hesitation in the city.[57]

Dante's fate as an enemy of the Blacks and the pope, if not already sealed by his priorate, was now finally decided. We should however be careful to avoid the conclusion that his political stand in 1301 was determined by any general opposition to ecclesiastical and papal power such as that inspiring the theories of *Monarchy*, written more than a decade later. The background of political events shows us that the papal–Florentine conflict of this period was caused by the tragic divisions of city faction manipulated by an aggressive pope, trapped by the multifarious difficulties of his own policy, with whom his Florentine enemies wished in fact to remain allied. There is no reason to suppose that Dante's position was anything more than that of an exceptionally determined and outspoken supporter of White policy, operating with the normal assumptions of Guelf diplomacy in a situation in which those assumptions were impossible to maintain.

There is a good, brief description of the entry of Charles of Valois, probably the closest in time to the events which survives, written by a contemporary Florentine on the cover of a book of accounts:

1301, November the first, Wednesday, at the third hour messer Charles entered Florence. With him were Count Guy of Auzerre [*Guillemo il conte d'Alzurro*], messer Musciatto and messer Nicoluccio dei Franzesi, the lord of *Neblans* [?] and messer Henri de Bar [*Ughes de Barret*] and other knights, French, Burgundian and Picard and from Champagne and Nevers. Four days later messer Corso Donati entered through the Porta da Pinti by San Pietro Maggiore and he broke the gate open by force. The Corbizzi did not have the courage to resist and surrendered unconditionally to him. Ranieri de' Pazzi received him and put his flag with his colours on palaces and towers. Gradually burning and robbery started everywhere in the *contado* and lasted four full days so that every man did the damage he wished to friend and foe of property and

[56] *Consigli*, ed. Barbadoro, i, p. 9; Archivio di Stato, Florence, Provvisioni Protocolli 2, fo. 31v.

[57] *Consigli*, p. 14; B. Barbadoro, 'La condanna di Dante e le fazioni politiche del suo tempo', *Studi danteschi*, ii, 1920, pp. 33–42.

person. Then on the fifth day the land was restored a little and the priors were removed and new priors made, messer Andrea da Cerreto for Porta Duomo and Baldo Ridolfi for Oltrarno and Tedice Manovelli gonfaloniere. And in this time all the prisons were broken open and the *podestà* was deposed and Cante Gabrielli da Gubbio was *podestà*.[58]

A great deal more information about the days of upheaval following 1 November is contained in the writings of Dino Compagni and other chroniclers and in the extensive city records, but the picture of a *coup d'état* carried through by the force of Charles's French army, by Musciatto de' Franzesi and by Corso Donati returned from exile is correct. At the end of a week it resulted in the establishment of a new Black priorate. Boniface probably hoped that intervention would bring about a reconciliation of families, marked by marriage between them, like the reconciliation Cardinal Latino had attempted to carry out in 1280. In December he sent Mathew of Acquasparta back to Florence to help with this process. But this was not what actually followed. The intensity of feeling within the city was maintained by another bloody episode: on Christmas eve, Corso Donati's son Simone attacked and killed Niccolò de' Cerchi just outside Florence and was himself killed in the scuffle. In January 1302 legal processes against the White leaders began, and the first banishments to exile were pronounced, including that of Dante. In the course of 1302, 108 men were condemned to fines and 559 to death, which meant in fact exile. They included members of notable families: Cerchi, Della Tosa, Adimari, Gherardini, Della Scala, Malespini.

The Cerchi went through a curious and short-lived reversal of fortune in exile because they were taken up as bankers by Benedict XI, the successor of Boniface VIII, in 1304. The papal intervention in Tuscany appears to have led to a certain number of bankruptcies of great companies: certainly the Ammanati of Pistoia, who fled from the papal court in January 1302,[59] and, possibly connected with these, the Nerli, the Abbati-Baccherelli, and the Ardinghelli in 1302–3. The Mozzi lost their contact with the papal court and began the decline which was to lead to their collapse and the loss of the palace in which they had once entertained popes: commercial success could be extremely fragile if it depended on political goodwill. The Franzesi too lost political influence and financial importance after the death of Boniface. An account of the Florentine Chamber for August and September 1303 gives some indications of the firms which were important in the city as lenders to

[58] Archivio di Stato, Florence, Diplomatico, Adespote Coperte di Libri; printed in *Cronica di Dino Compagni*, p. 271; but Del Lungo did not identify the Frenchmen, for whom see J. Petit, *Charles de Valois* (Paris, 1900), p. 58.

[59] A. Fliniaux, 'La Faillite des Ammanati de Pistoie et le Saint-Siège,' *Revue historique de droit français et etranger*, ser. 4, iii, 1924; A. M. N. Patrone, 'Clemente V, gli Ammanati e l'Abbazia die Montierneuf: Un episodio pittavino del fallimento degli Ammannati', *Studi in onore di Amintore Fanfani*, iii (Milan, 1962). On this and other failures, Davidsohn, *Storia*, iii, pp. 296–304, 429–30, 483–5.

the commune at that time, among whom the pre-eminent appear to have been the Scali, Peruzzi, Spini, Bardi, Mozzi, and Pazzi, though Lapo Cerchi, returned from exile in the summer, was also included.[60] The Spini prominence was also in fact not to last long because the papal patronage on which it depended was to come to an end. The prominence of the Bardi and Peruzzi, however, mainly dependent on trade with Naples and the support of the Neapolitan royal house, was probably relatively strengthened by the difficulties of the papal financiers.

From 1302 the Whites, in exile, were in much the same position as the Ghibellines had been after 1267. Although as yet distinct from the Ghibellines they tended to ally with them against the regime in Florence now dominated by Corso Donati, Rosso della Tosa, and Pazzino de' Pazzi. Their natural places of refuge were the Ghibelline cities of Arezzo and Pisa, and the city of Pistoia now dominated by local Whites like themselves. In the countryside around Florence they made alliances with old Ghibelline exiles like the Uberti, and with great country nobility like the Pazzi of Valdarno and the Ubaldini of the Mugello. In June 1302 Dante was present with other Whites at a meeting at San Godenzo, high up in the Apennines to the north-east. The *contado* was thrown into severe and dangerous upheaval such as Guelf Florence had not known for a long time. The Whites did not in the long run have very much success, but in the early years they looked as though they were a serious threat.

Dangerous but not very successful in their military efforts, the Whites were given a great boost that almost carried them back into Florence: the election of Benedict XI in October 1303. Benedict, a Venetian Dominican, was appalled by the devastation caused by Boniface's pontificate, the disastrous conflict of Black against White, Caetani against Colonna, pope against French king, and was determined to put an end to it. He therefore started a serious peace initiative in Tuscany and appointed a legate, Cardinal Niccolò da Prato, who arrived in Florence in March 1304. In contrast to Boniface's Black fury, Benedict's intervention was perhaps too friendly to the Whites to have a reasonable chance of success, but its main weakness was simply that it lacked the military backing of Charles of Valois or any other substantial force. Niccolò got as far as imposing a theoretical peace and bringing into Florence a group of exiled Whites and Ghibellines to lodge in the Mozzi palace and

---

[60] Archivio di Stato, Florence, Camarlinghi Uscita, 1303; A. Gherardi, 'L'antica camera del comune di Firenze e un quaderno d'uscita 1303 de suoi camarlinghi dell'anno 1303', *Archivio storico italiano*, ser. 4, xvi, 1885, pp. 341–2: repayments of loans, made for payment to Charles of Valois and for the army in the Mugello in accordance with the *provvisione* of 14 December 1302. To Lapo Ghini de' Malpigli for the Amieri, or Amieri-Scali co. 2000 florins; Maso Peruzzi for Peruzzi co. 2000 fl.; Bartolo di Jacopo de' Bardi for Bardi co. 1500 fl.; Gabriello Bertaldi Spini for Spini co. 2000 fl.; Giano di Bencivegna for Mozzi co. 1000 fl.; Manieri de' Pazzi for Pazzi co. 1000 fl.; Dardano di Consiglio for Lapo de' Cerchi 850 fl. This document, oddly neglected by Davidsohn, contains the earliest direct information about the Florentine Chamber. (cf. B. Barbadoro, *Le finanze della Repubblica Fiorentina* (Florence, 1929), p. 326).

negotiate with their enemies. The unheard-of re-entry of famous exiles was too much for some of the Black leaders. They created confusion by setting fire to houses of the Cavalcanti and Sassetti and a substantial part of the city. Niccolò fled. Rosso della Tosa and Geri Spini were summoned to the papal court but the pope died on 7 July 1304, before any further action could be taken.

Benedict's death was closely followed on 20 July by the exiles' most audacious move, an attempt to break into the city by force that misfired completely. The White forces were assembled under Baschiera Della Tosa at La Lastra, three miles to the north of Florence. They should have waited for reinforcements from Pistoia under Tolosato degli Uberti, which would have given them a decisive superiority, but a part of the White force made an unwise attack on the gates too soon and were driven back. This unnecessary failure led to the collapse of the enterprise, and Black Florence was to be safe for some years.

Its most alarming enemy was now White Pistoia. At the end of 1300, when Pistoia was still living under Florentine guardianship established by the agreement of 1296, the White representative there, Cantino Cavalcanti, had imposed a White priorate and expelled the Blacks. This led to alliances between White Pistoia and Ghibellines, and was no doubt one of the reasons why Boniface was so anxious to clear up Tuscany. When Charles of Valois had finished with Florence he moved on to subdue Pistoia, but in this he failed. In 1302 Pistoia, by this time employing as captain of war the Ghibelline Tolosato degli Uberti, was attacked again by Black forces under the command of Musciatto de' Franzesi. This also failed, and for several years Pistoia remained a disturbingly close centre of White and Ghibelline independence which the Florentine Blacks were determined to suppress. In 1304 the Florentines decided, together with their allies in Siena and Lucca, to mount a more ambitious assault by bringing Robert of Calabria, the son of the king of Naples, with Neapolitan troops, to act as captain of the Guelf League. Robert arrived in Florence in the spring on 1305. By the end of that year the siege of Pistoia had been severely tightened and the Blacks were waiting for the collapse which was to take place in the spring.

The end of the spectacular age of Boniface and the beginning of the French papacy with the election of Clement V in June 1305 thus saw Tuscany in a condition which was in some ways reminiscent of the period following the collapse of Hohenstaufen power forty years earlier. Not for many years had the power of Angevin Naples been so deeply involved in Tuscany. Facing an external threat widely distributed through the province, the Blacks, like their ancestors facing the Ghibellines, had decided that they could survive only by invoking Neapolitan help. The conditions were not in fact parallel because Florence had grown immensely in power and wealth and was more able to act as the dominant force in Tuscany and the superior paymaster of princely allies. But the division of Tuscany between hostile cities and hostile factions remained and was to remain for many years.

Historians have sometimes tried to play down the importance of the papacy's shift from Italy to France in 1305 on the ground that before that time popes had spent more of their time outside Rome, at Viterbo and other places, than in it.[61] This is true, but it is a gross misrepresentation of history to deduce from it that the move to France was not important. The election of 1305 involved two changes of enormous significance: first the move away from Italy, and second the transformation of the papal court into a French institution. In 1305 three-quarters of the cardinals were Italian and the papacy was strongly tied to Central Italy, but Clement V's creations at the end of that year immediately made the numbers of Italian and non-Italian cardinals equal. By 1310 the non-Italians were in a majority, and the shift in that direction continued thereafter. The consequences for Italy were very great. There was however a continuity of a quite different kind. In long perspective, the move to France has to be seen as arising from the development of papal connections with ultramontane Europe in the thirteenth century. After the pontificate of Innocent III at the beginning of the century, papal political power in Italy did not develop very greatly. The big change was the growth of the popes' power beyond the Alps. Part of this was financial. The Italian and Mediterranean enterprises of the popes—Clement IV's installation of the Angevins, Gregory X's crusade plans, Martin IV's invasion of Romagna, Boniface VIII's wars against the Colonna and in Sicily—were dependent on the enlarged capacity to tax the French clergy. The popes' influence was assisted by growing administrative and judicial rights, which enabled them to influence the appointment and jurisdiction of bishops. The aggressive exercise of these powers reached a climax when Boniface was met by the resistance of Philip IV of France. The check to Boniface's power which culminated in the French attack on him at Anagni was inextricably involved with the divisions that his war against the Colonna produced within the college of cardinals. These divisions dominated the conclave of 1304–5 and produced the election of a French pope acceptable to the French king.

Boniface claimed in 1302 that as a cardinal, unlike the others from Campagna, he had always been French rather than Roman.[62] There was something in this; while devoted to the private aggrandizement of his own family around Rome, he had been and remained an exponent of the expansion of papal power along the lines followed by the French rather than the Italian

[61] G. Mollat, *Les Papes d'Avignon (1305–1378)* (Paris, 1949), p. 11.

[62] 'Ego semper, quamdiu fui in cardinalatu, fui Gallicus, ita quod frequenter mihi improperatum a fratribus meis Romanis, a quocumque, qui est mortuus et etiam ab alio, qui est iuxta me, quod eram pro Gallicis et contra Romanos. Dicebant enim, quia semper alii cardinales, Campani fuerunt cum Romanis' (P. Dupuy, *Histoire du différend d'entre le Pape Boniface VIII et Philippe le Bel Roy de France* (Paris, 1655), p. 78).

popes. It was this policy pushed too far that brought him into collision with the French king. The first conflict arose in 1296 over the bull *Clericis Laicos* by which Boniface sought to prevent the grant of taxes to kings without papal permission. Philip, who was not sympathetic to Boniface's wish to use James II of Aragon to recover Sicily, reacted by preventing the export of money from France. Boniface had to climb down, especially when there was a danger of Philip supporting the Colonna, allowing the French king to collect clerical tenths and fawning on him by canonizing his grandfather Louis IX in 1297.

While the king's brother, Charles of Valois, was working for the pope in Italy in 1301 another crisis blew up in France resulting from the king's judicial condemnation of the bishop of Pamiers. In spite of his dependence on France it seemed essential to Boniface to reassert the clergy's independence of royal power. He did this forcefully in the bull *Ausculta Fili*, and then again in November 1302 in the bull *Unam Sanctam*, which proclaimed the superiority of papal to royal authority. Against the background of political theory based on canon law developed in the thirteenth century there was nothing new in Boniface's pronouncements. But the policy of the French court was in the hands of lawyers who were extremely hostile to ecclesiastical jurisdiction interfering with the supremacy of the king's courts. The most famous of these was Guillaume Nogaret, a Languedocian from a Cathar background. Nogaret led the band which broke into the pope's bedroom at Anagni in September 1303 in a final demonstration that papal authority had no material power. A month later, Boniface died.[63]

When the College of Cardinals met for the conclave following the death of Benedict XI in June 1304, they were divided sharply by views about the policy of Boniface VIII and the two Colonna cardinals, Peter and Jacopo, whom he had expelled. The head of the Bonifacian party was the old Matteo Rosso Orsini, who had been a cardinal since 1261. There were two relations of Boniface VIII whom he had created cardinals: Francesco Caetani, a great-nephew who had been a cardinal since 1295 and was a large territorial beneficiary of the pontificate, and Leonardo Patrasso; and Luca Fieschi, his former chaplain. There were also two distant relations of Matteo Rosso (Francesco Orsini and Jacopo Stefaneschi), and three devoted supporters of Boniface: Teodorico Ranieri of Orvieto, Peter of Spain, and Gentile da Montefiori, a Franciscan. The opposing party was also led by a member of the Orsini family—the much younger Napoleone Orsini, who had been an opponent of Boniface and was probably motivated by a greater willingness to compromise with France and by sympathy with the Colonna (his sister was married to a Colonna) and with the spiritual religiosity which Boniface scorned. He could count on four cardinals created by Celestine V (Landolfo Brancacci, Guglielmo Longhi, Jean le Moine, and Robert of Pontigny), on John Minio de Murrovale, the former Franciscan minister-general; and

---

[63] Accounts of Boniface's pontificate in Digard, *Philippe le Bel* and Boase, *Boniface VIII*.

Niccolò da Prato the Dominican who had acted as Benedict XI's legate in Tuscany. The division in the college appears to have been based essentially on the passions resulting from Boniface's policies. It was rooted in the Italian experiences of the papal court, and both parties were led by members of Rome's great Orsini family. The conclave was held in the buildings attached to the cathedral in Perugia.

Until the end of 1304 the cardinals appear to have been trying in vain to find a candidate within the college who could win a majority. Thereafter attention turned outside, in particular towards Bertrand de Got, the archbishop of Bordeaux, who had the merits of being known to some of the Bonifacians as a reasonable man (he had been at one time chaplain of Francesco Caetani), and also of being acceptable in France. It is not known what influence may have been exerted by King Charles of Naples who was at Perugia in the spring of 1305, or by a French embassy at about the same time. There is no evidence of French pressure behind Bertrand, though there may have been such pressure. The election must have been made with the advantages of a French candidate in mind, and it seems on the whole likely that there were exchanges between the French court, the cardinals, and Bertrand of which no record has survived. The completion of the work, however, appears to have been the result of Niccolò da Prato detaching three members of the Bonifacian party, including Francesco Caetani, by secretly suggesting three names—one Bertrand's, the other two impossible—with the pretence that he was acting independently of Napoleone Orsini. In this way Bertrand de Got won a majority on 15 June 1305—an election by manœuvres to overcome a paralysing split within the Italian college, but with the eventual consequence of destroying it.[64]

The cardinals certainly did not intend that the papal court should move to France. In the letter in which they announced his election to Clement V they exhorted him to come to Italy, recalling appropriately the examples of the two previous popes who had done so, Clement IV and Gregory X. Only his presence could save the papal state. 'The ship of Peter is shaken by the waves, the fisherman's net is broken, the serenity of peace turns to clouds, the disaster of wars devastates the lands of the Roman church and nearby provinces.' And in Italy his own position would be stronger:

There is no doubt that in the see of Peter you will reside more strongly, you will shine more brightly, in his land you will live with more tranquility and, distant from kings, princes and peoples, your position will be more admirable and you will acquire more fully their devotion and obedience. Everyone is stronger in his own house and calmer in his own church.[65]

---

[64] A good account is given by G. Fornaseri, 'Il conclave perugino del 1304–1305', *Rivista di storia della chiesa in Italia*, x, 1956, which refers to earlier discussions.

[65] J. D. Mansi, *Sacrorum Conciliorum Nova et Amplissima Collectio*, xxv (Venice, 1782), col. 125.

But the new pope did not come to Italy. The cardinals had to go over the Alps to meet him in France. It is impossible to determine what plans Clement originally had or what his wishes were,[66] but the circumstances of his pontificate—in particular the extraordinary pressure of the French king on the papacy, the Council of Vienne and his own sickness—argued strongly in favour of staying in France. The story of the treatment of the papal treasure left in Perugia when the cardinals went to France, only later and after many expensive vicissitudes transferred to Avignon,[67] shows what uncertainty there was about the papacy's eventual home. Whether or not Philip pressed for the election of Clement, whether or not Clement intended to remain in France, the result of the election of 1305 was that the process of absorption of the papacy by the greater power of France, which had been carried forward by the dependence of those earlier French popes, Clement IV and Martin IV, on French money, was completed, and Italy lost the papal court totally. In a remarkable letter written to the king of France in 1314, Napoleone Orsini, the leader of the party which had brought about the election of Clement, expressed his horror at the attempt to convert the church into a 'corner of Gascony' and the abandonment of Italy which had resulted from his work. He had not, he said, spent the eleven months of the conclave 'in prison in Perugia' to bring about the present situation in which 'Rome has fallen into extreme ruin, the see of St Peter is desolate, the patrimony of the church is despoiled by thieves posing as rectors, and the whole of Italy is given over to devastation.' It was not his intention to 'move the see from Rome or to desert the sanctuaries of the apostles'.[68] Italy may not have been quite as ruined as Napoleone made out, but Rome was certainly abandoned and desolate and Italy had lost the popes through the inability of the Italian cardinals to handle the ultramontane powers and responsibilities of the papacy which had been called into existence over the past century.

[66] For a good discussion, see E. Dupré-Theseider, *I papi di Avignone e la questione romana* (Florence, 1939), pp. 8–38.
[67] F. Ehrle, 'Zur Geschichte des Schatzes, der Bibliothek und des Archivs der Päpste im vierzehnten Jahrhundert', *Archiv für letteratur- und Kirchengeschichte des Mittelalters*, i, 1885.
[68] S. Baluze, *Vitae Paparum Avenionensium*, ed. G. Mollat (Paris, 1916–22), iii, pp. 237–41.

8

Tuscany Without the Pope, 1305–1316

THE pontificate of Clement V lasted from 1305 until 1314. For the greater part of that period, until 1312, the pope maintained a political relationship with Tuscany that was in some respects close to the policy of his immediate and short-lived predecessor Benedict XI (1303–4), but totally different from that of Boniface VIII and of the earlier popes stretching back for more than forty years. This was not simply a result of his being a Frenchman living in France, for later Avignon popes, equally settled across the Alps, reverted to a policy much more like the Guelf alliance of the late thirteenth century. But no doubt something should be attributed to the tendency of a French pope with an increasingly French college of cardinals and curia to withdraw his attention from Italian politics.

As far as the papal state was concerned, Clement followed a policy of extreme nepotism, filling the offices of rectors as far as possible with his own French relations.[1] Rather surprisingly he abandoned the custom followed by Boniface VIII and his predecessors of using Italians as cameral merchants with the duty of managing the routine finances of the curia and lending money when it was needed. The accounts with the papal chamber of the three Florentine firms which had managed papal finances during the vacancy of 1304–5, the Spini, Bardi, and Cerchi, were closed in September 1306, and no cameral bankers were appointed for the rest of the pontificate.[2] This change in financial policy, quickly reversed by Clement's successor John XXII, may have been the result of the pope's determination to avoid his predecessors' expensive involvement in large-scale warfare in Italy and thereby to keep out of debt. Apart from his intervention in Ferrara in 1309, Clement spent little money on warfare and was able to leave a substantial sum of money on his death.[3] With other changes in curial personnel, however, it had the effect of making it more difficult for Tuscan cities to influence the papal court than it had been for the previous forty years.

Not only was the papal court detached from Tuscany, it also followed a

---

[1] G. Ermini, 'I rettori provinciali dello stato della chiesa', *Rivista di storia del diritto Italiano*, iv, 1931, pp. 68–9.

[2] *Reg. Clement V*, nos 1151, 1152, 2271; Jordan, *De Mercatoribus*, pp. 143–7; Y. Renouard, *Les Relations des papes d'Avignon et des compagnies commerciales et bancaires de 1316 à 1378* (Paris, 1941), pp. 94–8.

[3] E. Göller, *Die Einnahmen der apostolischen Kammer unter Johann XXII* (Paderborn, 1910), pp. 1–4.

policy of pacification during the years 1305–12 which involved supporting the Ghibellines and Whites against the Black Guelf regimes in control of Florence, Siena, and Lucca. The explanation for this is probably to be found in the influence of cardinals Napoleone Orsini and Niccolò da Prato. These two men had been Clement's principal supporters in his election. After the election they were allowed to continue their anti-Guelf policy with papal support, and did so until 1312 when the success of the Emperor Henry VII in Italy forced the papal court back into alliance with France and Naples. This persistent reaction against the divisive Italian policy of Boniface VIII meant that for some years the Guelf cities of Tuscany found themselves not only out of touch with the papacy but also harassed by papal intervention in favour of their Ghibelline enemies. The contrast with the earlier system of Tuscan–papal relations is great. The Guelf cities were on their own.

The immediate objective of Florentine policy in 1305 was the suppression of White Pistoia, for which Duke Robert of Calabria had been engaged as captain of the Black forces of Florence, Siena, Lucca, and lesser towns. He arrived in Florence in April 1305, and the siege of Pistoia was tightened in the summer. One of the first actions of Clement V as pope was to send two French legates with the task of mediating between Blacks and Whites and ending the siege. They arrived in Tuscany in September and held long and difficult negotiations with the warring forces,[4] but were entirely unsuccessful in halting the Guelf attack which was pressed hard through the winter until Pistoia fell in April 1306. It was a cruel siege with cruel results. Dino Compagni, the Florentine chronicler, said that Sodom and Gomorrha had a better fate in sudden death.[5]

Meanwhile, in February 1306, Clement had appointed Napoleone Orsini as legate with wide powers. His mission lasted until the beginning of 1309. During those three years the considerable figure of the Roman cardinal acted as a rallying point for Ghibelline and White politicians around the eastern side of Tuscany. Napoleone was not only a fairly powerful politician, but also a supporter of the radical Franciscans.[6] One of his prominent employees in Italy was Ubertino da Casale the Franciscan author of the *Arbor Vitae Crucifixae*; as Napoleone's envoy it was with him that the Guelf cities had to negotiate in 1307. This was of course a personal attitude which had nothing to do with the policy of the papal court, but the combination of anti-Guelf politics with an appeal to radical religious earnestness was a message which

[4] For this and other events of the period starting in 1305 the best account is in Davidson, *Storia*, iii. More recent account in R. Caggese, *Roberto d'Angio e i suoi tempi* (Florence, 1922–30). The negotiations of the legates, the abbot of Lombez and bishop of Mende are recorded with exceptional fullness in their reports, partly printed by Davidsohn, *Forschungen*, iii, pp. 287–312 and by G. Calisti, 'Le relazioni fra Firenze e Pistoia nei primi anni del trecento', *Bullettino storico pistoiese*, xxi–vii, 1922–5, from the originals in Archivio Vaticano Collettorie, 443 and Instrumenta Miscellanea, 396 and 397.

[5] *Cronica di Dino Compagni*, p. 197.

[6] C. A. Willemsen, *Kardinal Napoleone Orsini (1263–1342)* (Berlin, 1927).

touched many Tuscan consciences. The rulers of Florence found it difficult to maintain a pose of Guelf loyalty to the papacy and hostility to the Whites and Ghibellines when they were under a papal interdict and fighting a papal legate who had religious appeal. They could not prevent many of the city's clergy from taking Napoleone's side. They complained to the pope that Napoleone wished to deprive members of the Buondelmonti, Della Tosa, Visdomini, Frescobaldi, and Pazzi families—prominent members of the city's upper ranks—of their ecclesiastical benefices.[7] Napoleone's legation must have given comfort to the rootless White exiles, as the legation of Niccolò da Prato had done in 1304. It is possible that his combination of politics with radical Franciscanism helped to incline Dante towards the religious enthusiasm which appears in his later writings.

The legation was a failure because Napoleone could not find a strong enough centre of support from which to menace the Guelf cities. His first resort was Bologna, which was in league with the Ghibellines and Whites when he was appointed. That alliance ended very quickly with an upheaval in the city which led it to change sides. The Florentines reacted fairly energetically to the threat, which they expected from him. Fearing a link between Napoleone and the Ubaldini family in the Mugello to the north of the city, they besieged the Castle of Montaccianico, which fell in July 1306. Napoleone moved to Imola in the Romagna and then to Forlì and Florence did its best to rouse the other cities of the Romagna against him. Napoleone moved to Faenza and then to Arezzo, the most serious Ghibelline enemy in eastern Tuscany, and there was warfare between Florence and Arezzo in 1307. Napoleone then moved south to Cortona, but his legation petered out for lack of effective support and military leadership.

In March 1309 Napoleone was replaced as legate by a papal nephew, Arnaud de Pellegrue. His Italian policy was less personal, and relations with the papacy improved. This was helped by Florentine assistance to Pellegrue in saving Ferrara from Venetian conquest, Clement V's only serious Italian initiative. The religious and serious-minded Robert of Calabria, who had been captain of the Guelf *tallia* against Pistoia in 1305, became king of Naples on the death of his father Charles II in May 1309 and tried to reconcile the pope to the Florentines on a visit to Avignon. By the end of the year the interdict imposed five years earlier had been lifted. By this time the new king of the Romans, Henry of Luxemburg, later Emperor Henry VII, had been elected in Germany and was preparing his descent into Italy; Florentine diplomatic efforts to prevent his election had failed, and a new effort was underway to divert him and to prevent the pope supporting him. The full seriousness of Henry's threat to the Guelf supremacy in Tuscany could not have appeared, however, before the end of 1310; it was then that his success in Lombardy began to be apparent. During 1309 and 1310, the old story of Guelf-

[7] Archivio di Stato, Florence, Missive I Cancelleria, 1, fos 96v–97v.

Ghibelline conflict went on in Tuscany with the same trivial successes and the same futility. If it was not stirred into conflagration by the effects of larger external forces—a Frederick II, a Boniface VIII, or, as it was to be, a Henry VII—the Guelf–Ghibelline conflict was a flickering fire or, to abandon the metaphor, a mode of life for families and small states without an effective government to control them.

During this period Florence was concerned with the possibility of an alliance against Pisa with James II of Aragon who was interested in conquering Sardinia, for which the city offered him 50,000 florins.[8] Fighting with Arezzo seems to have been practically continuous. A great future leader of the Ghibellines, Uguccione della Faggiuola, was building up his military reputation there at this time, but Florentine troops defeated him near Cortona in February 1310, to the jubilation of the city. Even at humbled Pistoia the fires of conflict were still alight: a Florentine captain of the city, sent there in November 1310, was driven out soon after his arrival.[9] So the normal petty conflict, deplored by chroniclers and preachers but infinitely important to the heads of ambitious families, went on.

The ambition of Henry VII was to re-establish a proper imperial authority in Italy of a kind which had been totally absent and not even very seriously promoted for over forty years. For the Ghibellines, who regarded themselves as the natural allies of the empire and who could be regarded as such with still more confidence after Henry's early alliance with them in Lombardy (where he arrived in October 1310), this was a cheering prospect. For the Guelfs— and particularly for Black Florence which had taken such a decided lead in anti-Ghibelline politics—it was menacing.

Florence therefore maintained a stance of absolute hostility to Henry's plans, even when the other Guelf cities of Tuscany were wavering and inclined to respond to Henry's generous personality, which was recognized even by the Florentine chroniclers Compagni and Villani. In the summer of 1310 Henry's envoys were received politely everywhere, even at Lucca and Siena, but not at Florence. One of the difficulties, however, was the attitude of Clement V, who, although heavily pressed by the French king, who was naturally suspicious of a Luxemburg prince trying to establish himself in Italy, was inclined to favour Henry as a pacifier of the country and to promote a Luxemburg–Anjou marriage alliance. The pope's dreams were in fact naïve but he clung to the idea of a general Italian pacification. Hence the bull of Clement V *Exultet in Gloria*, dated 1 September 1310,[10] the eve of Henry's arrival in Italy, in which he ordered the Italians to accept him. This had been preceded by a letter to Henry *Divine Sapientie*, dated 26 July 1309,[11] in which

[8] In addition to Davidsohn, *Storia*, iii, P. Silva, 'Giacomo II d'Aragona e la Toscana, 1307–9', *Archivio storico italiano*, lxxi, 1913.

[9] Archivio di Stato, Florence, Provvisioni, 14, fos 74v–76.

[10] *Reg. Clement V*, no. 6336.

[11] *Reg. Clement V*, no. 4302.

he accepted the division of power between the imperial and ecclesiastical authorities. It was therefore natural, in the autumn of 1310, to think of the pope and the king of the Romans as political allies. It was this assumption which lay behind Dante's letter to the princes and peoples of Italy in favour of Henry, probably written in about October 1310, which ends with the famous sentence: 'This is he whom Peter, the vicar of God, exhorts us to honour, and whom Clement, the present successor of Peter, illumines with the light of the Apostolic benediction; that where the spiritual ray suffices not, there the splendour of the lesser luminary may lend its light.'[12] Dante had been in exile for nine years among Whites and Ghibellines, for whom the arrival of an effective emperor was a heaven-sent blessing which they could hardly have expected, made even more satisfying and hopeful by the approval of the pope. The new turn of events introduced excitement and enthusiasm into Ghibelline circles.

At the end of 1310, Florence and the other Guelf cities sent substantial embassies to the papal court which remained there for a long time. Although they were honourably received, their arguments did not succeed in turning papal policy around. In letters addressed to Florence and to Henry written on the Apennine borders of Tuscany 'beneath the springs of the Arno' on 31 March and 17 April 1311, Dante denounced the Florentines with extreme vituperation, and urged Henry to proceed immediately to attack

the viper that turns against the vitals of her own mother . . . the sick sheep that infects the flock of her lord with contagion . . . the abandoned and unnatural Myrrha, inflamed with passion for the embraces of her father Cinyras . . . the passionate Amata, who, rejecting the fated marriage, did not shrink from claiming for herself a son-in-law whom the fates denied her [the reference is to Turnus, the enemy of Aeneas the founder of Rome in the *Aeneid*, connected in Dante's mind with Robert of Naples, enemy of Henry] but in her madness urged him to battle, and at the last, in expectation for her evil designs, hanged herself in the noose.

But Henry in fact lingered in Lombardy long after the submission of Cremona (which the Florentines had incited into rebellion) in April, and beyond the fall of Brescia in September: not until October did he move to Genoa, and not until March 1312 to Pisa. This delay may have been harmful, and Henry would probably have done better to follow the poet's advice.

Henry could naturally count on the support of Pisa, his wealthiest ally south of Lombardy, which was lavish in its enthusiasm and its help with troops and money.[13] Arezzo supported him. The hostility of Lucca and Siena, the main Guelf cities apart from Florence, was uncertain. Siena expelled Ghibellines from the city in 1312 for fear of a rising in Henry's favour,[14] and

[12] *Opere minori*, ii, p. 548.

[13] There is a modern account of Henry's expedition to Italy by W. M. Bowsky, *Henry VII in Italy: The Conflict of Empire and City State, 1310–1313* (Lincoln, Nebraska, 1960).

[14] *Cronache senesi*, ed. A. Lisini and F. Iacometti (Rerum Italicarum Scriptores, xv, part vi, 1931–7), p. 93.

was also disturbed by the presence in Henry's court of Niccolò Bonsignori, the head of the bank, whose debts were still causing trouble to the Sienese and who had married an Aldobrandesca countess. Henry also had in his train a number of prominent Tuscan Ghibellines—old enemies of Florence, including Ubaldini and Uberti—and of prominent White exiles—an Altoviti, a Cerchi, an Adimari, and others. He had with him legates sent by the pope to carry out his coronation at Rome. These included Niccolò da Prato. Florence could not count on the support of King Robert of Naples, who was still hesitating in face of the attractions of an alliance with Henry and had not committed himself to military support of the Guelfs. The arrival of Henry on Tuscan soil therefore presented an extremely dangerous threat.

Henry decided to make sure first of his coronation, and therefore moved through the Maremma to Rome, which he reached early in May 1312. By this time the pope had changed sides, probably at the end of March under French pressure; henceforward his letters were in favour of Robert of Naples. This was a dramatic change in the European background to the Italian struggle, which restored the papacy to its old place on the side of the Guelfs. However, it did not immediately affect Henry's position very much because he still had with him cardinals who remained sympathetic with his aims and anxious to carry out the coronation. Florence sent a considerable army of 4,500 to Rome to prevent it. But although he was prevented by Roman and Neapolitan resistance from getting to St Peter's, Henry was crowned at the Lateran by Niccolò da Prato on 29 June 1312. In August he left Rome to try to subdue Tuscany, and by 19 September, having come north by way of Arezzo, Montevarchi, and Incisa, he was at the gates of Florence. The presence of a German army outside the city was certainly the worst danger that the Florentine Guelfs had endured since the days of Manfred, but Henry was perhaps defeated chiefly by the illness which attacked him in the autumn and from which he never really recovered. In November he moved away to Poggibonsi, and Robert finally decided to come down on the side of sending troops to the Florentines. After that relations between Florence and Robert warmed rapidly, and in May 1313 the Florentines went so far as to give him the power of nominating the *podestà*, a very limited revival of Angevin lordship which did not amount to anything like a restoration of the position held by Charles I in the 1260s but nevertheless survived until 1322. The Emperor Henry remained desultorily in Tuscany, attempting without success to win over the lesser Guelf towns by negotiation or attack, until his death at Buonconvento to the south of Siena on 24 August 1313.

Eight months later, in April 1314, came the unmourned death of Clement V, disliked in the end by both Guelfs and Ghibellines. This was followed by a long vacancy, lasting until August 1316.[15] At some time during the conclave,

---

[15] Modern account by G. Tabacco, *La casa di Francia nell'azione politica di papa Giovanni XXII* (Rome, 1953), pp. 37–41.

Dante wrote a letter to the Italian cardinals (he mentioned in particular the Romans Napoleone Orsini and Jacopo Stefaneschi) urging them to take pity on the city of Rome, abandoned and deprived of all power both spiritual and temporal, 'a sight to move the pity even of Hannibal'.[16] It was a hopeless plea. Italian cardinals were now outnumbered sixteen to seven by Gascons, Provençals and French. Although the conclave was long and at times disordered, there could not be much doubt that the choice would be ultramontane. Jacques Duèse, who became John XXII, came from Cahors, though he had been a councillor of Robert of Naples. He therefore represented the Angevin alliance from a French point of view, and had nothing in common with the Roman cardinals to whom Dante appealed. John was a very powerful and active pope and the papacy, while returning to its Guelf and Angevin connections, was fixed in a French mould; it was thus fundamentally detached from the Italian interests and instincts which had moved Nicholas III, Nicholas IV, and Celestine V, and would at least have been comprehensible to Boniface VIII.

Although it came at a time when the pope had returned to his natural position on the side of the Guelfs, the death of Henry VII was not by any means the end of the Ghibelline revival in Tuscany. Pisa, his chief ally, took over the management of eight hundred of Henry's German cavalry, an alarming military force in the Italian world; and a month after Henry's death Uguccione della Faggiuola was given command of the city as *capitano di guerra, capitano del popolo* and *podestà*. During his period of power, until 1316, Uguccione was rather more successful than Henry had been, perhaps because he operated from a stable base at Pisa and was able to use the patriotic anti-Guelf enthusiasm of the Pisans more effectively. Guelf energies were weak after the end of the imperial crisis, and Robert's commitment to Tuscany was incomplete. Uguccione was able to make peace with Lucca and Siena in spite of Florentine opposition, and Lucca was disturbed by the return of Ghibelline exiles. In June 1314 Uguccione broke into Lucca and established a Ghibelline ascendancy there with his own son as *podestà* and captain-general, and this time it was the Guelfs who were exiled. A large dent had been made in the structure of Guelf Tuscany: the establishment of a Ghibelline alliance with powerful forces controlling the western end of the Arno Valley. It produced acute anxiety in Florence, and King Robert was persuaded to send his brother with cavalry to help. The worst point of the new crisis was reached on 29 August 1315 when the armies of Pisa and Florence met at Montecatini, to the west of Pistoia. This was the largest battle to take place in Tuscany for many years, at least since Campaldino in 1289, and it was a decisive defeat for Florence. Ten thousand men were said to have died, including a nephew of King Robert and many members of leading Guelf families—Tornaquinci, Della Tosa, Donati, and others. Uguccione's regime did not last long for he

[16] *Opere minori*, ii, pp. 580–93.

was driven out of Pisa at Easter 1316, but he had a successor in Castruccio Castracani of Lucca; the Ghibelline revival was not at an end.

The most dramatic event in the internal politics of Florence after the upheaval caused by the legation of Niccolò da Prato in 1304 was the death of Corso Donati in October 1308. In the last period of his life, Corso—the proud leader of the Black Guelfs in 1301—married as his third wife a daughter of Uguccione della Faggiuola and became suspected of attachment to the Ghibellines. The most remarkable leader of oligarchic faction became the victim of intense hatred by other oligarchs and of popular denunciation. Fleeing from the city, he was pursued by a detachment of Catalan mercenaries and eventually dragged to his death by his horse. Dino Compagni ends his history of Florence with reflections on the Black leaders who dominated the city around 1310.[17] The six he named, 'the chiefs of this discord of the Blacks', were Rosso della Tosa, Pazzino de' Pazzi, Betto Brunelleschi, Geri Spini, Tegghia de' Frescobaldi, and Gherardo Ventraia de' Tornaquinci. Two of them were connected with great mercantile families, the Spini and Frescobaldi, the others were members of ancient clans long powerful in the city. Rosso della Tosa 'who divided the entire Parte Guelfa of Florence as Whites and Blacks', a very prominent politician of the crisis era, lived beyond the age of seventy-five and, 'expected for a long time by God', died in July 1309 of a wound caused by falling over a dog. Betto Brunelleschi died in March 1311 of wounds inflicted by two young Donati in revenge for the death of Corso. The style of factional and family conflict which divided Tuscany was mirrored on a smaller scale in the feuds which divided families within the city and often erupted into violence.

In such a small place died five cruel citizens, justice being done and evil doers punished with evil death. They were Messer Corso Donati, Messer Niccolò de' Cerchi, Messer Pazzino de' Pazzi, Gherardo Bordoni, and Simone di Messer Corso Donati; and by evil death Messer Rosso della Tosa and Messer Betto Brunelleschi. And they were punished for their errors.[18]

While the politics of the city were never without violence, however, the political control of the Black oligarchy as a whole was in a sense stable. They were able to preserve themselves from both the irruption of the external Whites and Ghibellines and the internal class ambitions of the lower orders. The system of election of priors preserved the continuity of the rule of a relatively small group, partly by allowing the priors to nominate their successors.[19] The early decades of the fourteenth century might be regarded as the golden age of oligarchic rule in Florence.

Siena under the regime of the Nine—the elected magistrates, corresponding to Florentine priors, who acted as the signory between 1287 and 1355—had a

---

[17] *Cronica di Dino Compagni*, pp. 259–65.

[18] Ibid., p. 264.

[19] On the electoral system of this period, see Najemy, *Corporatism and Consensus*, pp. 79–84.

more broadly based government than did Florence, one distinctly less liable to be dominated by individual great men.[20] It was however frequently disturbed by the conflicts of the great. In March 1306 the Nine took powers to settle a dispute of the 'two parties of noblemen of the house of Tolomei and the house of Malavolti . . . who at the devil's instigation are known to have a quarrel and war between them'.[21] The entry of Henry VII into Italy caused repeated anxiety about the actions of Ghibellines, both within and without. In October 1311 the Nine were to investigate a sect of people threatening to overthrow the state.[22] In 1312 the Ghibellines were expelled.[23] The departure of members of the great Tolomei family from the city as suspect *grandi* in 1313 was one of the events leading to the formation of the order of Montoliveto by Giovanni di Mino Tolomei, whose sister, incidentally, was the wife of a Florentine Cerchi.[24] The Tolomei and Salimbeni, however, were fighting in the streets of the city in April 1315.[25] We have to picture the great Guelf cities, not to mention the lesser victims of their neighbours' expansionist avarice, such as Pistoia or Prato, as living throughout this period in a condition threatened by political instability although they were able to muster great sums of money to pay for armies of defence and offence. Communal regimes, based on broad electoral foundations in the cities, maintained a generally successful but always fragile government which could easily be upset by the actions of the great families. Every commune faced the danger of collapsing into the disruption caused by Uguccione della Faggiuola at Lucca. Florence had in a sense bought itself a greater internal peace by the total expulsion of Ghibellines and Whites, but that policy too was a source of external danger and opened up the danger of a *coup d'état* promoted from without.

Villani made the point that the defeat of Florence at Montecatini in 1315 did no harm to the city's economic vigour.

The Florentines were not dismayed by this defeat but vigorously reformed their city's ranks and force of arms and money and surrounded the boundaries for defence. . . . The Ghibellines and exiles of Florence found themselves deceived, believing that they had conquered the land by the defeat, for the opposite was the case; the damage was not so great that in Florence it appeared that there had ever been a defeat which did not allow the artisans to continue with their labours.[26]

[20] W. M. Bowsky, 'The *Buon Governo* of Siena, 1287–1355: a Medieval Italian Oligarchy', *Speculum*, xxxvii, 1962; idem, *A Medieval Italian Commune: Siena under the Nine, 1287–1355* (Berkeley–Los Angeles–London, 1981).

[21] Archivio di Stato, Siena, Consiglio Generale, 68, fo. 112; *Cronache Senesi*, pp. 86–7.

[22] W. M. Bowsky, 'The anatomy of rebellion in fourteenth-century Siena: from commune to signory?', *Violence and Civil Disorder in Italian Cities 1200–1500*, ed. L. Martines (Berkeley–Los Angeles–London, 1972), p. 241.

[23] *Cronache Senesi*, p. 93.

[24] F. Lugano, 'Origini e primordi dell'ordine di Montoliveto', *Bullettino senese di storia patria*, ix–x, 1902–3.

[25] *Cronache Senesi*, p. 105; G. Cecchini, *La pacificazione fra Tolomei e Salimbeni*, Quaderni dell'Accademia Chigiana, ii (Siena, 1942).   [26] Villani, IX, lxxiv.

Florence could write to San Miniato in 1314 of 'our merchants on which the
city of Florence for a great part depends [*ex quibus ... pro magna parte
consistit*] and without whom we cannot bear the burden of our expenses' who
'have in the city of Pisa almost immeasurable quantities of merchandise and
precious things'.[27] Trade was the lifeblood of the city, rarely mentioned in the
political chronicles but continuing to develop at a great pace in the midst of
political upheaval. The abolition of papal bankers for the decade from 1306 to
1316 was politically important and cancelled out one of the areas in which we
can normally see Tuscan finance working in a spectacular fashion, but there is
no reason to suppose that it did serious harm to the Florentine economy. We
are still very badly informed, however, about the nature of the Tuscan
economy. From the hundreds of Florentine and Sienese companies which in
this period apparently operated in international trade over large areas, only a
tiny number of account books survive to give us a clear indication of the
business they did. We have to put together a tentative picture drawn from
scattered hints.

The most spectacular commercial and financial activities of Florentine
merchants during these years were their relations with England and Naples.
In both cases the reasons were essentially the same. The kings of England and
Naples were active monarchs who, unlike Clement V, required the financial
help of merchants with substantial resources. In both cases, the native
mercantile classes were relatively backward and unable to provide this service.
But in both cases also there was a large export trade which provided suitable
merchants with the opportunity for recovering, both by participation in the
trade and by collecting customs dues, the sums which they lent the kings. The
kings therefore needed merchants who had large reserves of cash and
extensive trading contacts abroad to provide them with essential financial
services in return for commercially useful privileges. This was why Charles II
and Robert of Naples and Edward I and II of England depended on Tuscan
traders, and why they turned to the Bardi and Peruzzi and Frescobaldi. The
difference between the period around 1310 and the thirteenth century was the
movement of the rulers of these kingdoms, both economically relatively
backward in comparison with Northern Italy, France, and the Low
Countries, to almost exclusive dependence on Florentines. In late thirteenth-
century England, the most important commercial servants of the crown had
been the Lucchese Ricciardi. In Naples the Sienese and Lucchese had been
important as well as the Florentines. In 1310 the Bardi, Peruzzi, and
Frescobaldi were supreme. Their supremacy was itself important as a source
of money in Florence—it was the Bardi and Peruzzi who were able to pay for
Giotto's chapels in Santa Croce—but their wealth can only be explained as a
result of the more general consolidation of Florentine industry and trade in
France and Italy, which supplied them with the cash and the networks of

[27] Davidsohn, *Forschungen*, iii, p. 131.

commerce that made them more capable than the Sienese and Lucchese of providing commercial services. These commercial systems nearer home are less clearly visible to us, at least in the sense that they provide us with no global figures; but there is no doubt that they existed, and they must be assumed to be the reason for the dominance of the Florentines in the underdeveloped fringes of the continent.

The best recorded of the Florentine enterprises abroad is that of the Frescobaldi in England; many records of their relations with the crown have survived in the archives of the English Exchequer and Chancery.[28] The Frescobaldi had been trading in England since the 1270s, but their great period of prominence arose out of Edward I's turn to Florentine merchants after the collapse of the Ricciardi in 1294. Between 1294 and 1298, Edward borrowed from eleven Italian companies of whom eight were Florentine (Spini, Cerchi Neri and Bianchi, Bardi, Pulci and Rimbertini, Mozzi, Frescobaldi Neri and Bianchi), one Lucchese (Bellardi), one Pistoiese (Ammanati), and one Sienese (Bonsignori). The Cerchi loaned more than the Frescobaldi at this time. It was after this that the Frescobaldi became the king's special merchants, but the relationship did not develop fully until after 1303, when a new custom was imposed on wool exports to be paid at a higher rate by alien merchants and therefore offering good opportunities for raising money to pay back loans. In 1307 the Frescobaldi were petitioning for large sums, over £40,000, which they claimed were still owing to them from earlier loans. The best way open to them was presumably to get still further involved, and the high point of their connection with the crown was reached in the years 1309–11. During this period they were in complete control of the customs, which allowed them fairly easy recovery of loans. At an earlier stage they had managed a silver mine in Devon, and from 1307 Amerigo de' Frescobaldi was warden of the Mint. In 1307 they were also appointed receivers of the king's profits in Gascony, and Amerigo later became constable of Bordeaux. During the years 1304 to 1310 their loans to the crown were running at an average level of about £20,000 a year—at approximately 100,000 florins, a turnover which certainly put them among the most active of all Florentine companies.

The end of the Frescobaldi in England came in 1311, the result not of commercial failure but entirely of native political hostility to the financial system they operated and to the independence it gave the king. They moved in a fairly orderly fashion to Bruges and thence to the papal court at Vienne and Avignon, and to Florence. The account book published by Sapori was kept by Pepo di Bettino di Berto de' Frescobaldi at the papal court in 1312 after the flight and tells us nothing about dealings during the great days, an example of

[28] Story told by R. W. Kaeuper, 'The Frescobaldi of Florence and the English Crown', *Studies in Medieval and Renaissance History*, x, 1973; Sapori, *La compagnia dei Frescobaldi*; valuable survey by M. Prestwich, 'Italian Merchants in Late Thirteenth and Early Fourteenth Century England' in *The Dawn of Modern Banking* (New Haven–London, 1979).

the tendency of the surviving early Florentine accounts to be irrelevant to the issues which centrally concern the historian. But it does record the movement of wool and cloth south from Bruges, which was presumably a late continuation of Frescobaldi activity at the time of their greatness. After this period they disappear from the top rank of merchants, but there is no reason to suppose that this was due to commercial failure.

The Frescobaldi were not the most prominent Florentine merchants of this period. That title should probably be awarded to the Bardi and Peruzzi, and it was probably the result of their dealings with Naples. Naples is much less well documented than England but it can be seen that it offered great opportunities to foreign merchants for the movement of grain out of it and cloth into it. This trade was partly carried on by land. In 1314–15, representatives of the Peruzzi were complaining that seven *salme* of ultramontane cloth which they had sent to the widow of Charles II had been seized in the territory of Foligno by a man who was trying to recover an unpaid debt from the firm of Pulci and Rimbertini.[29] There was also of course extensive traffic by sea from Provence, Genoa, and Pisa. Although often interrupted by political difficulties, all this trade was within the geographical orbit of Italy. The king of Naples was a Guelf prince, active in Italian politics mostly on the same side as Florence, who was happy to provide commercial privileges in return for loans.[30] The dominance of three Florentine firms—the Bardi, Peruzzi, and Acciaiuoli, who seem to have acted in a relatively friendly manner towards each other quite unlike the cut-throat competition which often marked the actions of Italian merchants at the papal and English courts—is clear from the beginning of the reign of Robert in 1309.

Substantial loans from the Bardi and Peruzzi are reported on various occasions in 1309–11. Robert borrowed money, for example, for his trip to Avignon for coronation and the very large sum of 24,000 *oncie*, nearly 100,000 florins, in 1310 for his troops in Romagna. An account of 1310 also indicates that the Peruzzi had been regularly producing various small sums for the expenses of the king's household and for payments in Genoa, in Provence, and at Avignon. The war with Henry VII led to loans in 1313. In 1314 Robert accepted the obligation to repay the Bardi and Peruzzi the enormous sum of 116,000 *oncie*, more than half a million florins, borrowed in the previous two years. As the Mozzi had entertained Pope Gregory X on a visit to Florence, similarly it was in the Peruzzi palace that King Robert stayed. In recompense for the loans, the Florentines received the most extensive privileges in the way of offices and control of commerce. At the heart of this was the privileged position which they had in the essential export of grain, the primary

---

[29] Archivio di Stato, Florence, Mercanzia, 1030, fo. 31.

[30] G. Yver, *Le Commerce et les marchands dans l'Italie méridionale au XIIIe et au XIVe siècle* (Paris, 1903), esp. pp. 289–417; D. Abulafia, 'Southern Italy'; Davidsohn, *Storia*, IV, ii, pp. 789–818.

commercial produce of Naples, equivalent to wool in England. In 1311 Florentines exported 45,000 tons of Apulian grain, enough to fill fifty large ships. This was balanced no doubt by the less well-documented import of cloth. But the Bardi and Peruzzi undertook many other kinds of work, collecting taxes, running the mint, paying officials and troops as well as carrying on their trade. In the middle of the second decade of the fourteenth century they reached the height of their dominance of Neapolitan financial and commercial life, a supremacy which was to last at least for another decade. The early fourteenth-century Florentines in Naples, which was so easily integrated into their general Italian and Franco–Italian trade, are probably the most striking case of 'informal empire' in the Middle Ages.

We have very little knowledge of Florentine financial dealings with the papal court in the pontificate of Clement V. No doubt they were more restricted than they had been earlier, or than they were to be later in the pontificate of John XXII, because between 1306 and 1316 more papal money was transferred by clerks. Many payments to the papal chamber were still, however, being made by Florentine bankers,[31] not to speak of the endless movement of money for other people who had litigation at the papal court. And there were numerous dealings with other ecclesiastics. In 1321 the Order of St John of Jerusalem owed the large sums of 191,000 florins to the Peruzzi and 133,000 florins to the Bardi, debts built up over many previous years.[32] When we turn to ordinary business in France and Italy and industry in Florence itself, we are faced by a much more difficult problem because although we have innumerable limited pieces of information we have very few figures of the kind which enable one to make generalizations. The most famous is Villani's statement that in the first decade of the century, Florence had three hundred workshops of the wool industry making 100,000 cloths a year.[33] The statement was made in the course of a survey of Florence in the 1330s. We cannot provide detailed evidence about the industry at the beginning of the century. We know that Florentine products were important in the trade in cloth in many parts of Italy, probably next in importance after cloth from Northern France and the Low Countries, but we know very little about the industry. On the basis of lists of guild members and other scattered evidence we have to assume that Florence included an extensive and varied industrial world, but it cannot be quantified.[34]

The surviving account book of Alberti Del Giudice and Co., which starts in 1304, tells us of profits drawn from the company by partners but nothing

[31] Archivio Vaticano, Obligationes et Solutiones 2, fos 47v–62 records payments to the Chamber on behalf of clerics in the pontificate of Clement V after 1306 by the Cerchi, Peruzzi, Bardi, and Spini, and the Bellardi of Lucca.

[32] Davidsohn, *Storia*, IV. ii, p. 547; Lami, *Deliciae*, viii, pp. 258–9.

[33] Villani, XI. xciv.

[34] Hoshino, *L'arta della lana in Firenze nel Basso Medioevo*, pp. 52–4; Davidsohn, *Storia*, IV. ii, pp. 3–345.

about its trade. The same is broadly true of the Peruzzi account books, which start in 1308.[35] More interesting information is contained in the early records of the Mercanzia. The Mercanzia was a tribunal set up in the first decade of the fourteenth century by the guilds of merchants most interested in international trade (wool manufacturers, cloth importers, money changers, the silk guild, the apothecaries, and the spicers) to deal with the problems caused by debts due to the Genoese for grain brought to Florence during the shortage caused by the drought of 1302, and also by the debt problems caused by the many failures of international companies in this period, including the Franzesi in 1307, the Mozzi in 1308, and the Pulci and Rimbertini in 1310[36]—all, incidentally, companies which had at one time been important in papal finance; their fate indicated among other things the dangers of that kind of business. One of the documents in this archive which provides an early indication of the relative importance of different companies is a list of contributors to a sum collected in 1307 as a guarantee for debts to the Genoese. At the head of thirty-four contributors, all presumably keenly interested in doing business in Genoa, were the Scali, Peruzzi, Spini, Bardi, and Macci. At the bottom of the list are the silk company of Dino Compagni the chronicler, and the company of Uliviero de' Cerchi.[37] In impositions placed on companies in 1319 to pay the expenses of ambassadors sent to Pisa and Romagna, the Bardi, Peruzzi, and Scali paid the largest sums.[38] Information of this kind helps to put companies in perspective. No doubt it would be possible, by collecting the scattered evidence of judicial cases, to form some impression of the directions of movement of goods and the companies involved; but one would not get much idea of the size of business.

The earliest Florentine company whose activities can be seen fairly clearly in surviving accounts is Francesco Del Bene and Co., a Calimala company founded in 1318.[39] The main business of Francesco Del Bene was importing cloths from the Low Countries and France and selling them in Florence. The cloths seem to have come mainly from the centres of production, places like Malines, Douai, Brussels, Ypres, or Ghent, and many were paid for at the Champagne fairs. They were sent down through Avignon to the coast of Provence and thence to Pisa and Florence. Since many of them were white cloths they were often put out for dyeing in Florence. Francesco del Bene had a workshop near Or San Michele. The purchasers were sometimes merchants from various parts of Tuscany, sometimes Neapolitan merchants, sometimes Florentine firms, like the Scali, exporting to Naples. It is clear that quite a high proportion of the cloths were destined for the far south. One of the interesting

[35] *Alberti del Giudice*, ed. Sapori; *I Libri di Commercio dei Peruzzi*, ed. Sapori.

[36] A. Grunzweig, 'Le Fonds de la mercanzia aux archives d'etat de Florence au point de vue de l'histoire de Belgique', *Bulletin de l'Institut Historique Belge de Rome*, xii, 1932.

[37] Ibid., pp. 82–3.

[38] Archivio di Stato, Florence, Mercanzia, 4115, fos 148v, 149v.

[39] Sapori, *Una compagnia di Calimala*.

features of the accounts is the prominence of the Bardi. Francesco had a Bardi mother and one of his partners was a Bardi, so the connection was partly based on family ties. But it is also clear that the great extent of Bardi operations, with factors in many cities, enabled the Bardi to provide facilities which were essential for smaller firms like this, both in arranging the purchase of cloths in distant places and their transport and in providing for payments to be made over long distance by letters. One can see how the very large firm provided an international framework within which many smaller specialists could operate.

More valuable than any commercial accounts of Florentines which have survived from such an early date are the account books of the Gallerani of Siena, operating at London and Paris in the years 1305–8.[40] The Gallerani were probably not the wealthiest of Sienese companies, though the family was prominent in the city,[41] nor were they among the most prominent Italian companies at work in North-West Europe. The survival of their accounts is a lucky chance that reveals the multiplicity and complexity of financial operations carried out by Tuscans in a distant part of the world, in which a great many other companies of similar size but less well recorded must have been taking part at the same time. The activities recorded in the accounts are mostly concerned with movements of money between London, Paris, the Champagne fairs, the papal court, and Tuscany. The Gallerani did export wool and lead from England, but most of the actions recorded are simply movements of money. They were carried out for a large number of clients, including great Florentine houses such as Frescobaldi and Cerchi, Sienese merchants, a large number of clerics (usually having business with the papal court), and some laymen who were not merchants. The entries show the existence of a continuous business of international exchange, used by the English and French but carried out by Tuscans.

The chance survival of the Gallerani books should not, however, lead one to overestimate the importance of Sienese trade in the North. It is fairly clear that since their great days in international finance in the middle and later parts of the thirteenth century, the Sienese, like the Lucchese, had been replaced by the big Florentine companies that had risen to dominance in Naples and the North.[42] In the early fourteenth century they were no longer prominent in either sphere. The collapse of the Bonsignori *Gran Tavola* in 1298 seems to have been the end of the Sienese empire; the unpaid debts of that company caused endless trouble in France to Sienese merchants, who had in any case lost their grip on the international market. The massive growth of the

[40] *Les Livres des comptes des Gallerani*, ed. G. Bigwood and A. Grunzweig (Académie Royale de Belgique, Commission Royale d'Histoire, 1961–2).

[41] G. Cherubini, 'Proprietari, contadini e campagne Senesi all'inizio del trecento', in his *Signori, Contadini, Borghesi; Ricerche sulla società italiana del Basso Medioevo* (Florence, 1974), p. 249.

[42] G. Bigwood, 'Les Tolomei en France au xiv siècle', *Revue belge de philologie et d'histoire*, viii, 1929, p. 1110.

Florentine economy squeezed out the other Tuscan cities. Yet Siena remained wealthy. The first and second decades of the fourteenth century were a period of notable territorial expansion when Siena was able to put money into developing the new port of Talamone and buying new lands for the *contado*, for example the castle of Civitella Ardenghesca bought for 6,000 florins in 1317.[43] In the same period the fiscal expenditure of the commune was growing rapidly. This was in large part a result of needs forced upon the commune by the wars of Henry VII and Uguccione della Faggiuola, but it seems to be clear that the money could be found by taxation and borrowing.[44] Surviving sources have enabled us to be fairly well informed about Siena's communal income and expenditure. The information available about the economy of the city, as opposed to its communal income, is poorer than it is even for Florence. We know from the tax documents of other cities that Siena had a considerable exporting cloth industry, presumably the largest in Tuscany apart from Florence though considerably smaller than the latter, and indeed perhaps not more than a tenth of its size.[45] But we have little internal information about it at this period or about the financial basis of great families, such as the Salimbeni and Tolomei, who were prominent in the city. Did other great families who had formerly been active in international finance turn their attention, as the Piccolomini did in the late thirteenth and early fourteenth centuries,[46] to landownership? The obscurity of the Sienese economy may eventually be clarified, but in the present state of research little is known about the direction of Sienese economic development. The economic basis of the ambition which led the Sienese to enterprises of territorial expansion and at the same time grandiose plans for the physical improvement of the cathedral is somewhat mysterious: all we know is that the commune behaved as though its citizens were rich.

If we attempt to generalize about early fourteenth-century Tuscany we must conclude that it presents us with a picture which should probably be regarded as unusual. It was a world of desperate political divisions and almost everywhere of repeated bloodshed on a large or small scale. In spite of expansion by some of the greater cities political units were still small in area. Warfare between them was frequent. Internally they were often subject to greater or lesser upheaval, and the customs of the vendetta produced undiminished ferocity. But it was also a society in which republican government was highly developed, and industry and commerce on a world-wide

---

[43] W. M. Bowsky, *The Finance of the Commune of Siena, 1287–1355* (Oxford, 1970), pp. 23–5, 27.

[44] Ibid., pp. 46, 165, 300.

[45] Producing between 2,700 and 10,000 cloths in the 1340s, S. Tortoli, 'Per la storia della produzione laniera a Siena nel trecento e nei primi anni del quattrocento', *Bullettino senese di storia patria*, lxxxii–lxxxiii, 1975–6, p. 228.

[46] G. Prunai, 'Carte mercantili dei Piccolomini nel diplomatico fiorentino' in *Studi in onore di Amintore Fanfani*, ii (Milan, 1962), p. 560. Indications of territorial holdings of families in Cherubini, 'Proprietari'.

scale produced great wealth. We have said nothing of the maritime empire of Pisa or the industry of Lucca, which continued to be important at this period. The most remarkable point of growth in Tuscany was the industry and commerce of the Florentines, which would eventually lead to Florentine political domination of the whole province. In 1320 that political amalgamation had scarcely begun; Florence was the greatest but still only one of a number of proud and jealous powers. It is into this world of continual warfare mitigated by finesse in communal government, of primitive family enmities often supported by supreme financial expertise, and of physical brutality shamed by the ecstasies of mendicant piety, that we have to set the artistic masterpieces of Duccio, Giotto, and Dante. Around the artists, cruelty, intensity of passion and high civilization coexisted in a manner that is not found in more settled societies. It is important to remember this when we look at the crucifixions and read about the torments of hell.

9

Realistic Visual Narrative

THE papal revolution of the years 1303 to 1305 left Italy without a papal court. The Guelf communes of Tuscany survived the upheaval with scars but with undiminished wealth, and with increased intellectual and artistic isolation and independence. Florence and Siena were now cities coping on their own with the Ghibelline threat around them. The cultural axes linking Rome with those cities were gone. The new political situation involved a rather different world of artistic patronage. It is true that the rebuilding and painting of the lower basilica at Assisi continued partly with the help of cardinals' finance.[1] But the painting done here in the first two decades of the fourteenth century had relatively minor importance at this period, in comparison with the grand originality of the designs carried out by Giotto at the Arena Chapel in Padua and by Duccio in the *Maestà* at Siena. These two works incorporate the development of a new system of pictorial narrative which is the fruition of the beginnings at Rome, Pisa, Siena, and Assisi at the end of the thirteenth century. The introduction of classical inspiration into sculpture and painting lost the aegis of papal patronage and now took place almost entirely with the help of commercial finance. The continuance of the classical revolution with the introduction of a fully developed realistic pictorial narrative, which was in general to provide a new standard of art not to be surpassed for another century, is the subject of this chapter. We shall begin with Duccio's *Maestà* and pass from that to the central masterpiece by Giotto.

Siena in the late thirteenth and early fourteenth centuries, under the government of the Nine, was, by Tuscan standards, a relatively stable centre of mercantile power and wealth, a republic in which the problems of factional upheaval were brought under reasonable control for long periods. In contrast to Florence, where artistic patronage, including the control of building and decoration at the cathedral and the baptistery, were decentralized into the hands of guilds as well as families and religious orders, the Sienese commune maintained a remarkably unified control over the structure and appearance of the city. Well-known examples of this co-ordinated development are the statute of 1297, which laid down that all buildings looking onto the Piazza del Campo were to have windows with small columns and without balconies, to match the face of the Palazzo Pubblico; the surviving rectangular plan made in

---

[1] R. Simon, 'Towards a Relative Chronology of the Frescoes in the Lower Church of San Francesco at Assisi', *Burlington Magazine*, cxviii, 1976.

1306, to control the development of the recently acquired port of Talamone on the coast; and the ordinance of 1309 expressing the intention of acquiring open meadows to improve the beauty of the city.[2] The building of the Palazzo Pubblico started in the 1290s, though the great tower was not put up until forty years later. In 1316 plans were under way for an extension of the cathedral by building a new baptistery at the bottom of the hill below it, which foreshadowed the extraordinarily grand design to build a new nave to make the cathedral the largest in the world with the existing nave as a transept, a plan eventually halted by the Black Death. Sienese plans were not fundamentally very different from those of other Tuscan cities—notably Florence, where a new cathedral, palazzo pubblico, and great churches for the mendicant orders were being built at approximately the same time—but in relation to the resources of the city they were more ambitious than Florentine plans, and resulted from a more united devotion to the physical aggrandizement of the commune.

The greatest work of art commissioned by the commune in the early fourteenth century, Duccio's *Maestà* (Pls 23, 24), is the largest piece of panel painting of its age. It was intended as an extremely splendid glorification of the Virgin Mary, the patron of the cathedral and of the city, to whose intercession Siena was indebted for the survival of the great crisis of the battle of Montaperti in 1260 and more recent dangers and to whom the population looked for further favours which would preserve it in the future. The *Maestà* was placed in the most prominent position in the cathedral, on the high altar. It is not clear whether the high altar at that time was actually underneath the crossing of the church or just to the east of it.[3] It is certain, however, that the *Maestà* became part of the group of famous panels devoted to the Virgin, including the later paintings of the *Birth of Mary* by Pietro Lorenzetti (in the Museo dell'Opera del Duomo, Siena), Simone Martini's *Annunciation*, and Ambrogio Lorenzetti's *Presentation at the Temple* (both in the Uffizi, Florence), which were placed in nearby chapels. The ceremony in which the panel was taken from the workshop to the cathedral in 1311 is reported in a chronicle written thirty or forty years later.

On the day on which it was carried to the cathedral the workshops were closed and the bishop ordered a great and devout company of priests and friars, with a solemn procession accompanied by the Nine Lords and all the officials of the commune and all the people. One by one all the more worthy people were by the altarpiece with lights in their hands and behind them were the ladies and children with much devotion and they accompanied the altarpiece up to the cathedral, making a procession around the

[2] E. Guidoni, 'Roma e l'urbanistica del trecento', *Storia dell'arte italiana* (Turin, 1979–83), v, pp. 309–16.

[3] Contrasting opinions by A. Middeldorf-Kosegarten, 'Zur Bedeutung der Sieneser Domkuppel', *Münchner Jahrbuch der bildenden Kunst*, xxi, 1970, and K. van der Ploeg, 'Architectural and Liturgical Aspects of Siena Cathedral in the Middle Ages' in van Os, *Sienese Altarpieces 1215–1460*, i.

Campo, the bells tolling glory for devotion to such a noble altar-piece . . . All that day
they remained at prayer with much giving of alms to the poor, praying God and his
Mother who is our advocate to defend us with her great mercy from all adversity and
all evil and safeguard us from traitors and enemies of Siena.[4]

This unusual description of the installation of a work of art makes clear that
the patronage of the *Maestà* was an expression of the central importance
which the city oligarchy attributed to the Virgin as the defender and promoter
of the commune.

Duccio was an outstanding and original painter long before the *Maestà*, for
which the earliest surviving contract is dated 9 October 1308.[5] As artists
around 1300 go he is well documented, though there is little documentation
for his works. The earliest record probably referring to work done by him for
the commune of Siena is dated 1278. A contract of 15 April 1285 records the
agreement by which Duccio was to paint a Madonna for a Florentine
confraternity, the Society of St Mary the Virgin of Santa Maria Novella,
probably the *Rucellai Madonna* (Pl. 22) now in the Uffizi. There has been
considerable disagreement among recent historians about the works apart
from the *Maestà* to be attributed to Duccio;[6] this is a matter of connoisseur-
ship about which there can be no certain conclusion. If we follow the view of
the majority, however, we must accept the *Rucellai Madonna* and the small
Madonna of the Franciscans in the Siena Pinacoteca, recognized by all critics
as Duccio's work, and add to these the *Crevole Madonna* (Pl. 21) in the
Museo dell'Opera del Duomo in Siena, and the Perugia *Madonna*. Critics
place before us a small group of paintings, all madonnas, to represent the early
Duccio. He is an artist whose style is, to say the least, dramatically different
from that associated with Guido da Siena and the generation of Sienese artists
preceding 1280. We are struck in Duccio's work by the smoothly modelled,
soft features of the faces, giving a stronger appearance of real physical outline,
by the robustly realistic children, by the delicacy of the handling of transparent or semi-transparent clothing, by the detailed fineness of the Virgin's
clothes, sometimes making effective use of gold striation. This is an artist who

[4] *Cronache senesi*, p. 90.
[5] Three important and often conflicting studies of Duccio have been published recently: J. H.
Stubblebine, *Duccio di Buoninsegna and his School* (Princeton, 1979); J. White, *Duccio*; F.
Deuchler, *Duccio* (Milan, 1984). The archival documents for Duccio's life are conveniently
presented by White, op. cit., pp. 185–200.
[6] White accepts the *Crevole Madonna*, the *Rucellai Madonna*, the *Madonna of the Franciscans*,
the Boston Triptych, the National Gallery Triptych, the Perugia *Madonna*, and the Siena
polyptics nos. 28 and 47. Stubblebine accepts only the *Rucellai Madonna*, the *Madonna of the
Franciscans*, the Stoclet *Madonna* (whose whereabouts are now unknown), the Perugia
Madonna, and the National Gallery *Madonna* (not the Triptych). Deuchler's core list is the
Crevole Madonna, the *Rucellai Madonna*, the *Madonna of the Franciscans*, the Berne *Madonna*
and the Perugia *Madonna*. For another work, recently brought out of obscurity which may
conceivably be early Duccio, see A. Smart, 'A Duccio Discovery: An Early Madonna Prototype',
Apollo, cxx, 1984.

gives the appearance of working to new standards of particularly high technical refinement, presumably to please wealthy customers, possibly affected by Byzantine standards of panel painting, who has developed a more realistic style in the presentation of flesh and clothing. There is no doubt about the novelty of the style. The sources that inspire it present an enigmatic problem, probably because they were diverse and overlapping.

Although someone called 'Duch de Siene' was in Paris in 1296,[7] there is no evidence that the painter Duccio went north of the Alps. But small French art objects were well known in Siena in the late thirteenth century. Sienese manuscript illumination and stained glass show the influence of the French as early as the 1260s,[8] and no doubt French ivories and metal reliquaries were imported. It is therefore reasonable to suppose that the more supple shapes of the bodies of madonnas and angels in Duccio's paintings owe something to the influence of French models, as does the free and complex treatment of the folds of clothes so characteristic of his style. The question of Byzantine influence on Duccio is presented sharply by the two madonnas in Washington. The Kahn *Madonna* is now thought to be the work of an eastern artist trained in the advanced Paleologan style of the mid-thirteenth century but painting in Tuscany.[9] Byzantine art had recently introduced a new classical realism which greatly affected the painting of faces. It was probably this that inspired Duccio's new conception of the faces of the Madonna and the Christ-child which emerges in the *Crevole* and *Rucellai Madonnas*.

Still more baffling than the fairly obvious, if generalized, evidence of French and Byzantine influences is the problem of Duccio's relations with Cimabue and other members of the avantgarde who worked at Assisi. Two of the putti on the vault of the nave of the upper basilica at Assisi look very much, as has recently been observed, as though they were the work of the painter of the *Crevole Madonna*.[10] If that is so, and we have to imagine Duccio working at Assisi in the 1280s, then we must also imagine him as exposed to a range of Italian influences which would take him far away from his Sienese background. The *Rucellai Madonna* and Cimabue's *Santa Trinità Madonna*, undated but perhaps of about the same time, look like the work of two artists in competition with each other in the enterprise of creating a very large altarpiece of the Madonna and Child seated upon an elaborate wooden throne supported by angels. Duccio's altarpiece is indifferent to the problem of unified spatial realism, and his angels, beautiful figures in themselves, have a capricious relationship to the real body of the throne. On the other hand his

[7] Stubblebine, *Duccio*, p. 198.

[8] B. Tosatti Soldano, *Miniature a vetrate senesi del secolo XIII* (Genoa, 1978).

[9] H. Belting, 'The "Byzantine" Madonnas: New Facts About Their Italian Origin and Some Observations on Duccio', *Studies in the History of Art* (National Gallery of Art, Washington), xii, 1982.

[10] F. Bologna, 'The crowning disc of a duecento "Crucifixion" and other points relevant to Duccio's relationship to Cimabue', *Burlington Magazine*, cxxv, 1983, p. 337.

throne is physically more convincing than Cimabue's, and his Virgin sits more satisfactorily in a real position.

Another influence which must be taken into account is the sculpture of Nicola and Giovanni Pisano which, from the 1260s onwards, must have impressed itself upon the minds of all artists working at Siena. Pisan sculpture is remarkable for its command of the body and of drapery. The treatment of drapery is always outstandingly advanced in Duccio's painting, more ambitious and successful than his treatment of space. This is most obvious in the *Maestà*, for instance, in the figures on the main panel at the front (Pl. 23) or in the *Three Marys at the Tomb* (Pl. 28) at the back, which look very much as though they were influenced by the upright cathedral-facade statues of Giovanni. But to a lesser extent it is also true of his early madonnas and their children. Duccio appears therefore as a highly eclectic artist responsible less for carrying forward a single new idea than for absorbing a range of influences from the artists around him and impressing them with the stamp of a delicate sensitivity, anxious to incorporate into his art the most luxurious inventions of his contemporaries and to create out of them masterpieces of modern refinement for the delectation of his patrons.

Unlike the madonnas of his earlier years, the *Maestà* is a large and complex work made up of more than fifty panels joined together. It consists of the great frontal presentation of the enthroned Virgin with saints and angels on either side and apostles above with, in addition, a large number of panels containing a narrative of the lives of the Virgin and Christ. It is the second, narrative element that has great historical significance. The *Maestà* (known dates 1308–11) followed shortly after Giotto's Paduan frescos (probably c.1304–5 or a little later) which succeeded or perhaps overlapped the St Francis cycle at Assisi (c.1290–1307), and it should be considered as part of a group consisting of these three works. They have much in common—though they offer also many contrasts—because they established a new style of narrative painting that had great influence over European pictorial assumptions for the next two centuries. The essence of the new narrative was the combination of several separate characteristics. First, a limited grasp of spatial perspective of a distinctly pragmatic kind, without the mathematics of Brunelleschi, but intended to give both buildings and figures a fairly shallow space within which they could be placed to front or rear realistically. Second, a highly developed capacity for drawing figures with roundness and weight, especially when they were heavily clothed with folded draperies. Third, a surface design which gave paintings patterns emphasizing the main features of the action which the painting was portraying, for example the emphasis of the direction of movement of the figures by the patterns of lines in the partially realistic landscape. Fourth, a constant awareness of the allegorical, symbolical, or figural significance of the subjects of the paintings so that, for example, the scene of *Wedding at Cana* might be placed above the *Lamentation* over the dead body of Christ, as it is in Giotto's Arena series, because Christ's miraculous conversion of water into wine foreshadowed the eucharistic conversion of bread and wine into his body and blood as a result of the Passion.

The new narrative is thus a combination of ancient and modern features. The symbolism and the significant design were inherited from the past. The grasp of the physical world of space, building, and figure entered rather suddenly into Italian painting at the end of the thirteenth century. The combination was made up of elements which could exist separately, as spatial depth can exist in modern painting without symbolism. The coexistence of these features driven into relationship with each other around 1300 had the effect, however, of making a very powerful amalgam. The symbolic pathos of the Crucifixion and the Nativity was enhanced by a degree of realistic representation in which the bodies and faces could be seen as if they could be felt. Perhaps we should see the new realism as appealing to the sensitivity of a richer and more sophisticated audience, but it also presented better opportunities than the old style for presenting the subtleties of a complex story. The conflict in the Massacre of the Innocents, or the Betrayal of Christ, is more effectively conveyed by a scene in which the meeting of opposed figures can be imagined as surrounded by figures which inhabit a convincing space. An artist who constructs a long series of scenes in which there is a fair degree of realism can make an effective presentation of a narrative, with semi-realistic episodes backing each other up and contributing by their symbolic interrelationship to the whole pattern of meaning. Since the meaning of the Christian story was essentially mystical and symbolic—the significance of biblical narratives seen as allegorical and figural—the level of semi-realism introduced into painting in the early fourteenth century was appropriate to religious narratives; it produced a fruitful combination. Thus the style of religious narrative was established for a long time, arguably until the successful balance of realism and symbolism was destroyed by the extreme realism of Michelangelo and Raphael.

The carefully worked-out narratives of Assisi, Padua, and Siena were expensive. We know very little about their financing but we imagine them as being paid for in the case of Assisi by the pope and the worshippers in the church buying indulgences, at Padua by a rich merchant also supported by indulgence buyers, at Siena by the communal government. A great deal of money was needed to finance painting schemes on such a scale; the buoyancy of papal and commercial incomes at this period is an essential part of their background.

So much is clear, but when it comes to unveiling the professional as opposed to the financial background to Duccio's brilliant invention we are completely without information and have to speculate. The speculation is all the more difficult because Duccio's other works are all madonnas, and include no scenes that could inform us about the earlier development of his narrative technique. It is possible that Duccio had dealings with Cimabue, and he was familiar with the works of Giovanni Pisano in Siena—we happen to know that in 1295 they were both members of a committee to advise the commune about a fountain. We have no evidence to connect Duccio with Giotto. It is difficult to believe, however, that the painter of the *Maestà* had not learnt from both Assisi and Padua; indeed it is difficult to believe that the *Maestà* was not his deliberate contribution to the treatment of pictorial narrative he had seen presented at Assisi and Padua. The narrative of the *Maestà* contains more panels than either of the other series, but of course they are much smaller; a series of wooden panel paintings, with great attention to detail, not frescos. Such a detailed account of the Passion is without precedent. There is no obvious literary source, apart from the Gospels, as there is at Assisi and Padua. The suggestion has been made that the choice of scenes was based on illuminations in a Byzantine manuscript,[11] and the idea that Duccio turned to a source like that when given the opportunity to paint the *Maestà*, combining the Byzantine choice of episodes with the inspiration of his Italian predecessors, is attractive. But the sources remain unclear, and the narrative may be based simply on choice from the Gospels.

The most striking difference between Duccio's style and the style of Assisi and Padua is that he has a less systematic interest in space. Giotto at Padua has a strong tendency to a rather unified space in each scene, and a persistent interest in placing buildings obliquely to the picture plane. This tendency is seen at an earlier stage at Assisi, as White has shown. Duccio has a general interest in space but it is extremely unsystematic, as if his work were not guided by any definite theoretical principles. The spatial organization of his panels is often inconsistent. An extreme case is the scene of the *Gathering of the Apostles*, on the front of the *Maestà*. The two pillars on the left of this scene appear to support an arch which is parallel with the front of the picture and the back wall of the room. This is clear in the top half of the scene. But on the floor Duccio has placed the Virgin's bed and a trestle on which figures are seated, also parallel to the front of the picture, behind one pillar and in front of the other. The result is spatial nonsense of a kind avoided at Assisi and Padua, though the general feeling of the space of the room survives. Did this characteristic arise because Duccio had no experience of Roman classical painting but was simply responding to Assisi and Padua? It is impossible to say. It should be added, however, that Duccio produces one enterprising spatial experiment not to be found in Giotto: the attempt to show a complex spatial interior through a narrow door. It appears strikingly in the *Temptation on the Temple* on the back predella, and also in the *Feast at Cana* in the same sequence. It looks like a luxury detail, adding to the painting's power to give visual pleasure but it is clearly related to Sienese spatial developments later in the century.

[11] Stubblebine, *Duccio*, i, pp. 48–52.

It is interesting to compare Duccio's treatment of the human figure with Giotto's. His figures do not have the weight of Giotto's. They are also sometimes absurdly distorted by elongation: the youths at the front of the *Feast at Cana*, for example, or the blind man in the *Healing of the Blind Man* (National Gallery), both from the predella at the back of the *Maestà*. But, as in his earlier madonnas, his treatment of drapery is often complex and satisfying. This may be the result of observing the treatment of drapery in Giovanni Pisano's sculpture, a reflection of the primary importance and precocity of sculpture in the Sienese tradition. A good example is provided by the figures of the three Marys in *The Marys at the Tomb* (Pl. 28) on the back of the *Maestà*. They are impressive, immobile figures with rich, folded drapery which look very much, as we have said, as though they had been inspired by some of Giovanni's standing figures for the facade of Siena cathedral. Duccio's style, then, is very different from Giotto's, less deliberately concerned with space and the human figure, though interested in both; different also from the style of the St Francis series at Assisi. He apparently stands apart from the Roman–Florentine tradition, influenced by the paintings and sculptures he knew at Siena, by Byzantine panels and manuscripts, by his own luxurious interest in detail and refinement of texture rather than realistic structure. Nevertheless his intention in the *Maestà* was evidently to compete with the narrative systems of Assisi and Padua in a different medium.

The *Maestà*, intended to be placed on the high altar of the cathedral, is designed to be seen from the front by the congregation in the nave, from the back by the clergy closer to it in the chancel. In the front (Pl. 23) Duccio therefore concentrated on size and visibility, in the back on detail visible only by close inspection. The greater part of the front is occupied by the main panel in which the Virgin, with the Child on her knee, is seated on a broad marble throne. To either side of her are three rows of angels and saints. In the middle row to the left are St John the Evangelist, St Peter, and St Catherine of Alexandria, to the right St John the Baptist, St Paul, and St Agnes. The two female saints, the least important, were both Virgins. Below them are four kneeling figures of the saintly protectors of Siena: St Ansanus, St Crescenzius, St Savinus and St Victor. The emphasis is on the Virgin and the city. Above these identifiable people are the angels, a pile of faces of handsome young figures. Above the whole assembly around the throne, in a separate line of small panels, are ten apostles, clothed in the same colours in which they reappear in the narrative pictures on the back. Above the Virgin were two panels (now missing) which probably contained the Assumption and Coronation of the Virgin. The central part of the front of the *Maestà*—Virgin, angels, saints, apostles—is a development of the structure of earlier polyptych and madonna altarpieces, which often contained similar figures; but it is of course an enormous development—in its size, in the elaboration of the Virgin's marble throne, and in the introduction of the idea of placing angels and saints in a crowd within one space. The space is executed with a mixture of realism in the kneeling area to the front, and an unrealistic piling up of faces at the rear. The effect was not intended to be spatially realistic. It may well have been influenced by the appearance of the numerous figures on the pulpit of Nicola Pisano or in Cimabue's *Santa Trinità Madonna*.

The narrative sequence begins with the six panels relating to the death of the Virgin along the top at the front, intended no doubt to be related to the missing Assumption and Coronation which were above. They are the *Annunciation of the Death of the Virgin*, the *Arrival of St John*, *Gathering of the Apostles*, *Death*, *Funeral Procession*, and *Burial*. The scenes on the left all take place within the same room with its rather awkward arched doorway mentioned earlier. The scenes on the right include a very large number of figures. In the background of the *Funeral* scene are the walls of Jerusalem, rising above them a hexagonal church building, perhaps the Holy Sepulchre, which reappears in the scene of the *Entry into Jerusalem* on the back. The scenes on the right, extremely rich in other respects, show comparatively little interest in space.

The seven predella scenes below the main panel on the front illustrate the early life of Christ. In the middle is the rounded arch of the *Presentation in the Temple*, appropriately and symmetrically below the figure of the enthroned Virgin. To the left are the *Annunciation*, the beautifully coloured scene which has wandered to the National Gallery, portraying a businesslike, classically robed Gabriel, *Nativity*, and *Adoration*. To the right are the *Massacre of the Innocents*, the *Flight into Egypt*, and the *Teaching in the Temple* (Pl. 29). The latter is a complex scene. Christ sits on a parapet before an arched arcade, with winged classical figures in niches above the square pillars behind him. To the front are two rows of seated disputing elders, rather graphically portrayed. Behind one of the rows are Mary and Joseph who have come to recover Christ. The floor has an elaborate pattern. A large dark arch to the right appears to invite the viewer to move round behind the picture where the series will continue. It is also noticeable, however, that the effort to fit in the arch has led to the complete spatial confusion of the architecture.

We then move to the predella of the back (Pl. 24), the first scene of which, probably a Baptism, is missing.[12] Eight scenes from the Ministry of Christ survive: the *Temptations on the Temple* and *on the Mountain*, the *Calling of Peter and Andrew*, the *Feast at Cana*, the *Woman of Samaria*, the *Healing of the Blind Man*, the *Transfiguration*, and the *Raising of Lazarus*. Above the predella is the elaborate story of the Passion (Pl. 25) occupying most of the back of the *Maestà*. The story is dominated by the three wide panels of the *Agony in the Garden*, the *Betrayal of Christ*, and the *Crucifixion*, probably continued upwards by scenes (now lost) of the Ascension and perhaps Christ

[12] I follow the analysis of the *Maestà* by White, *Duccio*, pp. 119–34. It is to some extent controversial. For other views of the arrangement of the *Maestà* see Deuchler, *Duccio*, pp. 46–81.

in Glory. The story of the Passion begins in the bottom left-hand corner with the tall panel of the *Entry into Jerusalem* (Pl. 26) whose surface shape, Christ riding up the road diagonally to the entrance to the city in the top half, is balanced by the two panels of the *First Denial* and *Christ before Annas*, to the right of the centre, which are given a similar external form by the staircase across the *First Denial*, parallel to the road in the *Entry into Jerusalem*. The *Entry* looks as though it was painted in admiration of the delightful Entry attributed to Guido da Siena on a Lenten hanging (Siena Pinacoteca no. 8) adapted by recollection of the more rational arrangement of Giotto's *Entry* at Padua, which has a road rationally entering a city. But Duccio's panel has, characteristically, a much larger number of figures, giving the impression of a crowd at the gates, with a great range of carefully modelled faces, and a complex city behind the wall, crowned by the polygonal building looking like a baptistery.

Between the *Entry* and the centre are four smaller panels showing the *Washing of the Feet*, the *Last Supper, Judas Taking the Bribe*, and *Christ Taking Leave of the Apostles*. Duccio presumably wished to make a contrast between the purification of the *Washing*, with black sandals cast off, and the adjacent group of shifty old men with black feet bribing Judas. He also contrasted the excited scene of the *Supper* with the solemn, anxious group before Jesus at the *Leave-taking*. The magnificent broad scenes of the *Agony* and the *Betrayal*, with the long sweep of coloured robes emphasizing the repose and movement of the figures, take place in a similar rocky landscape, its tilt upwards to the right repeated but with the trees rearranged to fit different groups of figures, and the orange trees to the front removed to make the betrayal starker. In each of the two panels are three groups: Christ in Prayer, Christ and St Peter, and Sleeping Apostles, paralleled by Fleeing Apostles, Capture of Christ, and Peter Cutting Off the Ear of Malchus.

We move right to a group of six scenes showing the development of the Trial of Christ; the double panel of the *First Denial* and *Christ before Annas*, repeating the shape of the *Entry into Jerusalem*; the *Second* and *Third Denials*, both taking place outside the same room in which Christ faces Caiaphas and is later mocked; and a double showing of another room, once for *Christ Accused by the Pharisees* and once for *Christ before Pilate*. The arrangement of panels in this corner of the back of the *Maestà* is highly symmetrical. Caiaphas's room is more bare with an oblique throne and pointed arches. Pilate's room is expressly classical, with columns and lintels. The group of figures in Caiaphas's room is roughly repeated; so is the group in Pilate's.

The four panels at the bottom right-hand corner of the Passion sequence, full of scenes taking place in box-like rooms, are balanced by the similar four panels at the top left-hand corner in which the story of Christ's trial is carried further. Here we have first a pair of scenes of *Christ before Herod*, in a room more similar to that in which the Caiaphas scenes took place, and Christ brought again in a white robe before Pilate in his classical room, following the story in Luke xxiii. This is succeeded by a pair of scenes, again in Pilate's room, in which the *Flagellation* and the *Crowning with Thorns* take place. In the next pair of scenes, the first is again in Pilate's room, where he is washing his hands; but the second, the *Carrying of the Cross*, is a preparation for the dark terror of the *Crucifixion*. Here there is no architecture or landscape, only a dense crowd of moving figures behind Jesus, the cross carried ahead of him, Mary sadly following. And so we come to the great central panel of the *Crucifixion* (Pl. 27) itself, which presents a scene of terrible anguish. The light and carefully modelled, almost nude body of Jesus, which must owe much to the model of French and Pisan ivory sculpture, is nailed to the cross against a gold background. At the foot of the cross, Mary and her followers fall away to one side, the Jewish malefactors to the other. It is a scene of turbulent emotion under a dark and desolate sky, an earth-shattering event at the moment of the sun's eclipse.

To the right of the *Crucifixion* are six more scenes in which the square framing of the trial of Christ is abandoned, and the story returns to a diagonal upward movement which repeats the movement in the *Entry into Jerusalem*. The first pair of scenes in this section is the *Deposition*, in which the ladder placed against the cross balances the tilt of the cross in the *Carrying of the Cross*, and the *Entombment*, in which the figures are bent over a large tomb in front of a rocky landscape. The large and complex crowds of actors in the previous scenes are replaced by the small group of Christ's immediate followers. The next pair is the *Harrowing of Hell*, a resplendent, cross-carrying Christ trampling down a devil to release Abraham and other Old Testament figures from the dark cave of hell; and the beautifully composed *Marys at the Tomb* with the stately, robed figures of the Virgin, the Magdalen, and the Mother of James and Joseph leaning away from the symmetrical white angel above the empty tomb. The last two scenes—the *Noli me Tangere*, and the *Apparition on the road to Emmaus*—are both given a strongly tilted form, the lie of the sharp rocks behind the *Noli me Tangere* being parallel to the road tilted upwards to the equally parallel shape of the elaborate entrance to Emmaus.

The six surviving panels from the top back, above the Passion sequence, carry the story forward to Pentecost: the *Apparition behind Closed Doors* and the *Incredulity of Thomas*, both before a round-arched building with leaf-work lintels; the *Apparition on the Sea of Tiberias*, which repeats the scene of the *Calling of Peter and Andrew*, the *Apparitions in Galilee* and *at Supper* and finally the rounded group at *Pentecost*.

The core idea of the *Maestà* was to match the large-scale array of Madonna and Child with angels, saints, and Apostles on the front with the Passion sequence on the back, made up of a large number of panels but making a piece with much the same shape and size. The Passion sequence is carefully organized into a symmetrical arrangement dominated by the *Crucifixion*, the balance of square scenes at bottom-right and top-left and upward-moving scenes at bottom-left and top-right making it a unified picture. To grasp the unity, one has to take account not only of the story line, running left to right and lower to upper, but also of the surface balance of shapes over the whole rectangle, the static form of the square process scenes against the upward movement of the beginning and end of the sequence. No doubt the upward tendency would have been accentuated further by the two missing panels above the *Crucifixion*, probably showing the Ascension and Christ in Glory. The idea was to show the Saviour's return to heaven through the agonies of the Passion as both a sequential upward-moving story and a graphic representation. Above and below these main areas of the enthroned Madonna and the Crucifixion were assembled four shorter sequences of narrative: above the Virgin, the story of her death in preparation for her Assumption, below her the childhood of Christ under her guidance, below the Passion the earlier ministry of Christ, above it his apparitions after death in preparation for his ascension.

A much later commentator remarked that the *Maestà* is like a Trojan horse in Sienese painting. It was followed by a flood of highly original works by Simone Martini, the Lorenzetti brothers and others, many of which seemed to derive inspiration from aspects of the *Maestà*, making the first half of the fourteenth century a highly innovative period. It is probably wrong to deduce that the *Maestà* was a collaborative work in the sense that different panels were designed by different masters; White's analysis shows that it can best be explained as the development of the plans of a single master, who no doubt painted with the help of assistants. We have suggested here that the details of the work are explicable with reference to a careful master plan, which makes it difficult to believe that much of the structure of individual panels could have been left to the caprice of subordinates. Although it is not isolated in relation to later paintings, the appearance of the *Maestà* is curiously sudden—in this way unlike Giotto's Arena chapel frescos—in relation to its antecedents. We do not see preliminary stages in Duccio's work. The most likely explanation for this is that it resulted from an exceptionally lavish new commission which inspired him to work out a novel conception heavily influenced by contemplation of the painting at Assisi and Padua in which he had had no part.

The *Maestà* impresses because of the fineness of the flowing forms of its draped figures, its sense of pattern, the profusion of original faces, the acute sense of the drama of the Passion story. These features can all be explained in part by the background of the art of the Pisani, and Duccio's earlier command of paintings of the Madonna. The mastery of a highly developed realistic space, which we associate with Giotto, is only partly imitated. The Giottesque ability to represent dramatic relations between individual figures is hardly present at all. We therefore have to consider the *Maestà*, exquisite as it is in its craftsmanship and its firm grasp of the essentials of the Christian story, as only a partial encounter with the new art. For the essentials of the artistic revolution we have to turn to Giotto, and from him back to his Roman predecessors.

Giotto's early life, until a date after the upper basilica at Assisi and the Arena chapel at Padua were complete, is without documentary evidence and extremely obscure. He is mentioned in a document dated 4 January 1309 recording his repayment of a loan at Assisi. On 23 December 1311 he promised to make a payment at Florence. In 1312—this is the earliest reference to him in connection with his paintings—money was left for a lamp in front of his *Crucifix* in Santa Maria Novella. In the following year he appointed a proctor to recover household goods he had left in Rome. By this time, references of a different kind are beginning to appear in literary sources. About 1312 the chronicler Riccobaldo da Ferrara refers to work by him at Assisi, Rimini, and Padua. The passage in Dante's *Purgatorio* about his surpassing Cimabue as a painter was probably written not much later. From these documents we can deduce with confidence only that he was at Assisi some time before 1309 and at Rome some time before 1312, and that the Santa Maria Novella *Crucifix* was painted by 1312 when he was already a famous painter. We do not know whether he was born in the 1260s or 1270s, or how he was trained. The important stages in his development can be deduced only by speculation based on examination of works of art he may have painted.[13]

The early documents about the Arena chapel at Padua, which contains Giotto's masterpiece in fresco on its walls, do not mention him. They tell us that the land was bought in 1300, and that the pope granted indulgences to visitors to the chapel on 1 March 1304. On 9 January 1305 the construction of the church was sufficiently advanced for the nearby Eremitani monks to complain that Enrico Scrovegni, the owner of the Arena chapel, had built a bell tower for excessively large bells, and apparently that the church as a whole was too elaborate. Two months later Scrovegni was borrowing hangings for the consecration.[14] It seems probable therefore that the Arena chapel was painted perhaps about 1304–5, perhaps a little later.

Apart from the disputed paintings in the upper basilica at Assisi there are other notable surviving works by Giotto, or probably by Giotto, which may well have been painted earlier and therefore provide information about the advances in his style before his work at Padua. One of these, perhaps the

---

[13] P. Murray, 'Notes on some Early Giotto Sources', *Journal of the Warburg and Courtauld Institutes*, xvi, 1953; idem, 'On the Date of Giotto's Birth', *Giotto e il suo tempo* (Rome, 1971); V. Martinelli 'Un documento per Giotto ad Assisi', *Storia dell'arte*, xvii, 1973. Most of the documents are listed by G. Previtali, *Giotto e la sua bottega* (Milan, 1967), pp. 148–52.

[14] Documents translated by J. H. Stubblebine, *Giotto: The Arena Chapel Frescoes* (London, 1969), pp. 103–8. For a good account of the problem of chronology, see E. Borsook, *The Mural Painters of Tuscany* (2nd edn Oxford, 1980), pp. 7–8.

earliest, is the *Crucifix* in Santa Maria Novella (Pl. 30). The figure of Christ is a development away from the intense and diagrammatic crucifixions typical in the Tuscan tradition of the thirteenth century. It marks a new seriousness in the treatment of the male nude, with new aims: the torso is designed to reveal a more realistic rib-cage and stomach. The face hangs in suffering; it is a real face, not a series of twisted lines.[15] The similarity with the small-scale crucifix in the *Verification of the Stigmata* scene in the *St Francis* series seems to imply that the *Crucifix* is an early work, probably of the 1290s.

The *Ognissanti Madonna* (Pl. 31) in the Uffizi reveals a technical skill of a different kind. The Madonna is seated on an elaborate three-dimensional throne whose high sides and back have arches derived from Gothic sculptural forms, rather like the *ciboria* recently sculpted for San Paolo fuori le Mura and Santa Cecilia in Trastevere at Rome. But the most important difference from earlier madonnas is the sense of weight given to the figures. The Madonna herself sits heavily on the throne. The angels in the foreground have the appearance of kneeling squarely on the ground. The gravity of the faces, especially that of the Child, is perhaps what strikes the onlooker most powerfully, but the position of the figures in space is more important in the history of artistic style.[16] The Louvre *Stigmatization*, painted for San Francesco, Pisa, which has on the frame *Opus Iocti Florentini*, takes up the version of the stigmatization developed for the series in the upper basilica at Assisi and has a predella with three other scenes from Francis's life, also based on the paintings at Assisi.[17] If this is by Giotto or his workshop it is also important, like the Rimini *Crucifixion*, as evidence of his geographical movements at the beginning of the fourteenth century. It does not, however, have anything like the importance which the Santa Maria Novella *Crucifix* and the *Ognissanti Madonna* have in the evolution of artistic style. In these two latter works, Giotto took the two most prominent types of ecclesiastical panel-painting of the thirteenth century, the Crucifix and the Madonna and Child, and transformed them by the introduction of realistic figures. Instead of being symbolical expressions of religious ideas, depending for their power on the forceful use of stylized pattern and luxurious decoration, they became representations of the human body whose expressiveness depended on the visual realism of the shapes and the conveying of a real presence in a real place. The Crucifixion is a sad body, not twisted into an extremity of patterned distortion but showing its expression in the serious, modest endurance of its

---

[15] Previtali, *Giotto*, pp. 31–6, 330–3; C. Brandi, *Giotto* (Milan, 1983), pp. 64–6.

[16] Previtali, *Giotto*, pp. 83, 334–5; Brandi, *Giotto*, pp. 118–22; L. Marcucci, *Gallerie Nazionali di Firenze: i dipinti toscani del secolo XIV* (Rome, 1965), pp. 11–14.

[17] J. Gardner, 'The Louvre Stigmatization and the Problem of the Narrative Altar-Piece', *Zeitschrift für Kunstgeschichte*, liv, 1982. It may be that the Stefaneschi altar-piece is also a work by Giotto painted in the pontificate of Boniface VIII (J. Gardner, 'The Stefaneschi Altar-piece: a Reconsideration', *Journal of the Warburg and Courtauld Institutes*, xxxvii, 1974). But there are stylistic arguments for a later date (J. White, *Duccio*, pp. 140–50) which leave the question uncertain.

face. The Madonna is a majestic woman whose commanding strength is inseparably connected with the weight of her body. If we are right in thinking that these paintings precede the Arena frescos, Giotto had already shown himself to be an unparalleled master of the significant human body in a manner which was to be incorporated into later paintings but on which he did not improve greatly in the last thirty years of his life.

Historians have been repeatedly troubled by the question of whether the *Legend of St Francis* in the upper basilica of Assisi and the Arena frescos can both be the work of Giotto. There are strong arguments against giving the two series to the same man,[18] derived in part from differences between the painting of faces. The paler and smoother faces at Padua do not have the patches of deep shadow made by leaving dark underpainting bare, and the structure of drapery and limbs is in general cruder and less finished in the St Francis series. Still more convincing is the contrast between the structure of the individual scenes. The essence of this is that the Paduan scenes are more tightly organized. Figures are placed in significant relations to each other in a band across the front of the space in the composition. The background space, landscape, and architecture are limited, and in general rather closely related to the groups of figures often placed in front of them. At Assisi, on the other hand, the figures are often more clearly distinguished from the space behind, individuals are sometimes less clearly related to the action or idea which it is the main purpose of the panel to represent, architecture is less idealized, and landscape can be present in great stretches of hillside which have little relation to the main action. This contrast is striking. It has convinced some historians that it is impossible to imagine Assisi and Padua as different stages in the evolution of the same artist.

Emphasis on the contrast has probably paid too little attention to the difference between the size of the scenes, 270 cm. high by 230 cm. wide at Assisi, against 185 cm. by 200 cm. at Padua. With panels as large as these at Assisi it would have been difficult to establish the same relations between figures and background without multiplying the figures or grossly enlarging them. Apart from this, however, the differences between the scenes at Assisi and Padua cannot be understood without comparing the relationship of the paintings with the purposes for which they were composed. Both the St Francis series and the Arena frescos are closely related to precise literary sources and to general religious conceptions which they were intended to present. But the literary sources and the conceptions are extremely different. There is no better way to define and grasp the character of the great display at Padua than by comparing its intention with that of its predecessor at Assisi.

The St Francis series at Assisi is dominated by the simple and definite instructions which must have been given to the painter and his workshop. At

---

[18] Stated by R. Offner, 'Giotto, Non-Giotto', *Burlington Magazine*, lxxiv, lxxv, 1939, reprinted in Stubblebine, *Giotto*; and M. Meiss, *Giotto and Assisi* (New York, 1960).

the time when they were painted, the life of St Francis was the subject of bitter dispute within the Franciscan order. In choosing to represent it in the form of illustrations to a series of scenes drawn from Bonaventure's official *Legenda Maior*, the order was taking a deliberate stand, based on a particular literary source whose attitudes would have been disputed by the Franciscan spirituals in a quarrel of which everyone at Assisi was intensely aware. It would have been impossible to allow the painter to deviate from precise iconographical instructions. One notable addition to the *Legenda Maior* is in the last scene, the posthumous *Liberation of the Prisoner*, in which Francis, after the achievement of the Liberation, is ascending into the skies in a pose rather similar to that of Christ's *Ascension* on the entrance wall.[19] Bonaventure gives no authority for this final emphasis on the parallelism of the lives of Francis and Christ. In general, however, the content of the episodes as they were related by Bonaventure is followed faithfully, and a very short summary of each episode was put as an inscription under each scene.[20] The painter could not have been allowed to use his imagination in ways that might have undermined the precise intentions of the patrons.

Still more important is the general character of the story of Francis's life as reported in the *Legenda Maior* which had to be illustrated. It does not have a unifying structure leading up to the Passion, such as could be given to the life of Christ. It has no set of characters for whom a continuous story-line could be developed like Mary, St John and Judas, who have such large roles at Padua. Francis did have important relations with other people—for example his father, the pope, or St Clare—but they were not continuous or repeated relations. It was possible to emphasize themes in Francis's life, such as poverty, the rebuilding of the church, papal approval, the idea of Ascension, posthumous miracles. But, beyond this, his life was bound to be a series of fairly separate episodes, without the sense of continuous, ominous conflict which runs through the scenes at Padua. In most of the scenes Francis was bound, if one was to follow Bonaventure, to be a fairly isolated individual without the changing but continuous collection of friends and foes which gives unity to the scenes at Padua, and also allows each scene there to be a tightly knit drama of relations between significant people. These differences of purpose and dramatic structure in the dominant literary sources probably make it rather futile to work out the aesthetic contrast between the two series of paintings as if they were the work of artists operating under similar conditions.

In spite of the emphasis on the parallelism of the lives of Francis and Christ at Assisi and the literary pursuit of this motif, culminating in the late fourteenth century in Bartholomew of Pisa's book *On the Conformity of the*

[19] Mitchell, *Giotto e il suo tempo*, p. 123.
[20] The texts are set out by A. Smart, *The Assisi Problem and the Art of Giotto* (Oxford, 1971), pp. 263–93.

Life of the Blessed Francis to the Life of the Lord Jesus,[21] the contrast between literary sources has to be remembered. The structure of the life of Francis, as reported by Celano and Bonaventure, is quite different from the structure of the life of Christ in the Gospels. If Franciscan attitudes to a holy life influenced views of the life of Christ through the *Meditationes Vitae Christi* or the *Legenda Aurea*, it was an influence on the more life-like interpretation of individual scenes rather than on the general shape of the events leading to the Crucifixion.

The *Life of St Francis* opens on the north wall near to the crossing with a bay containing three preparatory scenes (Pl. 32): the *Homage of a Simple Man of Assisi* (I), *The Gift of the Mantle to a Poor Knight* (II), and the *Vision of the Palace* (III). The group is given symmetry by the dominant architecture in the two outer panels contrasted with the country landscape in the central panel. We then move on to a trio of scenes representing the call to Francis in the *Miracle of the Crucifix* at San Damiano (IV), Francis's *Renunciation of Worldly Goods* (V), and the *Dream of Innocent III*, in which Francis is supporting the church of St John Lateran (VI). At the centre of the bay are the figures of the nude and modest Francis facing his wealthy and angry father. The composition works back on either side from the central gap between them. Again the two outer panels have balancing designs of architecture in contrast to the central panel, which has two separated buildings rising above Francis and his father like the two tower-capped hills in the central panel of the first trio. The third bay (Pl. 33), representing the *Sanctioning of the Rule* by Innocent III (VII), the friars' *Vision of the Chariot* (VIII), and the *Vision of the Throne* reserved for him in heaven (IX), again repeats the same pattern. In the two outer panels the pattern of the roof of the pope's palace balances the row of thrones high in the air, while the central panel has a different shape.

The north wall ends with a larger bay, towards the entrance to the church, that contains four scenes: the *Exorcism of the Demons at Arezzo* (X), *Francis before the Sultan* (XI), his *Ecstasy* (XII), and the miracle of the appearance of the Christ-child at the *Christmas Crib at Greccio* (XIII). Though it appears less obviously, this bay also has a symmetrical pattern like those in the previous bays. At the centre the oblique position of the building in the ecstasy scene balances the opposite obliqueness of the canopy above the Sultan's throne. The mass of the church screen behind the scene at Greccio balances the mass of the buildings at Arezzo behind Silvester. There is a rhythm in the figures, the raised hands of Silvester and Francis in ecstasy interspersed with the flatter scenes of the Sultan and Greccio. On either side of the door (Pl. 34) the series continues with two scenes which have an appropriate similarity of structure: the *Miracle of the Spring* (XIV) and the *Sermon to the Birds* (XV). In both of these scenes the figures are set against a delightful rural

[21] H. W. van Os, 'St Francis of Assisi as a Second Christ in Early Italian Painting', *Simiolus*, vii, 1974.

background. Then follows the four-panel bay on the south wall (Pl. 35): the miraculous *Death of the Knight of Celano* (XVI), Francis's *Sermon before Pope Honorius III* (XVII), the miraculous *Appearance at Arles* (XVIII), and finally the *Stigmatization* (XIX). This completes the story of the ministry of Francis after the approval of the rule with which all the stories at this end of the church (X–XIX) are concerned. The scenes illustrate the variety of Francis's work: miracles, preaching to pagan and Christian, devotion to animals. The climax of the *Stigmatization* scene is emphasized by the bright area of white rock around Francis, surrounding him like a vast halo.

We now return to bays containing three panels. The first is concerned with his death: the *Death and Ascension* (XX), the *Vision of the Ascension* (XXI) and the *Funeral and Verification of the Stigmata* (XXII). The second (Pl. 36) is concerned with posthumous recognition: *Francis mourned by St Clare* (XXIII), the *Canonization* (XXIV), and the *Appearance to Pope Gregory IX* (XXV). The last is a group of posthumous miracles: the *Healing of the Wounded Man* (XXVI), the *Confession of the Woman of Benevento* (XXVII) and the *Liberation of the Prisoner* (XXVIII). With these bays we return also to patterns something like those visible in the early bays on the opposite wall, though rather less obvious. In scenes XX–XXII the shapes of the two outer scenes balance: in the *Death and Ascension* (XX) and the *Verification of The Stigmata* (XXII) the body of Francis lies outstretched near the bottom, with a crowd of figures above and behind him in the central band topped in the one case by Francis ascending and in the other by the crucifix. The central panel of the vision of the *Ascension* (XXI) has a different structure.

It is possible also to point to significant parallels between the scenes on the north and south walls. The first scene of Francis stepping onto the cloak offered to him in Assisi, the site emphasized by the approximate portrayal of the Roman building, faces the final scene of the *Liberation of the Prisoner*, where Rome is made easily recognizable by Trajan's column. Francis's story begins at Assisi, ends at Rome. Rome patronizes the Franciscan order in general and this basilica in particular. This is a Roman church celebrating a Roman saint. The raised hands of Francis in ecstasy in scene XII on the north wall and his position within the painting are repeated in his appearance at Arles in scene XVIII, almost opposite on the south wall. There are many parallels and repetitions of this kind. In analysis of the structure of the series, however, most prominence should be given to the fairly obvious breaking up of the story into chapters, as in the *Legenda Maior*, within which the scenes are related in a symmetrical fashion: preparation, establishment of the order, premonitions of saintliness, ministry culminating in the stigmata, death, recognition, miraculous powers. This was the message which the series was intended to convey. It offered a remarkable lesson in the arrangement of separate episodes within a pattern whose external, aesthetic significance helped to convey the internal, theological message.

The use of space and architecture in the St Francis scenes has been examined by White and Gioseffi.[22] The designer has advanced beyond the spatial systems used in the rest of the upper church partly by having a stronger general sense of the presence of groups within an open space, as for example in the *Crib at Greccio* scene: there is no attempt to present the total spatial structure of the church but the limited space behind the screen is given a convincing depth. There is also a convincing attempt to draw a group within a large, square room, seen from a position slightly right of the centre, in the *Sanctioning of the Rule by Innocent III* and the *Sermon before Honorius III*. Moreover many of the buildings are presented in an oblique view which gives a strong sense of the space to the two sides—most effectively in the *Miracle of the Crucifix* at San Damiano, where the interior of the building is shown as well. This experiment with space was not, of course, an attempt to present a mathematically correct focus for the whole space of the painting, such as Brunelleschi and Masaccio developed in the fifteenth century. It was probably based on an empirical imitation of the buildings in Roman paintings. Indeed, if one compares the spatial scheme within the panels and the painted architectural framework around them at Assisi with the classical Roman wall painting from Boscoreale in New York,[23] it is plain that the whole spatial system of the St Francis legend must have been based on Roman painting, probably on examples in Rome which have since disappeared. The spatial system was however also subordinated to the demands of the story, in the sense that oblique and frontal views were used to contribute to the patterned relationship of the panels.

Another marked feature of the St Francis legend was the painting of real, existing architectural settings. Not only Assisi and Rome in the first and last scenes, but also the ciborium in the *Crib at Greccio*, which appears to be based on the Gothic ciboria built by Arnolfo di Cambio at San Paolo fuori le Mura and Santa Cecilia in Trastevere. There are many references to recent architectural innovations and it is probable that if real buildings were better preserved we should be able to identify still more direct imitations.

The work of illustrating the St Francis legend at Assisi was in part repeated by Giotto about twenty years later at the Bardi Chapel in Santa Croce at Florence (Pl. 37), probably painted after 1317 (in view of the presence of St Louis of Toulouse who was canonized in that year) and well before 1329, when the work of Ambrogio Lorenzetti appears to show knowledge of the paintings in the neighbouring Peruzzi Chapel, generally thought to be later.

[22] J. White, *The Birth and Rebirth of Pictorial Space* (London, 1957), pp. 33–47; D. Gioseffi, *Giotto architetto* (Milan, 1963), pp. 16–32.

[23] Gioseffi, op. cit., p. 153. There is a more general study of borrowing from Roman painting by J. R. Benton, 'Some Ancient Mural Motifs in Italian Painting around 1300', *Zeitschrift für Kunstgeschichte*, xlviii, 1985.

Giotto painted the *Stigmatization* on the wall outside the chapel and six more scenes on the side walls within: on the left-hand side the semicircular painting of Francis's *Renunciation of Worldly Goods*, below it rectangular paintings of the *Appearance at Arles* and the *Funeral and Verification of the Stigmata*; on the right-hand side the semicircular *Confirmation of the Rule*, and below it *Francis before the Sultan*, and his posthumous *Appearance to the Bishop of Assisi and Brother Agostino*.

Comparison with the frescos at Assisi shows a studied concern for the design of the paintings to fit the shape of the space available. In contrast to Assisi, all the panels except the *Stigmatization* are much broader than they are high. The *Stigmatization* panel is rather similar in shape to the one at Assisi, and its general design is similar too. The main difference is that, instead of kneeling to face the seraph directly as at Assisi, Francis has been given a more complex pose, kneeling away to the right and twisting the upper part of his body back to the left to meet the rays from the seraph, a position more like some of the figures in Giovanni Pisano's sculpture. The painting in the Bardi Chapel is probably not all by Giotto,[24] but the figures in the other frescos too have a greater suppleness and freedom of movement than figures at Assisi— for example, the famous figure of the young friar looking out from behind the curtain in the *Appearance to the Bishop of Assisi and Brother Agostino*. More striking, however, is the way the figures are spread out across the breadth of the panels, each occupying a separate spatial position, in contrast to the less realistic piling up of figures at Assisi, for example in the *Renunciation of Worldly Goods*. This is partly a result of the broad shape of the composition but must also be partly a result of the command of space which Giotto had acquired at Padua. The architectural background of each scene is designed to fit and fill the space of the panel, hence the oblique block of the classical structure rising above the crowd to fit the semicircle in the *Renunciation of Worldly Goods* and the two side-pieces added to the main room in the *Sanctioning of the Rule*. The architecture and the architectural space are not particularly interesting, with the one exception of the grandiose irrelevance of the building in the *Renunciation of Worldly Property*, which suggests that the artist has an imaginative interest in drawing buildings rather like that shown by the artist at Assisi. Nor are the pictures remarkable like the Padua paintings for dramatic tension; in this respect they reveal, as at Assisi, the limitations of the Franciscan stories. The main aesthetic interest of the Bardi Chapel lies in its profusion of expert and advanced figure-drawing.

Comparing Padua and the Bardi Chapel one sees that the same artist can respond in different ways to different physical settings and different kinds of stories. If anything, the comparison makes one more inclined to believe that Giotto, the painter at Padua and Santa Croce, could have been involved at

[24] E. Borsook, 'Giotto nelle Capelle Bardi e Peruzzi', *Giotto e Giotteschi in Santa Croce* (Florence, 1966).

Assisi too. The progression from Assisi, through Padua to Santa Croce must be seen as a single line of development.

Though the scenes of the St Francis legend at Assisi are strong in space and landscape, they are relatively weak in drama, for the literary reasons mentioned earlier. The two panels of the Isaac, Jacob, and Esau story in the earlier Old Testament series on the north wall above the St Francis legend, however, are painted with an extremely telling dramatic sense. The first panel, *Isaac Blessing Jacob*, shows Jacob and a woman, probably his mother Rebecca, standing before the reclining Isaac who is feeling his falsely hairy hand. In the second panel, the *Rejection of Esau* (Pl. 38), better preserved, Jacob and Rebecca are moving out of the scene and the real Esau stands before his father offering him the savory meat, with another woman, perhaps a servant, behind him. The two scenes are both placed within a moderately realistic box-like room, open on two sides. It is, however, the figures which are important because their stance and facial expression establish a relationship between them. Esau bends forward offering the food, his face innocent and bewildered by the evident signs of rejection expressed by the hands of the dignified Isaac, while the woman behind him looks on with perhaps slightly guilty concern. The three figures are interrelated realistically, and describe precisely the moment when 'he said, I am thy son, thy first-born Esau. And Isaac trembled very exceedingly, and said, Who?' (Genesis 27: 32–3).

The names of the painters of the St Francis legend and the Isaac scenes are unknown. The probability is that several painters worked on the St Francis scenes. Whether Giotto was involved is beyond our knowledge. It is clear, however, that the upper basilica contains the materials, especially those based on the imitation of Roman painting, which were necessary before the step taken at Padua could be made: the presentation of realistic drama in the relationship of human figures, the advanced sense of space, the ability to manage a complex series of episodes with a complex visual interdependence illuminating a theological lesson, skill in fresco painting on a large scale. Whoever the painter or designer may have been, much of this technique has been directly transferred from Rome; the painting at Assisi is, as far as we can see, essentially an adaptation of classical methods which could only be learned at Rome. The Arena frescos at Padua, painted just after Roman patronage had collapsed, were probably a rich man's attempt to imitate the success achieved at Assisi in covering the interior of a church with fresco. The Arena chapel, with its smooth, uninterrupted walls and light from windows in one wall only, was built to be painted. It seems likely that Scrovegni, the patron at Padua, would have tried to attract someone who had been involved in the triumph at Assisi, and it may be regarded as certain, in spite of the contrasts between his style and those of the 'St Francis Master', the 'Master of St Cecilia', and the 'Isaac Master', that Giotto knew a great deal about what had been done at Assisi, and used that knowledge in his work at Padua. The exploitation of the Roman patterns provided the essential preparation for the use of the Roman lessons outside the Roman orbit.

The major purpose of the paintings at Padua is to tell the story of Christ, his family, the Apostles and the Passion. Certain elements in the events, however, are emphasized in an exceptional way which gives the story a particular colour. One of these emphases is on the figure of Judas,[25] who is prominently displayed receiving money from priests for the betrayal of Jesus in a vivid portrait of devilish avarice and treachery which balances the loving meeting of Mary with Elizabeth the mother of John the Baptist on the other side of the chancel arch (Pl. 39), and in another scene kissing Jesus at the time of his seizure. It may also be someone whose face deliberately resembles Judas's who sits in the temple receiving the blessing of a priest in the first scene while Joachim is expelled. In the *Last Judgement*, Judas hangs at a point between the cross and the entrance to hell roughly equidistant to the point on the other, redeemed side of the cross, where the donor kneels presenting the chapel to the Virgin. Around the hanging Judas are other damned in a clear association with money bags, as though avarice were an important part of the reason for their condemnation.

Still more important for the structure of the story told by the paintings is the apparent emphasis on the Immaculate Conception and Chastity.[26] The wish to emphasize this element in Jesus's story is the most plausible explanation for the generous amount of space given to the preliminary story of Anna, Joachim, Mary and Joseph, which fills the whole of the top level of the chapel (Pls 40, 41). Joachim and Joseph were both elderly men, incapable of procreation, and Mary and Jesus were born as a result of divine intervention. This is made very clear in the several scenes devoted to Joachim, who plays a prominent part in the whole sequence. This theme is continued in the prominence given to St John the Evangelist. In the *Wedding at Cana* John is the bridegroom and is seated on the left hand of Jesus, and in the *Last Judgement* he appears to be one of the three figures receiving the Arena Chapel from Enrico Scrovegni, the other two being the Virgin and perhaps St Ursula, following Scrovegni's endowment of a convent of Sant' Orsola.

The series begins at the end of the top level of the south wall at the chancel arch. On this level are the first six scenes showing the story of Joachim (Pl. 40), beginning with his humiliating expulsion from the temple for failure to be a father, and ending with the joyful meeting with his wife Anna at the Golden Gate when she is pregnant. Opposite, at the top level of the north wall are the six scenes of the early life of Mary (Pl. 41), from her birth to her return home. Then follows the *Annunciation*, shown by Mary and the Angel Gabriel facing

[25] U. Schlegel, 'Zum Bildprogramm der Arena Kapelle', *Zeitschrift für Kunstgeschichte*, xx, 1957, trans. in Stubblebine, *Giotto*.

[26] R. H. Rough, 'Enrico Scrovegni, the *Cavalieri Gaudenti* and the Arena Chapel in Padua', *Art Bulletin*, lxii, 1980.

across the top of the arch while the broad and delightful scene of *God the Father sending Gabriel* to make the Annunciation fills the arc between the arch and the vault (Pl. 39). The story takes off again at a lower level with the *Visitation* below the *Annunciation*, and continues at the same level on the south wall with five scenes of the birth and childhood of Jesus, ending with the *Massacre of the Innocents* (Pl. 42). The series continues along the north wall with five scenes of Jesus's ministry, ending with the *Expulsion from the Temple* and then the *Pact of Judas* on the chancel-arch wall (Pl. 43). The lowest level begins with the *Last Supper* on the south wall at the chancel end (Pl. 44). The five scenes on this side end with the *Mocking of Jesus*. The Passion story continues on the north wall (Pl. 45) with the *Way to Calvary*, and goes through the *Crucifixion* and the events following it to end with *Pentecost*. Finally, to complete the whole sequence, one must look back to the huge and dominating *Last Judgement* on the entrance wall. The Arena chapel thus tells the story of Jesus in a long series of scenes broken up into groups to fit the spaces available around the walls.

The Arena chapel was founded by Enrico Scrovegni, son and heir of the rich usurer Renaldo Scrovegni, whom Dante placed in hell. He was an intimate of Pope Benedict XI, who provided a bull of indulgence for the chapel. He was also a member of the lay order of *Frati Gaudenti*.[27] It may be that the story-line adopted for the chapel was intended to express the hostility to usury and the devotion to Mary for which the *Frati Gaudenti* were noted. In any case, the story involved recourse to literary sources outside the New Testament to provide material for the scenes.[28] Giotto appears to have used two popular texts composed in the late thirteenth century by mendicant authors that contain full and inventive versions of New Testament stories: the *Legenda Aurea* by the Dominican Jacopo da Voragine and the *Meditationes Vitae Christi*, probably by the Franciscan Giovanni de' Cauli.[29] The use of these sources, characteristic of the lively and realistic interpretation of the Bible in thirteenth-century Italy, can be seen as an influence of mendicant literature encouraging an imaginative interpretation of biblical events by the visual artist. They placed Giotto at Padua in a different position from the designer of

[27] Rough, 'Enrico Scrovegni'; J. K. Hyde, *Padua in the Age of Dante* (Manchester, 1966), pp. 101–2, 190.

[28] M. von Nagy, *Die Wandbilder der Scrovegni-Kapelle zu Padua; Giottos Verhältnis zu seinen Quellen* (Bern, 1962) is the best general investigation of the problem of literary sources but gives rather too much importance to Jacopo da Voragine's *Legenda Aurea* for the Joachim story and to the Gospels for the life of Jesus.

[29] *Legenda Aurea*, ed. T. Graesse (Bratislav, 1890). The *Meditationes Vitae Christi* can be found in old editions of the works of St Bonaventure to whom it was formerly attributed. An English translation of a fourteenth-century Italian version is in *Meditations on the Life of Christ: An Illustrated Manuscript of the Fourteenth Century*, ed. I. Ragusa and R. B. Green (Princeton, 1975). On the *Meditationes* and its author see C. Fischer, 'Die "Meditationes Vitae Christi" und ihre handschriftliche Ueberlieferung', *Archivum Franciscanum Historicum*, xxv, 1932; G. Petrocchi, 'Sulla composizione e data delle' "Meditationes Vitae Christi" ', *Convivium*, 1952.

the St Francis scenes at Assisi who had to stick closely to a precise and limited story. It seems probable that the scene in heaven—on the chancel arch above the *Annunciation*—a scene striking both for its beauty and for its originality, was inspired by the passage in the *Meditationes* (ch. 2), which describes a debate between Truth and Mercy in the presence of God before the decision on the Annunciation was made.[30] We cannot, however, see the Paduan frescos as a visual expression of mendicant story-telling (though this may be a general description true of them in some sense) because the source which appears to be most helpful for explaining the greater part of the most original scenes at Padua, those which convey the story of Joachim and Anna and the early life of Mary, is a much earlier text on which the *Legenda Aurea* was partly based, the apocryphal *Gospel of Pseudo-Matthew*. How Giotto or his theological adviser knew this less obvious source, or whether he was using yet another text which incorporated it more fully than the *Legenda*, is not clear.

Giotto has two scenes of encounters with angels during Joachim's exile from Anna, which he spent with his flocks. In the first, Joachim is kneeling before a burning animal sacrifice on an altar set obliquely. To one side, facing him, stands an angel with a hand raised, apparently in admonition. Behind is one of his shepherds with hands raised in prayer. A hand appears from heaven above the altar. In the next scene, Joachim is sitting asleep before a hut. An angel is in the sky with hand directed towards him. Two shepherds are entering the picture from the side opposite Joachim.

In *Pseudo-Matthew* we read of an encounter between Joachim and an angel who urges him to make a sacrifice. When Joachim takes a lamb for the sacrifice, the angel says that he would not have spoken without knowing the will of God and then ascends to heaven with the smoke of the sacrifice. Joachim falls asleep on his face; in his sleep the same angel appears to him, giving him the order to return to his wife.[31] He is then awakened by his returning servants; they too exhort him to go back to his wife. It is possible to imagine how Giotto could have evolved his two scenes recording the two encounters with the angel, one at the time of the sacrifice, the other when he was asleep, out of an imaginative consideration of this text. In both scenes, the pastoral element is prominent, with flocks and shepherds—the *Pseudo-Matthew* does not mention them at this point, but Giotto could easily have decided to make the pastoral scene the background of all pictures of Joachim in exile, following the information earlier in the text that he retired to his flocks and shepherds after his expulsion from the temple. The scenes of *Joachim's Expulsion from the Temple, Joachim among the Shepherds*, the *Annunciation to Anna, Joachim's Sacrifice, Joachim's Dream*, the *Meeting at*

---

[30] J. Gyarfes-Wilde, 'Giotto Studien', *Wiener Jahrbuch für Kunstgeschichte*, vii, 1930.
[31] C. de Tischendorf, *Evangelia Apocrypha* (Leipzig, 1876), pp. 58–60. The account of the same episode by Jacopo da Voragine in *Legenda Aurea*, pp. 587–8 is briefer and less helpful.

the Golden Gate, the *Presentation of Mary at the Temple*, the *Presentation of the Rods*, the *Watching of the Rods*, and the *Betrothal of Mary* all look as though they were based on *Pseudo-Matthew*.

On the other hand, *Mary's Return Home* seems to owe more to Jacopo da Voragine; and the elaborate scene of the *Birth of Mary* does not look very like any of the texts to which it has been referred. It may be that Giotto was following a source which is unknown to us, or it may be that he was following *Pseudo-Matthew* or something similar to it with considerable use of the imagination in designing the pastoral landscape of Joachim's exile and the house in which Anna received the Annunciation and gave birth to Mary. The probability is that the latter is the true explanation of the paintings we see in the top level of the Arena though the birth of Mary was a scene which had a well-established iconography. Giotto was given the task of presenting episodes in the story as contained in *Pseudo-Matthew* to show Joachim's religious modesty in withdrawing from his wife into the wilderness after his expulsion from the temple, and the similar modesty of Joseph in not pushing himself forward as a bridegroom for Mary. In both cases, miraculous intervention led to success: Anna conceived Mary, Joseph's rod was shown to be the one which entitled him to Mary's hand. Finally, the Annunciation led to the conception of Jesus. Giotto made these events into a continuous story with the help of a set of backgrounds which are repeated: the temple, the external shape of which may have been inspired by the Schola Cantorum at San Clemente in Rome,[32] the interior of the temple, the wilderness with flocks and shepherds, Anna's house.

The scenes from the life of Jesus, in which we move from a slow progress through relatively unfamiliar episodes to a rapid progress through a well-known sequence, are based principally on episodes recounted in one or other of the four canonical Gospels. Here again it looks as though Giotto has also been influenced by fragments drawn from another source, the *Meditationes Vitae Christi* or something like it. For example, in the *Flight into Egypt*, Mary and Jesus are accompanied by a group of four women whose presence may have been inspired by the mention in the *Meditationes* of the *bonae matronae* who accompanied them on the way back. For the *Wedding at Cana*, the *Meditationes* could have provided the suggestion that St John the Evangelist was the bridegroom, as he is in Giotto's painting, which fitted so well into the general structure of the narrative.

In addition to the links provided by Judas and the theme of the chaste husband, a certain continuity is also given to the story by the repetition of identical or similar groups of people. The shepherds in the Joachim scenes reappear in the *Nativity*. A similar group of ladies attending Anna and Mary appear in the *Meeting at the Golden Gate*, *Mary's Betrothal* and *Return*

[32] J. White, 'Giotto's Use of Architecture in "The Expulsion of Joachim" and "The Entry into Jerusalem" at Padua', *Burlington Magazine*, cxv, 1973.

Home, the *Visitation* and the *Flight into Egypt*. The bystanding priests hostile to the Holy Family are at the *Presentation of Mary at the Temple*, Jesus's *Entry into Jerusalem*, and the *Pact of Judas* and *Betrayal of Christ*. Eventually the lurking hostility which they represent from the beginning explodes in the scenes of the Passion, in which the latent cruelty engulfs the Saviour. The Arena paintings thus present essentially a dramatic story with the use of rather small groups of characters, small enough for the dramatic interplay between individuals to be clearly shown—unlike the large crowds which fill many of Duccio's scenes with pictorial rather than dramatic effect. Though divine intervention is of course supremely important, and is shown graphically in the very beautiful heavenly scene of God, enthroned above a crowd of angels against a blue sky, sending Gabriel on his mission to Mary, there is no emphasis on the sacramental implications of the Passion or the Eucharist. The story is about dramatic events, the interplay of personalities and the dominating power of Jesus.

Though the structure of the whole series has great aesthetic importance because it provides the artist with a continuity and a significant relationship between the individual figures quite different from those which are found in the St Francis legend at Assisi or in Duccio's *Maestà*, Giotto's powers are chiefly shown in the organization of the individual paintings.[33] The Paduan frescos are tightly organized, with a general avoidance of elaborate landscape backgrounds unnecessary for the story. The individual panels tend to be filled with figures and with just enough landscape or architecture to give them an appropriate setting. No space is wasted, though the buildings are often elaborately designed to make them pleasurably interesting; for example, the detailed pediments and moulding shown in the roof of Anna's house. Nearly all the buildings are in a position oblique to the front plane of the painting. This is most obvious when they are seen from the outside, but it is most important when they are interiors seen from one side and receding obliquely—as in *Christ Disputing with the Elders*, or the *Wedding at Cana*, where the oblique setting provides a realistic interior quite different from that which would be provided by a frontal position parallel to the front of the painting. Within the panels, the figures are set in a shallow space but one in which their spatial relationship is made clear—sometimes less realistically, as in the *Entry into Jerusalem*, where the tops of the figures are piled up on each other; sometimes very realistically, as in the *Mocking of Christ*, where each of the thirteen figures is placed satisfactorily in his own spatial position.

In addition to the spatial structure of the paintings, there is a tight organization of design, partly independent of space, to bring out the significance of the story. This is a matter of surface design rather than of space. For

---

[33] Valuable analyses by D. Frey, 'Giotto und die maniera greca: Bildgesetzlichkeit und psychologische Deutung', *Wallraf–Richartz–Jahrbuch*, xiv, 1952; White, *Pictorial Space*, pp. 57–71; M. Imdahl, *Giotto: Arenafresken, Ikonographie, Ikonologie, Ikonik* (Munich, 1980).

example, in the *Presentation of Mary at the Temple*, the pattern of the design is a pyramid with its summit at the pointed top of the roof of the temple. One side of the triangle is emphasized by the steps on the left-hand side, Mary at the top, Anna urging her forward from below, the arms of the priest receiving her in line with the triangle. On the right-hand side the pyramid descends sharply by the right-hand steps, down to the two doubting figures in the corner. Thus the triumphal ascent of Mary is emphasized and balanced by the depressed position of those hostile to her. In the *Flight into Egypt*, the forward movement of the group is emphasized by the ground surface below the ass being tilted upwards, and the outline of the hills behind. Together they form a wedge with its point in the direction in which the group is moving, the human figures and the legs of the ass tilted forwards to show movement. The head of Mary is at the exact centre of the painting horizontally, above the centre vertically. Her serious, forward-looking face expresses her clear determination to move in the direction which she must take.

Discord is shown as effectively as success. In the *Betrayal of Christ*, the heads of Jesus and Judas are near the centre of the panel, emphasized by the brightness of Jesus's halo and the light colour of Judas's broad robe. The importance of their expressive, contrasting faces is further picked out by the raised hand of a priest, whose arm and finger make a diagonal line pointing towards Jesus's unflinching eye. The background to the central couple is made up of converging figures, and the message of the picture is partly conveyed in the top half of the panel in which the confusion of waving weapons, rods, and clubs, pointing in different directions, creates a prevailing atmosphere of extreme discord around the unmoving figure of Jesus. A different atmosphere of discord is achieved in the *Massacre of the Innocents*, in which the limbs and faces of the attacked women and infants form a series of arcs pierced by the diagonal lines of the central murderer's sword and the outstretched hand of Herod. In this painting, incidentally, as elsewhere in the series, the contrast between classical and gothic architectural forms symbolizes the difference beween the old law and the new. Herod stands under round arches. Behind the women, his victims, rises a church-like building with double-arched gothic windows.

Most of the scenes at Padua can be analysed, and in principle much more fully analysed, in the manner which has been briefly indicated here. To take a final example; in the most famous scene, the *Lamentation*, the central importance of the heads of Christ and the Virgin is emphasized by the line of the hill running down from right to left and from background to foreground towards them, creating a wedge-shaped space. Around this central point the figures, limbs, and draperies of the lamenting onlookers create a series of arcs on a succession of planes, which surround the upper part of the dead body of Jesus with a rhapsodic circle of despair. The gestures of the wailing angels in the sky above are mirrored by the stretched-back arms of the bent John, the striking position of his arms probably inspired by a figure in the *Massacre of the Innocents* on Nicola Pisano's Siena pulpit, which was itself probably adopted by Nicola from a classical sarcophagus.[34] The areas of heavenly and earthly complaint converge again on the faces of Jesus and his mother. Giotto thus created at Padua a style of painting in which an advanced type of spatial realism was combined with a carefully controlled system of surface patterns heightening the emotional intensity of the subjects. Though we have separated them in discussion here, these two aspects of his art are not really separable in the paintings because the symbolic, patterned relationship of figures depends on their position within realistic space. This combination is the triumph of the new style of painting.

[34] A. Bush-Brown, 'Giotto: two Problems in the Origin of his Style', *Art Bulletin*, xxxiv, 1952.

10

Dante in Exile and the Poetic Vision

AFTER Dante's death, his poem the *Comedy* acquired the adjective 'divine'.[1] Its extraordinary power and beauty, combined with its complicated symmetry, have always tempted its admirers to think of it as the perfect and consistent creation of a celestial mind rather than the artefact of a troubled human existence. Although he is a shadowy and obscure figure, however, Dante was a real man whose life can be traced with slightly more assurance than Shakespeare's. His prominent and dramatic involvement in politics gives a substantiality to his intellectual biography which helps us to treat him as a real person. Dante is not the mythical spokesman of an age. He is a man whose changing ideas can be followed from year to year, very imperfectly of course, but with some confidence that we are seeing the understandable evolution of a soul buffeted by the torments of political and private fortune. The *Comedy* can and should be placed in a historical context which makes the development of its ideas intelligible.

The *Comedy* records in three *cantiche* the journey of Dante through hell (*Inferno*), purgatory (*Purgatorio*) and the heavens (*Paradiso*). The date of the journey, which is scrupulously observed both by the exclusion of the souls of those who were not dead at that date and by the description of appropriate movements of the stars, is Easter week 1300. Apart from the fact that it gave him an appropriate fictional age of thirty-five, Dante probably chose this date because it was when the political pressure on Florence, which led to his exile, was beginning to build up: it was shortly before the dramatic events of the Florentine condemnation of the Spini and the bloodshed of 1 May. He may

---

[1] The text of the *Comedy* used in modern editions is *La Commedia secondo l'antica vulgata*, ed. G. Petrocchi (Milan, 1966–7). Among recent annotated editions may be mentioned, in Italian, those by N. Sapegno, 2nd edn (Florence, 1968), and by U. Bosco and G. Reggio (Florence, 1979); and, with English translation, that by C. S. Singleton (Princeton, 1970–5). The text of *Monarchia* is that ed. by P. G. Ricci (Milan, 1965); edition annotated by B. Nardi in *Opere minori*, ii. Text of *De vulgari eloquentia* ed. A. Marigo and P. G. Ricci (Florence, 1957); edition annotated by P. V. Mengaldo, *Opere minori*, ii. Text of *Convivio* ed. M. Simonelli (Bologna, 1966); annotated edition by Busnelli and Vandelli, 2nd edn (Florence, 1964–8). *Epistole*, ed. A. Frugoni and G. Brugnoli in *Opere minori*, ii; ed. P. Toynbee, 2nd edn (Oxford, 1966). *Rime* ed. G. Contini, 2nd edn (Turin, 1946); also *Dante's Lyric Poetry*, ed. K. Foster and P. Boyde (Oxford, 1967). Allusions to people and places in the *Comedy* and Dante's other works can be conveniently followed up in P. Toynbee, *A Dictionary of Proper Names and Notable Matters in the Works of Dante*, revised by C. S. Singleton (Oxford, 1968), and a vast survey of Dante scholarship is contained in *Enciclopedia dantesca* (Rome, 1970–8). Because of the availability of references to scholarship in these works and in the annotated editions, footnotes are largely omitted in this chapter.

also have chosen it because he was actually in Rome at that time as a pilgrim profiting from the Indulgence; it has been suggested that *Purgatorio* ix presents the theology of the Indulgence rather than an allegory of the sacrament of penance.[2] Casella the musician, who came across to purgatory from the shores of the Tiber together with souls admitted because of the Indulgence (*Purg.* ii), gives evidence that Dante accepted Boniface VIII's power. It may well be, therefore, that we should see the fictional date as determined both by the civil crisis in Florence's politics and by the temporary grace of the indulgence at Rome, united in their significance by Dante's participation in both and thus presenting a suitable moment for his entry into the worlds beyond the grave to observe the fate of humanity and the truth of religion.

Unity is given to the *Comedy*, not only by its short time-span, by the tightly consistent verse structure, and by the many numerical patterns running through all three *cantiche*, but also by the figures of Dante's guides. It is clear as early as *Inferno* ii. 70 that Beatrice is the source of Virgil's mission to Dante. Virgil is his guide through hell and purgatory to the terrestrial paradise where Beatrice appears (*Purg.* xxx) to take his place and guide Dante up to the celestial rose (*Par.* xxxi), where she is replaced for the last few heavenly cantos by St Bernard. The evidence of structural unification in the *Comedy* is strong. In some cases it is probable that it was the result of later reworking. *Inferno* xix. 79–81 contains the prophecy that the time between the death of Nicholas III (1280) and that of Boniface VIII (1303) will be longer than the following period until the death of Clement V (1314), which presumably cannot have been written before 1314. Later in the same canto come references to the whore seated on the waters (Revelation xvii), a figurative reference to the pope, which are out of character with the thought of the rest of *Inferno*, though fitting for the poet of the mystical procession of *Purgatorio* xxix–xxxii. The extreme denunciation of Clement V represents a view which Dante held after 1312, and which he probably added to *Inferno* some years after it had originally been written. We can only conclude that while some passages which give structural unity to the whole poem may have been in Dante's mind from an early stage, others were probably added later to bring the work into order; which should not prevent us from observing changes in belief and interest in the long period of composition extending over some fifteen years.

The common modern opinion is that *Inferno* was mostly written between 1307, when Dante turned his attention to it from *Convivio*, and 1313.[3] At the end of 1313 or beginning of 1314 Francesco da Barberino made the first surviving reference to it. *Purgatorio* was probably begun earlier than 1313 and

---

[2] P. Armour, *The Door of Purgatory: A Study of Multiple Symbolism in Dante's Purgatorio* (Oxford, 1983).

[3] Worked out by G. Petrocchi, 'Intorno alla pubblicazione dell' "Inferno" e del "Purgatorio" ', *Convivium*, n.s., v, 1957.

finished soon after 1314. *Paradiso* was composed some time between then and Dante's death in 1321. This chronology is vague but it is possible to establish links between the *Comedy* and Dante's other writings, and between the *Comedy* and political events which give the hypothetical evolution of his thought more substance. The main external system of reference is provided by the Italian expedition of Henry VII, from his arrival in Lombardy in October 1310 to his death in August 1313, a political enterprise with which Dante was certainly very much concerned. Other important points of reference are provided by the alienation of Pope Clement V from Henry in the spring of 1312, which probably changed Dante's whole attitude to the papacy, and by the papal vacancy from April 1314 to 1316. The new importance in Dante's imagination acquired by both emperor and pope in the course of the expedition of Henry VII is probably fundamental to his intellectual evolution.

In addition to the external political events we have the help of a series of political letters in Latin, which can be dated either precisely or within limits, and which provide the firmest chronology for the ideas they happen to contain. The most famous are the letters connected with the early part of Henry VII's expedition and written in enthusiastic defence of it to the princes and people of Italy (probably in autumn 1310, when Henry VII appeared in Italy), to the Florentines (31 March 1311), and to Henry (17 April 1311).[4] Of great importance also is the letter to the Italian cardinals written some time in the vacancy between Clement V and John XXII.[5] From an earlier period came letters I and II, springing from Dante's attachment to the exiled Guelfs, addressed to Cardinal Niccolò da Prato and to counts Oberto and Guido da Romena in 1304. The precision of the chronological position of some of the letters contrasts with the extremely uncertain dates of the three important prose treatises which Dante wrote while he was in exile. *De Vulgari Eloquentia* (On vernacular expression), Dante's treatise on language and poetry, and *Convivio* (The banquet), an interpretation of some of his earlier poetry in terms of technical philosophy, were left unfinished. The probability, at least in the case of *Convivio*, is that Dante failed to finish it because he was turning his attention to the *Comedy*. These treatises contain no indications of date except for a few references to contemporary people. It is generally thought now that they were both written during the earlier part of his exile between 1303 and 1308. *Monarchy* is even more destitute of indications of date. Its passionate attack on papal and ecclesiastical claims to jurisdiction indicate that it belongs to the period 1312–14 when Clement V's rejection of Henry VII would have encouraged Dante to adopt this line of argument.

The documents other than the *Comedy* thus provide a fairly clear indication of the strength of Dante's attachment to imperialism during the expedition of

---

[4] Epistole V, VI, VII in both *Opere minori*, ii and Toynbee edition.
[5] XI in *Opere minori*, ii; VIII in Toynbee.

Henry VII and the effect this had in turning him into an anti-papal political theorist. Before the coming of Henry we have the highly original literary critic and vernacular philosopher continuing the work of Brunetto Latini, writing the learned *De Vulgari Eloquentia* and *Convivio* in the intervals of a life of exile which was probably very peripatetic. After the death of Henry the indications are less clear. The important letter to the Italian cardinals maintains Dante's criticism of the degeneracy of the contemporary church, rebuking the prelates in words which combine religious radicalism with reminiscence of Ovid: 'you, who are as it were the centurions of the front rank of the church militant, neglecting to guide the chariot of the spouse of the crucified along the track which lay before you, have gone astray like the false charioteer Phaethon'. But the main purpose of the letter is to urge that the papacy should resume its position at Rome, and this seems to imply that Dante has fallen away from the enthusiastic rejection of papal secular power he had expressed with such totality in *Monarchy*.

De Vulgari Eloquentia, *Convivio*, and *Monarchy* are all writings of dazzling originality, each of which exemplifies Dante's capacity for creating a new system of thought, unprecedented in the tradition in which he writes, by fitting together unexpected combinations of ideas. None of them, however, is a creative work in the sense in which that is true of the *Comedy*. It is the *Comedy* that lifts the Tuscan consciousness onto a new level with new horizons and contains the evidence of a new perception of man.

Dante expressed the anguish of exile realistically in a prose passage of *Convivio* I. iii:

Since it was the pleasure of the most beautiful and famous daughter of Rome, Florence, to cast me out of her sweet bosom—in which I was nurtured up to the summit of my life and in which, with its good will, I desired with all my heart to rest my tired spirit and end the days allowed to me—I have gone through nearly all the regions to which the Italian tongue extends, a wanderer, almost begging, showing against my will the wound of fortune, often unjustly held against him who is wounded. I have been truly a ship without sail or rudder, carried to many ports and straits and shores by the dry wind blown by grievous poverty, and I have appeared to the eyes of many who had perhaps imagined me, through a certain fame, in another way.

From such evidence as we can piece together of the early years of exile it is clear that Dante moved about considerably.[6] There is early evidence of links with the other White exiles at Gargonza and San Godenzo in 1302, after which time he may have moved briefly to the hospitality of the Ghibelline Della Scala far away at Verona and then back again to the exiles' centre at Arezzo. At some stage, perhaps 1304, he broke with the Whites, possibly because he became distrusted for bad advice which he had given. The break may have been followed by a move north again to the court of Gherardo da Camino at

[6] The best account of Dante's biography is the article by G. Petrocchi, 'Biografia', *Enciclopedia dantesca*.

Treviso. But in 1306 he was probably in Lunigiana and from 1307 to 1309 at Lucca, where he may have profited from the friendship of the lady Gentucca mentioned in *Purgatorio* xxiv. If Dante ever did, as Boccaccio thought, visit Paris, 1309 would be a suitable date, though the possibility seems slight. In Italy itself, however, the poet made considerable journeys; from these spring the complaints and the broad knowledge of Italian dialects so well demonstrated in *Convivio* and *De Vulgari Eloquentia*.

Among its numerous remarkable and memorable characteristics, *Inferno* displays one which is of supreme importance as an innovation in the literary perception of humanity. This is the presentation of major characters, in a form hovering between the realistic and the mythical, as complex personalities with an archetypal significance made up partly of the real or imagined events of their earthly lives, partly out of the implications these could have for Dante's own preoccupations. These are the characteristics we see most clearly in such major figures as Francesca and Ulysses, and to a lesser extent in many others. They involve a leap into the modes of perception of human character typical of the novelists and dramatists of later centuries. There is no obvious preparation for them in Dante's earlier writings or in other Italian literature before *Inferno*. If we look for a literary background which may have influenced them, we may think of the Bible, of Virgil's *Aeneid*, and of the French Arthurian legends, all of which were well known to Dante and all of which contain representations of individual human character which may have contributed to those found in *Inferno*. There is nothing in these works, however, which approximates closely to the poetic evocation of a character whose personal destiny emerges in a brief conversation and carries a weight of psychological and philosophical significance. The characters of *Inferno* are not allegorical fictions like those in Dante's earlier *Fiore*. They are figures, whether contemporary, historical, or mythical, presented for a significance their life embodies, closer to the characters of the Bible and the *Aeneid*. But their personal significance comes to the reader through what they say or do in *Inferno* before his eyes; it is character fictionally embodied in speech and act, in a manner which is novel in European literature. We have little or no information about Dante's movement towards these characterizations. We must assume that they emerged from a convergence of his reading of the Bible and Virgil and the Romance legends with his personal analysis of his own destiny. The experiences that lay behind it in his own biography were the political conflict leading to his exile and the religious upheavals of his reaction to courtly love poetry, which we read about in *Vita nuova* and *Convivio* and in the lyrics. The effort of reworking these experiences in his poetic mind seems to have resulted in the creation of the new literary appreciation of mankind caught in the turmoils of life. The most original literary novelties are woven into an elaborate poetic artifice because Dante was essentially a poet who expressed himself as a poet, though he was capable of powerful, rational expression in prose in other works. They are woven into a consideration of political events which troubled him, into an analysis of human virtues and vices owing much to the patterns of thought he knew as a Florentine, and into the allegory and symbolism of traditional poetry.

As far as its most valuable features are concerned, the genesis of *Inferno* is very largely a mystery. Dante can be seen moving towards some of its external characteristics in the last chapters of *Convivio*. The general scheme of hell, and therefore of *Inferno*, is explained by Virgil in *Inferno* xi. Above the two wanderers at this point are the six circles of lust, gluttony, avarice, prodigality, anger, and heresy through which they have already passed. Below them are three more descending circles of sinners whose wickedness has caused *ingiuria* either by force or, worst of all, by fraud, which is a perversion peculiar to man and especially offensive to God. Force leading to murder, suicide, and blasphemy is worse than the sins of incontinence above. Still worse is the fraud of hypocrites, thieves, corrupt politicians, and certain other types of sinners. Worst of all is treachery directed against the trusting, and thus Brutus and Judas are placed in the very pit of hell. Virgil explains this classification by referring to the division of evil dispositions into incontinence, malice, and bestiality in Aristotle's *Ethics*. But in fact Aristotle's division does not fit Dante's hell very well, and the crucial distinction between force and fraud was taken from Cicero's *De Officiis*, which is not mentioned.[7]

It happens, however, that Dante refers to Aristotle's *Ethics* and *De Officiis*, both works no doubt well known to him, in the same sentence in *Convivio* iv. xxvii, and this confirms they were present in his mind at the time he must have been planning *Inferno*. In the last chapters of *Convivio* iv. xxvi–xxx, Dante was interpreting the last part of the canzone *Le dolci rime d'amor*, which he had composed a decade earlier. This part of the poem lists the virtues proper to a noble soul in the various ages of life: adolescence, youth, age, and senility. In *Convivio* Dante elaborates this pattern. In youth it is proper for a man to be temperate, strong, loving, courteous, and loyal. A good example is Virgil's Aeneas. The next age is *senectus*, when a man is at his prime and should be prudent, just, generous, and quick in praise. This is the political age when men fulfil the Aristotelian requirement that man is a civil animal and become, in their prime, useful to others. This is the age for wisdom based on goodness, for good counsels and justice. *Senectus* begins at thirty-five, Dante's age at the fictional date of the *Comedy* and his actual age when he became a prior. In his letter *Popule mee* he claimed, according to Leonardo Bruni, that though he may not have been fitted for the priorate by prudence, by faith and age he was. At this point in *Convivio*, when he has not mentioned himself or his experiences for a long time, it is evidently in his mind that he had wished to live up to the Aristotelian precepts, which others had so signally failed to

---

[7] E. Moore, 'The Classification of Sins in the "Inferno" and "Purgatorio" ', *Studies in Dante*, Second Series (Oxford, 1899).

follow, and the cry breaks out, 'Oh, unhappy, unhappy country of mine, how often pity for you constrains me when I read or write of anything which concerns civil government!' (IV. xxvii). At this point the reader is surely being permitted a glimpse of the inspiration lying behind *Inferno*. We can say this partly because the catalogue of virtues in *Convivio* is in a sense the mirror image of the catalogue of vices in *Inferno*: both belong to the same classificatory approach to human character that was familiar to the Florentine tradition of thought. Partly because the classification of virtues in *Convivio* is evidently relevant to Dante's own experience of politics as the classification of vices was so clearly to be in *Inferno*. It was a natural step to move from the virtues to the vices.

Dante's most extended commentary on his fate in Florence is given indirectly in cantos xxi and xxii of *Inferno*, which contain his passage with Virgil through the circle of barrators, those guilty of corruption of office, for which he had been exiled. This episode is exceptional in the *Comedy* because it is plainly comic. The travellers are assailed by an absurd gang of burlesque demons with names like Calcabrina and Libicocco who quarrel so much that they themselves fall into the infernal pitch where they are tormenting the sinners. Dante is terrified of them. As the travellers arrive in the circle, the demons are bringing in a load of barrators from the city of Lucca. One of them says that everyone in Lucca is a barrator except one Bonturo, and that everyone sells his vote. As commentators both medieval and modern have pointed out, Bonturo Dati, the party boss of Lucca from 1303 to 1314, was notoriously corrupt. If this is a comment on the political morals of Lucca it means either that everyone there from the top down was rotten with corruption or that the distinction between the just and the unjust was in practice comically inverted. The Whites were expelled from Lucca by an order issued at the behest of the Florentine Blacks on 31 March 1309. Dante probably left the city at this time or not long before, seeing his Florentine political experience, after a happy interlude at Lucca, repeated. His experience of irrational communal injustice, we may suppose, reached its lowest level before the coming of Henry VII in the following year. His sense of the absurdity of the events was expressed by the comedy of the two cantos. This was his state of mind in relation to his political experience when he was composing *Inferno*.

The name of Florence is 'spread through hell' (*Inf.* xxvi. 3). The condemnation of Florentine politics is repeated and pervasive in *Inferno*. It appears first in Dante's encounter with the obscure Florentine glutton Ciacco in canto vi. Ciacco gives, in somewhat gnomic terms, a prophetic account of disputes to come in Florence in the two years between Easter 1300 (when the meeting takes place) and the expulsion of the White Guelfs, including Dante, in the early part of 1302: first the ascendancy of the Whites, then the victory of the Blacks with papal help. He attributes the ills of Florence to the evils of pride, envy, and avarice that dominate the actions of all but a few good men. In the upper circles of hell, Dante meets two further characters who help to fill out the picture. In canto viii, there is an arrogant *grande* among the angry whom Dante particularly disliked, Filippo Argenti of the Adimari family. In the circle of the Epicureans in canto x is that great character Farinata, the most famous member of the Ghibelline Uberti family exiled from Florence since 1267. Farinata died in 1264 but his cousin Tolosato, captain at Pistoia in 1304, was still prominent in Ghibelline politics when *Inferno* was written. Farinata's warning to Dante of the pains of exile which will follow the victory of the Blacks links the Ghibelline exile of 1267 with the White exile of 1302; and his magnanimity, shown in his refusal of vindictive action against his Florentine enemies, is an example of a spirit which is normally absent from communal politics.

Below the city of Dis, the circle of the sodomites in cantos xv–xvi contains a generous allotment of Florentines, perhaps because Dante regarded Florence as the new Sodom. The dominant figure here is Brunetto Latini, the master of rhetoric, who repeats the prophecies of Ciacco and Farinata, linking Dante's sufferings with the inherent savagery of Florentine political strife arising from the survival of the Fiesolan strain in the population beside the descendants of the Roman founders of the city. Also in the circle of the sodomites are Guido Guerra, Tegghiaio Aldobrandi, and Jacopo Rusticucci, three prominent Guelfs of the period of Guelf–Ghibelline conflict, distinguished in popular recollection by their decent behaviour. Much further down, the circle of the thieves in cantos xxiv and xxv carries the story of Dante's political experience forward because it contains Vanni Fucci's prophecy (xxiv. 139–51) of the destruction of the Tuscan Whites with whom Dante was associated immediately after his exile, referring obscurely either to the loss of Serravalle in 1302 or to the fall of Pistoia itself to the Blacks in 1306, which finally ended any hope of a White revival. And it turns out that the very lowest circles of hell have their Florentine politicians too. Among the traitors in canto xxxii are Gianni de' Soldanieri, the Ghibelline whose rebellion in 1266 led to the destruction of Ghibelline power in the city; Carlino de' Pazzi, who betrayed for money the fortress of Piantravigne held by the Whites in 1302, one of their first serious set-backs after the exile; and Bocca degli Abbati, who had notoriously betrayed the Guelfs at Montaperti in 1260. *Inferno* as a whole presents us with a rich evocation of the factional conflict characteristic of Florentine politics over the last half-century, related to Dante's experience as a victim of that political system.

Though Florentine politics loom so large in *Inferno* that it is almost possible to see in the poem a picture of a hellish city, there are of course other themes drawn from Dante's recent experience that also play a considerable part. The popes are present in canto xix, and in the story of Boniface VIII's dealings with Guido da Montefeltro in canto xxvii. The wickedness of disbelief in the immortality of the soul, which became a serious issue for Dante in his earlier dealings with the *Roman de la rose* and with the poetic scepticism of Guido Cavalcanti, emerges when he sees the heretics appropriately placed in their half-open tombs at the end of canto ix, and when he meets Guido's father Cavalcante Cavalcanti in canto x. *Inferno* is a general catalogue of sins much influenced by the political wickedness which Dante had experienced, and which appears at many levels from mere pride to deadly treachery, but still a general catalogue which covers a wide range of human actions and beliefs. Though there is good reason to suppose that Dante's obsession with wickedness sprang from the political misfortunes he had suffered, some of the most prominent characterizations in which his literary style appeared at its richest, springing out of his most profound interior disturbance, have little to do with politics. As examples of this style we may turn to the episodes of Francesca and Paolo, and of Ulysses.

Auerbach pointed out that Dante's elaborate use of syntactical connections gave his description of events a suppleness and complexity which had no precedent in earlier literature. The example that he used to demonstrate this was the meeting with Farinata and Cavalcante in lines 22–78 of canto x. Dante hears Farinata addressing him from the tomb as a fellow-Florentine. He then turns in fear to Virgil, who identifies the speaker and pushes him in among the tombs. Farinata rises before him, scornful of hell, and tells Dante of his family's exile. Then appears the shade of Cavalcante who asks Dante about his son Guido, still alive and not fit to make Dante's journey because of his disdain of Beatrice. Farinata speaks again, continuing his lament for his family's fate. The short passage contains a complicated meeting of four figures, a rising and falling of their physical bodies, an interplay of the themes of political behaviour in the mouth of Farinata and of the memory of disrespect for Dante's pilgrimage implied in Dante's reply to Cavalcante. Farinata begins with a high-flown address to Dante: 'O Tosco che per la città del foco . . .' In the middle of Dante's conversation with him comes the sudden interruption by Cavalcante introduced by the phrase 'Allor surse', (then there arose). Cavalcante's anxious questions are in clear contrast with Farinata's fearless assertiveness. As Cavalcante sinks back Farinata resumes his grand speech with its contempt for hell:

> 'S'elli han quell'arte,' disse, 'male appresa,
> cio mi tormenta più che questo letto.'

> 'If they', he said 'have ill learned that art
> [of recovery from banishment], that torments me
> more than this bed.'

This is not a simple series of events or observations. The scene is like a quartet of figures on the stage, their positions and speeches intertwined. The physical movement is connected with powerfully resonant theoretical statements that evoke fundamental preoccupations of the writer.

If we start from his predecessors, Dante's language is a well-nigh incomprehensible miracle. There were great poets among them. But, compared with theirs, his style is so immeasurably richer in directness, vigor and subtlety: he knows and uses such an immeasurably greater stock of forms, he expresses the most varied phenomena and subjects with such immeasurably superior assurance and firmness, that we come to the conclusion that this man used his language to discover the world anew.[8]

Dante's adaptation of Tuscan speech and poetic forms has given him the power to present his figures with a complexity of character and ideas related to their physical movements and at the same time evoking fundamental human problems.

The capacity for dramatic representation is seen at a great many points in *Inferno*. Though they are in hell, his characters are men whose shades retain the movements of their mortal bodies and whose personalities are unimpaired and express the ideal significance of their lives as Dante wishes to convey it to the reader. The stylistic skill appears in a slightly different form in the more extended presentation of certain individuals, and it is in this presentation of character that Dante's art reaches its height.

Among the lustful in canto v, Dante meets the souls of the adulterous lovers Francesca and Paolo in the form of birds, drawn together by their love but held apart by their flight on the air in eternal punishment for their sin. Francesca explains how she came to commit adultery with Paolo through the lust aroused in them by reading together the story of Lancelot and Guinevere, and at the end of her moving recital Dante faints with pity. This episode contains an association of ideas. Paolo Malatesta of Rimini was *capitano del popolo* at Florence in 1282 when Dante was seventeen. Dante had probably seen him and may have known him. The scandal was a famous one involving members of a great family in the Romagna with which Dante may have had dealings during his exile. Francesca was married to Gianciotto Malatesta, Paolo's brother, who slew both the sinners when he discovered their adultery. The story of Lancelot and Guinevere was a powerfully erotic account of their first kiss in a French version of the Arthurian legend, which was known to Dante. In his portrayal of Francesca and Paolo in hell, Dante is conveying with infinite delicacy his sympathy with their love, his realization that it was damnable, his pleasure in Romance stories of courtly love, and his rejection of the immorality which they contained. We have no idea how much he had added fiction to the story of their adultery. Certainly it must have been a story which had long been well known to him, perhaps given greater poignancy by acquaintance with the real actors. We do not know whether the association with Arthurianism was based on a reminiscence of Paolo's real liking for

<hr/>

[8] E. Auerbach, *Mimesis* (trans. W. R. Trask, Princeton, 1968), pp. 174–83.

literature of that kind, or whether it was a fictional embellishment. It is clear, however, that he must have taken two people who had characters known to himself and to the audience for which he wrote, and elaborated their personalities to convey a moving and subtle judgement upon the experience of love and upon the reading of a powerful and popular form of lay literature to which he had been addicted. The story does not have the length to give it the weight of meaning which might have been presented by a later novelist, but within a very short space it achieves a subtle adaptation of real characters to convey a complex amalgam of ideal meaning related not only to them but to the author himself. This powerfully meaningful realism is a literary invention.

The encounter with Ulysses is in one fundamental respect different from the encounter with Francesca: Ulysses was a remote and mythical figure to whom Dante gives a story which has no known source and which he probably made up. The implications of the story are also much less obvious. But the technique of elaborating the personality of a character to embody wide emotional significance is similar, and the beauty of the literary picture created is no less entrancing than in Francesca's case.

The meeting with Ulysses comes within the circle of evil counsellors in cantos xxvi to xxvii. The two main characters in that circle, to be seen in one respect as balanced against each other, are Ulysses and Guido da Montefeltro. Guido was the noble warrior from the Romagna who played a large part in the warfare of the late thirteenth century, mostly on the Ghibelline side, whose character would have been well known to Dante and his contemporaries. Near the end of his life in 1296 Guido repented of his past deeds and joined the Franciscans, but he was recalled from retirement in 1298 by Boniface VIII in order to give expert advice on the reduction of the Colonna stronghold of Palestrina. This is the episode emphasized by Dante, though not invented by him because it appears in other sources. Telling his own story, Guido confesses that his success had been due to the fact that his works were 'not leonine but fox-like'. Boniface, waging war with Christians, not Saracens or Jews, called him out of his religious seclusion for advice, claiming that his keys could open and shut heaven; and Guido, accepting this perverted representation of papal powers, gave what was asked of him. After his death, in spite of the intercession of Francis, he was seized by a black cherub as an unrepentent sinner and dragged down to hell. Ulysses' chief claim to fame was that he was the inventor of the stratagem of the wooden horse aimed against the Trojans, the people of Aeneas the founder of Rome, and his later voyage, which Dante recounts, was a pagan's effort to reach purgatory by terrestrial endeavour without the aid of Christianity. Ulysses and Guido are therefore balanced against each other, though this is not stated by Dante but must be understood by us, as men who had perverted the imperial and papal powers. Each had come from the other side, Ulysses from the anti-Trojan Greeks, Guido from the anti-papal Ghibellines, to embrace actions which expressed a sinful

misunderstanding of the new causes they had taken up, a heroic but disastrous
pressing of, on the one hand terrestrial, on the other hand celestial, powers
beyond their true capacity.

Ulysses' fate as told to Dante was quite different from, though based on, the
story in Homer. He did not return to Ithaca after leaving Circe but embarked
on a voyage of discovery into the Atlantic beyond the pillars of Hercules. Not
even his love of Penelope and his family could conquer his will 'to gain
knowledge of the world and of human vices and human worth'. Leaving the
straits for the unknown world of the Atlantic, he exhorted his crew in one of
Dante's most splendid passages of poetry:

> 'O frati', dissi, 'che per cento milia
> perigli siete giunti a l'occidente,
> a questo tanto picciola vigilia
>
> d'i nostri sensi ch'è del remanente
> non vogliate negar l'esperienza,
> di retro al sol, del mondo senza gente.
>
> Considerate la vostra semenza:
> fatti non foste a viver come bruti,
> ma per seguir virtute e conoscenza.'
>
> 'O brothers,' I said, 'who through a hundred
> thousand dangers have reached the West, to this so
> small vigil
>
> Of our senses that remains, do not choose to deny
> experience, behind the sun, of the world without
> people.
>
> Consider your birth: you were not made to live
> like brutes but to follow virtue and knowledge.'

After this they had journeyed on into the ocean until they saw before them a
mountain. Before they could reach it a tempest arose and the sea closed over
them.

Dante's invention of this journey of discovery may have been inspired by
the Vivaldi brothers of Genoa, who are reported to have set out in 1291 on
such a voyage into the Atlantic from which they never returned. It is an
example of his interest in scientific novelty and the keen sense he shows
throughout the *Comedy* of seeing the geography of the world in perspective.
But the story has other implications too. The mountain which Ulysses could
not reach was probably the base of the earthly paradise to be attained by
Dante later, after the painful ascent of purgatory. Ulysses has been transformed into a symbol of the excessively aspiring human spirit, attempting
misguidedly to reach by terrestrial effort a goal which can only be attained by

Christian repentance. And perhaps it is also right to see in Ulysses' yearning but proud recollection of the family whom his journey led him to neglect an echo of Dante's own realization that the rootless life of exile which he had chosen by his proud attachment to a cause was also an abandonment of ties to which he might have given greater devotion.

Inferno must of course be seen as part of a larger poem. The journey through the three *cantiche* is a single one, and the three worlds beyond the grave are balanced against each other. But the subject-matter of *Inferno*, Dante's greatest creation, is the world of interests which absorbed him in the early years of exile, before his mind became absorbed by the religious enthusiasms and the attachment to orthodoxy which are prominent in *Purgatorio* and *Paradiso*. *Inferno* contains his most original work because it gave him the best opportunity to present real human figures, accentuated by their hellish predicament, clothed in a poetic evaluation of their significance but not placed within an essentially religious framework. The pattern of sins is Dante's own, not the pattern of theological sins taken over in *Purgatorio*. It is an expression of his experience of men. The experience on which it is based was that of his own central period of earthly grappling with the problems of political order and religious truth, mostly in the years from 1290 to 1304. In the last decade of his life Dante probably became a still more isolated and introspective man, absorbed in eternal truths and cut off from the normalities of life. *Inferno* is a poetic explosion springing out of and reflecting the world of Florentine speech and life which he had known before 1302.

The interpretation of the second *cantica* of the *Comedy*, *Purgatorio*, is inseparable from consideration of Dante's main work of political thought, *Monarchy*. The subject-matter of the greater part of *Purgatorio*, is, in one sense, the overcoming of sin by repentance, prayer, and work. This is the process Dante observes as he climbs up the cornices of purgatory (cantos ix to xxvii) and in which he participates to the extent that he finally emerges from it with his own will 'free, upright and healthy' (xxvii. 140) to meet Beatrice again in the final cantos. The content of *Purgatorio* is also extensively marked by other particular preoccupations of Dante, such as his attitude to traditional poetry, which receives more treatment here than in either of the other two *cantiche*, and his highly original and beautiful conception of the earthly paradise.

Among the concerns which stand out most prominently in the *cantica* is Dante's interest in the contemporary problem of relations between ecclesiastical and temporal power. This could have been presented more fully in either *Inferno* or *Paradiso*; it is not entirely absent in either of them. *Inferno* contains the denunciation of the contemporary popes (canto xix), which was probably in part a later addition contemporary with *Purgatorio*. *Paradiso* gives a substantial account of imperial power in the mouth of Justinian (canto vi), rejects the Donation of Constantine (xx. 58–60), contains devastating condemnations of Boniface VIII and Clement V, and places Henry VII in the celestial rose (xxvii and xxx). But, although the justice of imperial authority and the wickedness of the papacy were clearly things in which Dante still believed when he wrote *Paradiso*, the problem of the precise relation between them and, in particular, the extreme denial of civil functions to the papacy, which he argued so forcefully in *Monarchy*, do not seem to have remained obsessions at this later stage. In *Purgatorio*, on the other hand, the condemnation of the contemporary papacy in the context of the whole of ecclesiastical history is presented at the dramatic climax of the whole work in the mystical procession. Dante's personal re-encounter with Beatrice, resuming the whole of his past life and misdeeds, stands together with the travails of the church at the summit of *Purgatorio* as, in a sense, the two matters towards which the poem climbs. This aspect of its structure should be connected with Dante's preoccupations during the expedition of Henry VII.

The question of the relations between ecclesiastical and temporal power appears most clearly at two points in *Purgatorio*. The first is when Dante meets an unidentified figure called Marco Lombardo among the wrathful (canto xvi). Dante asks him to explain why the world is so lacking in virtue. 'One places the cause in the heavens and another here below.' Marco replies rather wearily that the cause is certainly in ourselves, for men are granted free will. The nature of men also makes law necessary to guide the will. But now the law is not enforced because of bad leadership. The world is corrupted by the confusion of temporal with spiritual. 'Rome, which made the good world, used to have two suns, by which one road and the other were shown, that of the world and of God.' Now 'the sword is joined with the crook and the one with the other must perforce go ill, since, joined, the one does not fear the other.' Marco then refers to the corrupt condition of Lombardy, where only three particularly noble men maintain good old ways. In spite of the particular reference to Lombardy, Dante here seems to be putting forward a general view connected with the theories mentioned in his letter to the princes and peoples of Italy in 1310, in which he accepts the division between the two 'lights' of spiritual and temporal power; and in Book iii of *Monarchy*, in which he rejects the view, based on an interpretation of Genesis, that spiritual power is superior to temporal as the sun to the moon, and insists instead on the absolute separation and equality of the two. That he refers to the 'suns' in *Purgatorio* may suggest that the passage is inconsistent with *Monarchy*'s rejection of the biblical figure, but the recollection of their separation by 'Rome that made the good world' suggests at least a preference for the time before the Donation of Constantine that gave the pope temporal power.

The second important passage is Dante's vision when he awakes from the sleep that follows his confession to Beatrice (canto xxxii) and his cleansing in the waters of Lethe. Beatrice had appeared to him in the terrestrial paradise in a chariot, representing the church, drawn by a griffon whose double nature, half lion and half eagle, symbolizes Christ's humanity and divinity, surrounded by an elaborate collection of biblical and ecclesiastical symbols. After his sleep, this church triumphant is transformed into a chariot which suffers before his eyes a series of attacks, symbolizing the vicissitudes of the church in history. The chariot is attacked by an eagle, representing the Empire's persecution of the early church; then by a fox, representing the early heresies; and again by an eagle that leaves its feathers, representing the grant of power by empire to church in the Donation of Constantine; it is cloven by a dragon, for Muhammadanism; and then puts forth seven heads, perhaps representing the seven capital sins. Finally a harlot appears seated on it, kissing a giant; because she turns her eyes towards Dante, the giant scourges her and drags the chariot into the woods. The final scene was intended to represent the link between the papal harlot and the giant king of France, who captured the papacy in spite of its half-hearted yearning for the true faith represented by Dante.

Dante has already, since his cleansing, seen the tree, which probably represents divine justice, revered by the griffon and Beatrice. He has been told that he shall be 'a citizen of that Rome whereof Christ is a Roman.' In the next and final canto (xxxiii), Beatrice gives him a deliberately and expressly obscure prophecy of an imperial saviour to come and tells him that he is to publish the knowledge she has given him to living men. Dante is therefore presenting himself, at least fictionally, as a man who possesses arcane knowledge of the future course of world history which he is bound to impart to the world.

The attitude to the empire and the papacy expressed in *Purgatorio* is to some extent a poetic telling of the account which Dante had set out in rational prose in *Monarchy*, probably composed in 1312–14 under the inspiration given by the failure of Clement V to support Henry VII and the papal assistance to the anti-imperialists. Dante's earliest statement of imperialist views was contained in *Convivio* IV. 4–5, probably written about 1307. It was added almost irrelevantly to his commentary on the poem *Le dolci rime d'amor*, composed a decade or more earlier, and probably records a point of view to which he had been converted recently. The interest in imperialism was a new one, inspired in exile by his contact with Ghibellines before the coming of Henry VII. *Convivio* supports the two propositions that a universal monarchy is a necessity for earthly life, and that the Roman empire is ordained to have that universal power. It makes no mention of church or papacy, and is probably best understood as the romantic political dream of a victim of political conflict, impressed by the need for a more ordered management of Italian society, in touch with ardent imperialists, and far from thinking that relations between emperor and pope were the central issue of Italian politics. The situation in which *Convivio* was written was dramatically changed, first by the coming of Henry VII, which made imperial power a serious possibility; and second by Clement V's reversal of policy in the spring of 1312, which made the pope a bitter enemy of the imperialists. *Monarchy* was written under the strong influence of that last change.

Monarchy consists of three books which deal quite straightforwardly with three subjects. Book I is a philosophical defence of the proposition that a single world government is a necessity. It makes ingenious use of fragments of ideas derived from Aristotle. It stands on its head the Aristotelian system developed by St Thomas Aquinas and Egidio Colonna to justify the supremacy of papal power, making it instead a justification of a supreme lay power. It argues that the need for peace and justice to allow the full development of the potentialities of the human race requires a world empire. In Book II, Dante attacked the problem from a historical standpoint, arguing that, since the time of Aeneas, the Romans had been clearly marked out by providence to wield the supreme imperial power. These two books were essentially enlargements of the arguments used in *Convivio* IV, adding new defences but not essentially changing the approach.

Book III is different. It marks a new step in Dante's political thought: the attack on the temporal power of church and papacy. Unlike the first two books the argument is presented, not as a defence of a viewpoint, but in a different and polemical spirit, as an attack on the defenders of the opposite view. These are identified as the pope, the self-styled 'sons of the church' whose 'obstinate cupidity has extinguished the light of reason', and the *decretalistae*, that is, the canon lawyers who construct defences of papal power based on papal decretals (III. iii). Dante's main attack was directed against the figurative use of scripture in order to provide arguments for papal power, such as the sun and moon argument based on Genesis 1:16, not because he objected in principle to the mystical interpretation of the Bible but because he thought the particular cases of it used by the canonists were misinterpretations. Non-biblical arguments were also wrong, and in any case irrelevant since the nature of the church could be defined properly only with the help of texts drawn from the New Testament. There the church was defined simply as the apostolic body established by Christ and ordered by him to live in poverty and humility without gold, silver, or brass. In Aristotelian terms, the 'form' of the church, that which defined its nature, was the life of Christ. Dante therefore asserted an argument, which had never before been presented in similar philosophical terms (though only a decade later Marsilius of Padua was to present a different Aristotelian case for the same conclusion) in defence of the view that terrestrial power belonged entirely to the empire and that the church was totally excluded from property and jurisdiction. The intense polemic is most easily understood if it is seen as arising from the needs of a particular period in political controversy, probably between 1312 and 1314.[9]

[9] The argument for this date was well stated by L. Chiappelli, 'Sulla età del De Monarchia', *Archivio storico italiano*, ser. 5, xliii, 1909.

Dante's political position in *Purgatorio* was therefore based in part on the one he stated in prose in *Monarchy*. But that was not the whole of it. He appears in canto xxxiii also as a prophet entrusted with knowledge of a mysterious imperial saviour who was to come in the future. This prophecy has parallels in the prophecies in *Inferno* (i. 101) of the *veltro*, greyhound, which will come to save Italy from the she-wolf of avarice, and in *Paradiso* (xxvii. 61–3) of a future successor of Scipio. None of these three prophecies can be explained. They may all have had the same meaning, but the one in *Purgatorio* is the most developed and the one most prominently fitted into the structure of the poem. Taken together with the view of the history of the church presented by the image of the mystical procession, it leads naturally to the view that Dante was at that time under the powerful influence of a mystical interpretation of history which owes something to the Joachist theories of the Franciscan spirituals and contemporary expectations of a Last World Emperor.[10] This is a conviction, evidently strong, which has no precedent in Dante's earlier poetry or prose, and is indeed in unexpected contrast to the poetry and rationalism with which we would associate him before this time. We have no evidence at all to explain it, apart from the knowledge of Ubertino da Casale and Joachim of Fiore revealed by ambiguous references to them in *Paradiso* xii. 121–41. The most natural explanation is that during his wanderings in Ghibelline circles in the years between 1307 and 1314, Dante had encountered radical religious prophecy and been so impressed that he incorporated it into his own thought. It is a line of theory different from that found in *Monarchy*, but could easily have been added as an appropriate culmination of it.

The atmosphere of the whole of the end of *Purgatorio*, from canto xxvii onwards, suggests a revolution of thought, a new conviction or conversion which contrasts with the natural attachment of *Inferno* and most of the early part of *Purgatorio* to Dante's earlier preoccupations. When he left purgatory Dante saw the earthly paradise across the River Lethe. It was partially explained to him by the lady mysteriously called Matelda whom he saw gathering flowers on the other side of the river. She explained that it corresponded not only with the biblical Eden, but also with the golden age imagined by the classical poets. We can connect this with the passage at the end of *Monarchy* (iii. xv) in which Dante finally described the two aspects of life controlled by the empire and the church.

Ineffable providence has set two ends for man to strive towards: the beatitude of this life, which consists in the operation of his own virtue and is figured in the earthly paradise, and the beatitude of eternal life, which consists in the enjoyment of the vision of God, to which man's own virtue cannot ascend unless assisted by divine light, which

---

[10] B. Nardi, 'Dante profeta' in *Dante e la cultura medievale*, 2nd edn (Bari, 1949); M. Reeves, 'Dante and the Prophetic View of History' in C. Grayson, ed., *The World of Dante* (Oxford, 1980).

is to be understood by the heavenly paradise . . . We come to the first by the teaching of philosophy, if we follow it by exercising the moral and intellectual virtues; to the second by spiritual teaching, which transcends human reason, if we follow it by exercising the theological virtues of faith, hope and charity.

The two aspects of human life, the imperial–philosophical and the ecclesiastical–theological, are represented in *Paradiso* by the earthly paradise, a place of blessed innocence embodying the virtues accessible to man without Christian revelation; and the mystical procession, a vision of the possibilities of perfection and damnation opened to man by Christ. Putting aside their great poetic beauty, this is the essence of the message conveyed by the last cantos of *Purgatorio*.

We are left, however, with the most remarkable and the most inexplicable part of *Purgatorio*: the figure of Beatrice. Beatrice appears at three stages in Dante's writings. The first is *Vita nuova*, written in the 1290s, in which she is the dead woman he had loved without declaring his love. She had been an embodiment of celestial as well as earthly perfection. When she died she was welcomed in heaven. After her death Dante was temporarily attracted to another lady who was a revival of the erotic, courtly love imagery, but eventually the memory of Beatrice triumphed. In *Convivio* ii. xii, written a decade later, Dante tells us that after the death of Beatrice he endured a period of despair from which he was rescued by reading the philosophical works of Boethius and Cicero, and came to regard philosophy as a 'noble lady'. In this account Beatrice was replaced by another lady, clearly inspired by Boethius, and did not regain her hold over him; the rest of *Convivio* is devoted to his post-Beatrice attachment to philosophy. Some years later Beatrice appears for the third time (*Purgatorio* xxx), though she has of course, been mentioned earlier in the poem as responsible for Dante's pilgrimage, and remains with Dante for most of the rest of the *Comedy*.

> Guardaci ben! Ben son, ben son Beatrice.
> Come degnasti d'accedere al monte?
> non sapei tu che qui è l'uom felice?

> Look at me well! I am, indeed I am Beatrice.
> How did you think yourself worthy to climb the mountain?
> Did you not know that there man is happy?

In the lines that follow she reveals to Dante what he should know about church and empire, but she also makes him submit to a painful ceremony of confession. She denounces him for abandoning her after her death, following 'false visions of good' and devoting himself to 'a young woman or other novelty of such brief enjoyment'. It is only after his confession that Dante is fully cleansed and able to understand.

It is impossible to know what lapses Dante had in mind since the death of Beatrice in 1290. Presumably he was thinking both of infidelity to Beatrice, the woman he had loved, and philosophical disloyalty to the theological truths she had represented in *Vita nuova*. The main problem of interpretation, however, relates to the figure of Beatrice herself. How is it possible, the modern reader may wonder, for the erotic object of a man's courtly love to become the heavenly shade who recalls him to the Christian path?

Beatrice is not like the other characters in the *Comedy*. They, as we have seen, are extracted from life or myth and worked up into realistic or significant figures to represent in a heightened form fragments of character or idea particularly important to Dante. This is just as true of people like Cato or Forese in *Purgatorio* as it is of the characters in *Inferno*. Beatrice has a different role. She is derived from the idealized object of love in courtly love poetry. In that literary world the object of love was a unique figure, the reason for poetry's existence, not an example of normal humanity like the rest of the characters in the *Comedy*. The normal characters in the *Comedy*, we have suggested earlier, constitute one of Dante's great inventions. Beatrice is not to be included among them. She is an invention of a different kind. In the religious world of the *Comedy* she has a uniqueness as a moral force equivalent to the uniqueness of the loved one in earlier poetry.

The strange literary development of Beatrice, the womanly recall of man to repentance and truth, is one of the most powerful elements in the *Comedy*, but it stands apart from Dante's main literary developments. She is a transformation of an earlier figure of love poetry which haunted Dante the poet throughout his life, and which, in spite of its magnificence, is not part of the map of humanity seen in the new literary style he was unfolding in *Inferno* and *Purgatorio*. Though she is a powerfully feminine figure with attributes of womanhood in her beauty, her moral power over her lover, and her charming corrections of his simplicity, Beatrice is also an ambiguously religious character (as in her earlier appearance in *Vita nuova*, when she was greeted with the cry *Benedictus qui venis*, which met Jesus on Palm Sunday), and endowed with the superhuman power of the redeemed souls, which enables her to explain the secrets of mankind and the universe. As she passes with Dante through the circles of *Paradiso* she remains an all-knowing guide whose function in the poem is related entirely to the instruction and correction of Dante, not to her own past. She must therefore be distinguished from the other characters of *Inferno* and *Purgatorio*.

What we have said of the new Beatrice is to some extent true of the whole of the later part of *Purgatorio*. In spite of its remarkable poetic beauty, regarded from one point of view it is a falling away from the poetic realism which Dante had pioneered in the earlier poetry. Dante's new obsession with the truths of politics and religion, apparently inspired by his lonely, wandering, introspective attachment to the cause of Henry VII, had given him an interest in abstract truth that was to some extent a diversion from the interest in humanity so magnificently expressed in the earlier part of the *Comedy*. The explosion of a new literary vision of men in *Inferno*, parallel to and contemporaneous with the explosion of a new visual perception in the Arena frescos, has given way, not to an inferior poetic style (for the poetry of the end of *Purgatorio* is superb), but to a fundamentally less interesting and original obsession. That development will be carried further in *Paradiso*.

Paradiso has two main themes which are intertwined. The first is a scientific picture of the structure of the heavens. Dante and Beatrice move upwards through the spheres encircling the earth from the circle of the moon to the empyrean. Unlike hell and purgatory, which are entirely imaginary structures, the portrayal of the heavens is in accordance with what Dante regarded as scientific truth. It was normal to believe that the earth was at the centre of the universe and was surrounded by the encircling planets and stars. Dante gives a picture of this heavenly system which is in some ways eccentric but is intended to represent reality. We shall return to this theme later.

The second theme is a series of essays on important philosophical and theological subjects. They are related appropriately to the various circles in which they are expounded; they progress from relative philosophical rationalism, accessible to the unaided human mind, in the lower spheres, to theological truth accessible only by revelation in the higher spheres, in which the fictional Dante is more enlightened and better able to understand them. But the subjects are chosen not because they present an encyclopaedia of knowledge—it would be a mistake to see *Paradiso* as a poetic equivalent of a *summa*—but because they are topics in which Dante had had an interest earlier in his career, and often because he thought that his earlier statements about them had been incorrect. Looked at from this point of view *Paradiso* is a comprehensive correction of Dante's earlier philosophical and theological mistakes, a continuation of his confession to Beatrice, put forward in the interest of the theological orthodoxy that evidently became an increasing concern of his last years. Fortunately the earlier theoretical disquisitions, which have survived in *Convivio* and *Monarchy* provide us with enough information about Dante's philosophical development to enable us to see at least some of the opinions he was anxious to recast in *Paradiso*.

The only part of *Paradiso* to which this general pattern does not seem to apply is the encounter with Dante's remote ancestor Cacciaguida, in cantos xv to xvii. This is placed in the middle of the *cantica* to match the encounter with Dante's intellectual father Brunetto Latini in canto xv of *Inferno*. Brunetto placed Dante's fate in the context of Florentine politics but promised him an ultimate 'glorious haven', and Dante also thanked him for teaching him 'how man makes himself eternal'. Cacciaguida presented a much more elaborate account of Florentine society and of Dante's fate, and also urged him to proclaim in the world the knowledge which he had gained, without regard for the sensibilities of those who would be injured by it.

Before moving to the main sections of Dante's doctrinal exposition, this may be the place to mention also the subject-matter of the circle of the sun in cantos x to xiv. The main figures in this circle are the two great mendicant philosophers, the Dominican St Thomas Aquinas and the Franciscan St Bonaventure. They are accompanied by two circles of twelve lights, representing twenty-four philosophers and theologians whose works can be considered important contributions to Christian thought. In this circle particular attention is paid to King Solomon as the wisest of kings, and to other general philosophical issues; but the most prominent feature of the circle is the praise given by Aquinas to the Franciscans and by Bonaventure to the Dominicans. This general encomium of the mendicant orders is not preceded in Dante's earlier works by any other general consideration of them except by the very broad criticism of the mendicants and their behaviour included in *Il fiore* some forty years earlier. The references to Siger of Brabant (surprisingly included among the twenty-four for the ambiguously characterized 'invidious truths' which he uttered) and Solomon are also links with *Il fiore*. It is difficult to avoid the conclusion that in his glorious celebration of the friars in the circle of the sun, his praise directed towards their central aims and the moderate interpretation of them, Dante was making amends for the hostile dismissal of the mendicants in *Il fiore*. The retention of Siger of Brabant, an exceptional figure among the generally revered and accepted thinkers included in this circle, is a sign that Dante still attaches value to Siger's syllogisms, although their limitations are immediately emphasized a few lines later. Siger 'silogizzò invidiosi veri', (x. 138); 'difettive silogismi' are part of the 'insensata cura de' mortali' (xi. 1–2).

The lowest sphere of the heavens, the circle of the moon, occupies cantos ii to v. Here the main character is Piccarda de' Donati, a girl who entered a convent but was then dragged from it by her brother Corso to be married to Rossellino della Tosa. Because of her breaking of her vows she is condemned to be in the lowest part of heaven. This raises in Dante's mind the problem of will and violence. How can a man be condemned for breaking his vow when compelled to do so? Dante had earlier given the question of free-will prominence in *Monarchy* i. xii, where he argued that men must maintain their freedom from the compulsion exercised by a bad monarch. Free-will, man's greatest gift, could be diverted by an external power. In *Paradiso* iv. 73–114, to quieten the doubts in Dante's mind aroused by Piccarda's fate, Beatrice explains that the 'absolute will' cannot be compelled to change. It rises out of itself again like a flame, and is diverted only in so far as it accepts fear into itself. The argument of *Paradiso* is related to that found in Aristotle's *Ethics*, probably known to Dante in the version with Aquinas's commentary. It is an acceptance of Thomist orthodoxy in line with Dante's attribution of important imaginary philosophical statements to Aquinas in *Paradiso* xi. The relationship of *Paradiso* with *Monarchy* is complicated by the fact that *Monarchy* I. xii contains the only words which indicate the date of *Monarchy* and which suggest that it was written after *Paradiso*: 'as I have already said in *Paradiso* of the *Comedy*', referring to *Paradiso* v. 19–24. Since there are no surviving manuscripts of *Monarchy* written in Dante's lifetime, it is reasonable to suppose that the very strong general arguments in favour of dating it before *Paradiso*, as a product of devotion to the cause of Henry VII in 1312–14, are stronger than the evidence of one phrase which may well be a later insertion by an enthusiastic copyist. The probability is that in writing *Paradiso* iv Dante recalled words he had written earlier, which seemed to be in conflict with the absolute force to be attributed to a religious vow, and wished to present a different opinion.

In the circle of Venus in cantos viii and ix, Dante meets Carlo Martello, who died in 1295, the eldest son of Charles II of Naples and the brother of King Robert, ruler of Naples at the time of *Paradiso* and one of Dante's political enemies. Carlo had been a lover of poetry and met Dante by chance on a visit to Florence in 1293. He appears singing *Voi che' ntendendo il terzo ciel movete*, a famous canzone of Dante composed about that time, the first poem interpreted in *Convivio*. Dante puts to him the problem 'how bitter seed may come forth from sweet', a problem appropriate at this moment because Carlo and Robert were good and bad sons of the same parent. The question of the generation of the human soul had been treated by Dante earlier in *Convivio* II. 2 and IV. 21 and in *Purgatorio* xxv. In *Convivio* IV Dante had given an account which emphasized the importance of the natural elements in generation, that is the complexion of the seed and the disposition of the heavens, the possible intellect descending into the soul in accordance with its pre-existing natural quality. This was a naturalist interpretation heavily dependent on the neoplatonic tradition in scholastic thought.[11] In *Purgatorio* Dante corrected this view, distancing himself from the opinion of Averroes and emphasizing that God breathed into the human form the soul, which retained its complete existence after death. In *Paradiso* viii. 85–148, Carlo presents Dante with another version of this improved view. The divine mind operates with unerring power through the heavenly bodies. To be citizens, men must differ and must be made to differ. The divine power thus acts without reference to the natural destination of its effects, planting different souls in bodies of the same family.

In *Monarchy* I. xi, the longest chapter of the first book, Dante had presented justice as a good of social life that could be present to a lesser or greater degree, but would be most perfectly present in the work of a world emperor: 'Justice

---

[11] B. Nardi, 'L'origine dell'anima umana secondo Dante' in his *Studi di Filosofia Medievale* (Rome, 1960).

is strongest only under the Monarch'. As he and Beatrice enter the circle of Jupiter in *Paradiso* xviii, Dante sees the spirits of the just kings forming themselves into the opening words of the Book of Wisdom 'Diligite justitiam qui judicatis terram'. The narrative of the circle which follows is concerned primarily not with the human justice those kings have administered but with inscrutable divine justice, which has incomprehensibly excluded the righteous heathens from heaven but admitted the obscure figure Rifeo, pronounced just in the *Aeneid*; and the Emperor Trajan, who was alleged to have been saved from hell by the intercession of Gregory the Great. As they leave the circle (canto xx), Dante is reminded that the righteousness of God is not understandable to man, and that he can only will what God wills without knowing its cause. At this point Dante appears to be adding a vast (and to human understanding, arbitrary) new dimension to the idea of justice he had put forward in *Monarchy*, a book whose powerful philosophical doctrine of the supremacy of the lay state is unmentioned in *Paradiso*.

The longest section of *Paradiso* is the circle of the starry heaven (cantos xxiii–xxvii) in which Dante is interrogated by St Peter, St James, and St John about the theological virtues of faith, hope, and charity. Having passed through the circle of Saturn, which contains the contemplatives, and therefore risen to the level of understanding which they are able to reach, Dante can now see heaven and the redeemed and bear the smile of Beatrice: 'Open your eyes and look at what I am'. He is therefore ready to be questioned about theological truths not properly comprehensible to earthly men confined to the benefits of unaided reason. The confession of belief which Dante places in his own mouth in these cantos is marked by a belief that the teachings of the Bible and of Aristotelian philosophy fundamentally point in the same true direction. His belief in charity is 'by philosophical arguments and by authority which descends to us' (xxvi. 25–6), and in the lines that follow the two kinds of argument, Aristotelian and biblical, are made parallel. He believes in one God, the prime mover, through the proof of Aristotle and the Bible, in the trinity through 'evangelical teaching' (xxiv. 130–44). The statement of belief is a clear presentation of the view that Aristotle and the Bible are in concordance, but that part of the truth is contained only in the Bible. How far does this match with Dante's earlier philosophical essays in *Convivio*?

Convivio is unambiguous in its occasional statements about the superiority of Christian teaching to the understanding of the pagan philosophers. 'Christian doctrine has greater vigour [than that of philosophers and gentiles] and crushes all cavil thanks to the supreme light of heaven which illuminates it' (IV. 15). But the lady of philosophical doctrine in the first of the three *canzoni* discussed was expressly said to be in conflict with the dead Beatrice in Dante's mind; and it was the lady philosophy's teaching with which he was concerned in *Convivio*, although he did not doubt the supreme value of

Beatrice and faith (11. 7–9). *Convivio* is thus about philosophy, and is marked by an enthusiasm for the power of reason to carry men towards truth. If one ignored the statements about the superiority of Christianity to be found scattered here and there in the work, one could easily take some of the other passages to suggest an absolute capacity in philosophy to discover the truth by itself. When the three Marys visited the tomb they found not the saviour but an angel.

> By these three ladies can be understood the three schools of the active life, the Epicureans, Stoics and Peripatetics who go to the tomb, that is the present world and the receptacle of corruptible things and ask for the saviour, that is beatitude, and do not find it ... The angel is our nobility which comes from God, which speaks with our reason and tells each of these schools ... to go and tell the disciples and Peter ... that he will go before them in Galilee, that is that beatitude will go before us in Galilee, that is in speculation [IV. 22].

In another place Dante says that philosophical reason makes unreasonable marvels rationally understandable.

> Whence our good faith has its origin, from which comes hope for what we long for and foresee and by that is born the operation of charity. By these three virtues we climb to philosophize in that celestial Athens where the Stoics, Peripatetics and Epicureans by the tree of eternal truth unite harmoniously in one will [III. 14].

These strange concordances of biblical and Christian teaching with philosophy, set in a work that is essentially a presentation of philosophical instruction for the unlettered, present a very strong belief in the power of reason to advance if not to religious truths at least very close to them. *Convivio* makes comparatively little reference to Christianity and starts from Dante's abandonment of Beatrice, the earlier symbol of divine truth. It is probably correct to deduce that when Dante returned to Beatrice, as he tells us at the end of *Purgatorio*, he looked back to *Convivio* as a shameful expression of an excessive attachment to philosophy. Paradiso xxiii–xxvii does not conflict with *Convivio*, but it provides what would be regarded in the early fourteenth century as a more balanced concordance of philosophical and biblical paths to truth, in which the biblical is given a more positive role than it received in the earlier work. It should be seen as a statement of the arguments for the theological virtues by a writer who had recently swung over to a much stronger attachment to theology than he had had at an earlier stage in his career.

Other, smaller corrections could also be mentioned: for example the dark patches on the moon (*Par.* ii correcting *Conv.* 11. 13), and the hierarchy of angels (*Par.* xxviii correcting *Conv.* 11. 5). If more of Dante's writings survived it is probable that we should find still more evidence of *Paradiso*'s purpose of settling his account with theological truth. He aimed to present his ideas, which were earlier set down in a form which now appeared either rebellious or mistaken or one-sidely philosophical, within a framework which clearly accepted the Thomist balance of philosophy and revelation, both pointing in the same direction, essentially concordant, always assuming that the ultimate truths which mattered most were only available through revelation.[12] Although when he wrote *Paradiso*, Dante evidently continued to believe in a prophetic imperialism, he seems to have either abandoned or lost interest in the extreme assertion of imperial power at the expense of the slightest ecclesiastical jurisdiction, which had been the argument of *Monarchy* iii. This is probably to be taken as an aspect of the swing towards theological interests.

It is a curious fact that the general agreement of the doctrinal lessons of *Paradiso* with Thomist orthodoxy was accompanied by a view of the physical nature of the heavens, that leaned towards a neoplatonist interpretation and was difficult to reconcile with Christian ideas of creation. The neoplatonic conception of the universe depended essentially on the idea that it was made up of a scale of being extending from the simplest and purest in the divinity to the most complex and various in material objects. Most things, including celestial bodies, animals, and men, were at points on the scale between the two extremes. Emanation from the divine centre had power over material elements lower down in the scale. Conversely, the lower elements were drawn by love towards the higher and simpler elements. These were the forces that drew the universe together and enabled it to be controlled from the divine centre. When Dante looked up on entering the crystalline heaven to see a point of intense light at which Beatrice explained, 'from that point hang the heavens and all nature' (*Par.* xxviii. 41–2), and that it was the focal point of all time and space, she was essentially stating that the universe hung from the divine centre as the neoplatonists imagined. This doctrine was extremely influential in earlier medieval thought before the time of Aquinas, who was hostile to it. It was known to Dante, for instance, from the twelfth-century Arabic treatise translated as the *Liber de Causis*, which he quoted several times, and from the works of Albertus Magnus. A structure of ideas which was ultimately late-classical in origin had been incorporated for a long time into Christian thinking. The opportunity it offered for a beautiful conception of the physical structure of the universe, with the celestial bodies acting as intermediaries between the divinity and the world below, has made it attractive to many poets since Dante; and it was no doubt in part this aesthetic potential which persuaded him to make it a persistent part of his view of the world, and to give it the most delightful of all literary expressions in *Paradiso*.

The neoplatonic view is expounded fairly fully in *Convivio*. The circles of the celestial bodies descend from the Empyrean at the summit. Immediately

---

[12] cf. B. Nardi's essays 'Dal "Convivio" alla "Commedia" ' in his *Dal 'Convivio' alla 'Commedia' (sei saggi danteschi)* (Rome, 1960) and 'Filosofia e teologia ai tempi di Dante in rapporto al pensiero del poeta' in his *Saggi e note di critica dantesca* (Milan–Naples, 1966).

below it is the crystalline heaven or *primo mobile*, moving very fast around the Empyrean because of the intense attractive power which that still centre exercised over it. 'The principles of philosophy', says Dante, 'require of necessity a very simple *primo mobile*' (*Conv.* II. 2) because the source of movement in the heavenly circles below it must be simpler and purer than they are. At lower levels, creatures are affected by the divinity in accordance with their position in the scale of being between spirit and matter.

The goodness of God is received in one way by substances separated [from matter], that is angels, which have no material grossness but are almost diaphanous through the purity of their form; differently by the human soul which, although it is in part free from matter is in part impeded like a man under water except for his head and thus not entirely in or out of it; differently again by animals, whose soul is made entirely of matter but somewhat ennobled; by plants; by minerals; differently from all these by the earth which is the most material and therefore the most remote from and disproportioned to the first, simplest and noblest virtue which is entirely intellectual, that is God (*Conv.* III. 7).

In *Paradiso* the neoplatonic structure is implied immediately in the first tercet of canto i:

> La gloria di colui che tutto move
> per l'universo penetra, e risplende
> in una parte più e meno altrove.

> The glory of him who moves everything
> penetrates through the universe and reflows
> in one part more and in another less.

When Dante takes up the question of the dark patches on the moon (ii. 46–148) to receive Beatrice's correction of the earlier interpretation he had put forward in *Convivio*, he does so partly in order to provide an explanation more in keeping with the principle of emanation in the created universe. The differences which produce the dark patches are not differences in density but in actual substance. This is cosmologically important because the different parts of the heavens receive and reflect divine illumination differently as a result of differences in the materials of which they are composed. Beatrice states the general principle:

Within the heaven of the divine peace whirls a body in whose virtue lies the being of all that it contains. The heaven next following, which has so many things to show, parts this being through diverse essences, distinct from it and contained by it. The other circling bodies by various differentiatings dispose the distinctions within themselves to their ends and their sowings. These organs of the universe go, as you see now, from grade to grade, for they take from above and work on that below (ii. 112–23).

In this rather obscure passage Beatrice is describing a neoplatonic universe in which the power from the top works downwards through the circles from stage to stage, producing different results as it strikes different material below. The same doctrine can be found in other places in *Paradiso*, for example in the explanation which Aquinas, in the circle of the sun, gives of the process of creation:

For that living light, which streams from its lucent source so that it is not disunited from it nor from the love which makes three with them, by its goodness focuses its raying, as if reflected, in nine substances, remaining eternally one itself. Thence it descends to the ultimate potencies, down from act to act, becoming such that it makes only brief contingencies. These contingencies I mean to be the generated things which the moving heaven produces with seed or without seed (xiii. 55–66).[13]

This brief account of themes in *Paradiso* is designed to suggest that the interests exhibited in that work are interests in questions of philosophy, theology, and natural sciences, which can be given a place in Dante's biography if they are understood as continuations, completions, and corrections of earlier preoccupations, but which constitute a swing away from that interest in human character, in political life, and in the life of the poet which dominates *Inferno* and to a lesser extent the earlier part of *Purgatorio*. There are of course a number of important people in *Paradiso*, from Piccarda to St Bernard, but they have a static and abstract quality and are never presented with that fascinated vision of the individual soul reliving the key moments of its destiny and exhibiting the eternal significance of its actions which gives *Inferno* its supreme power. The power of *Paradiso* is equally great but quite different. It is the capacity, perhaps unrivalled by any other poet, to present difficult ideas with, at the same time, perfect precision and exquisite beauty. When Dante says that in creating the angels, creatures of pure spirit, 's'aperse in nuovi amor l'etterno amore' (the eternal love opened himself in new loves) (xxix. 18), he expresses a precise philosophical idea in words with rich implications. The same capacity is exhibited on a thousand other occasions, often with much greater complexity. The abstract ideas are moreover included within an architecture of the heavens successively opened up to Dante and Beatrice which has a ravishing beauty.

The philosophical poetry of *Paradiso* was written by a man who had become detached from the concerns of his early political life in Florence and the early years of exile. When in 1315 Dante was at last offered the chance of return to Florence on proper submission and payment of a fine, he rejected the idea as an affront to his honour. 'Can I not anywhere gaze upon the face of the sun and the stars? Can I not under any sky contemplate the most precious truths?'[14] This was not the language of the man who in about 1304 had asked for reconciliation in the last lines of *Tre donne*. Though the society and

---

[13] Dante's acceptance of neoplatonism is emphasized by P. Boyde, *Dante Philomythes and Philosopher* (Cambridge, 1981), pp. 265–9 and elsewhere. This book contains a full account of Dante's natural science.

[14] Epistola XII in *Opere minori*, ii; IX in Toynbee's edition.

politics of Florence were well remembered in the interview with Cacciaguida, they were now somewhat distant from Dante's mind. Through his long travail of introspective wandering, attachment to distant courts and new political and religious inspirations, the sun and the stars and abstract truth had acquired more importance than erring humanity in its everyday agonies of practical and moral choice.

The point of this characterization of *Paradiso* is to argue that the movement through the *Comedy* is not a consideration of different spheres of the afterlife by a writer working under the same conditions and with the same concerns, but a progress from one set of interests to another, which reflects the development in Dante's own life. Great as the poetry of *Paradiso* is, it therefore lacks the historical importance of the poetry of *Inferno*. It opens a world of philosophical and religious exposition with a new poetic skill, but the new felicity in the presentation of abstract ideas is a less notable innovation in literary techniques than the poetry of *Inferno*. In *Paradiso* Dante proclaimed his attachment to scholastic philosophy, the central philosophical tradition of the thirteenth century. In doing so he moved out of the Florentine world of ideas which had been the source of his greatest originality.

As the author of *Monarchy*, Dante was commonly regarded as an enemy of the church and the papacy by Guelf contemporaries. According to Boccaccio, *Monarchy* was burned by a papal legate a few years after its author's death and a Dominican opponent, Guido Vernani, writing about 1330, condemned Dante for undermining orthodox views both by that book and by the 'poetic figments and fantasies' of the *Comedy*.[15] This was a just judgement from one point of view, though an ironical fate for the author of the careful orthodoxy of *Paradiso*. Regarded in the light of history, the hostility in his own day, arising out of the political conflicts of that period, misses the point of Dante's ultimate significance as the creator, in *Inferno*, of a literary vision of humanity. This, we can now see, presented characters in a frame of reference which was highly original, and it was potentially the embryo of an alternative to the picture of humanity presented by the Bible, the church and scholasticism. Dante's successors would, in the very long run, provide humanity with an aesthetic view of human life.

It is equally ironical that *Inferno*, the poem which makes a masterpiece out of the speech and the ideas of Florence, should have been written by an exile who expresses bitter enmity towards his native city. The Arena chapel is also the work of an exile, though not one driven out of the city by politics. Florence's supreme monuments were created outside the city. This should not cause us to abandon the conception of a Florentine culture; it is too clear that our two greatest artists were rooted in the Florentine world of the epoch of

[15] N. Matteini, *Il più antico oppositore politico di Dante, Guido Vernani da Rimini* (Padua, 1958), p. 93.

Cimabue, Brunetto Latini, and Cavalcanti. But it does emphasize the physical smallness of the Florentine state, and the easy and frequent movement between political units in Central Italy. Dante is of course no more un-Florentine in *Inferno* because of his dislike of its political bitterness than Dickens is un-English because of his dislike of the English bourgeoisie. *Inferno* is the supreme expression of the experience, the ideas, and the aspirations of the educated Florentine of that age. It turned the provincial Florentine culture into the creator of a triumphantly novel artistic vision which was to dazzle and inspire successors at the centre of European life.

To see this implication of *Inferno*, we have of course to look far into the future. Dante's writings made a great impact on the other two most notable writers of the fourteenth century, Petrarch and Chaucer, but he did not establish a school. *Inferno* is a sudden and enormous explosion, blown out of the city life of Florence, revealing in a way which we can see only in long perspective, after experiencing the work of dramatists and novelists in recent centuries, the possibility of a view of life created by a lay society. In the content and the circumstances of writing the *Comedy* there is a curious mingling of the universal and the narrowly particular. The structure of the *Comedy* depends on a broad awareness of the physical and political structure of the world, more easily available to an Italian city-dweller than to anyone else in the early fourteenth century, and the Florentine crisis which caused Dante's exile and inspired his reflections was a focal point of European politics. But the vision of the afterlife is at the same time the personal dream of one man, inimitable and without parallels. *Inferno* is an isolated work pointing forward to potentialities of literature which were not to be exploited for a long time.

The lonely position of *Inferno* in the history of literature and its composition in detached exile should not blind us to the fact that it emerged out of the world of Florentine speech and thought and bears the heightened characteristics of that world. It is the product of Dante's experience of man in society. The base from which his writing rises like a tall beacon is the speech and thought of the Tuscan cities: the poets Cavalcanti and Guinizelli of Florence and Bologna, their less serious 'realistic' contemporaries Rustico di Filippo and Cecco Angiolieri of Florence and Siena, the notary Brunetto Latini, the annalist of political life Dino Compagni. These are the people who dimly foreshadow Dante in their use of poetic language and their imaginative perception of the individual. Without them he could not have written as he did. *Inferno* is an elevation of city language and perceptions onto a high artistic level.

The conditions of work of the painter were quite different from those of the poet. He was not a gentleman amateur writing for his own satisfaction but an artisan executing traditional subjects laid down by his patrons. It was inconceivable that Giotto should invent a totally novel structure for his painting analogous to that created in *Inferno*. Within the limits of his craft, however, Giotto made innovations which have some similarities with those of Dante. If we look, for instance, at the scene of *Judas's Kiss*, or that of the *Lamentation* at Padua, we see groups of figures which are realistic in their supple movements and relationships in space and significant in the emotional and mythical messages conveyed by the patterns of their bodies. There is a similarity between the use of figures in Giotto's panels and the use of people in Dante's cantos, in the relationship between Farinata and Cavalcante or between Ulysses and Guido da Montefeltro. The poet does not have the capacity to handle such large numbers of figures clearly within one setting, as a dramatist might have done, but he conveys a similar sense of their heightened realism combined with the archetypal importance of their emotions. We can imagine that Dante might have done better if he had been a dramatist and Giotto if he had been a painter of pagan subjects. Both were contained within limiting formulae of structure. But the techniques of poetry and fresco were both appropriate for presenting individuals at a point of combined realism and symbolic suggestion.

Like Dante's poetry, Giotto's painting looks far forward in the avenues of development in artistic realism which it opened. Looking at art with whiggish eyes, we see Giotto's inventions taken up by Masaccio a century later, after a long relaxation of artistic invention, and by his successors later still, as we see the work of Giovanni Pisano continued by Donatello and Michelangelo. These visions of long-term development are of course distortions of historical evolution, picking out high points from an infinitely complex detailed pattern. They are nevertheless indications of the movement of the European mind which we cannot neglect if we are looking at the past to see how new worlds have been created. The city civilization of Florence and Siena was a new kind of environment which had grown up very rapidly in the thirteenth century and, largely unrecognized by contemporary observers, was capable of creating new artistic forms which could be seen centuries later as fundamental innovations. We see the explosion of *Inferno* and the Paduan frescos as something suddenly created by an urban society which was a new force in Europe, and which had the power to give a new direction not only to art but to the perception of life.

Giotto, like Dante, was an artist who rose out of the Florentine milieu. Some of the background to his work can be seen in the paintings of Cimabue and the Master of Santa Cecilia. But in the evolution of his style the influence of classical models from Rome, brought into the Tuscan world through cooperative work at Assisi, was essential. It was in painting that the interaction between Florence and Rome was most obviously essential to aesthetic advance. As Roman art influenced painting, Sienese art influenced sculpture, importing classical influences through the work of Nicola and Giovanni Pisano to a wide Tuscan style. This was a contact with the classical past which depended on seeing existing classical remains, and on links between the Tuscan and Roman worlds which depended on the action of patrons. In literature, Dante's high style is unimaginable without his reading of Virgil and Ovid; but in this case the ancient works were easily available in manuscripts and required no special conditions of patronage or politics to make their impact effective. The contribution of the classics, ranging from Aristotle who was known to Dante to Plotinus who was unknown to him, is due to widely diffused manuscripts and operates through many channels without a sudden break in the central evolution of taste. The dependence of the medieval on the classical world works in a different way in literature and the visual arts.

We have presented both poetry and the visual arts as profoundly influenced by the relationships between the Tuscan and Roman centres of power in the late thirteenth century. The patronage of Roman art by Nicholas III, the programme of decoration at Assisi inspired by the papacy, the political crisis of Boniface VIII's intervention in Tuscany (which led to Dante's exile), and the departure of the papacy from Italy were all disturbances in the outer world which had an effect on the development of aesthetic ideas. The origins of Florentine literary and visual arts can be seen in perspective only against a background which takes account of the connections of the Tuscan cities with Rome. The title of this book is intended to emphasize the point. Florence and Siena were great centres of active, expanding city life developing their own attitudes and styles of expression which were expressions of that life. But they were not self-contained. Religious power was centred outside them in the great organization controlled by the Roman pope, which also had political interests in Tuscany, and in the popular religious movements of Umbria. Only by observing Central Italy from Bologna to Rome as a whole can one include all the important forces affecting the art world and define the connecting influences which made for rapid aesthetic change. *Inferno* and the Paduan frescos are intelligible only as parts of that world, not as creations of the city alone.

This book is about the very first stage in the creation of Italian Renaissance culture. We have watched the play just long enough to see the cast assembled. The destiny of the new artistic ideals lies in the future. As the popes moved to France they left the Tuscan cities to a century of more isolated evolution in which the realistic ideals of art and literature were to grow. When the Italian papacy was recreated in the fifteenth century, the interaction of urban Tuscany and ecclesiastical Rome was revived. The age of Dante and Giotto was the beginning of a long pattern of artistic creations which was to be propelled forward by similar inspirations of city life and ecclesiastical authority for two centuries until central Italy lost its independent pre-eminence with the decline of wealth, the destruction of republicanism, and the reformation of the papacy in the sixteenth century.

Index